The BOUNTIFUL CONTAINER

McGEE & STUCKEY'S

The BOUNTIFUL CONTAINER

A Container Garden of Vegetables, Herbs, Fruits, and Edible Flowers

ROSE MARIE NICHOLS McGEE

and MAGGIE STUCKEY

Illustrations by Michael A. Hill

WORKMAN PUBLISHING · NEW YORK

Design by Paul Hanson and Elizabeth Johnsboen

Library of Congress Cataloging-in-Publication Data
McGee, Rose Marie Nichols.
McGee & Stuckey's the bountiful container / by Rose Marie Nichols McGee and
Maggie Stuckey ; illustrated by Michael Hill.
p. cm.
ISBN-13: 978-0-7611-1623-3 (alk. paper)
1. Container gardening. 2. Kitchen gardens. I. Title: McGee and Stuckey's the
bountiful container. II. Title: Bountiful container. III. Stuckey, Maggie. IV. Title.
SB418.M32 2001
635.9'86—dc21   2001046769

On the front cover: The authors hold some of the many vegetables that can happily be grown in
containers. The large purple flowering plant at the far left is agapanthus; don't eat it.
The containers *Top (left to right):* pansies, dianthus, lavender.
Left (left to right): Bright Lights Swiss chard; lettuce mix; marjoram, oregano.
Right (left to right): Cherry tomatoes, golden sage, sweet basil, peppers, red Swiss chard.
Lower left (left to right); sweet savory; rosemary topiary; thyme, chives, marjoram, and rosemary;
sweet bay. *On the spine:* Rosemary, marjoram, golden sage, Kent Beauty oregano.

Workman books are available at special discounts when purchased in bulk
for premiums and sales promotions as well as for fund-raising or educational use.
Special editions or book excerpts can be created to specification.
For details, contact the Special Sales Director at the address below.

Workman Publishing Company, Inc.
225 Varick Street
New York, NY 10014
www.workman.com

Printed in the U.S.A.
First printing March 2002
10 9 8 7 6

*"Time spent
working in your garden
will not be deducted
from your life."*

—M. S.

ACKNOWLEDGMENTS

I n one sense, every gardener who came before us played a role in this book, for the knowledge passed down through time from person to person is the core of every garden book ever written. We acknowledge, with respect, our debt to them all.

Three specific individuals are owed profound thanks for their help in this project. Jim Gilbert, owner of both Northwoods Nursery (wholesale) and One Green World (retail mail order), is a mine of knowledge about fruit trees; it is our good fortune that he is also generous in sharing what he knows. Two experienced gardeners and garden writers—Teri Dunn, who lives near Boston, and Carolyn Clark, of Portland, Oregon—pitched in with valuable and much-appreciated assistance. Thanks to all for your good information and good cheer.

Thanks, too, to the creative cooks who kindly shared their recipes: Walter Chandoha, Rosalind Creasy, Thomas DeBaggio, Peter Kopcinski, Jan Roberts-Dominguez, Bruce Naftaly, Carole Saville, and Renée Shepherd. And to Barbara Blossom Ashmun of Portland, Oregon, author and garden designer, for her rosy suggestions.

CONTENTS

PART THREE:

PLANTS FOR THE BOUNTIFUL CONTAINER

PREFACE

Several years ago my mother, Edith Nichols, attended a family wedding in Greece. She returned home with many happy stories and descriptions of fruiting gardens and fresh-picked figs served right from the tree. In particular, she could hardly stop talking about her sister-in-law's balcony garden. In the heart of downtown Athens, my Aunt Athena was growing three vigorous tomato plants, a few cucumbers, a small lemon tree, and several herbs—all in containers. Whenever the mood struck, she could simply step out onto the balcony and harvest the makings of a Greek salad, absolutely fresh. What so amazed my mother was the productivity: "That little space was feeding all those people!"

Inspired by Aunt Athena's success, and mindful of the pleasure my mother derived from it, the next summer we helped her plan a deck garden of her own. She was a lifelong gardener, but arthritis had increasingly curtailed her activity level. As a family project, we built a small garden on her deck, using containers raised to a height that she could manage. Here she grew vegetables, herbs, and colorful flowers, and even when the famous Oregon weather kept her inside, she enjoyed the sight of her plants through the windows.

At my own home, I also have a deck garden set within a larger garden. On and around the deck, I have containers of alpine strawberries, small-fruited tomatoes, spicy peppers, and herbs. I cannot begin to count the meals our family has enjoyed on that deck over the years, in the shelter of several large evergreens, but I do remember the many times that we snapped off sprigs of fresh herbs to add to the chickens on the grill or plucked a few more tomatoes for the salad.

We also are fortunate to have an oversize yard, with plenty of space for all kinds of gardening. We grow vegetables in several beds out back, and somehow that always seemed to be the "serious" gardening. The plants on the deck, while equally productive and healthy, seemed a more playful and personal expression of the pleasures of gardening.

Then I met Maggie, a great gardener who was planting her new vegetable garden in containers. She was determined to incorporate the best plant varieties and gardening techniques in this endeavor. We had much to discuss.

—ROSE MARIE NICHOLS MCGEE
Corvallis, Oregon

POSTSCRIPT: In the spring of 1999, as we were beginning the serious work on this book, my mother passed away. I wish that I could feel philosophical about it, saying something profound about the cycle of life in all of nature, but the fact is that I still miss her terribly. The small deck garden we built for her still stands, and I will tend the plants as long as I can, until I pass it and her house into the care of a new owner. —RMNM

About two years ago, for reasons that made sense at the time, I moved from a house I had lived in for twenty-some years, with a garden I had nurtured and loved for almost as long, into a condominium whose only garden space is a concrete patio about the size of a picnic table. In my old garden I had spent most of my time with herbs and vegetables, and in my new home I wasn't about to give that up, at least not without a fight. If I couldn't have my "in-the-ground" garden, I decided, I could do it all with containers.

My first instinct when starting a new venture is to head to the library, and there I encountered my first difficulty: most books about container gardening deal with flowers. Vegetables, if they are addressed at all, are accorded a skimpy page or two, usually given over to tomatoes.

I was not deterred. I felt deep in my bones that much more was possible, that indeed a full kitchen garden could be created with containers, if only we gardeners could break free from this limited, tomato-based thinking.

At first, my results were underwhelming. I endured some old problems (the slugs that are the bane of northwest gardeners managed to find their way from my old garden to the new place) and made my share of new mistakes. Then, in a wonderful piece of serendipity, I happened to cross paths with Rose Marie Nichols McGee.

Rose Marie is president of Nichols Garden Nursery, one of America's best specialty seed companies, a business founded by her parents more than 50 years ago. She is extraordinarily knowledgeable about vegetables and herbs, and passionate about teaching the world to grow them. The day she agreed to collaborate with me, two nice things happened: (1) my little patio garden moved from a stubborn experiment to a reality, and (2) this book was born.

—MAGGIE STUCKEY
Portland, Oregon

FROM OUR GARDENS TO YOURS

Imagine stepping outside in the early evening and filling a basket with the ingredients of tonight's salad: bronze-leaf and dark green Simpson lettuce, arugula, and scallions, along with a few chives to garnish the soup. Picture an early-summer Sunday picnic in the park. You'll bring your famous potato salad, made from tiny new red potatoes and sugar snap peas and garnished with blaze-orange nasturtiums, and a big jug of lemonade intensely flavored with lemon balm and spearmint—all from your garden. Fast-forward in your mind's eye to late summer, and the gazpacho you will make from your homegrown vegetables: tomatoes so perfectly ripe they practically hum, crunchy bell peppers, and sweet-crisp lemon cucumbers.

Wait just a minute, you may be thinking. That's all well and good for you country types, but I live in an apartment building. I'd love to have fresh vegetables and herbs right at my fingertips, but all I have is a balcony so small I can hardly turn around on it.

Do not despair. Even if your only "garden" space is tiny, we're betting you have room for at least one large container. And with that one container and a little planning, you can do amazing things.

This is a book about growing good things to eat—vegetables, herbs, fruits, and edible flowers—in containers. It may come as something of a new idea that you can grow food on your balcony or patio, but stop and think for a moment: if you can grow pansies in a pot, you can grow peas in a pot. Both need about the same conditions, but one will give you dinner.

We wrote this book for everyone who aspires to have garden-fresh foodstuffs but has no yard in which to grow them. If you live in an apartment,

town house, or condominium, or on a houseboat, you may be a container gardener out of necessity. But we think this book will also be useful for those whose traditional garden area is not well suited to growing vegetables. We imagine, too, that even those with an existing vegetable garden might find it convenient to add containers on a porch, patio, or deck, close by the kitchen or the outdoor grill.

For all these situations, we invite you to consider the many advantages of growing your bounty in containers:

- With one exception, every facet of every gardening task is simpler because you are working in a small area. Preparing the planting area is a simple matter of filling a container with premixed soil; your tool of choice is a trowel, not a shovel or a rototiller. Your back will thank you. Harvesting is easier, too, because there is less bending over. Checking for early signs of damaging insects and other pests is simpler because the plants are close at hand, and preventive measures are easier to manage because you have a smaller number of plants.

  The one exception is watering. Whereas in the traditional garden it's a snap to set up an oscillating sprinkler and just let it spray the entire area for an hour or so, containers need individual attention. Making numerous trips back and forth with a watering can is a tedious chore, all the more tedious because containers dry out faster than garden beds. In Chapter 5, we suggest ways you can simplify this task.

- Containers are mobile. You can move them around like furniture, grouping and regrouping them into combinations that give you pleasure, offer convenience, and take advantage of changing growing conditions as the season progresses.

- You can completely eliminate one worry that haunts traditional vegetable gardeners: soilborne diseases that persist in the ground year after year and are nearly impossible to eradicate.

- Container gardens almost never have weeds.

- Because your space is limited, you are forced to think about what you really want and how much of it you can realistically use. You're less vulnerable to the common error of overplanting.

Container Gardens You Can Eat

We have observed that, for whatever reason, most of the books and magazine articles about container gardening assume that you want to grow only flowers. We have nothing against flowers, but we think it's time for vegetables to come out of the closet.

In this regard container gardens and in-the-ground gardens are alike: vegetables get no respect. All too often they are relegated to the rear of the house, away from public view, considered too homely and too messy to be presentable. Recent interest in nicely designed kitchen gardens, with their endearing country charm, and the more sophisticated *potagers* has begun to dislodge this notion, and it is no longer considered startling to suggest that some vegetable plants are attractive enough to be integrated into the perennial border. But these approaches are only at the bud stage. The prevailing notion with vegetables still seems to be that people like the results but don't admire the horticulture.

This is keenly apparent with container gardens, where vegetables have frequently been a mere afterthought, and no attention has been devoted to their aesthetics. Even people who have created a handsome container garden gloriously filled with ornamental plants seem to include only one vegetable, if that: a lonely tomato, hidden away in an inconspicuous corner, not pretty enough to be part of the real garden. It is this way of thinking that we hope to influence.

Getting the Most from This Book

Here's a quick guide to how the parts of this book are arranged.

The chapters in **Part One** are designed to help you organize your thinking. All gardens involve some sort of trade-off between what you want and what is possible, and in many ways the delicate balance is even more delicate with container gardens. So in these first chapters, we look at the aspects you need to consider: what kind of space you have, what you'd like to grow, and ways to make it beautiful as well as bountiful. We believe that all gardeners, experienced and otherwise, will benefit from walking through these steps.

The chapters in **Part Two** deal with the how-tos of making and maintaining a successful container garden. If you have been gardening for a while you probably know most of what is presented here, but if your experience has been with the usual in-the-ground gardens, it wouldn't hurt to quickly scan these chapters for pointers specifically geared to container gardening.

The heart of the book is **Part Three**: individual descriptions, organized encyclopedia style, of the vegetables, herbs, fruits, and edible flowers that can be grown successfully in containers.

The **Appendix** includes the **U.S.D.A. Hardiness Zone Map** and **Mail-Order Sources** of plants, seeds, and garden supplies.

Throughout, you will find descriptions of special **Theme Gardens,** where several different plants are grouped together, in either one large container or several smaller ones, to create a special look or feeling. We describe the interrelationships of the plants, why we chose them, and how they work together to enhance one another, but do not go into detail about growing the individual plants; that information will be found in each plant's own encyclopedia listing. So if you already know about growing rosemary, for example, you might want some new ideas for combining it with other plants but don't need the full how-tos; on the other hand, if you've never tried growing rosemary, you will want to study the basics in the Herbs chapter and then explore the several theme gardens that incorporate it.

Every plant in every theme garden is edible; nothing is included in this book, in fact, *unless* it is edible. However, while we name the plants that make up these theme gardens, we see them only as suggestions and idea-starters. It is our intention, and our hope, that you will let your own imaginations fly free and create your own theme gardens.

A Word About Garden Terminology

Part of every new adventure is learning its vocabulary. Gardening, like all other adventures, has its own language.

In home gardens, all plants belong to one of two major categories: edibles and ornamentals. **Edibles** are plants grown to be eaten: vegetables, herbs, and fruits. In recent years, we have added edible flowers; in this case, "edible" implies both palatable and nontoxic. **Ornamentals** are plants grown for their visual appeal, whether that appeal comes from flowers, striking foliage, interesting bark, or what have you. In this book, where the word "edible" doesn't seem quite right in a sentence, we sometimes use the one word "vegetables" as a kind of shorthand for the bulkier, all-encompassing phrase "vegetables, herbs, fruits, and edible flowers."

We also find it necessary from time to time to contrast container gardens with regular, in-the-ground gardens. The term we use most often for the latter is **"traditional garden."** If you have such a garden but hate the idea of being thought traditional, remember that this is just another bit of writers' shorthand—no disrespect intended.

Another way that garden plants are distinguished from one another is by their growth cycle. We say that plants are annuals, biennials, or perennials. **Annuals** go through an entire cycle—from seed to new plant and all the way to producing seed for another generation of plants—in one growing season. **Biennials** live two years: the first year they make mostly foliage; the second year they produce flowers and then seeds for the next generation. **Perennials,** in the garden sense, are plants that live more than two years. Technically, this would mean that trees are perennials. But as gardeners use the term, it applies to plants that are *not* trees, *not* shrubs, and *not* bulbs but that still live for several years. Usually, the word refers only to plants that die back to the ground in winter and sprout new growth in the spring.

Why do you care? Because it affects your planning. If you want to grow a perennial that is tender (meaning easily damaged by very cold weather), you'll be happier if you put it in a small container by itself so that you can move it to shelter in winter. If you want to grow perennial herbs and annual flowers in the same container, just be careful not to damage the roots of one when you're planting the other. And so on.

As a broad rule of thumb, most vegetables are annuals, most herbs are perennials, fruit trees live many years, and edible flowers are a mix of annuals and perennials. Some plants that would technically be classed as biennials or perennials are, as a practical matter, usually treated as if they were annuals. That is why in the encyclopedia listing there is a specific heading: "Grow as."

Finally, perhaps the biggest terminology bugaboo of all is Latin names. They are critically important to botanists, horticulturists, breeders, and all other plant professionals; it's the only way to know for certain which specific plant is being discussed. Many home gardeners enjoy knowing and using the scientific names, which often have a very interesting etymology, but many more are confused and intimidated.

Here's a quick refresher. The Latin name has two main elements, which are italicized: the **genus** (spelled with a capital letter) and the **species** (lowercase), as in *Salvia officinalis* (culinary sage). Each genus can have, and usually does have, several species. When two or more species of the same genus are discussed together, the genus name is abbreviated after the first mention, as in *S. elegans* (pineapple sage).

In this book, we elected not to use scientific names except where confusion could otherwise result or where the information being discussed called for it. Generally, genus names are not necessary with edible plants: a carrot is a carrot is a carrot. Even where species names differ (as in the two sages named above), in edible gardens the common names almost always suffice. What is frequently important, however, is identifying a particular cultivated variety, or **cultivar,** which is written in roman (not italicized) type, with the first letter(s) capitalized. If you are designing a large container with a pink color scheme, for instance, you want to be sure you get a monarda with pink blossoms (Marshall's Delight, maybe) rather than red (Adam, or Jacob Kline).

The urge to watch something grow, to help it along, is a powerful, almost primeval impulse. So is the deep human need to beautify our environment, to take what we find and make it better. And so too is the yearning to link ourselves with nature, to know that some part of the natural world, no matter how small, is just over our shoulder.

All these threads of human desire come together in making a garden. By surrounding ourselves with growing green things, we make nature accessible, we put beauty at our fingertips, and we experience the joy of witnessing and nurturing our plants' development. Like a midwife, like a parent, we help them come healthy into the world, begin to grow, and finally flourish. It is that sense of wonder, the visceral pleasure of direct physical contact with beauty, that makes gardeners what they are.

Both of us love gardens and gardening for all these ethereal reasons. But we hold a special reverence for gardens that produce food. In these gardens we get to witness, over and over through the season, that proud moment when a seedling elbows itself up through the soil and demands its rightful place in the world. We revel in the taste, texture, and shining good looks of beautiful vegetables harvested just moments ago. We appreciate the safe feeling of knowing where our foodstuffs came from and under what conditions they were grown. Food is life, and growing your own is an experience of immense enrichment and affirmation.

None of this is any less true for people who live in large cities. The yearnings to watch something grow, to be connected with nature, are not diminished because the opportunities are fewer but may, in fact, be felt even more strongly.

It is our hope that with this book you will find the inspiration and encouragement to create a garden even if you have no land. From your bountiful containers, you will soon have the very great delight of serving a meal made of fresh things from your own garden, grown with your own hands and heart.

PART ONE

You and Your Garden

CHAPTER 1

MANAGING YOUR SPACE

E very gardener since Nebuchadnezzar, the visionary responsible for the Hanging Gardens of Babylon, has had to begin
at the same starting point: evaluating the physical characteristics of the garden space itself. Now, as then, the challenge is
making the most of what you have to work with.

As a container gardener, you actually have an easier time of it than
your compatriots with a traditional garden. Because the overall space of
your garden is probably smaller, you have fewer variables to take into
account. And if corrective action is needed, your task is simplified by virtue
of being confined to a smaller area. One very big advantage you have over
dirt gardeners is that you can skip the tedious, backbreaking work of creating new beds and digging in soil amendments with spade and garden fork
(you may add amendments to your potting mix, but we'll show you a simplified approach). Keep this in mind if you start to feel envious of your
friends who have large yards to garden in; after many hours of double-
digging in heavy clay soil, they're probably extremely envious of *you*.

Sunlight

S unlight is the most critical factor a gardener has to consider: it's the one
feature that plants cannot live without, and the one you cannot control.
Plants can't live without water, either, but you can add that. And they may
not survive bitterly cold weather, but you can provide protection against
that or plan around it. You cannot, however, manufacture sunshine.

In fact, while all plants need sunlight for survival, it's particularly
important for vegetables; some of the most popular types need a minimum
of six hours per day in order to produce their bounty. Generally speaking,
if a plant makes a flower before it makes the part we eat (such as tomatoes,
squash, peppers, eggplant, and all fruits), it needs at least that six hours. If
the part we eat is a leaf (lettuce, spinach, chard, kale, and so forth), or grows

Fooling Mother Nature

All gardeners have to contend with protecting their plants against the elements. At the extreme ends of heat and cold, you're at nature's mercy. But with a little ingenuity, you can adjust and enhance the physical environment around your containers, making your small garden work well even when the weather is not fully cooperating.

Too Much Sun. On a balcony, roofed patio, or houseboat deck, suspend a regular window shade from the ceiling, overhang, or top railing. Raise and lower it as needed.

Plant a trellis with beans and position it so it faces the sun; then put small containers of shade-loving plants at the base of the trellis on the opposite side (in the shadow zone).

Too Little Sun. Paint a wall bright white and position your containers where they'll catch the light that bounces off. If you cannot paint the wall, paint a free-standing screen bright white and position it in the same manner.

Too Hot. When the soil inside a container gets too hot, the plant's roots suffer. If your summers are long and hot and your garden area faces south, take precautionary measures. Stick to larger

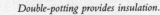
Double-potting provides insulation.

containers, which retain soil moisture better. Use double-potting: put one plant-filled container inside a larger container and fill in the gap with peat moss or wood chips, kept damp; this insulating layer will give some protection to your roots. Group pots in clusters, and they'll provide shade for one another.

Too Cold. If your growing season isn't quite long enough to grow all that you want, you can gain some time by babying your containers through the cool days of late spring and early fall. Wrap the pot in a blanket or burlap or heavy dark fabric. Use black containers, or paint the ones you already have dark colors. At night cover the entire container, plants and all, with a lightweight protection such as a pillowcase. Or invest in a package of row cover, which

Wrapped for warmth.

is an extremely lightweight, translucent material designed to cover an entire row of growing plants in a traditional garden (often referred to by a familiar trade name, Reemay). Row cover acts like a blanket, warming the entire area a few degrees, but it allows sunlight and water to pass through it. Cut it into lengths that will loosely cover your containers, and tuck the ends under the pots.

Protection against cold is particularly important with perennial plants because you must find some way to keep them alive through the winter. For more ideas on this, see page 288.

underground (scallions, radishes, etc.), it can get by with three to four hours of sunlight. At the other end of the spectrum, it's possible to have too much sunlight and/or too much heat for certain plants (chervil, arugula, kale).

Your first task, therefore, is to assess the sunlight quotient of your garden space. This is primarily a matter of paying attention to sun patterns and making mental notes. Start by noting the direction that your garden area faces. All other things being equal:

- Southern exposures receive the longest period of strong sunlight.
- Western exposures are next (you'll often hear gardeners say that a west-facing area gets "afternoon sun").
- Eastern exposures are next (with "morning sun").
- Northern exposures receive the least amount of sun.

Take note of nearby obstructions that might interfere with sunlight. Even if your balcony faces west, you won't get much afternoon sun if trees or a large building casts a shadow. Remember, the amount of sunlight is critical for many favorite vegetables, so if you've never given this much thought, it's worth your time to track where the sun falls at various stages throughout your growing season.

Wind

As you ponder where to site your container garden, keep the wind factor in mind. A strong wind can blow over top-heavy containers, especially if the plants they contain are tall, and even mild breezes will dry out the soil in your pots.

Protect tall plants by attaching their containers to a nearby wall, stair rail, or some other sturdy anchor with a strong wire or chain. If you have room, set up a row of dwarf evergreens in pots to block the wind. On page 85 you'll find another solution: plant pole beans to grow on a secured trellis, and site it where it can serve as a windbreak.

Anchor containers on windy balconies. Put smaller pots on the lee side.

Weather Cycles and
Hardiness Zones

What is your weather like? Extended periods of below-freezing temperatures in winter? Hot, humid summer months? Mild winters and long, damp springs? Whatever your climate, some plants will do better in it than others. It is possible to modify the effects of climate somewhat (see page 4), but as a gardener you'll be happiest if you plan in concert with the weather rather than trying to fight against it. Some vegetables actually do better in cool climates, while others thrive in the hot summer sun. Take a look at the lists on page 79, and plan accordingly.

Nearly 40 years ago the U.S. Department of Agriculture developed a nationwide system of cold-hardiness zones, built around the average coldest winter temperatures. The system is continuously refined and updated, and today there are 11 main zones, with the lowest numbers denoting the lowest average temperatures; parts of Alaska are in zone 1, south Florida is in zone 10 (see the map on pages 414 to 415). This numbering system has been widely adopted by horticultural industries, and zone information for individual perennial plants is included in most garden-catalog descriptions (as in "this variety hardy in zones 6–8" or "to zone 8").

Note that we specify *perennial* plants in the previous sentence. This is one of those points so basic it is often overlooked by new gardeners: zone information will tell you which plants should make it through your *winters;* it's completely irrelevant for annuals, which die at the end of one growing season anyway. For gardens of edible plants, hardiness zones mostly apply to fruit trees and perennial herbs and flowers; check catalog information when ordering one of these. We've chosen not to include zone information for individual plants in this book for two reasons: first, so many of the plants here are annuals, and second, container gardeners have much more control over the vagaries of winter weather because their gardens are much more easily protected against, or moved away from, severe cold. We can, in other words, more easily push our gardens into a warmer zone.

This cold-weather information is certainly critical for many kinds of gardening, but as any gardener will tell you, it's not the full story. Severe heat can stress plants just as much as severe cold. Just a few years ago, the American Horticultural Society tackled this information gap by producing the AHS Plant Heat-Zone Map. The country was divided into 12 zones, reflecting the relative number of so-called heat days, when the average temperature is so hot that plants are damaged. The zones range from 1

(Alaska), with no heat days, to 12 (southern Texas and Florida), with more than 210 heat days annually.

The two systems in tandem give gardeners all the information they need to choose varieties of plants that will accommodate to their weather patterns. The heat-zone map, however, is still quite new; not all plants have been coded, and not all published information reflects the codes. As the heat-zone system becomes better established, look for catalogs and books to provide both sets of weather data. Plants that have been coded for both hardiness and heat zones have a double set of numbers (such as 6–5), with the hardiness zone always being the first number.

At the moment, the hardiness-zone information is still the standard system, and you will find it handy to know what zone you live in (see the map on pages 414 to 415). Hardiness-zone information can also be found in a number of other places. Often, mail-order companies will put your specific zone number of the address label of gardening catalogs. You could also inquire at the local garden center, ask a neighbor who's a serious gardener, look at the map in a seed catalog or a gardening book, call your local agricultural extension service (look in the County Government section of the phone book), ask a librarian to help you research the information, or log on to www.usna.usda.gov/Hardzone/.

While you're at it, also find out two other useful items: the last spring and first fall frost dates in your area. This refers to the average last day in spring and average first day in fall when the temperature hits 32°F—cold enough to kill tender plants. The period between these two dates is your growing season. (In this book, we use a shorthand terminology: "spring frost date" or "fall frost date.")

Be aware that climate information is always imprecise. If your garden is on a patio, deck, balcony, or front entryway, it's probably protected from the severest weather by its proximity to a building. And even if this is not true in your case, you still have more control over weather whims than traditional gardeners: it's easier for you to cover containers against an unseasonably cold night, to shift pots into the sunniest spot, or to move tender plants into a sheltered corner.

Water

If you have the luxury of choosing among several sites for your container garden, and if they are equally well endowed in terms of sunlight, pick the one with the closest access to water. Even if containers are positioned where rain falls freely on them, you'll still have to water in the summer.

Size and Structure

Consider how big your gardening area is, and what architectural possibilities it provides. Unless you own your home, you'll also need to ask the owner of the building about any tenant restrictions that might affect your plans. Frame your request in terms of how much more attractive the building will be, and try to anticipate any questions about damage or liability.

Measure the overall dimensions of your future gardening space. Take note of other structural elements that you can incorporate into your garden. If it's a balcony, for instance, what is the railing like? Is it flat on top, to accommodate planter boxes? Can you add hooks to the ceiling for hanging baskets? Would you be able to add posts at one end and attach a trellis? What about bolting a trellis to the wall of the building? Is the flooring material likely to be damaged by water? If so, could you install something on top, such as wood decking? Are you able to paint any part of the balcony, or the building wall? How will you make sure no water drips onto your downstairs neighbor's balcony?

Specific Space Considerations

We passionately believe that anyone with a speck of outdoor space can enjoy some kind of container garden. In the following list, we have tried to anticipate the main environmental concerns you'll need to address for various settings.

BALCONY OR PORCH. Sun orientation—whether your porch faces west, south, east, or north—is critical. Since most balconies are rectangles with two short and two long ends, and since one of the long sides is usually the wall of the building (which does a good job of blocking any sun), plants get full sunlight only about 25 percent of the day, when the sun is directly facing them. If there is another balcony above you, make sure you know how much vertical space you have to work with before planting something that will eventually grow tall, or be prepared to pinch and prune.

Porches call for the same sort of evaluation, except that they are usually larger than balconies and therefore receive more sunlight over a longer period of the day.

If your only outdoor space is a fire escape, you may be tempted to put a few containers there. Before you do, check the fire department regulations in your city. You must not block firefighters' access, and in some communities that means *nothing* on the fire escape.

PATIO OR DECK. In most cases, the sun hits three or sometimes all four sides of a patio as it moves through the sky, so sun orientation is less of a concern than it is with balconies. If your patio is made of concrete, however, you'll need to watch for reflected heat in summertime. And be sure to think about access to water.

DECKS AROUND POOLS. Since most pool decks are concrete, your siting concerns will probably be similar to those mentioned above for patios. Most pools are located where they will get maximum sunshine, which is good for swimmers but maybe not so good for plants. Watch carefully for overheating; see page 4 for ways to cope.

ROOFTOP. Anyone who lives in a tall building and is able to develop a rooftop garden is fortunate indeed. You will no doubt have a wonderful, large space to work with, and you'll be blessed with sun from all sides. But there are several problems you should be aware of. One is the curse of high winds. Walking on some roofs will damage them and cause leaks below, and weight can also be an issue. If the floor is a kind of blacktop, the heat reflection in summertime can be fierce. And then there is all the toting you have to do to get supplies and materials, and perhaps water, up there. Many big-city dwellers happily make those trade-offs in exchange for a big garden spot.

HOUSEBOAT DECK. Weight is a real concern for houseboats. They usually have a deck, rather like a roofless porch, along one or more sides, so there's plenty of room for containers. But several large, heavy containers massed in one spot can throw the boat off balance.

FRONT OR BACK STEPS OR ENTRYWAY. One thing you have to think about here is the size of the containers—make sure you leave room for humans to pass. Look for containers that are tall rather than wide, with a small footprint. If you're concerned about vandalism, here are a couple of antitheft suggestions:

- Loop a chain or strong wire around the pots and tie it to a handrail.
- Before you fill the container, lay a short, fat dowel or length of pipe crossways in the bottom and thread a chain or metal cable up through the drainage hole, then slip the dowel through a link of the chain; if the drainage hole is not large enough to accept a stout chain, use metal cable instead and tie it to the dowel. Fasten the other end of the

chain to something solid, like a drainpipe or handrail. This provides good protection against spontaneous thievery, with the extra benefit of being mostly invisible.

Of course, nothing will stop a really determined thief; do what you can, and then try not to worry.

Front-entry gardens provide something no others do: a way to welcome your guests with fragrance. Fill the containers with sweet-smelling plants (lavender is a personal favorite); as visitors climb the stairs they brush against the plants, releasing a heavenly aroma into the air.

WINDOW BOX. Fastened onto an exterior wall underneath a window, window boxes have some of the same limitations of sun orientation as do balconies, but to a lesser degree because there is no roof blocking the sunlight as there is on a balcony. Also, because window boxes have so much surface area in relation to their depth, it's hard to keep them moist. Be sure you know how to get water to them. If you can't reach a window box from the ground, does the window open?

HANGING CONTAINER. Baskets brimming over with cherry tomatoes or nasturtiums add a wonderful bright splash to patios, balconies, or porches. Remember that a large container filled with soil mix and then plants can be surprisingly heavy; choose your location carefully, and make sure your hook or bracket is strong enough and secured firmly.

INDOOR WINDOWSILL GARDEN. Plant choice is critical, as is finding a window with good sunlight. Most of all, manage your expectations; you won't have the same luxuriant growth as you would in an outdoor container.

OUT IN THE GARDEN. People who have traditional in-the-ground gardens often find it extremely useful to integrate container plants into the overall garden scheme, to fill in seasonal gaps or to take advantage of specialized minienvironments. With this approach, you can stand the question of site on its head, putting each container where it fits best—in the right amount of sun or shade, for instance—and then moving it aside when the harvest production is done.

CHAPTER 2

PLANNING FOR GOOD TASTE

A certain genteel madness often comes over new gardeners as they set about deciding what to grow. Giddy with possibilities, they devour dozens of mail-order catalogs, turning down page corners and marking fat circles around the seductive photos; ultimately, agonizingly, they will place orders with several companies, only to have their decisions thrown into sweet turmoil when a new catalog arrives in the mail. Then, a few weeks later, the madness attains a new level, when young plants start showing up at local garden centers. Now the temptations are three-dimensional, with in-your-face color, texture, and fragrance, and it is a strong soul indeed who can resist. "I'll just get one of those," they think, "and that, and that . . . " and soon the shopping cart is spilling over with baby green things.

If you had all the room in the world, and all the time, none of this would matter. You could plant all the seeds in all the packets, and all the transplants, and wait to see what happened. Gradually, through trial and error, you would learn what is successful in your climate and what you really love, and could leave the rest behind with only a small smile of regret.

But as a container gardener you do *not* have all the room in the world, and you're probably short on time as well. We want you to enjoy success in your first year. In the limited spaces of container gardens, there is less room for error, so your first decisions have to be well considered.

Your planning doesn't have to be as formal as it would for a full landscape design (although you may enjoy the process of creating one), but we recommend you do the exercise of putting your thoughts down on paper. First, figure out what you like to eat, what your garden conditions will support, and what your lifestyle will permit; then use that information to put together a garden plan.

What You Like to Eat

If you don't know where to start, a big fat seed catalog is an excellent reference. Most catalogs organize their inventory of vegetables and flowers alphabetically, so a fast run-through will serve as a good checklist of all the possibilities. Now your task is to narrow the choices down to a manageable number.

The first rule is, Be honest. Do you *really* like spinach, or do you simply think you should because it's good for you? If you don't really enjoy the taste of something, you're unlikely to feel differently just because you grew it with your own hands, so eliminate from consideration the things you realize you don't like.

At the same time, you'll want to leave room for experimenting with new items (see box at right). Selecting old favorites you know you love, plus new temptations you want to try, will give you a good start on a working list.

What Your Garden Conditions Will Support

Read up on the items on your wish list (in seed catalogs and the individual write-ups later in this book) and compare what the plants need with what you can give them. Key considerations to look for are climate, amount of sunlight needed, and how much time the plant takes to produce its bounty.

For example, many vegetables need at least six hours of sun a day. If your only garden space is a balcony that is blocked from all directions by tall buildings, you'll have trouble with tomatoes and peppers, but you can create a splendid salad garden with all kinds of gourmet lettuces and Asian greens.

Then there's the question of weather. If you live where growing seasons are short or summers cool, you might as well forget vegetables that need a long time to mature. This information is spelled out in later chapters and in most catalogs, which tell you how long it takes from the time you sow seed (or set out transplants—read the fine print) until the first produce is ready to be picked, expressed in days, as in "80 days." Compare that information against your growing season; in the case of a mismatch, you probably should choose something else.

Try Something New

One of the pleasures of growing your own vegetables is that you can try unusual and gourmet varieties that may never show up in the supermarket or, if they do, are days old and expensive. Here are some suggestions.

Snap peas. Don't confuse these with the flat edible-pod peas called Chinese snow peas. Snap peas are round, fat, crunchy, and unbelievably sweet; you eat the whole thing, pod as well as the peas inside, and then you swoon. They are making their way into stores across the country, but they are very expensive and it's worth having your own private supply.

Mizuna. A very pretty addition to your salad garden. The plant makes a large rosette shape, with extremely frilly individual leaves.

Winter purslane. An unusual salad green with small, succulent leaves, also known as miner's lettuce.

Salad burnet. Another pretty rosette-shaped plant, with very attractive round leaves that taste like cucumber.

Cinnamon Spice basil. Very different from the plain green type, with a spicy-sweet fragrance and purple stems.

Garlic chives. The "leaves" are flat with a strong garlicky taste.

Fava beans. You may have had them dried, but if you grow your own you can enjoy them fresh—an entirely different taste.

Beets that are solid yellow or red-swirled.

Purple tomatillos. Yes, purple.

Jingle Bells sweet peppers. When fully grown, these cute little guys are about 2 inches in diameter, so they reach maturity faster than regular bell peppers.

Reality Check for Container Gardens

In any garden, deciding what to grow is a balancing act between what you want and what conditions will allow. In a container garden, that balancing act is even trickier because you must also factor in questions of space and size.

This truth you cannot avoid: you have limited space to work with, so you have to make very efficient use of it. We've found that one very good way to decide what to grow is to focus on those edibles that are best when eaten absolutely fresh or absolutely ripe, and on those that you cannot readily find in the market.

Not Worth the Trouble

Wisdom, it has been said, consists in knowing what you can and cannot do, and having the sense not to waste time on the impossible or the pointless. Obviously we think container gardening is a wonderful idea, but we would be doing a disservice if we did not point out that some things just don't work well in containers. Either the plant is too large, or the amount of produce you get from the plant is too small to make it worth your while. For these and other reasons, we think you're probably better off avoiding these:

■ **Full-size fruit trees.** You simply won't have room for the root system; choose instead dwarf varieties, which have the added advantage of producing fruit when very young.

■ **Watermelon and most cantaloupes.** The vines are large and sprawly, and the melons need a long, hot summer.

■ **Pumpkins and winter squash.** Same problems as with watermelon: they need too much space and too long a growing season.

■ **Corn.** Plants are too tall for most containers, and you need several plants for good pollination.

■ **Cabbage.** Too big for most containers; inefficient use of space (one head of cabbage per plant).

■ **Traditional mammoth sunflowers.** Another too-tall plant. If your heart is set on growing sunflowers, there are many new smaller varieties to choose from.

■ **Beefsteak-type tomatoes.** The tomatoes themselves are huge and wonderful, but they're too heavy for most container arrangements and need a long growing period. But if you can't do without them—and many tomato fanatics cannot—try just one plant and pamper it.

Another consideration is plant size. You may be extremely fond of a vegetable that is unrealistic for container gardening simply because of its size. If you've never seen cabbage growing, you'll be amazed at how large a full plant is. For container gardening, you would be better off with something like kale, a much smaller cousin. Another example is corn. There's no denying it's best when fresh-picked; in fact, country gardeners put the water on to boil before they head out to the corn patch. But the plants are simply too tall for most containers.

Are You Willing to Make a Commitment?

Another kind of reality check is also needed, the kind where you must look inward. Container gardening requires more of your day-to-day attention than in-the-ground gardening. In the dead of summer, watering often needs to be done daily. Heavy feeders need a regular regimen of fertilizing. And when the beans and peas are at their peak of production, they really should be picked every day or so.

The most common problem seems to be daily watering. You can help yourself by using self-watering pots, drip systems set on a timer, and water-holding gels (see page 66), but there inevitably comes a time when someone has to turn on the faucet. If you're out of town often, could someone else fill in for you, perhaps a neighbor or a family member? If not, how about planning a garden around plants that do not need quite so much water—a Mediterranean herb garden, for instance? If you already know you'll be on vacation when the beans come in, arrange for a friend to pick them, and the vines will still be producing when you get back.

The point is that with a little preplanning, you can accommodate the special attention that container gardening demands—as long as you're honest about what you can and cannot do. Don't plant containers you won't be able to care for.

Planning for Maximum Impact and Continuous Good Looks

Mentally or on paper, examine all these factors and follow where they lead:

1. Start with what you know you enjoy eating.
2. Leave some room for experimenting with new things.
3. Eliminate whatever your garden space will not permit.
4. Eliminate whatever your climate and other environmental conditions will not permit.
5. Eliminate whatever your lifestyle will not support.

Now you have a well-thought-out list, but you don't have a garden plan. For that, you need to consider aesthetics and style (which are covered in the next chapter), and you also need to think about timing: what gets planted when. You owe it to yourself to get the maximum impact from your garden—both in terms of the food it produces and the visual pleasure it gives you—and that comes only with careful planning.

To give you a small taste of what is possible, we're going to introduce you to a concept that farmers call succession planting: continuously planting seasonal crops in the same space, intermixing fast-growing plants with slower growers, and replacing plants whose production peak has passed with new ones that are just coming into their best season. The goal is to have no bare spots in your container. Succession planting is an ideal way to get maximum use from your containers and to keep them looking their best.

To get you started, here are three plans for multiseason gardens, along with a few alternatives.

Succession Garden 1

START WITH A LARGE CONTAINER, AT LEAST 2 FEET WIDE AND 3 FEET DEEP.

SPRING. In early spring, as soon as weather permits, sow seeds of **mustard spinach** (or any Asian green of your choice) in the center of the container. Plant seeds of **bush snap peas** in a circle, 3 inches in from the rim. Between, add transplants of blue and pale yellow **pansies.**

SUMMER. As the weather turns hot, the peas will stop producing and start to die, and the greens will be past their peak. Cut off the pea vines at ground level (the roots will continue to provide nitrogen to the soil) and remove the remnants of the greens. In late May, or whenever the weather has really warmed up, plant one **tomato** plant in the center and add a stake for it. The pansies will soon be overtaken by the tomato, but may put on a new set of blossoms in the fall.

The tomato will continue to produce on into the fall, but the leaves at the bottom of the plant will probably turn yellow and in any case they are not doing you any good. Around the first of August, trim them off to create some room for a new layer: direct-sow seeds of Tuscan **kale.** Thin the young seedlings so the mature plants are about 6 inches apart.

FALL. The tomatoes continue, and the kale gets a good start in their shadow. When the tomato plant is on its last legs, cut it off at the base, leaving the roots in place so as not to dislodge the kale, which will continue to grow until winter and perhaps even on into the spring if your winters are not bitter cold.

Using a narrow trowel or a dibble (a fat, squat planting tool with a pointed end), plant bulbs of yellow **tulips** wherever there is room. Early

SPRING

EARLY
SUMMER

LATE
SUMMER

LATE
FALL

With succession gardening, you can have an almost continuous harvest in just one container, from early spring to late autumn. As the crops of each season begin to fizzle out, plant new ones in the same space. The above illustrates Succession Garden 1.

next spring, they will come up through the kale—a very pretty color combination.

Succession Garden 2

IN A BROAD, SHALLOW CONTAINER, ABOUT 8 INCHES DEEP AND 1½ FEET WIDE:

SPRING. Direct-sow seeds of **looseleaf lettuce, chervil,** and **calendula.**

SUMMER. Toward the end of May, when the weather and soil are truly warm, transplant one small **hot pepper** into the center of the pot. Most of the lettuce plants will be ready to come out, and the chervil will be looking pretty sad too, but the calendula may well keep going into early fall. In the space where the lettuce was, sow seeds of **cilantro.**

FALL. For a fall crop, in early August do another sowing of leaf lettuces, **arugula,** and **scallions** (Hardy White Bunching onions).

17

Design Your Own Succession Garden

Spring	Summer	Fall
Plant March or April, or February in mild-winter areas	*Plant May to early June*	*Plant mid July to August 1*
Razzle Dazzle spinach	parsley	fennel (bulb type),
Lollo Rossa or	cucumbers	together with Alaska
Rossimo lettuce	scarlet runner beans	nasturtiums
orach	Chinese kale (gai lohn)	purple-flowering bok
arugula	dwarf sunflower (Sunspot	choy, together with
peas	or Teddy Bear)	mustard greens
chives	eggplants	potatoes from true seed
parsley	golden purslane	Red Giant mustard
	red Malabar climbing	winter purslane
	spinach	edible pod peas
	basil	

Succession Garden 3

IN A MEDIUM-SIZE CONTAINER, ABOUT 18 INCHES IN DIAMETER AND AT LEAST 10 INCHES DEEP:

SPRING. Direct-sow **spinach beet** (perpetual spinach). Sow seeds of Misato Rose **Asian radish.** In mid spring, add a few **nasturtium** seeds near the edges.

SUMMER. In mid- to late May, plant two or three seeds (or one transplant) of **summer squash.** The spinach beet will still be producing, and nasturtiums will be reaching the point where they can spill over the edges; by July the squash will Bigfoot over everything.

FALL. For a fall crop, trim away the biggest and oldest leaves of the squash plant in early August, and sow a **mesclun** mixture around the edges. When the squash is finished, or when you've had enough, remove it by cutting at the soil line and sow another circle of mesclun seeds.

CHAPTER 3

MAKING YOUR GARDEN BEAUTIFUL

A beautiful garden does not happen by accident. It is the result of a graceful alliance of research, planning, and sure-handed understanding of the principles of good design. This is true whether it is an estate garden encompassing many acres or a container garden on a tiny patio. And it is as true for edible gardens as it is for ornamentals.

For those who equate vegetable gardens with long, boring rows, it may come as a surprise to learn that vegetables and good design can co-exist. Delete that image of long rows from your memory; in container gardens you will do things differently.

Design Fundamentals

The primary tools of garden designers are color, shape, and texture, combined in ways that produce pleasing contrasts and a sense of rhythm. In a thoughtful design, all these elements work together to create a handsome garden that reflects the owner's intentions. Garden design is an art of subtlety. Stepping into some gardens, you might feel a strong sense of serenity; others call up a mental picture of lively socializing. The more strongly you feel this emotional response, the more likely it is that the gardener designed for it.

Garden design is by no means simple. Designers must think about the color, shape, and texture of every single plant they consider: trees, shrubs, perennial and annual flowers, and ground covers and lawn. In this regard they work like artists, with one crucial extra dimension: the plants don't stand still, but change their appearance with the seasons. Perennial plants and trees continue to grow in size each year.

Designing a container garden is light-years easier. For one thing, many of the ingredients of a large garden—most trees, large shrubs, broad sweeps of lawn or ground cover—simply do not apply. For another, because a container garden is a smaller, more concentrated space, you are not overwhelmed with too many options. And since most plants in a garden of edibles are annuals, you have very few long-range decisions to make.

A full course in garden design is, we think, more than you need. If the subject interests you, a visit to your library or favorite bookstore will deliver some excellent books on the topic.

To create containers that are beautiful as well as productive, focus your attention in these areas.

- Accent the plants' best features.
- Learn to use color well (for both plants and containers).
- Create groupings for spatial impact, to make a strong visual statement.
- Guard against clutter.

A small note of caution: any garden represents a series of compromises between an ideal vision and the limitations of reality. You may develop a delightful design that your growing conditions simply will not support. Our goal is to lay out ideas that may be helpful as you begin the planning process; take the ones you can use, and leave the rest.

Accent the Plants' Best Features

We believe fiercely that edible plants are intrinsically beautiful and provide the raw ingredients, so to speak, of an artful composition. Even the humblest vegetable plant has at least one gorgeous quality, and most have many. Consider:

- The large, lusty blossoms of squash plants, almost tropical in their voluptuous excess.
- The deep green leaves of the kale plant, their edges delicately and perfectly ruffled as by a master seamstress.
- The elegant purple skin of an eggplant, so smooth you cannot resist caressing it.
- The dark green leaves of Swiss chard, held erect by broad-shouldered stems in jewel tones of ruby, garnet, and gold.

How can anyone think these plants plain looking?

Train yourself to take note of each plant's most attractive aspects. Then, when designing your container garden, try to envision an arrangement that takes advantage of the plants' best features. For example, mizuna, a very pretty salad green, grows in the shape of a frilly rosette, which is best appreciated when viewed from above; this would be a good plant to put in one of your lowest containers. Red Swiss chard is noteworthy for its beautiful garnet-colored stems; this variety would be best placed closer to eye level, and with nothing underplanted that would block the stems from view. Scented geraniums have insignificant flowers, but their aromatic leaves invite touching; position them where they can be easily reached.

If this is your first garden of any kind, you may not already know what the plants look like. In that case, turn to the best friend a gardener has: mail-order catalogs with color photographs. In the Appendix, you'll find addresses of numerous companies that sell seeds and plants by mail; they don't all have color pictures (in fact, some of the best do not), but at the moment we are using the catalogs only as visual aids. Collect as many as you can get your hands on, and study the pictures.

When you have narrowed down your choices, try this designer's trick: cut out the photos and lay them out on a plain piece of paper, moving them around until you get a combination you like. With a little experience, you'll be able to make your own mental pictures from the written descriptions in the catalogs that do not show color photos but offer interesting varieties.

The Powerful Effect of Color

Working with color—or rather, playing with color—is the most joyous, exhilarating aspect of planning your garden. Do you remember the childhood thrill of opening a brand-new box of crayons, the excitement of all those delicious colors waiting for you, so many to choose from? Designing a garden invokes that same thrill, and in fact the process is not all that different. Spread out all your colors—which are plants rather than crayons—and experiment with different combinations until you hit on something that feels just right. With artful color choices, you can achieve many moods, many looks: soft and romantic (pastels); lively (lots of bright, saturated colors); restful (just a few dark tones and hues); vivid (strong yellows and oranges); serene (monochromatic); or playful (unusual juxtapositions of color).

In plants, color comes from flowers, fruit, foliage, and bark. In container gardens, bark is usually insignificant as a visual component, so we can

Planning Your Garden by Color

To get your creative imagination going, here is a small sample of the many color possibilities for your container garden palette; many more will present themselves to you in the chapters on individual plants.

Color	Spring	Summer	Fall
blue	borage (flowers); rosemary (flowers)	blueberries; sage (flowers)	pansies
lavender/violet	thyme (flowers); lavender; chive (flowers)	purple-podded snap beans (flowers)	Lilac Belle peppers
orange	calendula	Sungold tomatoes; daylilies	nasturtiums
pink/magenta	Tricolor sage	roses; pink monarda; Malabar spinach	pansies
purple	pansies; violets	eggplant; purple snap beans	saffron crocus; Sharon Roberts lavender
red	red-leaf lettuce; tulips	scarlet runner beans; tomatoes; orach; bergamot (flowers)	red Swiss chard; pineapple sage (flowers); Red Russian kale; Red Giant mustard greens
white	sweet woodruff (flowers); apple blossoms	roses; begonias; Asian Bride eggplant	feverfew (flowers)
yellow	tulips; golden sage; violas	summer squash; Gold Nugget tomatoes	marigolds; apples

focus on the other three. (See the box above for a starter guide to choosing plants for their colors.)

FLOWERS. The flowers of most vegetable plants are only a minor attraction; exceptions include squash, scarlet runner beans, and purple-podded snap beans. All fruits are preceded by flowers, in a brief but lovely show. Most herbs produce flowers, usually small and subtle but occasionally flashy (calendula and monarda, for instance). With edible flowers, the blossoms are the whole story, and just about every color is possible.

FRUITS AND VEGETABLES. Except for edible flowers, the splashiest and longest-lasting color show in your container garden will come from fruits and vegetables: red strawberries, yellow apples, dusky blue blueberries. Beans in tones of green, purple, and yellow. Peppers wearing flamboyant coats of green, red, orange, yellow, creamy white, violet, and purple. Tomatoes that are yellow, orange, pink, and green-striped, in addition to jump-in-the-mouth red.

FOLIAGE. Sometimes we tend to think that all leaves are simply green. It's only when we look carefully that we notice the many different shades and hues of green, and the splashes of other colors intermixed with the green (known as variegation). You'll find interesting coloration in the many varieties of red-leaf lettuce; in variegated thyme, sage, and scented geraniums; in the luminescent stems of Bright Lights Swiss chard. And don't overlook the design possibilities of all-green plants that show different tones: green so dark it seems almost black, rich kelly green, blue-green, bright apple green, chartreuse—every one is a different color, a different crayon for you to play with.

The first step is to become aware of which plants offer which colors; the next step is to ponder how to combine colors in ways that are pleasing to the eye.

Think back to the color wheel that you learned in grade school. Colors that are directly opposite each other on this wheel are called complementary: yellow to purple; blue to orange; red to green. Complementary colors look good together. When we run into trouble, it's often because we are working with colors that are not pure hues but have undertones of another color. So even though green and red are complementary, it doesn't mean that any red works well with any green; a red with undertones of blue will look better next to a bluish green than it would near a green with undertones of yellow.

Another valuable guideline: colors that are next to each other on the wheel also look good together.

Red, orange, and yellow, and all the tones between, are called hot colors; the cool colors are blue, green, and violet. Hot colors appear to be closer; cool colors seem to recede. Hot colors therefore catch the eye sooner, especially the strong, deep, nonpastel tones. This is why some gardeners say they find yellow and orange hard to work with; in a broad expanse of garden, those two colors jump out at you, overwhelming everything else.

It's useful, and also fun, to know these abstract concepts about color. But as a practical matter, in a vegetable garden Mother Nature starts you off with many choices already made. The dominant color is going to be green. Most of the accent colors will be hot: reds, yellows, or oranges—that's because most of the vegetables we grow, if they are not green, are one of the hot colors. Only a few are pink, purple, or lavender, and they'll look best combined with other plants that show pink, purple, and lavender. The strongest color effects will be provided by edible flowers; fortunately, they come in just about every color you could wish for.

Don't forget that in container gardens, the containers themselves are a big part of the visual impact. Especially early in the season, while the plants are still babies, the containers may be your only source of extra color. This is a good thing if the colors are attractive and well coordinated, and it's a bad thing if they are a discordant jumble. See the box above for ideas on helping the containers enhance, rather than fight, the overall look of the garden.

Create Groupings

Working in the limited areas that usually characterize container gardens, you'll no doubt want to get maximum efficiency and maximum visual punch from your space. An excellent way to accomplish that is to create a grouping of several containers at various heights, in effect "painting" an area with plants. This gives an integrated design with a strong focal point and, in addition, offers several practical advantages. It allows you very efficient use of your space; maintaining the plants is easier than it would be if they were scattered around; and you can create combinations of plants that need different kinds of care and thus would not do well in the same container.

The difference between a well-planned group and a jumble of individual pots placed here and there at random is the same difference as that between a collection of framed artwork in a tasteful, cohesive arrangement and a bunch of pictures hung haphazardly on the wall. No doubt you've seen examples of both at some point in your life, and there is no question which one is more pleasing to look at.

What makes these plant groupings work is the variation in height. Here are some suggestions:

- Simplest of all, set a container on top of an empty container of the same size, turned upside down, or on top of a concrete block.
- Create a tiered effect with concrete blocks; in the rear, stack two blocks and put one container on top. In the middle row, set one block with a container on top. In the front, set a container on the floor. Each concrete block (wonderfully utilitarian but not exactly gorgeous) is hidden by the plant in front of it.
- Take that same idea a bit further if you have the space. Make your tiers longer by resting wooden planks on concrete blocks, and set the plants on these "benches."
- Place three containers of the same height on the floor in a triangular arrangement; then set a fourth container on top, resting on the rims of the three below.
- Use a stepladder to display a series of small or medium-size containers; if the ladder is wooden, first paint it a compatible color. Remember that the rungs of a ladder are not wide; choose pots with an appropriate size at the bottom, and fasten them in place using the dowel-and-chain technique described on pages 9 to 10. Another solution is to add an extra board atop each rung, making them wider.
- If you have basic carpentry skills or can sweet-talk someone who does, build a two-tiered box-within-a-box, like that described on page 34.

Another device for taking advantage of all available space is a trellis. Several kinds are described in Chapter 4, but for now we simply want you to keep in mind that a trellis makes a wonderful focal point.

The overall design is always a matter of balancing the size and arrangement of the containers with the structural look of the plants themselves. Keep these guidelines in mind.

- In window boxes, include some upright plants and some that trail down.
- In containers that will be viewed from all sides, put a tall plant in the center, with smaller upright plants at its feet, and surround everything with plants that cascade over the edge.
- If the container backs up to a wall, put the tallest plants in the rear, fronted with smaller plants, and then something that trails down.

Keep Everything Looking Neat

A defining characteristic of container gardens, in comparison to traditional ones, is that they tend to be smaller, more compact, and closer at hand. Because they are right under our noses, so to speak, it's easier to admire their delights and, in the case of edible plants, savor their produce. But by the same token, flaws are more obvious. Whereas in a traditional garden, ratty-looking foliage and dead flowers are lost in the overall view, in containers every disagreeable problem is right there, in your face.

All of which means that to preserve the beauty you have so artfully achieved, it's important to keep up with maintenance. If you don't use all your edible flowers in cooking, be sure to pick off any dead blossoms, a chore given the endearing name "deadheading." Snip away any dead or holey leaves, and keep the soil surface clear of plant debris. All these little attentions will also help to discourage plant pests and diseases.

This is not a major operation. As you stand by your containers, admiring and praising the plants for how well they've grown since yesterday, just run a quick critical eye over everything and take care of any problems you see.

In terms of the overall appearance of your garden, there is another kind of clutter: the visual chaos of mismatched, unattractive containers stuck here and there with no thought. This kind of disorder tends to creep up on you as in your enthusiasm, you succumb to new plants and new containers on every trip to the garden center. Before you know it, you have a real mess: empty containers stacked up in one corner, along with half-used bags of potting mix and compost, a watering can with a broken handle, and all those small nursery pots you can't bear to throw away. It takes real discipline to buy only containers that blend well with the ones you already have. It may seem like too much trouble to create a storage space for all your supplies, but do it anyway. In the long run, you'll be happier.

Putting It All Together

It has been said that beauty is in the eye of the beholder. It has also been said that Mother Nature is the best garden designer. That's a bit like saying water is wet—true, but not very helpful. Sometimes it's hard to know where to start when building a garden where none now exists. This summary may help.

1. Your first step is to analyze the space you have available for gardening, following the information in Chapter 1. Everything else depends on this fundamental question: what growing conditions do you have to work with?

2. Using the ideas in Chapter 2, make up a wish list of the plants you would like to grow—things you already know you enjoy, plus any new temptations you think it would be fun to try.

3. Compare the two. Read up on the horticultural requirements of the plants on your wish list (consult the individual plant chapters), and eliminate those items that simply will not grow in your space.

4. Now for aesthetics. What do you know about the colors, textures, and shapes of the plants you like? Are there special varieties that will provide unusual visual interest? As you look over the list, considering color for starters, what combinations suggest themselves to you? Or try thinking in terms of a theme: if you're mad for Thai food, for instance, can you create a container with ingredients that are often used in that cuisine? Many suggestions for Theme Gardens are spread throughout this book.

5. Double-check your plant selections: do those you visualize growing beautifully together need the same growing

conditions, or will they have to be in separate containers? If you spot a potential problem, can you substitute another plant that provides the same visual effect (color, texture, or whatever)?

6. Incorporate into your imaginings the visual effects of man-made elements: containers, trellises, any decorative additions that enhance your theme. Will painting the containers a dark purple pull your color scheme together? Would a grouping of containers look better at varied heights, and can you create some kind of platform to provide that? If a trellis is part of the plan, what should it look like: a rustic creation of twigs and branches, sleek bamboo, or perhaps wood, painted a compatible color?

7. Be prepared to be surprised. Some of the effects you planned so carefully will turn out differently—and maybe much better. One very cooperative feature of containers is that they are portable. If you don't like the way things are turning out, move your containers around, adjusting their positions to take better advantage of the sun or to create a more pleasing group. Even the containers that have several plants growing together can be fine-tuned during the season. If something dies, replace it; if the begonias turn out to be a different color from what you expected, move them. Make a few notes for next year, and then don't fret. Put your energy into enjoying what you've accomplished. You have every right to feel proud.

PART TWO

Down-to-
Earth Basics

CHAPTER 4

HARDWARE

CONTAINERS, TRELLISES, TOOLS, AND STORAGE

Your first venture into a large garden center can be overwhelming; there is simply so much *stuff*, how can anyone know what's what? Even when focusing on just one item—pots, say—there's enough variety to make a person dizzy. And that's before you take even the first peek at the plants. In this chapter and the next, we'll help you sort it all out.

Containers

Nearly all containers are fabricated from one of five materials, each with its advantages and disadvantages: clay, plastic, wood, paper pulp, and metal.

CLAY. The classic terra-cotta flowerpot that you've seen a million times is made of unglazed pottery clay. Clay pots are heavy and relatively fragile; they break and chip easily. Unglazed pots are porous, which is both good and bad. It's good because air circulates more easily to the root zone; it's bad because soil moisture evaporates more rapidly and you'll need to water more often. (Even that has a positive side because evaporation is a cooling process, and so plants in clay pots have some summertime protection against ultrahot soil, which can burn the roots.)

Perhaps the biggest drawback is that in winter, wet soil or even water trapped in the pores of the pot can freeze, expand, and crack the container.

Many gardeners, however, willingly overlook all these faults because of aesthetics: in any size, shape, or condition, terra-cotta pots are beautiful. Even the markings left by fertilizer residues and moss are considered a plus by many people, for weathered pots add an antique charm, especially in rustic or "country" gardens.

A variation on this basic theme is glazed clay. Applied to the outside, the glaze serves to give color and also seals the clay, creating a smooth surface. Because glazed-clay pots are therefore less porous, evaporation is less of a problem than with unglazed clay. The primary attraction of these pots is their beautiful colors. You may find them in solid colors, in both bright and muted tones, and in many swirled blends. Some may have been specially painted to create an antique look; others have colorful designs painted on a solid neutral background, similar to painted china. As you might imagine, with all that artistic attention, these pots are more expensive than the equivalent sizes of plain terra-cotta. Because they are less porous, glazed pots are not so vulnerable to winter freeze, but they are still breakable; you'll want to handle them carefully.

Classic terra-cotta pots come in many handsome styles.

PLASTIC. Plastic is inexpensive, lightweight, and nonbreakable. It is nonporous, and so holds water well. In practical terms, these qualities make it an ideal material for plant containers. Where plastic pots tend to fall short is in aesthetics, although that has improved in recent years. Most plastic containers are white or dark green, and they come in many shapes: the traditional tapered flowerpot, wide shallow bowls, square or rectangular boxes, and so forth.

You will also see plastic pots in bright decorative colors. Used carefully, they provide a strong color theme and a sleek, modern look; used haphazardly, they can easily overwhelm the

New high-tech plastics have the look of stoneware but not the weight.

plants in visual impact. A jumble of uncoordinated colors and textures looks like a kindergarten gone berserk; stick to one color or one color family, and you can create something quite stunning.

Some inexpensive plastic pots are modeled after terra-cotta in both shape and color. Whether or not they work for you is a matter of personal preference.

Strawberry Pots

One specific kind of container you'll find at many garden centers and retail nurseries is a tall, urn-shaped planter with several pockets on the sides. It is called a strawberry pot because that was its original purpose: individual strawberry plants went into the pockets, making it possible to grow berries in a very small area by using vertical space. In theory, strawberry pots should work just as well for any other small plants, but in practice many people have had very disappointing experiences with these pots.

The problem is watering—it's hard to get water (which runs straight down) out to the edges, to the roots of plants growing in all those little side pockets. Also, strawberry pots are usually made of clay, whose high evaporation rate only exacerbates the problem.

Here's a solution. In the plumbing section of the hardware store, find a piece of plastic pipe at least 1 inch in diameter and have it cut to a length that is just a bit shorter than the height of your pot. Then, with an ordinary drill, drill holes all over it. Tightly close off the bottom with a cork or sink stopper, set the pipe down into the pot, slightly off center (don't block the drainage hole), and fill the strawberry pot with potting soil. Now when you pour water into the pipe opening, it will ooze out sideways through the holes.

Rose Marie says: Plastic that looks like plastic is fine, and has a respectable place in my garden, but I have no patience for plastic that pretends to be something it's not. On the whole, I still prefer wood or clay for pots.

Maggie says: They aren't so bad, and besides, the price is right. I'd rather put my money into the plants.

The black plastic containers that nursery plants come in can also be used. (We're referring to the heavy-duty plastic pots in 1-, 2-, or 5-gallon sizes, *not* the thin plastic used for small 2- or 4-inch transplants.) The smaller heavy-duty ones work especially well in window boxes (with plants in individual pots, you can move them in and out) and in groupings where you need to separate plants that require different care.

The newest players on the scene are handsome containers made from various high-tech plastics: polyester or foam resin, polyethylene, fiberglass, high-density polyurethane. All these space-age materials are very durable and amazingly lightweight; you can lift with two fingers a large urn that looks as if it is made of concrete. The containers have the appearance of cast concrete and antique terra-cotta, but none of their fragility. They aren't inexpensive, but they do last for years and are gorgeous.

Making Your Own

Wooden containers are the favorite of many gardeners, both for their beauty and for their lasting qualities. If you have basic tools and moderate skills (or have leverage over someone who does), you can make your own. Not only is this vastly satisfying and economical, but you also end up with containers that are exactly the size you want.

Building a container is a simple woodworking project: an open box with no lid. For something that will last for years, use rot-resistant lumber (cedar or redwood) or apply a wood sealer to other types of wood. (We know someone who makes them out of discarded wooden pallets.) For ease of maintenance and 100 percent resistance to rot, you could ask at the building supply store for the new composite material made of recycled plastic and wood waste products such as sawdust; one popular brand is Trex. Most commonly used for decks and other outdoor projects, it comes in the same sizes as dimension lumber, and can be cut with a power saw.

A box-within-a-box holds deep-rooted and smaller plants in one compact space.

To avoid ugly rust streaks, use galvanized nails, screws, and bolts. Add wooden "runners" at the bottom, to raise the container an inch or so and provide air circulation. And be sure to drill holes in the bottom for drainage.

A Box Within a Box. This two-story container provides space for tomatoes, with their deep root system, along with shallow-rooted vegetables in a broader, lower box. The bottom box can be any size; the drawing shows a 2-foot cube. The top is a bottomless 1-foot cube. Fill the lower container with potting mix, then set the top box in position and fill it; now you have a total planting depth of 3 feet. To make the tomatoes very happy, you might want to add four stakes to the corners of the top box, providing the skeleton of a 3-foot tomato cage.

A Plant Tower. This tower consists of a series of progressively smaller boxes, each one turned 90 degrees from the one below so that it rests on the edges of the larger box below, and presents four triangular-shaped planting spots at each level. With an arrangement such

The plant tower, a simple carpentry project, makes very efficient use of a small space.

as this, you can grow a large amount of produce in a small space. A tower is particularly attractive planted with trailers and danglers.

Wood. Containers made of wood are intrinsically beautiful, if you happen to love wood for its own sake (as we do), but somewhat more problematic than clay or plastic. Wood containers are usually heavy (compared to plastic in an equivalent size), and over time they will rot from the damp soil. If you are buying ready-made wooden containers, look for those constructed from redwood or cedar, which are naturally decay-resistant. If you are making your own, either use one of those two woods or, if that's not practical, use other wood but apply a sealer to the inside and outside surfaces of your finished product.

The natural look of wooden containers complements most plants. For longer life, choose rot-resistant woods.

Paper Pulp. These pots look like they're made of thick, bumpy cardboard, and in fact that's essentially what they are—paper pulp (often made from recycled paper) pressed into shape. They are very lightweight and quite inexpensive, but not long-lasting. With care, you can usually get three years' use out of them, especially if you elevate them off the floor to give them a bit of breathing space.

Metal, Concrete, Wire. Containers of brass (or faux brass) or other metals work better for houseplants than for outdoor gardens. Large tubs or rectangular planters made of cast or poured concrete are found in the pages of gardening magazines more often than in a normal garden; they photograph well but are very heavy to work with, and can get hot enough to cook your plants. Hanging containers (often called baskets even if they aren't) made of wire can be used only if first lined with something that keeps the soil from dribbling through; see page 64 for planting techniques.

All the containers we have listed so far have a tendency to drip onto whatever surface they rest on. A wide drip tray underneath the pots will offer some protection for your new wood deck, or your neighbor's balcony one floor below.

Grow Bags. Very popular in Europe, the concept of grow bags is now finding its way to America. These are large bags filled with rich potting soil; slits are cut in the bag and the plants are grown directly in place, without any other containers. Large bags of commercial potting mix can be used the same way. One main drawback is looks: until the plants get big enough to cover it, you can see the bag underneath—advertising label and all. The other drawback to grow bags is their shape: they have to be laid flat on the floor or another broad surface, so you're limited as to where you can put them. But they are excruciatingly simple, and if you want a quick way to get going, this is it.

We recently found an ingenious product that operates on the same principle as grow bags but is much more attractive. These are long, narrow bags made of heavy-duty nylon-reinforced plastic (black or dark green) with precut planting slits and a loop at the top for hanging. When we first saw them, they had been hung in a vertical arrangement on the posts framing a doorway, four on each side, so that the whole post seemed to be made of flowers. The same company (see the Appendix) also makes a double bag that can be looped over a balcony rail like a saddlebag, so passersby (along with the owner) get to enjoy the garden.

An old toy box, with the top opening down, makes a charming storage unit for supplies and display for small plants. Coat with polyurethane for weather protection.

HOUSEHOLD ITEMS AND FOUND ART. Between the two of us, we have some of just about all the kinds of pots described so far, but we both also have our share of containers created mostly out of ingenuity—items that weren't originally designed as planters but that have great potential. Keep your eyes open whenever you're in a hardware store, secondhand store, or thrift shop, the household goods section of a large general merchandiser (such as Kmart, Target, or Home Depot), or at a garage sale or flea market, and continually ask yourself, "How could I use that?" For instance:

- In the "$1 only" section of a large variety store, Maggie found round white plastic tubs about 2 feet in diameter. "I had no immediate plans, but I knew they would make great planters so I bought five of them."
- Rose Marie discovered large plastic buckets (probably intended for laundry or general cleanup) in her local

discount outlet, and was attracted to three nice features: they're deeper than they are wide (good for deep-rooted vegetables), they have handles (easy to move around), and they come in several attractive colors.

- Empty 5-gallon paint buckets left over from your own or a neighbor's house-painting project are the perfect size for growing tomatoes. (One caution for all plastic containers: make sure they are fully opaque; if they are transluscent enough to admit sunlight, the plant roots can burn in hot summers.)

- A child's wooden toy box will hold plants on top and your garden supplies inside. Try setting it on its side, with the top opening downward, and see if it seems strong enough and stable enough to hold plants on top (which is really a side); if it is, you'll be able to get into the storage without having to move the plants. If the box looks nice in the condition you find it, you won't need to do anything except give it a protective coating of polyurethane; if it has seen better days, give it a new coat of paint.

- If you have a friendly connection with a restaurant, ask if they'll save some of those really large cans for you. Several grouped together make a pretty planting of salad greens (especially if painted; see box on page 24). You can also use them effectively in a window box or other planter where you might want to move plants in and out during the season. If nothing else, they make an inexpensive platform for lifting some of your containers to a modest height.

- In a category all by themselves are wine and whiskey barrels. You may find them for sale at garden centers— either the real thing or reproductions—but if you are fortunate enough to live near a wine-growing region, inquire about buying old barrels that are no longer in use. Last summer Rose Marie purchased some whole barrels from a nearby winery, and then worked out a trade with a neighbor: he sawed them in half; she cooked him a fabulous dinner. Try to find the kind known as true Burgundian barrels, which have wooden bands holding the staves together rather than rust-prone metal; or paint the metal black with a rust-resistant outdoor paint like Rustoleum.

Some of the most satisfying and interesting containers are those you find at thrift shops and yard sales—items that were never meant to hold plants but nonetheless do so very nicely. To be successful in this approach, you need a good eye and an explorer's soul.

Maggie, who can smell a good yard sale blocks away, found these treasures on a recent Saturday; grouped together, they create a miniature kitchen garden with a rustic charm.

- A very large wooden salad bowl (about 20 inches across) with little round feet. It had originally been painted red on the outside, but paint had chipped off and the inside was so badly scarred with knife marks that the varnish was flaking off—in other words, no one in her right mind would use it for salad. But with drainage holes drilled in the bottom, it made a very handsome planter for salad greens, which have shallow roots. "And," says Maggie, "the symmetry of growing salad in a salad bowl pleases me."
- An old wire market basket with handles, badly rusted but otherwise intact. "I spray-painted it with dark red Rustoleum, lined it with 3-mil black plastic, and filled it with herbs."
- A large, restaurant-size colander that had seen better days. Lined with the same heavy black plastic, it very nicely holds mizuna, which grows into a low, rounded mound, with an outer fringe of radishes. (It could also have been made into a hanging container, using the handles.)

Rose Marie, who lives in a more agricultural area, went looking for unusual containers in preparation for this book and found gold in a local junk shop:

- An old metal washtub. With drainage holes drilled in the bottom, it held a small, self-contained herb garden: thyme, several basils, rosemary, chives, dill, and parsley.
- A large commercial mop bucket made of galvanized zinc. Rose Marie planted it with a staked tomato and lemon cucumber spilling over the edge.
- A chicken feeder—a tall cylinder, slightly tapered at the bottom, that rests in a wide, shallow pan. Farmers add feed to the top and a small amount drops into the bottom

through narrow openings; as the chickens eat the feed in the pan, opening up space, more seed dribbles in. Those same narrow openings serve as drainage now that it's converted to a planter.

On any day of any week, you can find clever containers in your favorite thrift store, for example:

- An old spatterware washbasin with rusted-out holes in the bottom.
- Large, decorative food tins, especially if the design is printed directly on the metal, rather than on a paper label.
- For a child's garden, large old toys like a dump truck with missing wheels, a child's wheelbarrow, a toy wagon.
- Scads of straw baskets in all shapes and sizes, with handles for hanging (add liner first).

QUESTIONS OF SIZE. Most containers are measured by their diameter at the top. In the familiar tapered flowerpot shape, broader at the top than at the base, the height is usually the same dimension as the diameter of the top. (When your favorite nursery advertises "6-inch plants," it's not the plant that is 6 inches but the pot.)

As a general rule, you'll be better off with larger containers because they don't dry out as quickly. The trade-off is that to get a broad surface area, large enough to do a serious planting, you may also be getting depth, which makes the container quite heavy. Some vegetables need that deep soil (tomatoes are a classic example), but many others are happy in just 8 to 10 inches; the extra depth of soil is wasted. (For ways to fill up some of that space, see the planting tips in the box on page 62.) Taking all this into account, your best bet is to have a collection of sizes and shapes to enable you to match plant size to container size; if you're not sure how much root room to allow for, err on the side of too much rather than too little.

Imagine the final weight of a very large container, filled with soil, in the larger context of your entire planting area. If there's a chance you might want to move the container—maybe to make room for a picnic table later in the summer, or to move a young tree into a more sheltered spot in winter—then you'd be smart to plan now for mobility. Garden centers sell plant bases with wheels, or you can easily create your own from scrap lumber and casters.

ONE ABSOLUTE RULE. No matter what material the container is made from, or what size or shape it is, it *must* have drainage holes in the bottom. No exceptions, no excuses, no arguments. Anything you see in the garden center that does not have holes is meant to be used as a decorative outer container (called a cachepot), with another, usually plainer pot set inside.

Keep this in mind for found art and other household items that you plan to use as containers: you have to be able to add holes. Plastic and wooden containers can be drilled with an ordinary household drill; the size of the drill bit determines the size of the hole. If you're recycling large tin cans, make holes around the bottom edges with a church key, the kind of can opener that makes triangular pouring spouts.

Trellises

A trellis is any kind of structure onto which plants are encouraged to grow upward; it can be a free-standing tower or, more commonly, a flat form that works best when attached to something like a wall or a large container. Because they take advantage of vertical space, trellises are a good idea in all gardens and a lifesaver for container vegetable gardens.

You can buy commercial trellises at your favorite garden center, home improvement center, or lumberyard. They are made of wood (stained, painted, or left natural) and also plastic, and come in several basic shapes and sizes. In the same retail locations you'll also find lattice screening, made of

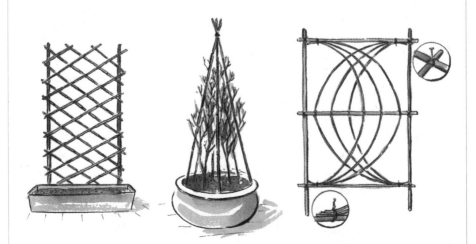

Trellises can be made from many materials, adding aesthetics and practicality to your containers. From left: lengths of bamboo from the garden center, tall stakes from the lumberyard, branch trimmings from a neighbor's spring pruning.

very thin wood strips fashioned into a diamond pattern or square grid. By themselves these lattice panels have little structural integrity and are intended to be nailed onto some kind of framework. But you may also find this latticework already made up into framed panels, and they work very well for trellises; panels in narrow widths are especially versatile, and can be combined into many arrangements. Also available commercially are flexible trellises made of nylon string or plastic gridwork; these, too, have to be nailed onto something.

Freestanding trellises made of wood or metal are another way to go. They represent more of an investment, but they often have a strong architectural or decorative look that will add a significant design dimension to your garden.

Of course you or your favorite handyperson can construct your own trellis, in just the right size, from dimension lumber; check out the styles at the garden center, and copy the format you like best. This is a great opportunity to explore the wonders of a real hardware store and let yourself be dazzled by all the items you didn't know existed.

How about a custom-made trellis handcrafted from bamboo (individual lengths are sold at the garden center), or from tree branches rescued from a tree-trimming project? All you need are strong garden twine, a good pair of pruners, and your creative eye.

A very clever tent arrangement can be made with two trellises and two rectangular planters. The trellises should be at least 4 feet tall, and the planters 8 to 10 inches deep. Set the planters about 2 feet apart and position the trellises so they angle inward from the outside edge of their planters toward the space between the two, then fasten the tops together to form a sort of A-frame tent. Because of the triangulation, this is an extremely strong construction. Pole beans, peas, or cucumbers, in all their rambunctious glory, climb up

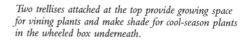

Two trellises attached at the top provide growing space for vining plants and make shade for cool-season plants in the wheeled box underneath.

over the trellises and down the other side. To really use your space well, grow cool-season vegetables like spinach or lettuce in the shade underneath the trellises. To make it easier to reach them, you might construct a flat box with wheels, and set the shade containers on it. This is also a good way to recycle

Not Your Mother's Apple Tree

E ven in a space that at first seems too small, you might be able to grow fruit trees if you can set up an espalier. They are a perfect combination of utility and good looks: not only do you have your own apples a few steps away, but you've also created a very beautiful decorative arrangement.

First, pick your spot: a sunny wall. Make sure you can add bolts to the wall, and don't forget that once the tree is growing, you won't easily be able to move it. Attach large eye-bolts up the wall in at least five rows that are 18 inches apart vertically, and string heavy-duty wire through them horizontally. In spring or fall, plant the tree in a container at least 2 feet deep, and cut the trunk back to about 2 inches above your lowest wire. When it begins to branch out, pick out the three best-looking sprouts and prune away the others. As these sprouts grow into small branches, ease two of them downward and tie them onto the horizontal wires; allow the third to grow upward to the next highest wire. As soon as it reaches the next wire, which may be later this season or next year, repeat the process. Keep going this way until you reach the top wire, where you will cut away all signs of new upward growth.

As the tree grows it sends out very short stems,

called spurs, where the fruit will form; prune away any that are facing into the wall. Also, be alert for signs of new branches forming where you don't want them; if one of these renegades shows up, snip it completely off.

Choose dwarf or semidwarf varieties of fruit trees, and check the individual plant descriptions in the Fruits section for specifics about caring for them.

Start your espalier structure by attaching heavy wires to a sunny wall, about a foot and a half apart.

As the tree grows, force branches laterally on each wire, and remove those that grow between wires.

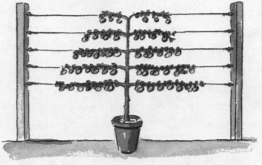

Enjoy many years of fruit.

a child's toy wagon or an old skateboard your teenagers have outgrown.

A nice alternative to a flat trellis is a demicage made of wire fencing. At a hardware store, lumberyard, or well-stocked garden center, buy a length of wire fencing or concrete-reinforcing wire. The piece should be at least 4 feet wide (more is better), and as long as two-thirds the circumference of your container. Thus if your container is 20 inches across (a good size for large vining plants like squash, cucumbers, and tomatoes), buy a 40-inch length of 4-foot or 6-foot fencing material. Make sure the grid opening is large enough for you to get your hand through.

Set the wire fencing in a semicircle around your container, with one end resting on the ground. Secure your "fence" to the container with two lengths of heavy-duty picture wire, threaded through the grid and twisted together in front. Gloves and wire cutters make this easier. (Yes, you do have wire cutters. Look at your basic pliers; there's a wire cutter just forward of the hinge.)

The vines will climb the fence as they grow (with a bit of encouragement from you in the beginning). The produce will be more prolific, cleaner, and less apt to rot because it's not resting on damp ground. And because the fence does not completely encircle the container, you can easily reach in through the open side for planting and picking.

Many other configurations are possible; you're limited only by your imagination. Look over your garden space and think "Up." What can you create? Here's one example from Maggie's garden.

Grow large vining plants (like squash and tomatoes) upward on a half-cage of heavy-duty wire grid with fist-size openings.

Maggie says: I think snap peas are the greatest thing since homemade bread, and I can't imagine a garden without them. But I like the productivity of pole peas, and they need to grow up on something, and besides you already know how tiny my patio space is. So I thought it would be fun to try growing them outside my living room window in what is otherwise unused airspace. First I nailed a row of galvanized nails, 2 inches apart, into the top and bottom window frames, and strung 50-pound monofilament (i.e., fishing line) between them. Then I found a small plastic storage cabinet that just exactly fits under the windowsill (it is intended by its manufacturer to be hung on a wall, but it works just as well sitting on the patio floor). On top of the cabinet (which holds my garden supplies) sits a rectangular planter box that is planted with peas at the rear (closest to the window) and pansies at the front. The peas are quite happily growing up the monofilament, and at the same time they create a very pretty green curtain; I love the way they look with sunlight coming through the leaves.

Unless your container is very deep, simply sinking the legs of the trellis into the soil will not hold it securely enough to withstand strong winds or heavy cucumbers, especially if the trellis is tall. Bolt or screw the legs either to the container (which means you can move container and trellis together as a unit) or if possible to an adjoining wall, which means you can fasten it at the top as well as the bottom. The second method is preferable for a very tall trellis, which in windy situations can act like a sail, causing the whole thing to topple.

One other thing to consider: what will you be growing on the trellis? Not all plants like all kinds of trellises equally well; it depends on how they grow.

- **Peas** send out short, thin tendrils that wrap themselves tightly around thin supports like a wire or string but cannot easily fit around something wide or fat like a thick bamboo pole or 1-inch wood strips.
- **Pole beans and tall nasturtiums** grow on vines that wind themselves, stem and all, around a pole or stake; they will also wind around a thin wire, but something with a wider diameter uses your space more efficiently (see page 82). They have an easier time with wood, with its slightly rough surface, than with smooth plastic or bamboo.
- **Climbing roses** do not twine themselves on their own, but need to be tied in place with household string or garden twine. Squash and cucumbers also make tendrils, like peas, but they're not stout enough to hold the heavy fruits; you'll need to tie the vines in place. The diameter of the trellis pieces is not as critical as strength is; no wimpy trellises here.

Gear Boxes

It is said of many things in life that half the battle is having the right gear, and this is certainly true of gardening. We suggest you invest in two large storage bins made of heavy-duty plastic, with lids, and consider them your gear boxes, one for tools and one for potting soil components. Tucked discreetly off to the side, they will neatly contain nearly everything you need for your gardening projects.

One bin holds hand tools (trowel, pruners, etc.), a couple of spray bottles, packages of fertilizer and other consumables, unused pots, and a heavy-duty dropcloth (or plastic tablecloth) to spread on the floor or picnic table while you're working.

The second bin holds your soil mixture and any leftover ingredients. On one trip to the garden center, buy everything that will go into your potting mix (see pages 49 to 53), then use this second bin as a mixing tub. When all your planting containers are full, store any leftover mixture, plus partially used bags of the individual elements, in this bin.

If space limitations mean you have to stack the bins, put the soil box on the bottom because you'll probably be getting into it less frequently.

A specialized type of trellis is the one used to espalier fruit trees (espalier can be done with many types of plants, but fruit trees are most commonly used). Through careful pruning, espaliered trees are trained to grow in a more or less flat plane, rather than in all directions. This allows trees to grow in spaces that are otherwise too narrow, and it also creates a very beautiful look. There is a real botanical advantage as well: fruit trees send off their short fruit-bearing stems from branches that are horizontal, so by creating an espalier, with its strong horizontal lines, you're encouraging the tree to produce fruit.

It is possible to espalier plants onto a freestanding support, but usually they are attached to a wall or fence, and that is the assumption with our directions (see page 42). Espaliered trees are more or less permanent additions to the garden, so they are best for people who are ready to stay put for a few years.

Finally, even though they're not exactly trellises, those round wire supports known as tomato cages serve the same purpose. They don't provide the height of a full-size trellis, but they are adequate for tallish vegetables that have a tendency to sprawl in all directions. Many gardeners have learned the hard way that these cages are actually too flimsy for vigorous tomatoes, but you may find them a handy way to corral tall herb plants and some vegetables. They're inexpensive, so it doesn't hurt to keep a few on hand.

Tools

Here's a piece of good news: container gardeners need far fewer tools than traditional gardeners do, and none with long handles. Only two things are really essential, a trowel and gloves, and if you don't care whether your hands get dirty you don't even need gloves.

TROWEL. A multipurpose tool you will use for mixing potting soil ingredients, loosening up crusted soil from last year, digging holes for seeds or transplants, and levering out dead things. Don't buy the cheapest kind you see; it will probably bend out of shape the first time you try to do any serious digging. A broad trowel is the most versatile, good for almost every task, but narrow ones are very handy for snuggling in a small transplant between existing plants, or for bulbs.

GLOVES. When you start mixing together components of your potting soil or planting three dozen tulip bulbs, you'll be glad to have a good pair of gloves. As to what type of glove, you have a choice of fabric, leather, and rubber. Leather gloves are more expensive but last longer; fabric (usually cotton) is inexpensive and washable, up to a point.

This is a subject about which gardeners tend to have strong opinions.

Maggie says: My favorite pair now is something I was originally very skeptical about. They are heavy rubber in a distinctive orange color, with a fabric lining and long length that gives protection halfway up to your elbows. They're sturdy enough to resist thorns, yet flexible enough that you can pick up seeds (that's the part I didn't believe, but it turns out to be true).

Rose Marie says: I hate gloves that make my hands feel sweaty and clammy. The ones I like best are made of breathable knit fabric that has been dipped in green latex on the palm side only, so your fingers and palms are protected but your hands stay cool.

PRUNER. A small hand pruner or trimmer will come in handy for trimming away dead or ugly leaves as well as for actual pruning. We don't consider them as essential because often you can do those chores with just your fingers or your household scissors, but the pruner gives a cleaner cut that's important if you are growing something with a tough stem such as rosemary. And if you have roses or fruit trees, a pruner is fairly essential.

CULTIVATOR FORK. A hand tool with tines at its business end. The tines may be either straight or bent 90 degrees so they're perpendicular to the handle. This tool is useful for loosening up soil before planting, and for drawing a shallow furrow in case you want to plant seeds in a straight line.

Good tools make life easier. Clockwise from top: two trowels, one regular and one narrow; gloves; dibble; cultivator fork; pruners.

DIBBLE. A T-shaped digging implement with a pointed end, used to make large holes, as for planting bulbs.

HOUSEHOLD ITEMS RECYCLED. Lots of the items that normally pass through your kitchen can be put to use as garden tools; not only do you save resources, but you get to feel terribly clever. Here are a few of our favorites:

- **Chopsticks.** These make great tools for seed planting, for staking short plants, and for holding frost covers up off tender seedlings. Restaurants are usually required to throw out the wooden kind because of health codes, so you don't need to feel guilty about bringing them home after your meal.
- **Plastic milk or water jugs.** Trim away the bottom and most of three sides, but leave the top and handle, and you have a scoop for mixing and transferring soil. Or cut off the base and leave everything else in place, and you've created a cloche to protect baby tomatoes, peppers, or eggplants from cold nights. A sharp knife cuts plastic very easily.
- **Panty hose.** Cut old panty hose into short, narrow strips, and use them to tie plants to a stake or trellis. They are wonderfully stretchy, and don't cut into plant stems the way some twine will. You may consider this funky or silly, but in truth it's hard to find a commercial product that works as well; hide them discreetly under the foliage and trim away the excess, and no one has to know.

Storage

If you can't find room indoors for your garden supplies, or if you'd like the materials closer to your container garden, here are some tidy ideas for storing them outdoors.

Spend some time in the housewares section of your favorite store, investigating the many shapes and sizes of plastic storage bins with snap-on lids (Rubbermaid makes them, as do many other manufacturers). Most of the ones we've seen are rectangular, which is more space efficient than round tubs; some are broader than they are tall, while others are tall but narrow, like oversized wastebaskets. Some have concave lids to allow stacking—a nice feature. The bins work well for holding your supplies and for mixing and then storing potting soil; one or two provide the basis for a more or less permanent workstation (see box on page 45).

The bins themselves are fairly neutral in appearance, and they would be perfectly acceptable tucked off in a corner. You might want to stack two and put a planted container on top if you don't mind moving it to get into the storage bins. Even better, build a deep bench from outdoor plywood, or assemble one with wide wood planks and concrete blocks; tuck the bins underneath, and display your containers on top.

In that same housewares section, check out the selection of plastic

Gear boxes keep small necessaries together and neatly tucked away underneath a display bench.

storage cubes. They're about 18 inches square and come in all sorts of colors, the sides are open grids, and usually they don't have tops. If they are strong enough—and this is what you have to ascertain—you can use them to create an inexpensive storage unit. Set two side by side with the opening facing out, then set two more on top. Now you can place medium-size planted containers on the top, and put your gardening supplies inside the cubes. They're not completely out of sight, but they are tidy looking.

Rubbermaid makes a line of outdoor storage lockers (large) and indoor/outdoor snap-together cabinets (medium to small) in an unobtrusive tan color; probably other manufacturers do as well. The small cabinet that Maggie used for her pea trellis is one example.

CHAPTER 5

SOFTWARE
SOIL, SEEDS, AND PLANTS

We said earlier that container gardening is light-years easier than traditional gardening in the ground. In this chapter you'll find out why.

Soil

In a garden, everything begins and ends with soil quality. Good soil allows both fast drainage *and* moisture retention. The only way around this apparent catch-22 is a soil that has an almost perfect blend of ingredients that provide both qualities—and that also has adequate nutrients and the right structure to allow good aeration.

Traditional gardeners rarely start out with that kind of soil; they must create it through hours of extremely difficult physical labor. And if they skip that step of preparing the soil, or even if they do just a halfway job, they might as well find another hobby because they'll never get satisfactory results.

Container gardeners, on the other hand, have it much easier: all we have to do is make a trip to the garden center, buy a big bag of good potting soil, pour some into our containers, and then try not to smirk.

When it comes to choosing potting soil for containers, there are basically two ways to go: dead easy and almost as easy. Dead easy is selecting a high-quality potting soil and using it straight from the bag. Almost as easy is buying any all-purpose potting soil and adding other things to it to fit your specific needs. (A third choice, not as easy, is to purchase each separate ingredient and mix your own planting medium from scratch. This is not terribly practical for container gardeners, and for most people it's not necessary; the end result would be something very like either of the other two choices.)

The difference between the two basic options—the product you can use as is, and the one you might want to amend—is mostly one of degree. Speaking very generally, the basic ingredients are much the same, but the higher-quality material has smaller, finer pieces of the main constituents and lesser amounts of coarse filler material. Usually, but not always, price is a good indicator.

Again speaking broadly, commercial potting mixes are a combination of (1) something that holds water well (commonly either peat or ground bark) and (2) something that keeps the first ingredient from compacting tightly (usually either perlite, vermiculite, or pumice, or some combination thereof). If you check the list of ingredients on the label, you'll see other things listed as well. Mixes may have regional variations depending on locally available materials. We've seen some that include earthworm castings, compost, ground fir bark, and sand.

One item you will probably *not* see listed is actual soil. Gardeners use the term "potting soil" out of habit, but in fact almost all potting mixes are soilless.

So which way should you go: straight out of the bag, or your own blend? It's partly a question of your budget, and partly what's available on the day you go shopping. Compare two brands. With any luck, the bags will have some areas of clear plastic and you can look inside. A high-quality mix has ground peat moss (looks like soft, dark brown dirt) combined in about equal measure with either perlite (looks like tiny white rocks), vermiculite (shiny flat bits), or some of each. Large pieces of bark or other shredded plant parts are often a clue to lesser quality. So is a smaller proportion of perlite or vermiculite. One very respectable approach, and quite affordable, is to get a large bag of the lesser-quality mix and a small bag of the amendment it seems to lack: ground peat moss, perlite, or vermiculite. At home, you will mix the bags together.

You'll want to avoid two things. Don't buy potting mixes formulated for one specific type of plant (roses, rhododendrons, orchids, and so on) unless you're growing that particular plant. And don't buy bags of topsoil (garden soil), which is too dense for your purposes. It's

What Do We Call This Dirt?

Don't let yourself get too tangled up in terminology. The manufacturers may name it potting mix, container mix, potting soil— it's all basically the same thing. Most of your gardening friends will call it potting soil, even though it contains no literal soil. In this book, too, we often use the term "soil" as a kind of shorthand, meaning the stuff your plants are growing in, the stuff that gets under your fingernails.

probably labeled "topsoil," but one good way to check is to lift the bag; if it is heavy, especially in comparison to another soil-mix product of the same size, you don't want it. Good potting mix has various ingredients that aerate it, making it very lightweight.

Using actual soil, straight from someone's yard, is not a good solution. Even if it is nutrient rich and well balanced, the very structure of garden soil presents some special problems for container gardeners. Because it is heavy (the gardener's term for soil that is dense, which also makes it literally heavy), it will not drain well from a container, which usually has only one drainage outlet. As you water, this soil compacts more and more, which means that roots will not get enough oxygen for growth, will not be able to take up fertilizers and other nutrients, and will be subject to rot. Furthermore, garden soil contains a host of microorganisms that exist in a natural balance in a garden plot, but can easily get out of balance in the confines of a container.

Then, to your basic potting mix, you may wish or need to add other ingredients.

FERTILIZER. The ingredients of fertilizer are described on pages 67 to 70. We recommend that you use a double-dose program of liquid fertilizer and timed-release granules, described on page 67. Those granules are easiest to apply if you mix them in as part of your soil mixture.

MICRONUTRIENTS. If your timed-release fertilizer does not include the important micronutrients, you will need to add them separately. An easy way to do that is with a material called greensand (described on page 68), mixed into the potting soil along with everything else.

LIME. The relative acidity or alkalinity of substances is measured on the pH scale, which stands for "potential Hydrogen" and is written with a lowercase p and an uppercase H. Low numbers are very acidic (lemon juice is 2); high numbers are very alkaline (baking soda is 8); 7 is neutral. Most vegetables do well at a soil pH of 6.5. Commercial potting mixes that have a high proportion of peat moss or ground tree bark (which are naturally acidic) usually also include some agricultural lime (which is alkaline) to produce the proper pH. Examine the label or check with a knowledgeable salesperson. If you have reason to think the pH might be too low, buy a small amount of agricultural lime or ground dolomite and work it into your mixture. You can also just sprinkle it on top of the soil after planting, like a fine coating of powdered sugar.

Incidentally, a few things that you might have in your garden

Saving Your Seeds for Next Year

It has only been fairly recently, as these things go, that horticulturists have made a business venture of producing seeds to sell to gardeners and other growers. For most of civilization farmers saved seeds of their crops from one year to the next, always choosing the strongest plants and best-tasting vegetables, and thus gradually improving and enhancing the garden for future generations.

Even today, enthusiastic gardeners still do this to make sure their most successful plants are preserved, and to share their discoveries with friends near and far (seeds are easy to mail). If you save seeds, you'll be participating in an ancient and honorable tradition. Here are the steps:

1. Clip the mature seed heads from the plant and shake them into a small paper bag, loosening the seeds till they fall in. Do not use plastic, as it retains moisture. Set the bags, with the tops open, on a high shelf for about a week to make sure all residual moisture evaporates.

2. When seeds are thoroughly dry, roll up the bags and label them with the varietal name and the year.

3. Place about two tablespoons of powdered milk (which acts as a desiccant) in the middle of a paper towel, fold it tightly into a small rectangle, and place it in the bottom of a large glass jar.

4. Place the paper bags in the jar, and store in a cool spot away from sunlight.

Seeds that carry over well include arugula, dill, marigold, parsley, and cilantro. (With early-season cilantro, you don't even have to wait until next year; as soon as a plant produces seeds, immediately plant them for a continuous harvest.) Don't bother with root crops or members of the cabbage family, and don't forget that letting squashes and cucumbers go to seed is counterproductive: you won't get any more vegetables.

Saving tomato seeds takes work but can be very rewarding. Start with a very ripe tomato. Chop up the inner pieces that hold the seeds and put the seeds, along with some of the flesh, into a glass jar. Set it aside until the contents ferment, which will take about four days in summertime.

The viable seeds will drop to the bottom, and the mushy tomato residue will rise to the top. Pour off all that residue, add some extra liquid to the jar, then rinse the seeds several times. Spread the seeds out on a paper plate to dry, then store them in paper bags as described above.

Keep in mind that since many of today's tomato varieties are hybrids (also true of peppers), the tomato you get next year may not be just like this year's.

(blueberries, for one) actually prefer an acidic soil; we'll tell you how to deal with that in the specific plant chapters.

WATER-HOLDING CRYSTALS. These granules (see page 66) start out small and dry, then absorb water and gradually release it. They, too, are easiest to apply if you work them into the soil mix before planting. Note that some manufacturers add micronutrients to the crystals; if the brand you choose has these, that's one thing you won't have to add.

Somewhere on the label of the potting soil you bought is an indication of its volume, usually measured in quarts. The packages of the other ingredients give you application rates: so much of their product in so many quarts or gallons of soil, or so many square feet, and so on. You'll probably have to do some converting; remember that 1 gallon is 4 quarts, and 1 cubic foot (an area 12 inches by 12 inches by 12 inches) holds 6.6 gallons.

Seeds and Plants

Planting seeds is not hard; you learned how in the first grade. Neither is setting out transplants; we discuss this later in this chapter, but the fact is, it's pretty self-evident even if you've never done it. What is not so obvious is deciding whether you should start with seeds or transplants.
Buy seeds if:

- The items you want, or the varieties you're interested in, aren't available any other way.
- The items don't transplant well: beans, peas, carrots, beets, and radishes, for example.
- You're trying to stretch your budget, especially if you can split seed packets with another gardener.
- You don't mind that you'll have to start some seeds indoors (a fairly tricky operation) in colder climates (see pages 54 to 60 for directions).
- You enjoy the convenience of making small repeat sowings of things like lettuce, mesclun, radishes, cilantro, and spinach; just tuck in a few seeds whenever an empty space appears.
- You don't want to miss the fun of witnessing a very dependable, very accessible miracle.

Buy transplants if:

- Your growing season is short.

■ You want to grow plants with a long maturity. In most
parts of the country, that means they'll need to be started
indoors early, and you may rather have someone else—like
a commercial grower—do that part.

■ You want only one or two of certain plants, not a hundred.

■ Something dies and you need a fast-track replacement.

As a practical matter, nearly everyone is better off with transplants—either
from your own windowsill or a commercial greenhouse—for these plants:

■ Tomatoes	■ Chives
■ Peppers	■ Perennial herbs
■ Eggplant	■ Pansies, violets, violas
■ Basil	

And you usually have to start these from seeds:

■ Peas	■ Radishes
■ Beans	■ Nasturtiums
■ Carrots	■ Sunflowers
■ Beets	■ Cilantro

Many others are in a go-either-way category; the decision has largely to do
with your climate. It is not hard to grow these plants from seed, provided
your growing season is long enough and the gods are smiling:

■ Cucumbers	■ Lettuce and other salad greens
■ Squash	■ Leafy green vegetables
■ Scallions	■ Marigolds

In the case of edible flowers, often the seed-versus-transplant question
simply doesn't arise: for tulips and begonias, you have to start with bulbs;
for roses, with a rosebush; and so forth. And, of course, with fruits you buy
a small tree.

Starting Seeds Indoors

Inside your house or apartment, it's nice and warm even when the outside temperature is chilly. You can get a jump on the season by starting
seeds indoors, then transplanting them into your outdoor containers when
the weather is right.

Fair warning: this is not dead simple. It's a fairly fussy operation,
and it involves a very tricky piece of timing. But if you are patient and have

a nurturing temperament, the results can be satisfying indeed. Besides, for certain out-of-the-ordinary varieties, you simply have no choice—they can't be found in a nursery.

It's an old farmer's axiom that to get off to a good start, seeds need a cool head and warm feet. In more prosaic terms, for good germination seeds have two requirements: even moisture and heat.

Here are the steps for starting seeds indoors:

1. FIGURE OUT WHEN TO PLANT THE SEEDS. In general, you want to plant far enough in advance that the seedlings are ready to go into outdoor containers when the weather is ready to receive them—and not

before. A common mistake is starting the seeds too soon; they hit transplant time before the weather is warm enough. Unless you take special protective measures (see the box at right), they will die outside; and if you try to keep them indoors longer, they'll get leggy, rot, or succumb to fungal diseases.

Obviously you have to know your own weather patterns, and you have to know the seeds' approximate germination time. Where we live it usually isn't warm enough for tomato seeds to germinate outdoors until early June, and if there's a killing frost in September, which there sometimes is, that doesn't leave enough time to produce anything other than a fulsome crop of green tomatoes. So we buy good-size tomato transplants at the garden center in late May or June, or start our own seeds indoors in April (that's how long it takes a tomato seedling to reach a transplant size large enough to do any good).

In the box on page 57

Pushing the Planting Season

Many of our favorite summertime vegetables need hot weather to do their best: cucumbers, squash, peppers, eggplant, tomatoes. If your weather is not cooperative, you can stretch the growing season by prewarming the soil.

To warm the soil, set the yet-unplanted container where it gets the most sun and wrap the whole thing in black plastic. Let it sit that way for a few days.

When you plant transplants, you may want to keep the plastic around the pot and cover the plants with a floating row cover, which acts like a lightweight blanket. While young plants are still quite small and nights are still chilly, cover each plant at night with a protective hotcap or cloche, perhaps cut from a plastic milk jug; remove the covering in the morning.

Protecting young plants during cool weather.

you'll find some general guidelines on timing. We have included only the seeds that are easiest to start indoors. Do a bit of checking on your local climate patterns, and adjust these guidelines as needed. Also, note that with some extra care, described on page 55, you can fool Mother Nature into thinking it is warmer than it really is, and can move your plants outdoors sooner.

2. COLLECT YOUR EQUIPMENT. Essentially you need:

- **Seed-starting medium.** We recommend buying a bag of mix specifically designed for starting seeds (it will be labeled as such). This mix is very lightweight and contains very finely milled bits of peat or perlite, or both—nothing large enough to thwart a tender seed trying to unfurl. The most important concern for seeds is that the medium they are planted in be completely sterile (thus free of any disease agents). Some regular potting mixes are sterile, some not; but usually you can count on seed-starting mixes to be free of microscopic troublemakers. One bag will probably be enough for all your seeds for a season; it's a good investment.

- **Something to put the medium and seeds into.** Small pots made of dried, compressed peat (round or square, in several sizes) are handy. When the seedling is ready to go outside, plant the whole thing, pot and all; the roots grow right through the sides of the pot, thus minimizing transplant shock.

    You can also reuse small nursery containers that you saved from last year, as long as you clean them thoroughly with a mild bleach solution to kill any residual pathogens.

    A very simple alternative is a product called Jiffy pellets, which are circles of compressed peat encased in a very fine netting. These serve as both pot and soil, and they go straight into the garden without any repotting, which is easier on you and the plant as it avoids transplant shock. When dry they are flat, about the size of a silver dollar. Soak them in water and

Timing Is Everything

To start seeds indoors successfully you have to get the timing right, so research the weather patterns in your area (see page 6). The critical information is the date, on average, when the average lowest nighttime temperatures are those listed in the second column below. Then count back by the number of days given in the third column, and cross your fingers that this year's weather is reasonably close to average.

	Nighttime Lows	Start Seeds Ahead
Asian greens*	35°F	30 days
basil	55°F	45 days
cucumbers**	50°F	30 days
eggplants	55°F	50 to 70 days
kale*	35°F	30 to 45 days
lettuce*	35°F	20 days
peppers	55°F	50 to 70 days
squash**	50°F	30 days
tomatoes	55°F	50 to 70 days

* Indoor starting is not essential for cool-season vegetables, which can be direct-seeded outdoors quite early in the spring; many gardeners do both (direct-seed and indoor starts), for convenience and to give themselves a bit of insurance.

** These items germinate so quickly that there's usually little advantage to starting them indoors, but it can easily be done.

they expand to about 2 inches high, with a little dimple on top where the seeds go.

- **A drip tray** to catch the excess water. (If you're using Jiffy pellets, place them on a cookie sheet.)
- **Clear plastic** to hold in humidity while the seeds are germinating. Any clear plastic bag will work, but don't use the stretchy film that clings to itself.
- **Something to label the containers with** (all baby seedlings look alike). Garden centers sell small wooden and plastic sticks that you can write on with a permanent marker.
- **A source of heat** (not essential but very helpful). You can purchase propagating mats or grow-mats if you're planning to start a lot of seeds indoors; or you can use a regular

household heating pad, as long as it's approved for moist heat. Keep it at the lowest setting, and set your trays on top. Another heat source you may already own is a food-warming tray, the kind you use on a buffet table; first cover it with a folded towel, and again, keep it at the lowest setting.

As well as these individual items, your favorite garden center undoubtedly stocks several types of complete seed-starting kits, which are very handy; many mail-order catalogs carry similar items. The kits often mimic the setup in commercial greenhouses: they consist of broad, shallow plastic trays divided into small squares, with a clear plastic lid and a drip tray. All you add is the seed-starting mixture and the seeds.

> *Maggie says:* Being essentially lazy, I have settled on just one very simple system: it consists of Jiffy pellets and those foam trays that supermarkets package their meat in. When I find a good price, I buy large quantities of Jiffys because they have an indefinite shelf life, and I save only the meat trays that are narrow enough to fit on my windowsills. When I'm ready to start seeds, I soak a whole sinkful of Jiffys at one time, then fill meat trays (which I sterilized by rinsing with bleach) with as many as will fit, and write the seed variety names on the edge of the trays with a permanent marking pen.

3. PLANT THE SEEDS. First, dampen the seed-starting mix thoroughly and let it drain. Then add the seeds and cover lightly with more damp mix. If you have a source of heat, put the seedling pots and drip tray on it now.

4. COVER LOOSELY WITH CLEAR PLASTIC. This will help keep the surface of the seed-starting mix from drying out. Use chopsticks, pencils, or small twigs to prop up the plastic and hold it away from direct contact with the soil and the tiny sprouts. The plastic should not be airtight; you want air to circulate.

5. MAKE SURE THE SEED-STARTING MIX STAYS MOIST. If you have covered the pots with plastic, you can easily tell if they are moist because water beads will form on the inside of the plastic. When the mix gets dry, water gently with a mister; it's important not to disturb the surface while the seeds are germinating. You can also pour water into the drip tray, and it will be absorbed up from the bottom.

Up to this point, light has been irrelevant. Seeds sprout in the dark.

What's What

The live part of a seed is encased in a **seed coat,** which opens up a bit like a clamshell once the germinating seed emerges from the soil. The two halves of the opened seed coat remain attached to the tiny stem, and sometimes are mistaken for leaves, but they are not. We speak of **true leaves** to distinguish the first actual leaves, distinct from the seed coat.

A **seedling** is the first flush of growth from a seed, whether that seed was planted in a greenhouse propagation bed, a tray on your windowsill, or directly into its ultimate garden home.

A **transplant** is a young plant that has passed beyond the seedling stage; the difference is relative, with no precise dividing line. Many gardeners call them by the homier name of **starts,** signifying their immature stage of growth. The young plants that you buy in a nursery, in 2-inch or 4-inch pots or in six-packs, are transplants; they may have been direct-seeded in those small nursery pots, but more likely they were germinated in a large propagation tray and then, as seedlings, moved into the intermediate containers.

Larger nursery plants (say, in 1-gallon containers) are technically transplants because you'll transplant them into your own pots when you get home, but at that stage most people just call them plants.

But once a seed has sprouted and formed its first set of true leaves (see box above), the process of photosynthesis, upon which all green plants depend, has begun, and sunlight is necessary for it to continue.

6. REMOVE THE PLASTIC AND ENSURE GOOD LIGHT. Carefully lift the plastic so it doesn't disturb the growing seedlings, and check your light source. If you don't have good sunny windows, move a fluorescent lamp close by. Special full-spectrum grow lights are available but not really necessary.

7. THIN THE SEEDLINGS, IF NEEDED. If you planted lots of seeds for insurance and they all germinate, you will soon have a crowded forest of baby seedlings. You have to sacrifice some of them, or none will do well. The roots are extremely tender, and pulling out seedlings can injure the ones you wish to keep. A better technique is to snip off the discards, at the soil line, with something like manicure or embroidery scissors.

8. PROTECT AGAINST DISEASE. Very young seedlings are particularly susceptible to a fungal disease called damping-off. It's a greenhouse version of sudden death syndrome: one minute the seedling looks fine; the next minute it has keeled right over. This fungus is rarely a problem with direct seeding, but it seems to find an easy foothold in the indoor environment. The best way to prevent damping-off is to water from the bottom by filling the drip tray with water in which you have dissolved a fungicide. For a homemade organic version, brew a batch of chamomile tea and water the seedlings with it; chamomile contains a natural fungicidal ingredient.

9. MOVE SEEDLINGS INTO A LARGER POT. Sometimes seedlings grow to an intermediate size while it is still too cold to put them outside, a common dilemma with heat lovers like tomatoes, eggplant, and peppers. If they stay in the original indoor seedling bed too long, their root growth will be stunted and they will never develop into healthy, thriving plants. So you need to move them into a larger interim container, where they'll have more room to grow.

Rule of thumb: when a seedling has three sets of true leaves, it's ready to come out of the seedling tray. If it can't go into the outdoor container, it needs to be moved into a larger temporary pot. Carefully remove the seedlings, taking as much seed-starting mix as possible; if they are in one broad flat, slice out a block of mix with a table knife, as

If seedlings are ready but the outside temperature is not, move them to an intermediate pot to prevent legginess.

if you were cutting a pan of brownies. Plant the seedlings in larger pots filled with the same sterile seed-starting mix. Be delicate; the baby plant is still quite tender and needs to be handled with great care.

At this point, start feeding the babies with a balanced fertilizer dissolved in water; balanced fertilizer is one in which the three numbers (see Chapter 6) are approximately the same.

10. GRADUALLY ACCLIMATE PLANTS TO THE OUTDOOR CLIMATE. It's easy to be seduced into premature action come the first sunny day. But don't move tender seedlings directly into their outdoor containers; the shock of drastically different temperatures would be too much for them. Instead, acclimate them gradually, in the process known as hardening off: day 1, set them outside for one to two hours, and then back into a sheltered location (a porch is ideal); day 2, outside for three to four hours, then back; and so on. After four or five days, they'll be ready to stay outdoors.

Buying Good Plants

If you decide you'd rather let someone else do the work of sprouting seeds and want to buy potted transplants at the garden center instead, you'll get no argument from us. In this case, your task is to get really healthy little plants.

In choosing healthy plants, short and compact is better than tall and lanky. Avoid plants that are leggy (with long stretched-out stem sections and relatively few leaves). Small, perky-looking plants with lots of green leaves will soon take off in a good environment like your containers; leggy ones always seem to have difficulty getting established, no matter what you do.

Roots growing out the bottom of the nursery container are a sign that the plant is rootbound. Vegetables and annual flowers in very small nursery pots or so-called six-packs often show this condition because commercial growers, eager to produce a large volume of plants in a short time, encourage fast growth, and at the retail nursery the plants just keep growing until someone buys them. It's not a perfect situation, but it's also not disastrous; just tear away the heavily matted roots before you plant. But if you have a choice between a six-pack that is rootbound and one that is not, choose the latter.

If you're buying a plant for its flowers, it's good if one of them is open so you can see the actual color, but in general look for a mass of buds rather than a mass of blossoms.

For all plants, check the stems and undersides of leaves for any indication of insects or disease. Most of these signs are obvious (discolored or misshapen leaves, for example); you may not know exactly what is causing the problem, but it's clear that some kind of problem is present.

Planting the Containers

Your beautiful new pots are empty and waiting; your special potting soil, with all its additives, is mixed up and ready to go; you've accumulated a nice selection of seed packets and a flat of eager small plants. Now what?

If you have already figured out that your large containers are deeper than your plants' roots will need, start by filling in some of the extra space (see box on page 62); the containers will be lighter and easier to move should you later wish to do so.

Fill the containers with potting soil up to about 2 inches from the top, and water them thoroughly; now you're ready to plant seeds or baby plants, or both.

Planting seeds directly into the container where they will grow, known as direct sowing, is simplicity itself; just follow the instructions on the seed packet for how deep to plant them and how far apart. A seed should usually be planted as deep as its own largest dimension. That means that very tiny seeds just get pressed down into the mix with your fingers; very large seeds, like some beans, might require a depth of as much as an inch.

Deciding where in the container to place the seeds is mostly a question of your ultimate design for that container. If you want a fringe of carrots around the edges of a large round container, plant the seeds close to the rim. If you want a semicircle of bush peas at the rear, fronted with an inner crescent of beets, plant the seeds in that pattern. On the other hand, if your container will have just one item—salad greens, for instance—spread the seeds over the entire soil surface in a way that maximizes the space. In rectangular containers, plant in tight rows; in oval or round containers, in concentric circles. There are no hard-and-fast rules about this; common sense will guide you. Just remember that young seedlings will fare much better if they are not moved, so plant the seeds where you want the mature plants to be.

And thin the seedlings with small scissors once they sprout (see page 59).

Space Fillers

If you have a 2-foot container into which you're planting vegetables with 6-inch roots, you could waste a lot of soil and make the pot heavier than it needs to be. Instead, fill up some of the extra space using one of these techniques before adding the potting soil:

1. Put one layer of empty soft drink cans, standing upright and upside down, on the bottom of the container. They're lightweight and readily available.

2. Add a thick layer of those Styrofoam peanuts used as packing material. We all hate them, but they come into our lives anyway and this is one way to put them to good use. This is a good system for pots you expect to reuse, soil and all, for several years; but it's an awful nuisance if you later dump this soil out and start over, because those little peanuts fly all over the place. (The new, environmentally friendly peanuts are not suitable for this purpose as they're made of cornstarch and dissolve in water.)

3. Save the large foam blocks that your new CD player came packaged in, and carve them into shapes that fit down into your containers. The blocks cut very easily with an ordinary kitchen knife, and this is one way to keep nonrecyclable foam pieces out of the landfills.

Moving transplants into the container takes a little more attention, but not much. Make sure the mix in the container is lightly and evenly damp; also, thoroughly water the small pots holding the baby plants and let them drain while you proceed. With your trowel, dig a hole about as deep as the small containers. Slide the fingers of one hand around the base of a baby plant, and turn it upside down so that the plant and all its soil slide out into your other hand. If the plant doesn't come right out, tap the rim of the small pot against something solid and try again. The thin plastic pots that many nurseries use for transplants will often release their contents if you simply squeeze them.

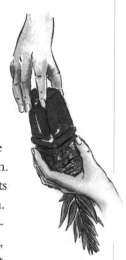

When removing a small plant from its nursery pot, try to keep the soil intact.

Try to keep intact the soil ball around the transplant. If you see a thick mat of roots twisted at the bottom, untangle them with your fingers and trim back the longest ones. Fit the plant and its soil ball into the hole you prepared, and fill in with the extra potting mix. Tamp the soil lightly with your hand, and move on to the next plant. When everything is in, water the entire container to help the plants settle.

Do this, if possible, on a cloudy or overcast day; bright sun is hard on tender transplants. Best of all, do your planting when cloudy weather is forecast for the next several days. If that means waiting a few days, keep the flat of transplants in a sheltered outdoor location in the interim. Don't keep them inside your warm apartment. Store them outdoors in a sheltered location, and check every day to make sure the soil doesn't dry out.

If you have chosen a variety that you expect to tumble prettily over the edge of the container, gravity will eventually take care of it, but you can help things along with this planting technique: put the plant in the container leaning sideways, at approximately a 45-degree angle, with the tip of the plant pointing toward the edge; the roots will find their way down into the soil, and the new foliage growth will take off downward, as you intended.

Unless you have specific instructions to the contrary, plant bulbs twice as deep as their diameter. Most of the bulbs suggested in this book are planted in the fall and bloom the following spring; if you also want to sow some early-spring seeds in the same container, be careful not to dig up the bulbs as you prepare the soil.

PLANTING IN WIRE BASKETS. So far we have been working with containers that have solid sides. For containers made of wire grid, different techniques are needed. Commonly seen in the form of hanging baskets, wire is also used for certain styles of window boxes and even some free-standing planters. Because the sides of wire planters have lots of openings, a liner is needed to hold the potting soil in place. Plants go in not only at the top, as with solid-sided containers, but also through the sides for an all-around burst of color.

You have several choices of lining material. The classic is a thick layer of moss, but the results can be disappointing; it is sometimes difficult to keep everything from drying out. Newer products that hold moisture better are made from recycled wood products and recycled wool, ground up and pressed into a mat. Heavy plastic liners work fine but are rather unattractive until the plants grow large enough to cover the liner completely. Burlap works well, although it doesn't usually last more than one year.

We have experimented with shade cloth (a heavy nylon mesh normally used in greenhouses to provide shade), and so far it looks promising as a liner. It will last for at least two years, and because it is flat black rather than glossy like plastic sheeting, it tends to disappear visually. A similar material is weed barrier, a permeable black plastic fabric designed to block out weeds in large garden plots. Both shade cloth and weed barrier have openings fine enough for water to drain out and air to circulate through, but they're not large enough for soil to leak through. Both are sold at garden centers, and both are easily cut with scissors.

If you're working with a basket that has a rounded bottom, set it down into an empty pail for stability while you work. Put the liner in place, all the way up to the rim; leave an inch or so of excess at the top to allow for settling, and trim it off at the very end. You are going to work

Set a round-bottom planter into a bucket for stability. Cut planting holes all around the liner, and add plants to all sides as well as the top.

in layers: add a few inches of damp soil, slit openings in the liner, wiggle a plant into position, add in some more soil, make more planting slits, and so on until the entire outer surface is covered with plants.

CHAPTER 6

KEEPING
A HEALTHY
GARDEN

W eeding? None. Hoeing and other heavy cultivating? None. Bugs? Sometimes, but easily spotted. Diseases? Less than in traditional gardens. Pruning? Not often. General tidying up? Sure, but not a big chore in such small spaces. Fertilizing? Yes. Watering? Yes.

Ongoing maintenance is not an overwhelming task in container gardens; it's nothing like maintenance in traditional gardens. You have only two major areas to worry about—watering and fertilizing—but those two are absolutely critical.

Watering

In the ground, plants have a wide soil area from which to draw moisture. Even more important, the surrounding soil acts as an environmental buffer for the plant roots, tempering the drying effects of wind and hot sun. In a container, a plant has a limited area of soil, and there is nothing beyond the container but air. If that air is hot and dry, it will quickly pull moisture from the plant and soil. In the dead of summer, it's not at all uncommon that containers need to be watered twice a day.

If you are to be successful with containers, you must be prepared with a good irrigation system and the discipline to use it. The system does not have to be high tech—a simple watering can is perfectly acceptable— but it does have to be used faithfully.

Your life will be a great deal simpler if you can run a hose to the area where your containers are. This may take some ingenuity on your part, but don't give up without investigating all possibilities. We know a dedicated gardener who, while temporarily living in a large city with only a balcony for garden space, added a Y-shaped fitting to the water pipe in her laundry area. The washing machine attachment fastened to one side of the Y, and from the other she ran a hose through the apartment and out the door to the balcony.

A long wand (a rigid extension that fastens to the end of the hose) is useful for reaching hanging containers. A hose attachment that allows you to switch from a hard, tight spray to a broad mist is convenient. Another handy hose gadget, called a bubbler, disperses the solid stream of water so it doesn't gouge a hole in the soil.

But if all you can do is fill the watering can and make lots of trips, then that's what you'll have to do. One way to make things a bit easier on yourself is to mix moisture-retaining polymers into the potting soil before you plant anything. Fairly new on the market, these are very small crystals of clear gel that start out about the size of coarse salt. They absorb water, swelling in size manyfold, and then slowly release the moisture back into the soil. A variation on this idea is a thin mat made of similar material that absorbs and then gradually releases water; you cut the mat to size and place it in the bottom of your container. Using these products is no substitute for watering, but they may buy you a little extra time, and that couldn't hurt.

Several companies offer so-called self-watering pots—containers with a built-in water reservoir. The reservoirs can hold up to several quarts of water, which is gradually wicked up into the soil. The containers are more expensive than plain pots of equivalent size, but may be a good solution for people who travel often.

And if you really want to go all the way, purchase a drip watering system: long flexible tubing with a series of offshoots, each of which ends in a water emitter that fits down into the top of a container. The best systems have small screens behind the emitters to keep small pieces of grit from clogging the ends. For the ultimate in convenience add a timer to the system, a small box that fastens to the faucet and opens and closes the valve according to the programmed instructions. You can set the system to water all the containers once a day for 30 minutes, or several times a day for shorter periods, or whatever works best for you, and you can vary the settings as the plants grow and the weather changes. As you might imagine, this is an expensive solution, but it is basically foolproof and does allow you to have extended vacations without imposing on the neighbors.

Fertilizing

Fertilizing and watering are interconnected chores. Fertilizers dissolve in water—that is the only way plants can absorb them, through the roots. With all the watering you must do, you are also washing away fertilizer, and so you need to replace it. That is true for all container plants, but it's particularly critical for edibles for this reason: you have only so much time in any one growing season to produce the food, and so you must get maximum growth out of the plants during that time.

We recommend that you start off with potting soil into which you have mixed a slow-release granular fertilizer—solid fertilizer encased in small coated pellets about the size of BBs (Osmocote is one popular brand). With repeated waterings, the fertilizer gradually dissolves into the soil. For those who prefer the all-organic route, timed-release fish pellets are available but harder to find. The granules last several months before they gradually dissolve away to nothing. This gives you a good fertilizer foundation, so to speak, but by itself is not sufficient; you need to supplement with a regular program of additional fertilizing. What kind should it be? To answer that, we need a short lesson in plant nutrition.

Plants need three main nutrients for healthy growth: nitrogen (which promotes healthy foliage), phosphorus (for flowers), and potassium (for strong roots and overall vigor). On fertilizer packages they are represented by three numbers, always in that sequence, and always prominently displayed. Thus a label that reads 10-15-8 signifies that 10 percent of the contents is nitrogen, 15 percent phosphorus, and 8 percent potassium. The numbers never add up to 100, which would be too strong a concentration; the balance is composed of other nutrients (which we'll address shortly) and inert filler. Fertilizers that contain all three primary nutrients are called **complete** (if one of the numbers is 0, it's not complete); they are said to be **balanced** if the three are in roughly equal proportions.

It's helpful to think of formulations in terms of *ratio:* the proportion of each primary nutrient in relation to the other two. A 20-10-10 formulation has the same *ratio* as 10-5-5, but has more fertilizing power. In the later sections of this book we often suggest fertilizers by ratio, because in different parts of the country you will find different formulations on the shelves. And by the way, arithmetic precision is not paramount: by ratio, 10-20-8 fertilizer is not significantly different from 5-15-6 or 8-20-5.

If you are growing vegetables mostly for the leaves (salad greens, for instance), you would want a fertilizer that has more nitrogen than anything else (a larger first number). But if you're growing plants that flower first (tomatoes, squash, blueberries, and so on), you want a higher proportion of phosphorus (a higher middle number). So you might want to have two formulations on hand: something like 20-10-10 for leafy vegetables and 10-20-10 for vegetables that flower. Or if simplicity is your goal, choose just one all-purpose formula with a somewhat higher middle number (such as 10-15-10), and use it for everything.

Another way to go, almost as simple: use one balanced fertilizer (such as 12-12-12) for everything, and then *add* a nitrogen booster for leafy plants and a phosphorus booster for flowering plants (these boosters are described below). This last technique works especially well with tomatoes, which often put on a burst of leaf growth early on and then fizzle out when it comes time for developing flowers and fruit; the phosphate helps them kick in to full production.

Commercial fertilizer comes in the form of either liquid or powder concentrates, both meant to be dissolved in water; the label will give you the correct dilution rate. You can make a weaker batch, but if you go stronger you're asking for trouble.

In addition to the Big Three of nitrogen, phosphorus, and potassium, plants need certain secondary nutrients and micronutrients, called trace minerals, for vigorous growth. The secondary nutrients are calcium, magnesium, and sulfur. The main micronutrients are iron, manganese, copper, chlorine, boron, zinc, and molybdenum. Plants need only small amounts of these nutrients, but without them they do not thrive.

One way to make sure your plants are getting everything they need is to search out all-purpose, complete fertilizers that also contain the secondary nutrients and micronutrients. Manufacturers are required to list all the ingredients, by percentage, on the package label. Another way is to start with a basic complete fertilizer and then add one or more of the "boosters" described here. The advantages of this latter approach are that you can fine-tune your containers for your particular plants, and it's easier to maintain an organic garden, if that is important to you. The disadvantage is lost convenience: you need to purchase all the various ingredients individually, and find a space to store what you don't use.

Here are some of the items you might find in a well-stocked garden center, starting with the organic products.

Greensand is a powder of finely ground rock that contains potassium, magnesium, and many micronutrients, and also helps improve the tex-

Fertilizer Chart

Name	Organic/ Inorganic	Form	Main Nutrients	Other Nutrients
blood meal	organic	powder	nitrogen	
bone meal	organic	powder	phosphorus	nitrogen
bulb food	inorganic	powder	phosphorus	nitrogen, potassium
dolomite lime	inorganic	powder	calcium	magnesium; also raises pH
fish emulsion	organic	liquid	nitrogen	phosphorus, potassium
greensand	organic	powder	potassium	magnesium, micronutrients
liquid seaweed	organic	liquid	potassium	nitrogen; many micronutrients
magnesium sulfate	inorganic	powder	sulphur, magnesium	
rock phosphate	organic	powder	phosphorus	micronutrients
superphosphate	inorganic	powder	phosphorus	sulfur

ture of the potting mix. The name is a bit misleading; it does indeed have a texture like very fine sand but is not itself green. Long popular with European gardeners, greensand is now becoming more widely known in America.

Bone meal, a fine powder, is indeed made from ground-up animal bones. It is an organic source of phosphorus (usually about 4-12-0). **Blood meal,** another slaughterhouse by-product, is an organic source of nitrogen (12-0-0).

Fish emulsion comes as a brown liquid, very concentrated and very fishy smelling. It provides mostly nitrogen, in proportions that vary by manufacturer.

Liquid seaweed, also a liquid concentrate, has light amounts of nitrogen and potassium and a wide range of critical micronutrients; it is especially valuable for helping seedlings develop strong roots.

Rose Marie says: In our business we use liquid seaweed constantly, for almost everything. I can't stand to see any plant die, and I have successfully rescued many a wilted, puny specimen by dribbling liquid seaweed, full strength, around the rim of the pot and watering it well. I simply can't imagine gardening without it.

Rock phosphate is really made from a rock deposit that is high in phosphorus, finely pulverized. It releases its phosphorus slowly, which is an advantage in container gardening. When sulfuric acid is added to rock phosphate, you have a product called superphosphate, which takes us to the inorganic side of the aisle.

Superphosphate provides a strong shot of phosphorus (approximately 0-20-0) in a form that plants can readily absorb.

Bulb food is a synthetic commercial fertilizer that is high in phosphorus.

Magnesium sulfate (commonly known as Epsom salts) provides magnesium (9.6 percent) and sulfur (14.5 percent), two secondary nutrients.

Dolomite lime is ground limestone (calcium carbonate) to which magnesium has been added, and thus it is another source of those two nutrients. Lime also increases soil pH, and this is the purpose for which it is most commonly purchased.

Here's a routine we like; it is simple and generic, and is grounded in the assumption that you do not need extra boosts of any one nutrient. When you first prepare your containers in the spring, mix some greensand and granules of a balanced slow-release fertilizer into the potting mix. Then, when the plants start actively growing and producing, apply a complete, balanced fertilizer in a half-strength formulation once a week. If you replant for a fall garden late in the season, add some new slow-release granules, and then start adding liquid fertilizer once the new plants take off. Incidentally, if you have a container with a plant already established, such as a fruit tree or perennials, you can sprinkle new fertilizer granules right onto the surface of the soil once or twice a season.

Pruning

A task that terrifies so many gardeners, pruning is virtually nonexistent in vegetable gardens. It's important for fruit trees and some perennial herbs, and so is covered in detail in those chapters, but with vegetables it is seldom needed. If you do any pruning at all, it will probably be with

What About Organic?

Literally, the word *organic* refers to something that is, or once was, alive. In the gardening world, the term is used primarily to describe certain fertilizers and pesticides, and means that those products are made with ingredients derived from the natural world. They may be homemade, as in compost from your compost bucket, or commercial items whose manufacturers use organic ingredients. Those products are always labeled organic, often in large, proud letters.

The opposite term is *inorganic,* meaning that the constituent ingredients are synthetic rather than natural.

These words are emotionally loaded, and lead to some common misconceptions. Many people tend to think that "natural" is automatically better than "synthetic." But the synthetic ingredients of a commercial fertilizer, for example, have the same chemical composition as the organic counterparts, and therefore have the same effect on the plants.

Many also assume that "organic" means "nontoxic." Not true. Commercial organic insecticides and fungicides can be every bit as poisonous as inorganic ones; pyrethrum, for instance, is manufactured from a flower in the chrysanthemum family, but that doesn't mean you can drink it.

Speaking very generally, organic products tend to have a lower concentration of active ingredients and take longer to do their work in the garden. Also speaking generally, their effect on the overall environment is gentler.

The organic-versus-inorganic debate is more relevant to traditional gardeners than container gardeners. Organic fertilizers such as manure and compost not only provide nutrients to the plants, they also significantly improve the texture of the soil, which is extremely beneficial for both the short and long term. Container gardeners, who mostly use commercial potting mix, have little need to be concerned with long-term soil texture. Similarly, people with an in-the-ground vegetable garden often have a traditional lawn and flower garden to care for also, and they are careful to separate herbicides that kill weeds in the lawn from their vegetable crops.

In your favorite garden center there are organic and inorganic versions of nearly everything you would ever need in your container garden; later in this chapter, we also show you how to make your own from ordinary household products (see page 76).

Don't let yourself become paralyzed over the question. Try two different items, if you wish, and compare the results. It is important to note here that for many people the choice is a matter of principle, a personal decision that we respect.

tomatoes and rampant vines that threaten to overgrow their trellises. In any case, it will be helpful to get the basic principle fixed in your mind.

Plants grow from the top, not the bottom. If you remove the growing tip, side branches will develop. If you then remove the growing tips from *those* branches, they will branch out yet again. In this way you can encourage compact, bushy growth, which is a good thing in tight spaces. Most of the time you can just pinch off the top with your fingers. This technique will come in handy if your pole beans are heading for the roof or your tomatoes are bursting out of their cages.

Pinching the growing tip promotes bushiness.

Preventing and Treating Problems

Right from the get-go, you have one *big* advantage over traditional gardeners: because you are using sterile potting mixes, you completely avoid those soilborne diseases that are so hard to spot and even harder to get rid of. For instance, an extremely common problem with tomatoes is a fungal disease called verticillium wilt, caused by a pathogen that lives in infected soil and enters the plant through its root system; container gardeners using potting mixes that contain no real soil neatly bypass the problem. For extra insurance, or if you're reusing a container from last year, select disease-resistant varieties; good catalogs include this information.

You may, however, experience other plant diseases that travel through the air or are carried in by insects. And you may be visited by any of a variety of damaging insects, but even here your life is easier because you'll have fewer of them and because you'll notice them sooner, while they are still relatively easy to take care of. In this section we introduce you to some of the worst troublemakers. First, though, we'll give you a bit of perspective on the matter and point you toward a source of expert assistance.

A Gardener's Way of Seeing

It may seem, as you scan through all the problems described in this section, that the gods are aligned against you; how can you possibly be successful if all these malevolent forces are gathering on the horizon? The truth is, in all likelihood you'll experience very few of these problems, and quite possibly none of them.

If you do see signs of a problem, we hope you will pause before taking action. Don't rush to the store for pesticides the first time you find a few holes in the escarole. That poison will do you a lot more harm than whatever of God's creatures is munching on your salad greens. First, try to figure out what you're dealing with. Be a detective: check the plant thoroughly, especially the back sides of leaves and the stem down at the soil line. Then consider how critical the damage is and how far you are willing to go to correct it. Research the various treatment possibilities, and decide which one makes the most sense for you. (Excellent help is waiting at your local county extension office; see box on page 74.)

Taking the broader view, strong toxins constitute a threat to the environment, some of them in ways we do not yet realize. Many diseases can be avoided by choosing disease-free or disease-resistant varieties of plants. Many garden insects are actually beneficial, and most of the others can be controlled through nontoxic measures.

Here's how we see it: anything you ultimately plan to put in your mouth should be treated tenderly and respectfully; we use toxic controls only as a last resort. Even then, we try to use products that break down quickly and are the least harmful.

Harmful Insects

APHIDS. Tiny little devils no bigger than a comma that suck the juices out of plants, eventually killing them. And even if they don't kill the plants themselves, they sometimes transmit other diseases. They're especially partial to tender new growth, so you find them clustered near the growing tips, on the stems, buds, or underside of leaves. They like hot weather.

> *Maggie says:* Except for slugs, there's nothing I hate worse than aphids. Just the sight of them clambering all over each other gives me the willies.

You don't usually see just one aphid but a whole clump of them. To get rid of them, spray that clump *hard* with the hose; the goal is to knock them off. You can also just rub them off with your thumb (gloves are nice). If that doesn't get rid of them, go to the next level: spray with insecticidal soap, pyrethrum, or rotenone (described below). A plant that is very severely infested should be dug up and disposed of, before the infestation spreads.

Keep an eye out for a line of ants marching into your containers; that's an early warning signal of aphids. The aphids secrete a sticky sweet substance that ants like, and so they (the ants) draw in aphids and keep them in place, rather like a herd of cows.

All members of the cabbage family, like kale, seem to attract black aphids at the soil line. The best controls are insecticidal soap, pyrethrum, and rotenone.

County Extension Offices

Every state has a land-grant college, chartered by Congress, with a school or department of agriculture. Each of these colleges has created, in every county in that state, an extension office through which research and information are shared and made available to all. The original mandate of extension offices was to be a close-at-hand source of information for those involved in some form of commercial agriculture: farmers, nursery owners, plant breeders, and so on. However, as public institutions they also have an obligation to serve the general public, and do so through an extensive system of publications and staff assistance. You will be amazed at the wealth of information that is available, either free or at very low cost.

To find your county extension office, check the government section of your telephone book and look under the name of your county. The staff person you want will have the title Home Horticulturist, Urban Horticulturist, Home Garden Specialist, or something like that. Ask that person about plant diseases prevalent in your area, about good resistant varieties, and about recommended controls.

In some states, extension offices also sponsor a wonderful program called Master Gardeners. The program offers sophisticated, in-depth training in gardening skills to anyone, in exchange for volunteer hours later. Some Master Gardeners do their volunteer duty on the Garden Hotline, and if you live in a county with a Master Gardener program, your call to the extension office may be routed there. If they don't know the answer, they can find it for you.

Insecticidal soap. This is a soap by chemical definition (the product of an alkali reacting with a fatty substance), but don't confuse it with dishwashing detergent—it is a poison, although safer and less environmentally harmful than many synthetic pesticides. Dilute it with water according to the directions and spray it where you see insects; you may have to repeat applications.

> *Rose Marie says:* At our nursery we add a few drops of essential oil of orange to the sprayer along with the soap. It helps the soap stick and is itself a natural insecticide, effective against ants and scale, and it smells nice.

Pyrethrum. An insecticide made from crysanthemum flowers; it is safe to use on food crops, and readily breaks down in the soil without toxic residues.

Rotenone. Another insecticide derived from natural sources, this time from certain legumes, and also safe to use on edible plants.

For all controls that are applied as a spray, use these directions. Make up the solution according to the instructions on the package label; resist the temptation to make it stronger. You can use a small spray bottle, but if you have access to a large tank sprayer, it works better. Wear gloves. Direct the spray to all parts of the plant, and don't overlook the undersides of leaves. Don't spray when it's very windy or in bright sunshine. Check after a few days; repeat if necessary. Wait a day or so after application before harvesting, and wash your produce well.

SLUGS AND SNAILS. Truly disgusting creatures that chomp big holes in almost every kind of plant, slugs and snails are large enough to see easily, but they do their dirty work mostly at night and hide below soil level in the daytime. They are prevalent where the environment is cool and damp, so be especially watchful in the spring, unless like us you live where practically the entire growing season is like that.

Organic gardeners favor hand-picking them and dropping them into a container of salty or soapy water. Copper strips, attached to the outsides of containers, are effective deterrents; slugs get an electric shock when they crawl over. Snip off a section of a copper scouring pad and use it to block access through the drainage hole. A new type of slug bait, made of iron phosphate in granular form, works well with slugs but it is not harmful to pets. Find it at your garden center (brand name is Sluggo) or mail-order (Escar-Go!, from Gardens Alive!).

FLEA BEETLES. These are black and very small, about the size of fleas, and they jump like fleas. They eat tiny holes in leaves; eggplant and arugula are particularly vulnerable. Spread a row cover over the entire plant early in the season, and you can keep them out. It also helps to raise your containers up off the ground several feet, out of reach of these jumpers. Flea beetles also feast on weeds and dead leaves, so keep these cleaned away.

CUTWORMS. You usually don't see these worms, just their results—the stem is sliced off at the soil line, and the plant topples over. Organic gardeners with large gardens protect young seedlings with some kind of collar, like a bottomless tin can pushed around the stem. In a container, you are less likely to have these pests, and if you do you won't know it until the young plant suddenly keels over. If that happens, dig around the potting mix at the base of the plant, looking for brownish caterpillar-like worms. Pick them out by hand and put them in the garbage, then run to the nursery for a replacement plant.

TOMATO HORNWORMS. If Walt Disney ever did an animated film about gardens and bugs, this fellow might be a star: you can easily imagine a playful rendition of this fearsome-looking critter, with his fat striped body and sharp horn. Hornworms eat big holes in tomatoes and chomp away at the leaves. They are well disguised, the exact color of tomato leaves, so you'll have to go looking. Fortunately, they're large enough that once you find them you can just pick them off and dispose of them.

Plant Diseases

MILDEW. Big splotches of mildew—grayish patches on leaves that seem to leach out the green color—are unsightly and also unhealthy. There are two types: downy mildew, which occurs in cool, damp conditions; and powdery mildew, which occurs when the weather is hot and humid. You usually see downy mildew in early spring, with peas, beets, and other cool-season vegetables; powdery mildew hits in late summer, especially with squashes and cucumbers. Cut off the most severely affected leaves, and spray the rest with a mixture of 1 teaspoon of baking soda dissolved in 1 quart of water. You may have to repeat sprayings every few days to keep the problem from spreading.

BLOSSOM-END ROT. The sign is impossible to miss: at the blossom end of the fruit (where the flower used to be, not the end that is now attached to the stem), a big, ugly, sunken black spot develops. It doesn't actually rot, but it definitely ruins the fruit. Two things seem to be responsible: a lack of calcium in the soil, and uneven watering. To control this disease, correct those two faults and throw away the blemished fruits. See more information in the chapters on tomatoes and peppers, which are the primary targets of this malady.

Preventive Care

Of course, the best control for all problems is prevention: clean away dead leaves and other debris that collects on the soil surface, and remember to run a critical eye over your plants while you're admiring them, checking for early signs of a problem. If you spot something suspicious, move that container away from the others while you figure out what's wrong. And remember to keep a healthy perspective.

> *Maggie says:* I have a rather unconventional philosophy about insect and disease problems: if you can't fix it easily, toss it out and start over with something else. Life's too short to make yourself crazy over things like this.

> *Rose Marie says:* Amen.

PART THREE

Plants for the Bountiful Container

CHAPTER 7

VEGETABLES

A recurring theme of this book is that people who grow their own vegetables enjoy multiple benefits: not only is the food fresher and tastier, and conveniently located just a few steps from the kitchen, but gardeners can enjoy unusual varieties that are not widely available. What's more, gardeners have the fun of watching the entire growing process and the satisfaction of knowing that they had a role in it.

None of this qualifies as news, of course. All vegetable gardeners know it is infinitely more satisfying to make a delicious meal using produce they grew themselves. In earlier times in our history, people had little choice in the matter. Our great-grandparents might smile if they could hear us make such a fuss over beans or lettuce from our garden, but we know that as delicious as they are, homegrown vegetables are a rare treat today, repaying us many times over for our small effort.

In this section we present an array of vegetables that are appropriate

Vegetables in Three Seasons

The lush harvest of fresh vegetables is not limited to summertime. Many favorites actually grow better in cool weather, which means both spring and fall. And some can span the entire growing season. With some planning, therefore, you can enjoy homegrown delights in three full seasons.

Cool-Season Vegetables	Warm-Season Vegetables	Extended Harvest
lettuce	tomatoes	green onions
spinach	squash	parsley
kale	snap beans	carrots
chard	lima beans	potatoes
Asian greens	eggplant	chives
peas	cucumber	leeks
fava beans	peppers	Malabar spinach
radishes		
collards		
beets/spinach beets		

for container gardens, including some tried-and-true varieties and some that may be new to you.

One thing you should keep firmly in mind is that across the board your final yield from a container garden will be smaller than what you would get from a comparable number of plants in a traditional, in-the-ground garden. On the other hand, you *do* get vine-ripened tomatoes and gourmet salad greens and luscious edible flowers and all the chives any normal person could possibly use. And that's good enough.

All-America Selections

One of a gardener's very great joys is perusing the pages of each year's crop of mail-order catalogs, bursting with temptations. This can also be a source of great frustration, especially for those who are somewhat new to gardening, for the sheer number of possibilities is overwhelming. It isn't enough to decide you'd like to order some bean seeds; you also have to figure out what type of bean you want, and then what specific variety or cultivar of that type, when all you have to go on is (maybe) a pretty picture and some luscious-sounding description. Fortunately, there is a better way.

Through the hard work of a nonprofit organization called All-America Selections, new seed varieties are intensively tested at trial gardens located throughout North America and the results evaluated by plant experts who volunteer their time as judges. The judges in each test garden score each new plant, and only those with the very highest scores are named All-America Selections winners. New introductions that are deemed to be truly groundbreaking (not simply an improved version of an older type) are given a Gold Medal, and usually only one or two are awarded per decade.

With vegetables, the judges look for taste, quality, earliness to harvest, ease of harvest, and resistance to diseases and pests. Because the test sites are located in many climate zones, and because the scores are averaged, it's a safe bet that any seed that has been named an AAS winner represents the best, sturdiest, and tastiest variety of that particular vegetable. The organization claims that it "take[s] the guesswork out of finding reliable new varieties," and that is true. You really can't go wrong by choosing AAS winners.

Almost all seed catalogs designate their offerings that are AAS winners, sometimes in the written description, and often by displaying the red, white, and blue AAS shield beside the listing.

If you have access to the Internet, you can check for each year's winners, plus other interesting information, at this website: www.all-americaselections.org

Vegetables

Beans

GROW AS: **annuals**

PLANT SIZE: **up to 8 feet (pole beans); 12 to 18 inches (bush beans)**

START WITH: **seeds**

HARVEST SEASON: **mid to late summer (early summer for favas!)**

SUN REQUIREMENTS: **full sun**

MINIMUM SOIL DEPTH: **6 inches**

I f the only fresh beans you've ever eaten came from the supermarket, you are in for a treat. Growing them yourself has it all over store-bought, and not just because of freshness. For one thing, you won't have to be limited to the standard green variety. For another, the plants are handsome and can be used (the pole types, that is) as a living curtain outside a window or as a windbreak for a windy balcony.

Yet another bonus is that the beans themselves are preceded by pretty little flowers, which are also edible and make a charming garnish, especially the lilac blossoms of purple-podded types and the bright red flowers of scarlet runner beans. And beans are among the easiest vegetables to grow. All in all, they are a very satisfying choice for your patio garden.

Bean Basics. All beans belong in one of two big categories: pole and bush; there are several types within each category, and many varieties of each type. Pole beans are long vines, 8 feet tall or more, and need vertical support. Bush beans are short, stocky plants that do not need support. Both types are very appropriate for container growing, but you do have to know which type you have, so pay attention to the mail-order catalog description and the information on the seed packet. If you plant pole beans without some kind of trellis to grow on, pretty soon you'll have a big mess. All other things being equal, bush types produce beans earlier than pole beans, but pole types continue to produce over a longer period of time.

Planting. You will almost never find baby bean plants for sale, so you have no choice but to grow beans from seed. The seeds are large and easy to handle, germinate readily, and grow quickly. Some pointers to keep in mind:

1. Plant seeds directly in the container, but wait until the weather is really warm (with nighttime temperatures of 60°F).

2. For pole beans, put a cluster of three or four seeds in front of each vertical member of your trellis. (In many books, this cluster is called a "hill," a term that has nothing whatsoever to do with height.) For bush beans, space individual seeds 4 inches apart. In both cases, plant the seeds approximately 1 inch deep and cover lightly with potting soil or moist peat moss.

3. All beans (peas, too) will benefit from a preplanting treatment with an inoculant. Functioning like a booster shot, it enhances the plant's natural ability to convert nitrogen from the air into nitrogen in the soil, which is important because nitrogen is one of the three primary nutrients that plants need for vigorous growth.

The long and the short of it is, beans that are inoculated grow stronger and produce more beans. Inoculant comes in the form of a powder, which you dredge the seeds in before planting. It also comes in the form of granules, which you sprinkle directly into the soil along with the seeds.

Success with Beans. Beans are quite easy to grow. Not many diseases haunt them, and insect pests are minimal. (An exception is the fava bean, which aphids love.)

Your biggest concern should be watering. Beans do best with a steady, even amount of moisture. If your summers are hot and dry, check the soil every day. Never let it go completely dry, or the plants will simply shut down. Once the first tiny beans form, begin a regular program of fertilizing.

Better Bean Poles

Pole beans are essentially vines, born with the innate urge to twine themselves around something. They do this without any help from us, as long as there is something nearby for them to wind around. They will grow on something as thin as string or wire, but that produces a long, stretched-out growth that is taller than most containers can accommodate.

Not so good: thin wire for beans.

In containers, pole beans do much better with vertical supports that are at least an inch in diameter. This produces a more concentrated growth pattern, with the full length of the vine condensed by the wide circles and the beans themselves bunched up thickly together, which is what you want when your space is limited.

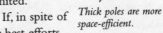

If, in spite of your best efforts, the vines insist on overgrowing their support, pinch out the new leaves at the very tip; this will control the growth pattern and also encourage the vine to send out side branches.

Thick poles are more space-efficient.

Harvesting. First the pretty little flowers wither and dry, then overnight, or so it seems, there's a miniature bean where the flower used to be. The first time you notice it, it's maybe an inch long and about as big around as a baby's shoelace. The next thing you know, it's a full-size bean, and pretty soon they're coming on faster than you can count.

It's very important to keep the beans harvested. Left too long on the vine, not only do the pods become tough but the plants stop producing.

Use two hands for harvesting. Grasp the stem with one hand and gently pull the beans away with your other hand, using an upward motion. Don't yank; bush beans, which are shallow-rooted, may come up out of the dirt, and pole vines may be ripped off the trellis.

Over the full growing season, you can expect to harvest approximately 1 gallon of beans (the full pods) from each plant of the bush type, and 1 to 2 gallons from each pole plant, including favas. For those beans that you shell (and discard the pods), the actual yield will obviously be less.

Varieties. One of the hardest things about beans is also the most fun—becoming acquainted with all the wonderful types and varieties. If you had a large farm garden, you could grow some of everything, but with container gardens you are forced to choose. It's important, therefore, to pay attention to key words in the catalog description, and to make your choices based on what is most impor-tant to you: taste, color, growing period, and so forth.

Here are the basic types, and sug-gested varieties of each:

■ **Snap beans.** Also known as string beans, these are your basic green bean.

For pole beans, we like:

Blue Lake (60 days). Stringless, tender pods with excellent flavor; long yielding.

Kentucky Blue (65 days). All-America Selection. Long, straight pods combine flavor from two classic vari-eties: Kentucky Wonder and Blue Lake. Vigorous and productive. Needs a hefty trellis.

Cascade Giant (60 days). Long, tender pods are light green streaked with scarlet and purple, and have a unique meaty flavor. Produces an early harvest at base of plant, with later crop on vines.

For bush beans, we like:

Blue Lagoon (60 days). Fine fla-vor, very productive, and a concen-trated harvest from compact plants.

Bush Blue Lake (60 days). Same classic flavor as the pole type.

Tendercrop (54 days). Vigorous, good flavor, and very popular.

■ **Purple-podded beans.** A varia-tion on regular green snap beans, these are green on the inside, but the exterior of the pod is an amazing rich purple that turns green when cooked. The flowers are lovely, in shades of lilac and lavender. Again, both bush and pole types are available:

Purple Queen (bush, 52 days). Beans are flavorful and a uniform deep purple. Leaves and flowers also have strong purple coloring.

Purple Peacock (pole, 60 days). Vigorous, productive vines make an attractive summer screen.

■ **Italian beans.** Compared to standard snap beans, Italian pods are wider and flatter, almost as if pressed in a book. You can eat them as young snap beans or let them get larger and shell them. **Romano** (70 days) is a good pole type; **Varoma** (58 days) is one of several flavorful bush varieties.

■ **Wax beans.** In a three-bean salad, these are the yellow ones.

Two good bush varieties are:

Roc d'Or (54 days). Productive, superior flavor, and tolerant of cool, wet growing conditions.

Gold Crop (56 days). Stringless, tender, with good flavor; sets pods well in hot weather.

■ **Scarlet runner beans.** A longtime favorite for the brilliant red flowers, but also valuable for the beans themselves, which can be either eaten fresh or left on the vine to dry. The term "runner" implies a vine, and most scarlet runner beans do grow as vines, but these are not the same as pole snap beans; they are their own species. Runner beans can be started sooner than regular snap beans, and thrive where summers are on the coolish side, like New England or the Pacific Northwest. The cheerful flowers look splendid in a salad or garnishing a bowl of steamed spinach.

These beans are lusty growers, with large, lush, dark green leaves; the vines will quickly cover a trellis or wall, giving you shade or a screen in addition to perky flowers and tasty beans.

For pole types, good varieties include:

Scarlet Emperor (70 days). Fully mature pods are 10 to 12 inches long, but for best table quality and a steady production of red flower sprays, pick beans before seeds begin to swell, when they are about 7 to 8 inches in length.

Painted Lady (90 days). The beautiful flowers have a scarlet hood and white base.

The terminology is confusing, but there are also bush runner beans that don't form runners. A nice one is **Dwarf Bees** (80 days). This dwarf variety, only 18 to 24 inches tall, needs no staking. Like all the runner types, it produces brilliant flowers and tasty beans. Seeds may be somewhat hard to find.

■ **Filet beans.** Tiny, delicate beans also known by their French name, *haricots verts.* Filet is a particular type of bean, not, as some people think, an immature snap bean. We recommend the variety called **Straight 'n Narrow** (53 days), a compact bush type.

■ **Dried beans.** Kidney beans, black beans, black-eyed peas, garbanzos—all the ones we normally buy as dried beans—can also be grown at home. With the limited space you have for gardening, however, you might decide it's easier to buy dried beans at the supermarket.

High-Rise Windbreak

If your garden space is subject to strong winds, a very common problem with high-rise apartment buildings, a thickly planted bean trellis is a nifty solution. Position the planter-trellis combination in the path of the prevailing wind. In addition to a nice crop of beans, you'll have a handsome, living windscreen that blocks the breezes from your other, more vulnerable plants.

The wind will not damage the beans, but you need to take precautions with the trellis itself. Use sturdy materials, and make sure the trellis is strongly anchored. Bolt it to the container and an adjoining wall, if possible. For extra security, screw eyebolts into something solid (a nearby door frame, windowsill, balcony railing, floor deck) and run guy wires from the bolts to the trellis.

Lima beans. The southerners' favorite, for good reason: limas need a long growing season. If your growing season is short but you love the taste, try a bush type, which matures faster.

Two good ones are:

Thorogreen (68 days). Vigorous 18-inch plants bear till frost.

Fordhook 242 (85 days) High yielding, heat tolerant, and easy to shell.

Fava beans. The sweetly fragrant flowers of fava beans make them a welcome addition to the culinary container garden. The individual beans are very large (their other name, broad bean, is quite apt) and have a dense,

meaty texture. Rich in protein, fresh and dried favas have long been a favorite of European families, and in recent years the fresh beans have become popular with gourmet cooks here. If you want to try them fresh, growing your own is your best bet. Unlike limas and even snap beans, favas prefer cool, damp weather; plant them in spring, about the same time as peas. The plants grow to about 3 feet tall, so a short trellis is a good idea.

Aphids can be a problem in the spring. One easy control is to just pinch off the growing tips where they tend to cluster. This has the advantage of forcing plants to put energy into maturing the crop of newly set beans. Harvesting occurs at several stages: pick the first pods when no more than 4 inches in length and beans are slim and flexible. Cook like snap beans, either whole or sliced. When the pods gain size and begin to droop, they are ready for eating as fresh shell beans. Steam for three to five minutes, then serve hot with butter or cooled for salads. If the seed coat on the bean has matured, slip it off before serving. At season's end, allow the beans to dry and store for soups.

A few people of Mediterranean heritage have a rare genetic allergy to favas. If you have never eaten them, start with a very small portion to see if they agree with you.

Good varieties are:

Broad Windsor (75 days). Large beans, four to five per pod, with good flavor.

Aquadulce (85 days). Hardy; in mild-winter climates, plant in fall for a spring crop.

T alk to any longtime gardener, and you'll find a common theme: almost all of them started gardening as a child. They speak with great fondness of summer days in the garden, working alongside their parents, their grandfather, a favorite aunt; they smile at the memory of pulling up their very first radish, eating sun-warmed tomatoes right there in the garden patch, surviving their first encounter with a ferocious-looking hornworm.

Theme Garden

A Kid's Garden

Of course, childhood experience isn't a prerequisite; many people first discover the pleasure of gardening as adults. But the reverse is universally true: anyone who learns about gardening as a child is hooked for life, even if circumstances sometimes intervene. By introducing children to gardens, you're equipping them for a lifetime of enjoyment. And even without that lofty parental goal, helping children start their garden is its own reward because they have so much fun and you have the even greater pleasure of watching their enjoyment.

Children are naturally attracted to small things of all species; just think how they go silly over new puppies or fuzzball kittens. They exhibit that same sense of delight when a seed they planted with their own hands breaks through the soil and pokes its head up to say hello.

Containers provide the perfect way to start children gardening because the very chores that make them lose interest in larger gardens are practically nonexistent in containers. For maximum success:

1. Let the kids make the decisions about what to plant, based on what they like to eat, but point them toward varieties that grow fast.
2. Set them up with their own container and gear; as much as possible, let them do the work.
3. Be flexible, and don't expect picture-perfect results.

We suggest two gardens here: one for toddlers and one for older children.

A GARDEN FOR TODDLERS

Everything in this garden is easy to grow and produces the good stuff at a young child's eye level.

For details on
growing the plants in
this garden, see

Beans, page 81
Carrots, page 93
Pansies, page 382
Pumpkins, page 158
Radishes, page 147
Sunflowers, page 401

Easter Egg **radishes** are a blend of several varieties in one seed packet, producing radishes in different colors: white, red, pink, and lilac. Harvesting them is always a surprise; you never know what colors you'll get.

Thumbelina **carrots** are small and round, rather than long and skinny. Even children who don't usually like carrots like these because of the fun shape.

Pansies are especially attractive to small children if they can see a cat's face in the flower. This mimicry is most obvious with bicolor or tricolor flowers, in small or medium sizes. Very large flowers in solid colors are quite pretty, but they don't look like kittens.

Wee-B-Little **pumpkins** are perfect jack-o'-lantern miniatures, about 3 to 4 inches across. The plant grows as a semi-bush, and will basically fill the container by mid summer. If several children claim this garden, you might want to let them create "autographed" pumpkins. When the fruits are about the size of a baseball, have each child write his or her name on a pumpkin with a felt marker. Then you go over the writing with a nail or the tip of a sharp knife, cutting lightly down through the skin. The cuts will scar over, and each mature pumpkin will be personalized.

Start with a container at least 18 inches wide. In early spring (as soon as pansies show up at the garden center), set out pansies and sow seeds of radishes and carrots. It's okay if the seeds get mixed together; in fact, many people deliberately plant radishes, which germinate very quickly, in with other, slower seeds to keep the soil surface loose. The radishes are ready to eat in less than a month; as they come out, space is opened up for the carrots. The pansies will still be looking cute through early summer.

In early June plant a few pumpkin seeds in the center of the container. Or, if your growing season is short, start seeds indoors in early May and transplant into the container in June. In either case, by mid summer the plant will stretch across the entire container, which is okay because everything else has been harvested. The pumpkins start forming in August, and are ready for decorating the table (or eating) by Halloween.

As an alternative, if your kids have an old toy dump truck or something similar that they no longer use, plant a few pansies in the truck's bed and set the truck right on top of the container. As the pumpkin vine grows and threatens to overtake the whole container, move the truck down to the floor and keep it watered; in the fall, when the temperatures turn cool, the pansies will put on another burst of flowers.

To add a playful element that will keep children entertained and also keep birds away, search out a colorful whirlygig. Older wooden ones in antique stores are very endearing, and very dear. New ones can be charming, and even the inexpensive plastic versions captivate young children with their movement and bright colors.

A GARDEN FOR OLDER CHILDREN

Children who enjoy eating sunflower seeds as a snack get a big kick out of growing the flowers and seeing the seeds form in autumn. And if your mental image of a sunflower is something 10 feet tall, you'll be glad to know about dwarf varieties. Three good ones are Teddy Bear, Sunspot, and Big Smile **dwarf sunflowers.** They seldom top 2 feet—just the right height for a child, and for a container.

Purple-podded **beans** are remarkable for their color; the outer skin of the pod is a dark purple that turns green when cooked. The taste is the same as regular green beans', which means the children either will or will not like to eat them, but kids are guaranteed to enjoy the magic show when the beans turn color. They are available in pole and bush forms, but choose a bush type for this garden.

Jack-Be-Little **pumpkins** are perfect pumpkins in miniature, 3 inches across and 2 inches high. Their tiny size is especially appealing to very young children, but we've chosen this variety for older children because the pumpkins form on a vine and thus need to be on a trellis, too high for toddlers to watch them growing.

This garden works well in a medium to large container, 14 to 18 inches in diameter. Position a strong trellis at the rear for the pumpkin vine to climb.

Easter Egg **radishes,** described above, can be planted and harvested several times from March through May. In late May, plant bean and sunflower seeds in among the last of the radishes, and pumpkin seeds just in front of the trellis legs.

Vegetables

Beets

GROW AS: **annuals**

PLANT SIZE: **6 to 8 inches**

START WITH: **seeds**

HARVEST SEASON: **early summer, again in fall**

SUN REQUIREMENTS: **full sun to partial shade**

MINIMUM SOIL DEPTH: **6 inches**

In almost every respect, beets are a perfect choice for the container garden: they're easy to grow and fast to mature, they don't take up much room, they can be resown for several harvests per year, they don't need a lot of maintenance, they taste significantly better than canned, and you can eat the entire plant.

The only drawback seems to be that for whatever reason, people don't think of growing them. But even if beets are not high on your list of favorites, we urge you to include them in one of your containers for all the reasons above, and two more: you'll get to enjoy the tops, which are wonderfully rich, smooth-tasting greens, and you can grow delightful varieties you'll never find in a supermarket.

Beet Basics. From one plant you get two crops: the round red root that you envision when someone says "beet," and the leaves that grow above ground. The most reliable way to find beet greens is to grow them, for even fresh beets in the supermarket often have the tops chopped off. Very young, tender leaves are wonderful raw in a salad, and older leaves can be cooked like spinach; even people who don't usually like cooked greens often enjoy beet leaves, with their soft, mellow flavor.

Planting. Beets are a cool-season vegetable, which means you can start them early in spring and resow several times, up till early summer, and then again in late summer for a fall/winter crop. In very general terms, that means mid March to early June for the first sowings, then again during the first three weeks of August for the second crop. You can even start seeds indoors ahead of time, should you get garden-restless in February. Germination takes one to two weeks.

To speed germination, soak seeds overnight, then plant directly in the potting soil ½ inch deep and 1 inch apart. The hard, bumpy seeds are actually clusters of several seeds, so you'll get several seedlings sprouting from each one. When the seedlings are about 2 inches tall, thin away all but one in each cluster. (Rinse the thinnings and add them, whole, to any mixture of sautéed greens.)

Success with Beets. The secret of tender, tasty beets is to keep them growing fast, and that means consistent watering and fertilizing. Add a balanced fertilizer once a week, and keep a close eye on soil moisture. If the soil dries out, or if there is an alternating pattern of too dry, then too wet, the beets will become tough and woody.

Harvesting. Start harvesting the roots when they are about an inch in diameter; to get an estimate of size, brush away the soil from the shoulders of one plant. Beets have a very cooperative nature: they are ready to eat when very small, but they also keep growing without loss of quality. If you make a second sowing in August, you may well be harvesting fresh beets right through the winter.

To cook beets (the roots, that is) without their bleeding, leave about an inch of stem in place and add a tablespoon of vinegar to the cooking water. When the beets are done, slip off the peel and the stem ends. For full, deep flavor, try baking beets in the oven.

Varieties. The classic beet is round and red, but that's only the beginning of the story. The fun part of growing beets is having access to unusual types: beets that are long and thin like carrots, or golden yellow, or pink-swirled inside like candy.

Scarlet Supreme (50 days). Outstanding on almost every front: it matures earlier than others, produces lots of bright green tops, and is sweet and tender.

Golden Beet (55 days). Another heirloom type, with a sweet-tasting root that is a lovely golden yellow and dark green leaves with yellow ribs. Popular with gourmet cooks because the color doesn't bleed. Plant more thickly than other varieties, to compensate for lower germination rate.

Detroit Dark Red (55 to 60 days). This standard, classic red beet is an heirloom variety, and the most popular for home gardens.

Chioggia (55 days). This heirloom variety produces roots with a pretty pattern of concentric circles of red or pink, alternating with circles of white or cream color. Grated raw into salads, they add a zap of color and texture; the flavor is unusually sweet.

■**Cylindrical beets.** These are a perfect example of the joy of growing your own food: you can have an unusual treat with no more effort than is involved in growing the ordinary kind. Rather than the familiar round globes, cylindrical beets are long and slender, like a carrot if carrots were beet red. Because of this narrow shape, they need less growing room; in the same amount of container space, you can get up to four times the yield. Another nice feature is that the mature beets can be sliced crosswise into rounds of uniform size for a very attractive salad presentation.

The downside is that they are a bit slower to mature; you might think about growing some of both types for a long, delicious harvest.

Two very nice cylindrical varieties are **Formanova** and **Forona,** both 60 days. If you plan to try these, use a slightly deeper soil depth than for round beets: 8 inches minimum.

Heirloom Vegetables

Something in our nature yearns to return to simpler times; the more complex the world becomes, the stronger this yearning is felt. In the matter of food and gardening, we see this most prominently in the recent interest in what are called heirloom vegetables. The term has a warm, homey sound with overtones of old-fashioned goodness, but what does it really mean? Like many other labels, this one has been used so freely by so many that a precise definition that all can agree on is hard to come by.

For the purposes of this book, we have followed the lead established by Benjamin Watson in his excellent book *Taylor's Guide to Heirloom Vegetables,* in which he defines an heirloom as one that meets these three criteria:

1. It is a standard, open-pollinated variety, rather than a hybrid, and thus its seeds will reproduce faithfully. A hybrid, which is the result of deliberate cross-fertilization of two different varieties in a breeder's greenhouse, has the characteristics of both parents, but any seed from it will not produce a plant that is like itself, or, in the phrase used by many longtime gardeners, it "doesn't come true from seed." You can plant the seed of a hybrid, but there's no telling what you'll get. Open-pollinated plants, in contrast, are pollinated by natural forces (bees, wind, and so forth), and their seeds reproduce accurately.

2. It was introduced at least 50 years ago. Many heirlooms are much older, of course, but all contribute to this sense of history and continuity.

3. It has its own unique history. Many heirlooms were saved by individual farmers, their seeds passed down through the generations; some represent the horticultural endeavors of famous people; some are associated with specific events. But all, in one way or another, mean something in the history of gardening.

All this is appealing to students of history and botany, but for most people the attraction of heirloom vegetables is their flavor. Heirlooms have passionate fans, firm in their conviction that these varieties have superior taste. This is the sort of fruitless debate that no one can win, since questions of taste can be determined only by the individual. What we can say for sure is that heirloom varieties provide us many delightful vegetables not otherwise available, with wonderful flavor, unusual colors or shapes, and marvelous stories.

They also play an important role in maintaining plant diversity, preserving the unique package of genetic material that each variety represents and from which the next generation of discoveries must come. For the sake of a healthy environment and a nutritious future, it behooves us all to support those businesses that are dedicated to preserving heirloom varieties. To support them is simple and wonderfully self-serving: buy heirloom seeds; grow the plants; eat the results. Enjoy.

Vegetables

Carrots

GROW AS: **annuals**

PLANT SIZE: **6 to 12 inches, both above and below ground**

START WITH: **seeds**

HARVEST SEASON: **summer through fall**

SUN REQUIREMENTS: **full sun**

MINIMUM SOIL DEPTH: **8 inches**

Fresh, sweet tidbits with a true carrot taste, frilly foliage that is pretty in its own right, and delightful varieties that have never seen the inside of a supermarket—are those enough reasons for growing your own carrots? If not, think of them as a way to introduce children to gardens, with a vegetable they probably already like in shapes they never saw before. Adults who think a carrot is a carrot is a carrot will change their minds when they first taste one that is truly fresh.

Carrot Basics. It's a bit of a challenge to sort out all the choices among carrots because of the way they are named. Seed catalogs describe individual varieties as being, for instance, "a

Chantenay type" or "early Nantes." Chantenay and Nantes are names of older varieties that have now become generic terms for different types of carrots; the distinguishing trait is their shape. Long and thin Imperator is the one you usually find in the supermarket. Chantenays are tapered, with a broad top and pointed tip, and can grow to very large size. Danvers are also tapered, a bit smaller. Nantes types have straight, untapered sides and blunt ends. Two other generic types, with more logical names, are round and finger carrots, and they are what you would think: round like golf balls, and finger-shaped. Rounds, fingers, and Nantes are best for containers.

Planting. Carrots germinate best when the soil is 70° to 80°F, but they can be started much sooner, as long as temperatures don't sink below 45°F. The seeds are quite tiny, and in cooler weather they take a long time to germinate; in the meantime, it's essential that they be kept moist. Carrots don't transplant well, and so must be sown in place. All this adds up to something of a challenge when it comes to getting them started. Here are some tips:

1. Make a mixture of carrot seeds and radish seeds, and plant the mixture; the radishes germinate rapidly, keeping the potting soil loose for the teeny carrot seedlings and serving as place markers. Check the soil every day; add water if needed. Use a gentle mist so you don't dislodge the seeds.

Keep the moisture level up even after the radishes begin to grow; the carrot seeds still need it, and it will keep the radishes tender and crisp.

2. Alternative for different taste buds: mix one part carrot seeds with three parts bok choy seeds. In 30 to 45 days, depending on the variety, you'll be harvesting the bok choy and the carrots will be just developing; as the bok choy comes out, it opens up room for the growing carrots.

3. If you'd rather not mix things, sow the carrot seeds alone (about ¼ inch deep) and take extra measures to keep them damp. Cover the seeds with wet burlap, a thin layer of sphagnum moss or peat moss that you presoaked, or even something like damp paper towels if that's all you have. Keep the covering layer damp, and keep checking underneath; at the first sight of feathery green seedlings, remove the covering.

Either mixed or plain, you can continue sowing carrot seeds in batches for an extended harvest season. It doesn't have to be a precise system: when you've pulled up about half your carrots, plant some more.

Because the seeds are so small, you cannot help but plant them very thickly, which means that you'll need to do some serious thinning once the tops are about 2 inches high. For long, slender types, thin seedlings to ½ inch apart; the round ones need more room, about a 1-inch spacing.

Rose Marie says: With these root crops you don't have to be too precise about the thinning. Just keep getting in there and picking out the largest ones, which creates room for their smaller brothers to grow. The first tiny thinnings can be added whole to salads—the tender young foliage is good to eat. Just rinse, and pinch off the threadlike root at the growing tip.

Success with Carrots. Once you get past the germination challenge, carrots are extremely easy to grow. Keep them watered and fertilized with a balanced fertilizer, and you can turn your attention elsewhere.

Harvesting. You can start harvesting anytime the carrots reach the size you want. There is no particular trick to it; just be sure you have a firm grip on the stems, near the shoulder of the carrot root.

If you sow in the summer for a winter crop and carrots are still growing when the weather turns cool, you can leave them in place and have the fun of pulling fresh carrots at Thanksgiving. Cover the soil with protective mulch in very cold areas; sphagnum moss, this time in a thick layer, will work fine.

Varieties. Two round ones we like for containers are **Thumbelina** (60 days), an AAS winner, and **Parmex** (70 days). Both are sweet, bite-sized treats that make children smile.

Scarlet Nantes (70 days). A full-size Nantes carrot, approximately 6 inches long. **Touchon** (75 days) is an heirloom Nantes type that is nearly coreless and very juicy.

Little Finger (65 days) is a Nantes type in shape but smaller overall, like your little finger. **Minicor** (55 days) is very similar.

Vegetables

Cucumbers

GROW AS: **annuals**

PLANT SIZE: **3-foot diameter (bush types) or 6-foot vine**

START WITH: **seeds**

HARVEST SEASON: **summer**

SUN REQUIREMENTS: **full sun**

MINIMUM SOIL DEPTH: **10 inches**

Cucumbers that are allowed to grow on the vine until they are just-right ripe have a rich, full, cucumbery taste that is as different from supermarket cucumbers as a fresh pineapple is from a picture of a pineapple. If you love cucumbers, you'll want to grow your own, for that wonderful flavor and for the unusual varieties available (lemon cucumber is pictured above). Just remember: they do take up room—more than, say, carrots—so be prepared.

Cucumber Basics. In the minds of people who sell us the seeds, cucumbers are grouped into two large categories, based on how they are used: picklers and slicers. Picklers are short, stubby, and bumpy. Slicers are the familiar long green vegetables that we slice raw for salads and crudités. Many catalogs group into another category the types known as "burpless," specially bred to eliminate the enzymes that make digestion difficult for some people (burpless is also the name of a specific variety, as well as the name of a subcategory). And some catalogs create a separate category for Asian cucumbers, which are unusually long and thin, mild, and crunchy.

Deep in their genes cucumbers are vines, but plant breeders, constantly searching for new items to offer customers, have developed several types that maintain a compact bush shape. The vine types need to be grown on trellises, the bush types do not; be sure you know which you are getting. In catalog descriptions and on seed packets, bush types will be indicated as such; the vining types may not say anything in this regard.

Planting. Cucumber plants are heat lovers; they simply won't germinate until the temperature hits 70°F. For direct sowing, wait until the weather, and thus the soil in your container, is really warm. Plant six to eight seeds in a cluster, about ½ inch deep; when they have two sets of true leaves, thin to the strongest two or three seedlings. Pinch the others off at the soil line to avoid damaging the roots of the keepers. Be ruthless about doing this; it really is important.

Cucumbers grow so fast once they get started, it usually doesn't help much to start them indoors. However, if you find small transplants at the garden center, you can plant them in your containers a bit early with some nighttime protection; see page 55 for ideas.

Success with Cucumbers.

Consistent water and lots of fertilizer—that's the secret to success. You are going to be surprised at how fast cucumber vines grow when the weather is to their liking. To support that growth, especially once they start setting fruit, give the plants a balanced fertilizer once a week and make *sure* the potting mix never dries out—that's what produces cucumbers that are bitter, hollow, or otherwise unpleasant.

To help hold moisture in the soil, cover the surface with a light mulch of peat moss or florist's decorative moss. This has the extra benefit of keeping any surface roots from drying out.

Cukes do extremely well trained to a trellis (see Chapter 4 for ideas). In a 20-inch container with a 4-foot demicage, you could plant up to six cucumber vines. Not only do you get maximum use of your space, but long, thin varieties like Suyo Long or Sweet Success grow into an attractive straight shape, instead of being twisted and curled.

Cucumbers are susceptible to a large array of plant diseases, most of them caused by pathogens that live in garden soil. As you study seed catalogs you'll see that breeders have been hard at work developing disease-resistant varieties. In containers you'll miss most of those problems, but you could very well encounter powdery mildew late in the season; see page 76 for treatment.

Harvesting.

With cucumbers we get an easy lesson in one of Mother Nature's fundamental principles: the goal of a plant is to reproduce itself. Annuals, which have only one season in which to do so, have an innate drive to produce seeds. One cucumber is a veritable seed factory; all you have to do is slice one vertically to realize how many seeds are inside. If we leave that one fruit on the vine, all the seeds will reach viable size, and the plant, having done its job, will stop producing cucumbers. But if we interrupt that cycle and pick the fruit before the seeds inside are mature, the plant will desperately make more cukes.

The moral of the story: pick cucumbers while they are small and tender, or the vines will shut down. Be vigilant; in the height of summer, the fruits grow astonishingly fast. If one gets away from you (you'll know it's overmature if you see yellow skin), remove and discard it.

Most cucumber plants produce both male and female flowers; the male flowers, which sit at the end of a short stalk, appear first, several days before the first female. Don't be surprised when the first flowers fall off without showing any signs of producing fruits; those are the males. Female flowers have a small bulge behind the flower, where it connects to the stem.

Varieties.

The whole point of growing pickling cucumbers is to make pickles, but it's necessary to grow a *lot* of cucumbers to make that project worthwhile—more than you can reasonably grow in a container. We're going to assume you're more interested in growing the slicing type, and there are many fine varieties to choose from.

Lemon (60 days). Almost everyone laughs with delight the first time they see a lemon cucumber, so different is it from the classic, long green item. Very reminiscent of lemons in size, shape, and color, they nonetheless taste like cucumbers, with a mild, almost sweet flavor. This is a very old heirloom variety, first introduced more than 100 years ago. Harvest lemon cukes while they're small and show just a trace of yellow at the blossom end. They need a trellis.

Suyo (62 days). These wonderful Japanese-style cucumbers are just as easy to grow as the ordinary kind, and the results are extraordinary: the long, slender fruits are crisp, not very seedy, and quite delicious—a real conversation piece. They need a strong trellis.

Salad Bush (57 days) is an All-America Selection with good disease resistance and the perfect shape for containers: short, very productive vines. Cucumbers are about 8 inches long, with smooth, dark green skins. **Fanfare** (63 days), another All-America winner with a compact growth habit, is very appropriate for containers. Good yield of slender, extra-crisp fruits.

Sweet Success (50 days) is an example of a fascinating development in plant breeding: gynoecious cucumbers, with self-pollinating, all-female flowers. The fruits are seedless (or virtually so; you may see the faint outlines of undeveloped seeds inside). If they are grown side by side with regular cucumbers, some cross-pollination occurs and seeds will form in these "seedless" fruits. But if you harvest them early, while they are young and tender, the seeds will not have developed to a noticeable stage. Sweet Success is an All-America Selection, and produces a steady crop of slender, 10- to 12-inch cucumbers. They need a trellis.

Human Honeybees

If the first cucumbers (or squash) that develop are lopsided, your plant has been the victim of poor pollination. In some parts of the country, a couple of nasty mites are killing our honeybees, and you may be in an area with a shortage of these natural pollinators. All is not lost. In fact, the solution to this problem is easy and extremely satisfying.

Visit your garden early in the morning with a small, soft artist's paintbrush. Insert the brush into an open flower and swirl it around with a circular motion. Then go on to the next blossom, just like a bee. What you are doing is transferring the pollen from the male flowers (those on a short, thin stalk) to the female blossoms (with a slight bulge at the base of the flower); in a day or two you'll see a tiny cucumber forming. The bee, of course, doesn't discriminate, buzzing from flower to flower in search of nectar and transferring pollen as he goes. We humans can be a bit more deliberate, making sure to move from male to female flower.

Gardening is as subject to trends as any other human endeavor. Spend some time in your local library's periodicals room, browsing recent issues of several gardening magazines, and you'll soon realize that you've seen the same general topics over and over. What makes gardening trends so interesting is the frequency with which the newest "hot topics" turn out to be very old ideas.

Take kitchen gardens, for example. A few years ago, they were the trend du jour in gardening publications; there was even a mild flurry about the elegant French version of a kitchen garden known as the *potager*. The ultimate kitchen garden is a happy, floriferous mélange of good things to eat, all growing lustily together: vegetables and herbs side by side with flowers and fruit trees. Our great-grandmothers grew their food just this way, and they never thought to call it anything special.

Theme Garden

Country Kitchen in the Round

Today most gardeners would love nothing better than to have their great-grandmother's garden, but many of us simply do not have the space. It is for these admirers of country gardens and country cooking that we designed this particular container garden, which provides a great bounty of good food in a small area. In a circle just 5 feet across, an astonishing variety of edibles can be grown. To put it another way, in a space no bigger than many kitchen tables, you can have an entire kitchen garden bursting with all the good things you like to eat.

What makes this garden work so well for so many situations is that it is planted in six different containers, so you can arrange them in whatever configuration best fits your garden site. In the drawing here, for instance, the pots are arranged in a semi-circle against the wall, and the tomato uses the fence as a support. You can also move them during the season, as the sun and weather patterns change. This is a very flexible concept, so we'll give only general suggestions before turning you loose to plant whatever you truly love.

POT 1. In the center, in full sun, a large (24-inch) container. Sturdily staked in the middle of the pot is one luscious **tomato.** On the edges, plant your favorite **cucumber** and some trailing **nasturtiums.** As an option, encircle the entire container with a wire trellis made from concrete

reinforcing wire with a 6-inch grid. It should be tall enough to extend another 24 inches or so above the rim. It supports not only the tomato and the cucumber in the large container, but some of the other containers' plants as well.

In a circle around Pot 1 are five smaller containers, 14 to 18 inches in diameter, with assorted plants. Here are some suggestions.

POT 2. One or two Asian **eggplants** at the rear, with three or four **basils** on the outer edge. Place this pot in full sun.

POT 3. One sun-loving summer **squash,** fronted with **lettuce.** By the time the summer heat knocks out the lettuce, the squash will be at its prime.

POT 4. Climbing **nasturtiums** at the rear, **peppers** near the front; this is another sun lover.

POT 5. Bush **peas** on the inside, **lettuce** circling the outer edges. Bush peas don't absolutely need a trellis, but will appreciate the extra support. Around the first of July, direct-sow seeds of bush **beans** in among the pea plants; by the time they germinate, the peas will be ready to come out (cut off at ground level and leave the roots in place). This container can go on the shady side of your circle.

POT 6. A small herb garden for fans of Paul Simon: **parsley, sage,** trailing **rosemary,** and **thyme;** sun or part shade.

If you add the wire trellis to the center container, many of the plants in the smaller containers will grab onto it. This is fine if you don't plan to move anything later on, but if you do, you can accomplish the same results by using individual short trellises in the smaller containers. In particular, pots number 2, 4, and 5 would benefit from a bit of trellis support.

Vegetables

Eggplant

GROW AS: **annuals**

PLANT SIZE: **2 feet tall**

START WITH: **transplants**

HARVEST SEASON: **late summer**

SUN REQUIREMENTS: **full sun**

MINIMUM SOIL DEPTH: **10 inches**

Very few people are ambivalent about eggplant. Either you like it or you don't, and if you don't, then you're not likely to develop a fondness for it just because you grew it with your own hands. But if you do like it, or if you're ready to try something new, the small Japanese or dwarf varieties are terrific—beautiful while they're growing, delicious when cooked.

If you've never seen eggplants growing, you're in for a treat. The plants are extremely attractive, with elegant leaves, pretty little flowers, and rich, lustrous fruits that may be regal purple, ivory, lavender, blush pink, or lime green, depending on the variety.

Eggplant Basics. It's convenient to think of eggplants in two major groups: the familiar fat shape, and the long, slender Asian types. Seed merchants have provided us with many choices, including smaller, miniaturized versions in many luscious colors.

Planting. These are hot-weather plants, and need temperatures of at least 75°F to germinate. Germination takes two to three weeks; add another couple of weeks to reach transplant size, and then another two to three months to start producing the fruits. It's clear, then, that you won't have time for direct sowing. If you are lucky enough to have a garden center stocked with unusual vegetable varieties, you can buy your eggplant transplants in May and June. But if you don't, your only choice is to start seeds indoors ahead of time.

Backtrack eight weeks from the time when daytime high temperatures usually reach 80°F in your area. Plant seeds ¼ inch deep in peat pots or pellets; keep the tray very warm (see pages 57 to 58). Depending on your climate, you may have to move the seedlings into larger, intermediate pots before the soil outside is warm enough to receive them. Be sure to harden off the seedlings (see page 60) before planting outside.

To give the babies the best chance, keep containers in full sun and cover with black plastic a few days ahead to really warm up the potting soil. For the first couple of weeks, when nighttime temperatures are not reliable, you may need to provide some protection for the tender plants. Blanket them with plastic sheeting, held up off the plants with short stakes; or cover them with milk-jug cloches (see page 47) at night.

Success with Eggplants. Your biggest problem will be timing—getting transplants into the container when the weather is ready. Otherwise, eggplants are generally hardy plants that present few troubles for the container gardener. Occasional problems include aphids, flea beetles, or Colorado potato beetles (eggplants are in the same family as potatoes), but all are manageable (see Chapter 6). Raising the containers up off the floor seems to help deter flea beetles.

Put the container in your sunniest location, keep the soil moist, and fertilize every two weeks. If the roots are warm, you'll have a little eggplant factory at work.

Harvesting. Eggplants that are overmature are not very appealing; if anything, you may want to pick them a bit ahead of time. The outside skin should still be glossy and smooth. Cut off each eggplant with clippers or a sharp knife, taking a bit of the stem. To keep the plant producing, it's important to keep up with harvesting. If even *one* fruit sets seed, the plant will slow down significantly.

Varieties. Traditional varieties, the ones that produce the familiar big, round, dark purple eggplants, don't work very well in containers: the eggplants they produce are simply too large and too heavy. Fortunately, we have other varieties to explore.

Two general categories of eggplant are excellent for containers: the Asian types, which are by nature long and slender, and the dwarf varieties, which are the traditional oval shape but much smaller.

■ **Asian type.** Ichiban (61 days) has long, slender, dark purple fruits—the classic Japanese eggplant. **Asian Bride** (70 days) has a similar shape as Ichiban but a different color: a delicate white with beautiful lavender streaks. **Green Goddess** (63 days) is an extremely productive type with fruits that are 8 inches long, 2 inches in diameter, and a knockout color: lime green. **Neon** (65 days) is a modified Asian type, with medium-long fruits slightly swollen near the end. It is well named: the outer skin is a rich, intense, deep pink that glows like neon against the bright green leaves.

■ **Dwarf varieties.** Bambino (75 days) produces lots of small round fruits, 1 to 1½ inches in diameter, deep purple in color. It is particularly good for containers because the plant itself is smaller than most. **Little Fingers** (65 days) has dark glossy purple fruits, short and slender, 3 to 4 inches long.

Rosa Bianca (75 days) has roundish fruits, rather like a softball that got squashed at one end, and mild flavored, but the real delight is their gorgeous color: soft lavender streaked with white is an heirloom variety from Italy. **Comprido Verde Claro** (72 days) has small and slender fruits, 3 to 4 inches long, and notable for their amazing color: leaf green at first, gradually turning orange.

Vegetables

Leafy Greens

GROW AS: **annuals**

PLANT SIZE: **4 to 24 inches high**

START WITH: **seeds or transplants**

HARVEST SEASON: **late spring through winter**

SUN REQUIREMENTS: **full sun to partial shade**

MINIMUM SOIL DEPTH: **8 inches**

because many of these plants are beautiful to look at and contribute delicious, unusual flavors to the dinner table. Southern European gardeners have built their cuisines on these easy-to-grow, nutritious powerhouses, and American cooks are now beginning to wise up.

Note that in this section we've included the green leafy vegetables that are usually eaten cooked (except for spinach, which has its own section). The specialty greens that usually go raw into salads are found in the Lettuce section. We admit that the distinction is subtle and a bit arbitrary, and some items could as well go in one section as the other. If you don't find something you expect to see here, check under Lettuce or Spinach.

Rose Marie says: My Greek grandmother loved going out to her field to harvest mustard greens, fresh and tender with a little bite. She prepared an endless variety of cooked salads: single or mixed greens, coarsely chopped and sautéed briefly in olive oil, then served with wedges of fresh lemon. Delicious hot, cold, or warm.

The virtues of greens are many: they are easy to grow, thrive in almost any kind of weather, excel in containers, produce a crop quickly, and provide more vitamins per square inch than anything in the garden. But like many things that are good for us, they are often overlooked by gardeners as being not particularly glamorous. That's a shame,

Greens Basics. Speaking in general terms, which we have to do in this consolidated section, greens are cool-season vegetables that are grown for their leaves. One very cooperative trait is

Recipe: Pasta with Summer Vegetables

Tom DeBaggio, owner of DeBaggio Herbs in Arlington, Virginia, has introduced several herb varieties to the United States and is the author of two books: *Basil, An Herb Lover's Guide* and *Growing Herbs from Seed, Cutting, and Root*. Tom says: "My cooking tends to be spontaneous and performed out of need. Ingredients are chosen on the basis of what is available that night in the garden."

This recipe makes use of two early-summer vegetables: kale and peas. If fresh tomatoes are not yet available, use good-quality canned tomatoes.

1 cup chopped fresh or canned tomatoes

1 tablespoon finely chopped fresh basil

1 pound pasta

1 tablespoon extra-virgin olive oil, plus extra for serving

1 cup shredded kale

1 cup shelled fresh peas

½ cup finely chopped ham (optional)

1 teaspoon chopped fresh thyme or oregano

1. Place the tomatoes in a bowl. Stir in the basil and set aside.

2. Bring a large pot of water to a boil. Add the pasta and cook until al dente.

3. While the pasta is cooking, heat 1 tablespoon of the olive oil in a large skillet over medium heat. Add the kale, peas, and ham, and sauté until the kale begins to soften, about 5 minutes; then add the thyme or oregano. Continue sautéing until the kale and peas are tender-crisp, 5 to 10 minutes more.

4. Drain the pasta and place in a large bowl. Top with the hot kale mixture and the tomato-basil mixture and toss thoroughly. Serve in wide bowls, and drizzle each serving with a little olive oil if desired.

Serves 4

their long period of productivity: they germinate just fine in cool weather, keep producing during the summer, when lettuce and spinach wimp out, and go on through fall without blinking. Even a light frost doesn't bother them—in fact, many people think frost improves the taste—so they can continue into the winter and even winter over in temperate areas.

Planting. As soon as nighttime temperatures are no longer cold enough to freeze your container soil, you can direct-sow seeds for these greens. The seeds are generally quite small, and thus should be planted only about ¼ inch deep. Because small seeds are difficult to space evenly, you're bound to get lots of baby seedlings that will need thinning; if you like, you can replant the thinnings into another container. As a group, greens transplant very successfully, so you can start seeds indoors three to four weeks before your spring frost date to get a jump on your first planting.

Because greens do transplant easily, you're also likely to find some of the better-known types for sale as young transplants at your garden center early in the season. This is a good way to go with these plants: you get the benefit of someone else's greenhouse work, but you don't have to worry about the weather being too cool to set out plants, as is sometimes the case with other vegetable transplants being sold at the same time.

Success with Greens. If you want tender, succulent greens, keep the plants growing fast. That means lots of water and steady fertilizing; since it's the foliage you're interested in, use fish emulsion or a fertilizer high in nitrogen (the first number). Most greens are relatively trouble free, but you may have to contend with slugs and snails in the spring and aphids in the summer; see Chapter 6 for controls.

Harvesting. All these plants can be harvested when they are still quite young, and you'll have baby chard or baby bok choy or baby whatever, just like the baby vegetables you'd pay a pretty penny for at the gourmet greengrocer. Otherwise, keep them growing fast for tasty full-size leaves. Take care, however, not to let them get too large. Most of what shows up in the produce aisle is overgrown, giving nongardeners a false impression of what these plants really taste like. If some of the oldest leaves on your plants get too big and tough, just remove and discard them to keep newer growth coming on.

Harvest the outermost leaves, just enough for tonight's supper, and your plants will keep producing. Pull away the leaves or slice the stalks at the base with a sharp knife. The technique for kale and collards is a bit different: if you slice leaves from the crown (the center of the plant), the plant will form new branches with more new leaves; use a knife for a clean cut.

Varieties. We offer just a few suggestions for each of the plants, even though many of them have many varieties and all are very fine container plants. Spend a few minutes with seed catalogs, and you'll realize the astonishing range of intriguing possibilities. The reputation of leafy greens as unglamorous country cousins will be banished once and for all. Most plants in this chapter belong to the cabbage family and share significant family traits; once you have experience with one, you can confidently grow its relatives.

■ **Swiss chard.** Botanically, chard is a first cousin to beets, but gastronomically it's closer to spinach. It sends up tall, upright leaves on thick, succulent stalks; both the leaves and stalks are delicious. The crinkly leaves are larger than spinach and the taste is more robust, what some people describe as earthy. Chard is a vitamin factory that just keeps going from spring till frost, and even through to the next spring in mild-winter areas. But when all is said and done, the main reason we're attracted to it is its looks: chard plants are some of the most beautiful vegetables you'll ever see. Don't be surprised if your visitors mistake them for a rare specimen of some exotic ornamental.

Two long-familiar types are red chard and white chard—a reference to the color of the stems. **Fordhook Giant** (60 days), the classic white chard, has been grown in America since 1750; **Ruby Red** (60 days), sometimes sold as Rhubarb Chard, is also an heirloom variety, having debuted in 1857. Several other varieties are offered by seed catalogs, all of them fine, but a real treat is the new

type called **Bright Lights** (55 days), an All-America Selection for 1998. What makes this such a stunning variety is the brilliant colors of the stems: they may be hot pink, orange, red, golden yellow, purple, white, or magenta-and-white striped. Each color is so richly luminous it seems impossible.

Maggie says: One summer, I constantly found my neighbors gathered at the edge of my patio, gazing at the containers of Bright Lights chard and whispering to each other. It was so much fun, I could hardly bear to harvest any of it.

Johnny's Seeds, which introduced Bright Lights, now has isolated the yellow strain in a new variety named **Bright Yellow** (60 days).

The color of the stem stays true through light cooking; you can also harvest leaves while they are still young and slice the colorful stems crosswise like celery for a salad surprise.

■ **Collards.** Anyone raised in the South is familiar with "a mess of greens," which invariably means collard greens. Collards are large plants whose upright blue-green leaves taste somewhat like cabbage. They are very closely related to kale (see below), but because they tolerate heat better, collards are the greens of choice in the South. Like other cabbage family members, collards grow nicely in cool weather, and a summer planting will produce a fall crop that collard lovers swear tastes better when "sweetened" by frost. The clas-

sic variety is **Georgia** (80 days).
Vates (80 days) is very similar.

■ **Kale.** You've seen kale in the
supermarket: the large, dark blue-
green, extremely frilly leaves next to
the cabbage. You've also seen decorative versions in the garden center,
perhaps labeled "ornamental cabbage": very pretty curly rosettes with
a blush pink or lavender center. (Yes,
you can eat them, although the taste
is mediocre; they also make fine garnishes.) But you may not have seen
the flat-leaved, nonfrilly types that
are such nutrition-packed standouts
in the home garden. "Flat" is a relative term in this case—not as flat as,
say, the leaf of a maple tree, but side
by side with the supermarket kale,
curled within an inch of its life, you
would definitely see a difference.
Kale is delicious cooked like spinach
or, in true Italian fashion, sliced into
hearty soups.

Among our favorites are two
very handsome kales that are heirlooms: **Red Russian** (50 days) is
thought to have been brought to
North America across the Bering
Strait by Russian traders around
1850. The leaves resemble the foliage
of oak trees but are much larger; the
plants reach a height of 2 to 3 feet.
The basic color of the leaves is a
grayish green, but in cold weather,
which kale survives very nicely, the
stems and veins turn a beautiful
lavender color. **Lacinato** (62 days), an
Italian heirloom also known as Black
Tuscan, sends up very dark green
leaves with a puckered surface and
edges that curl under. Overall, the

plant grows in a fountain shape, 2 feet
tall, and looks stunning as the centerpiece of a container garden.

Dwarf Blue Curled Scotch (55
days) has the deeply frilled leaves that
you expect from kale, in the more traditional rounded shape; a real knockout of a plant.

■ **Mustard.** It is all but impossible
to draw a sensible line between
American mustards and the many
Asian greens that are also mustards.
Let us begin with **Southern Curled**
(48 days), an heirloom dating from
the 1740s, which produces the
hearty-flavored leaves traditionally
favored in the South. It is particularly
attractive paired in a container with
Red Giant (45 days), which has a
sharper flavor and a scrumptious coloration: dark green leaves overlaid
with a translucent purplish red.

Osaka Purple (45 days) is quite
similar but smaller overall. Both of
these red mustards are heirlooms, and
because of their colors make a very
nice accent in mesclun salads.

For a gentler taste, we like
Tendergreen (45 days); this heirloom
variety is sometimes called mustard
spinach, and aptly so, for the flavor is
somewhere between the two. It is
slower to bolt and go to seed than
other mustards, another nice feature.

■ **Asian greens.** With the popularity of stir-fry dishes and our unflag-
ging enthusiasm for healthy eating,
Americans have fallen in love with
Asian foodstuffs. Catering to those
interests, many supermarkets now
carry a nice variety of Asian greens;

however, sometimes you have to buy more than you can use, and then eventually you'll have a slimy green mess to get rid of. How convenient it would be to have a supply of these wonderful green vegetables right outside your door, always ready, always the right amount.

Bok choy (also spelled pac choi or pak choi—same thing), perhaps the most familiar Asian vegetable after Chinese cabbage, is very easy to grow in containers. The large white stems are sweet and crunchy, the small, dark green leaves are tender and mild-flavored. Among several fine varieties we especially like are Mei Qing Choi (45 days), a dwarf type that stays small, and Joi Choi (45 days), a vigorous producer that does well in both warm and cool weather.

Also try komatsuna (40 days), very leafy with just a hint of tanginess in its taste; Green in Snow mustard (50 days), with tasty leaves and an irresistible name; Chinese kale (50 days), also known as Chinese broccoli and by its Chinese name, gai lohn, which sends up lots of edible flower stalks; tat soi (45 days), with very dark green leaves that grow in a flat rosette shape—very pretty; and mizuna (35 days), a rounded, frilly rosette that is delicious steamed like spinach and also wonderful fresh in salads. It isn't afraid of cold weather, and also can sail through summer heat if kept well watered.

Maggie says: The first year I grew mizuna, it was love at first sight. The leaves are bright green and very frilly, with slender, juicy white stems. It grows in a soft mound that is especially beautiful when you're looking down on it. The whole plant is so pretty I would happily grow it just for looks if I didn't know how great it tastes. And I must have very stupid slugs in my container garden, for they ate the boring old regular lettuce and left the mizuna alone.

Vegetables

Lettuce and Other Salad Greens

GROW AS: **annuals**

PLANT SIZE: **8 to 10 inches**

START WITH: **seeds or transplants**

HARVEST SEASON: **spring through early summer, again in fall**

SUN REQUIREMENTS: **full sun to partial shade**

MINIMUM SOIL DEPTH: **6 inches**

If the Garden Fairy challenged you to limit yourself to just one container with edibles, and in it you could plant only one item, you could not go wrong if you chose lettuce. In fact, lettuce may be just about the perfect container vegetable: easy to grow, with a short time to harvest, lovely to look at, and just exactly the type of thing you want to be able to pick fresh for each salad. The one drawback to growing lettuce—that it doesn't like hot weather—is actually a bit more manageable in containers because you can pick up your garden and move it into the shade.

Lettuce Basics. Looking through some of the catalogs, it's easy to feel befuddled by the sheer number of lettuce offerings; but when you consider that more than 800 varieties are recognized in the United States alone, the range of catalog varieties is actually rather modest.

Generally speaking, lettuce is grouped into four categories based on shape. Romaine lettuce makes tight heads of long, narrow, crisp leaves. Butterheads form rosettes of very tender leaves with a small, loose head at the center. One early variety was named Bibb, in honor of its developer, and today that has become a generic name for the whole category. Crisphead lettuces have a large, tight ball of a head inside looser outer leaves; Iceberg is one variety. Looseleaf lettuces do not form a head of any kind, just layers of individual leaves in an overall rounded shape.

Each type has its charms, and if you had unlimited space we would encourage you to grow some of everything. But for container gardens we advise you to stick with the looseleafs, primarily for economy of space. Unlike the other three types, which are harvested one entire head at a time, looseleaf lettuces can be harvested one *leaf* at a time. Thus you can pick just enough for tonight's salad and leave the plant to keep producing more. Also, most looseleaf lettuces are cut-and-come-again plants: snip off leaves and others grow in their place. But we wouldn't be making this recommendation if the looseleafs weren't also outstanding in other important respects: taste and looks.

Planting. Lettuce is most definitely a cool-season plant; it germinates better, and grows better, in cool weather. Even though breeders have worked hard to bring us varieties that handle warm weather better than some others, the improvement is relative, and you should still think of lettuce as a spring and fall crop.

If you can find a good selection of lettuce starts at the garden center, by all means use them; it will make your life considerably easier. However, some of the very best varieties can be obtained only as seeds.

Start seeds indoors about a month before your spring frost date, and move the seedlings outdoors after hardening off (see page 60), when they are 1 to 2 inches tall. Try to do this on a cloudy day, and provide the seedlings with some shade the first few days.

Direct sowing in spring is an easy alternative in mild or temperate parts of the country, for the seeds germinate readily at temperatures as low as 40°F. (In fact, there are reports of seeds germinating on melting ice.) For a steady supply of lettuce, make several sowings two to three weeks apart. As the seedlings grow, gradually thin them until you have about a 6-inch spacing.

If you have some containers with potting soil from last year, and it's so early in the year that you haven't planted anything else yet, loosen up the soil surface and sprinkle on a few lettuce seeds; they'll be up and going while you're still deciding on your summer plans.

To grow lettuce in the cool days of autumn, you need to sow seeds in late summer—which is a problem because the seeds don't germinate well in hot weather. To get around this, simply prechill the seeds and the potting soil. You can chill the seeds by refrigerating them for seven days in a zip-top bag mixed with a small amount of moist potting soil. Or if you have some seeds left over from the spring, put the partially used packets into a moisture-proof container and store it in the refrigerator or freezer until late summer. When you're ready to plant, water the potting mix well (this has the effect of chilling it) in the evening, and plant your seeds in that damp, cool soil.

Success with Lettuce. Lettuce turns bitter when the soil dries out; keep the plants evenly moist, and they'll grow fast and sweet. Cool, damp environments are perfect for lettuce—and for slugs. Be vigilant, and use the controls suggested in Chapter 6 if you see their trademark: big holes in your leaves and silvery trails on the soil.

One final problem: in hot weather lettuce will bolt. That's the term for a sudden spurt of growth—

where once there was a nice pretty mound of lettuce, there's a very long stem with just a few leaves, and it seems to have happened overnight. It's as if you reached deep down inside the plant, grabbed an invisible center knob, and pulled upward. Instead of being tight together, the leaves are spaced out all along the stem. Eventually the plant will flower and make seeds, but in the meantime it is basically worthless, for the leaves now have a very bitter taste. Pull out the plant and make way for the next crop.

Slow-bolting varieties have been developed (some catalogs list them under Summer Lettuces), and they are modestly successful. You can also help by providing some shade for your lettuce plants during hot weather. But the only sure way to prevent bolting is to grow lettuce in the cool "shoulder seasons" of late spring and early fall.

Harvesting. The beauty of loose-leaf lettuces, as we have said, is that you can just take a few leaves without pulling up the entire plant. Work from the outside in; grasp the bottom of a leaf (its stem end) and pull it off with a sideways motion. If you are growing mesclun or salad mixes (see pages 114 to 115), use scissors to snip off as much as you need, in the cut-and-come-again technique (see page 112). And don't forget that the larger seedlings that you pull up for thinning can be eaten as "baby lettuce."

Varieties. One of the earliest, most reliable, and tastiest lettuces is also one of our oldest: the heirloom **Black-Seeded Simpson** (45 days) has been cultivated in America for more than 100 years. It's a bright, clear green, with pretty ruffly leaves, and tolerates heat better than many others. It is too delicate to survive shipping to market, so only home gardeners can enjoy this tasty lettuce.

Deer Tongue (60 days) is an even older heirloom, dating from the 1740s; the name comes from the shape of the leaves, extended triangles. A very attractive variation is **Red Deer Tongue,** with red-tipped leaves.

Oak Leaf (40 to 45 days), another heirloom, is also named for its leaf shape. Over the years breeders have developed several variations on the oak leaf theme, so that the word has come to be used generically as well as for a specific variety.

Among these "oak leaf types" are some real beauties. **Salad Bowl** (50 days), an All-America winner, and **Red Salad Bowl** (50 days), with green and red leaves respectively, make a nice pairing. **Brunia** (50 days) is mostly green, with bronze coloration on the tips. They make a handsome trio.

Red Sails (55 days) is extremely beautiful, easy to grow, and slow to bolt: no wonder it was named an All-America Selection. The leaves are bright green at the base, gradually blending to a rich red near the edges; viewed from above, the whole plant seems a striking burgundy red, a color that becomes more vibrant with maturity. A good choice for fall as well as spring.

Lollo Rossa (55 days) is like no other lettuce. The outer edges of each leaf are very heavily frilled, so much so that looking at the plant, you cannot see down into the center. The entire plant is exquisitely decorative, all the more so because of its beautiful coloration: bronze red over bright green. The plants grow into compact, well-rounded mounds that make a handsome border around the rim of a large container. Be prepared for your visitors to go nuts over this one. Two traits you should be aware of: this variety is prone to bolting, and it also responds well to cut-and-come-again treatment; the latter takes care of the former.

For a stunning color palette, combine Lollo Rossa with two new varieties: **Lollo Bionda,** with soft green leaves, and **Impuls,** a dramatic cranberry red.

OTHER SALAD GREENS

As American tastes become more sophisticated and interest in healthful eating habits continues to grow, we have seen a great surge of interest in some of the more unusual greens for salad. In fact, in many larger cities it is no longer noteworthy to find once-rare items like arugula and mâche in the neighborhood supermarket.

No longer rare, maybe, but still pricey. Grow these gourmet greens yourself—for thriftiness, for freshness, and for the sheer fun of it.

Most of these salad greens are like lettuce in their growing needs. They do well in cool or moderate temperatures, not so well in very hot weather. Most are cut-and-come-again plants. In all likelihood you'll have to order seeds, but generally you're spared the agony of sorting through many varieties because catalogs tend to offer just one or two choices. Start seeds indoors around February, or direct-sow in containers starting in March, or both. Keep them well watered, watch for slugs, create some shade in mid summer, and enjoy.

■ **Arugula,** also known as rocket (42 days). The plant is not among the most gorgeous, but who cares—we're not after looks but taste. The pleasantly sharp tang is unmistakable and unsubstitutable. If you love that taste, you'll want to grow your own. It's quite easy and extremely convenient, since you can simply pluck off leaves as needed. Like most other salad greens, arugula is susceptible to bolting in very hot weather, but all is not lost. The leaves get more pungent after bolting, and the pretty little edible flowers add a touch of spiciness to salads.

Cut-and-Come-Again

Several lettuces and other salad greens can be harvested in the cut-and-come-again method. This means just what it sounds like: you cut off some of the leaves and others grow in their place. Start this continuous harvest when the plants are 3 or 4 inches tall.

Here's the procedure: grab a handful of leaves in one hand; with the other, use scissors to cut them off about ¾ inch from the soil line. Eventually new growth will sprout in that spot. In the meantime, make your next handful-harvest from another spot. Cut-and-come-again leaves can regenerate up to three times.

New on the American scene is **Italian Wild Arugula** (55 days), also called Rucola, a hot-weather substitute. It's actually a separate species from regular garden rocket but has a similar flavor—that robust, piquant taste we associate with arugula— and stands up to summer heat. The leaves, stems, and flowers can all be used in salads, although you can extend the harvest period if you continually cut back the plant to hold off flowering.

■ **Endive, escarole.** These two plants are virtual twins in a genetic sense, although they look very different. Both are bitter-tasting, though not unpleasantly so.

Endive is familiar and easy to recognize: very frilly, almost lacy leaves with long white stems. It is *not* Belgian endive. Leafy endive is very popular in France, where it is known as *chicorée frisée,* and Americans have adopted *frisée* as a synonym for endive (it means "curly" and is the source of our word "frizzy"). The white stems are crisp and succulent, and longer than you would find on, say, a ruffled lettuce leaf.

Commercial growers cover the center of the plant to make more of the stem area white and also to soften the taste, a process called blanching. You can easily do this yourself if you care to: either tie the leaves together at the top or cover the center of the plant with a plate or something similar. Both methods block sunlight from the heart of the plant, thus preventing the photosynthesis that turns plant material green.

A classic endive variety is **Green Curled Ruffec** (90 days), an heirloom. **Très Fine Frisée** (60 days) is a real charmer, a 6-inch miniature with mild flavor and extremely lacy leaves.

Escarole is a broad-leaved endive (or endive is a narrow-leaved escarole, depending on your perspective). **Broadleaf Batavian** (90 days) is an heirloom variety dating from the mid 1860s.

Both escarole and endive belong to the chicory family, and in that group are the plants whose roots are roasted, ground, and added to coffee in New Orleans. Also in the family is the salad green with the bright red heart—radicchio, described below.

■ **Mâche,** also known as corn salad and lamb's lettuce, is quite popular in Europe and is becoming more familiar here. It has a mild flavor that many describe as nutty, and is so hardy it can be sown in early fall for a winter salad green. This is one of those plants for which we recommend keeping seeds around; when ever you have a vacant patch in a container, tuck in a few.

Blonde Shell-Leaved (50 days) has small, round leaves that are slightly cupped, like shells. **Large-Seeded Dutch** (50 days), with large leaves, is very productive.

■ **Purslane.** Two different plants, with no other botanical relation aside from their common names, are called purslane.

Mesclun and Other Salad Mixes

Foods, like fashions, come and go, experiencing cycles of popularity. At the moment salad green mixtures are the rage, and it's easy to understand why: a sophisticated blend of tastes, textures, and colors is far more appealing in a salad bowl than monotone, monochrome, monoflavored lettuce.

In the market, these mixes are often made up of who-knows-what greens, prepackaged in quantities that you may or may not find convenient, and priced at something approaching the per-ounce cost of gold dust. If ever there was a reason for setting up a small container garden, this is it: with no more effort and no greater cost than growing plain old lettuce, you have an immediate, ongoing supply of elegant mixed salad greens just outside your door.

Mail-order seed companies have responded to the enthusiastic interest in unusual salad greens by creating their own mixes. In one packet you'll find seeds for several different types of greens. You plant the mixture, and everything grows up together in a luxuriant, free-spirited medley.

Two kinds of mixtures are available: (1) lettuce blends and (2) mesclun, a combination of lettuces plus other kinds of salad greens. Grow them just as you would the individual components: sow in cool weather, and keep well watered and lightly fertilized. Harvest them in superconvenient cut-and-come-again fashion (see box on page 112).

Lettuce Mixes. The seed packet may contain as many as half a dozen different types of lettuce, primarily the looseleaf types, for their growth habit best lends itself to the happy jumble that these mixes create. You'll probably have to thin the seedlings, but don't bother trying to separate them into types—that would defeat the whole purpose. Start cutting

Winter Purslane (40 days), also known as miner's lettuce, has a fresh taste and juicy texture. Sow seeds in late summer for fall and winter. It has a distinctive leaf pattern: two small leaves, approximately heart-shaped, are joined in pairs at their base, making a ripply edged funnel that encloses a small white flower. Snip off what you need, and new growth soon follows.

Golden Purslane (50 days) produces fleshy, succulent leaves with a tart, tangy taste and an upright growth pattern; it thrives in hot weather, and is sometimes called summer purslane. Both purslanes have

been considered weeds by some misguided souls who don't know what they're missing.

▪ **Radicchio.** Enormously popular with chefs and creators of "designer" salad mixes, the brilliant red radicchio deserves a place in every garden. It has a toothy texture, a zippy, tart taste, and knock-your-socks-off color. For visual impact, nothing else will do.

Rose Marie says: The slightly bittersweet juiciness of these greens is absolutely addictive.

while they are still young, at the extra-tender "baby lettuce" stage.

Mesclun. The food world has generated so much talk of mesclun in the last few years that some people are under the impression that it's the name of a specific variety of lettuce, something new and wonderful. It isn't. The term is used to describe a collection of greens grown together to produce a variety of tastes and textures. At its best, every bite tastes a little different. It *is* wonderful, but it's not new.

The concept of mesclun originated in Europe, where the cooks of France and Italy have been sowing their favorite salad greens together for many years. Several distinct regional variations became established, so that even in the traditional gardens of Europe, mescluns follow no one pattern. (Nor even the same name; strictly speaking, mesclun is the French version and the Italian version is called *misticanza*.) One thing, however, is always true: mesclun contains one or more types of lettuce *and also* one or more other greens—arugula, chervil, dandelion, cress, radicchio, endive, and other chicories are the classic choices.

In America, specialty seed companies have responded to the great interest by developing their own mesclun seed mixes. Some echo the traditional European blends, while others are new creations that expand the possibilities to include additional tasty greens: purslane, mâche, orach, komatsuna, mizuna, and other fast-growing Asian mustards. The best catalogs specify the individual ingredients of their various offerings, and describe their taste themes.

Growing mesclun is like growing lettuce or lettuce mixes with one extra twist. Because the various greens grow at different rates, the early harvests will not taste the same as the later ones. That's part of what makes this salad garden fun: it's never the same from day to day.

Traditionally, radicchio has been grown in a two-step process: seeds planted in spring produced a large head of green leaves by summer's end; that head was sliced off a little above ground level and in a few weeks small heads sprouted around the decapitated stem. In the cool days of autumn, the small new heads developed the strong red color that, for Americans at least, today defines this vegetable.

In recent years, new varieties have been developed that produce a red head without the extra step, although sometimes it is hidden inside an outer covering of green leaves. Some catalog descriptions point out certain varieties that do not require "cutting back," meaning one-step production.

Milan (78 days) is one of the most reliable varieties of a vegetable that, despite the best efforts of skilled seedsmen, is still not entirely predictable. **Firebird** (74 days) is described as an excellent variety for those who haven't grown radicchio before.

Castelfranco (85 days), an heirloom, forms heads without being cut back, as does **Chioggia** (60 days).

The next time you're in the supermarket, trying to select the prettiest lettuce from all those displayed before you, think about this: the lettuce was grown in a farmer's field that may be 100 miles away, if lettuce is in season in your region, or 1,000 miles away if it is not.

Once harvested from the field, it was taken to a packinghouse, where it was cleaned and packed in boxes bearing the packer's brand name. The packer sold that lettuce to a broker, who also buys lettuce, along with all kinds of other produce, from other packers. The broker used a refrigerated truck to bring the produce to your area. Once it arrived, the broker's representative sold the lettuce either to a local wholesaler, who then sold it to your market, or to a supermarket chain. The supermarket chain received it at its distribution center, and later moved it into the individual stores.

Where it sat for an unknown period until you came along.

At home, you put the lettuce into your refrigerator. You will use some for tonight's dinner, but you almost never use it all; the rest will stay until you finish it or it turns to green slime, whichever comes first.

Theme Garden

The Salad Basket

Now consider this alternate scenario: instead of dragging yourself to the market to buy ordinary lettuce that may be as much as five days old and that is almost certain to be more than you need, you step outside onto your patio or balcony or you open the window to your window box. From your container garden of beautiful salad greens, you pick just enough for tonight's salad. You choose two kinds of lettuce, maybe bright green Simpson and burgundy Red Sails, some arugula, a few leaves of escarole, and a bit of fresh chives. They are fresher than fresh and have not been sprayed with dubious chemicals; they look beautiful and taste fabulous. Tomorrow you can do it all again, with a completely different combination of tastes.

We think salad greens are just about the perfect container edible. They are dead easy to plant (just sprinkle the seeds on the soil in your container), grow quickly, and have a terrific ratio of produce to growing space since you eat the whole plant, not just its fruit. Size is not a determining factor: you could have a tiny salad garden in a window box, a large medley of greens in a wine barrel, or anything in between. You

can grow unusual salad greens, including many gourmet types that are not commercially practical and thus can be enjoyed only by home gardeners, just as easily as you can the more prosaic ones.

In your salad garden you can feature any of the delicious things you like to put in your salads. Here we suggest only two combinations, but many other possibilities will come to you as you scan through this book. You might want to include some of the many kinds of lettuce, spinach and spinach alternatives, mustard greens, beet greens, Swiss chard, kale, mâche, escarole, endive, arugula, the wonderful Asian greens, scallions, green garlic, chives, even salad flowers like nasturtiums.

THE CLASSIC SALAD BASKET

This selection fits nicely in a rather small round container or a window box. Plan an arrangement built around the various heights of the plants. In the center, the two tall plants: **scallions** and **chervil.** The chervil will get about a foot tall, the scallions a bit shorter. Around these two, set out two different kinds of **lettuce** chosen for their contrasting shape, color, and texture. One suggestion: Black-Seeded Simpson, a bright green looseleaf lettuce with frilly leaves, and Red Deer Tongue, with smooth, triangular-shaped leaves tipped in red. In a round container, you might want to do one circle of green and one of red, or intermix the two. In a rectangular window box, put the two tall plants in the center and the two lettuces arranged down both sides.

The anise-tasting chervil leaves are a delightful addition to salads. Chervil usually has to be started from seed because nursery plants are rare. Sow the seeds right in the final container, starting as early in spring as you possibly can (as soon as the soil is no longer frozen). You can plant scallion seeds at the same time, although transplants are not hard to find and will get your garden off to a fast start. Lettuce transplants are a common sight in garden centers in the spring, but to be sure of the varieties you have selected, your best bet is to order seeds and start them indoors early (see pages 54 to 60).

The lettuces will be at their peak from mid spring through early summer; once hot weather arrives, they will bolt (shoot up tall and spindly, with bitter leaves) and nothing you can do will stop it. The chervil will last somewhat longer, but eventually it bolts also. The scallions will remain all season, and in fact will multiply for next year as long as you don't harvest them all. When the lettuce and chervil have passed their peak, pull out the plants and replace them with hot-weather crops (see page 79 for weather-specific lists).

A WINTER SALAD BOWL

Many salad vegetables grow best in cool weather. Often gardeners think in terms of spring—probably because they are so eager to get going after the winter—but they shouldn't overlook the possibilities of fall gardens. In milder climates, those gardens can extend well into the winter months. With that kind of climate in mind, we suggest the following winter salad garden. This garden works best in a round container, medium size to large, but you could also use a window box as long as it is a fairly good size. Sow seeds or set out transplants in August, and you could be serving fresh salads from your garden as late as Thanksgiving.

Imagine a circle made of four rings, like a bull's-eye target; you're going to fill those rings with plants in alternating green and red colors. In the very center, one **mizuna** plant. This Japanese beauty is delicious as a cooked vegetable or raw as a salad green, and it is exquisitely beautiful. Its bright green leaves are extremely feathery, on long, crisp white stems, and they arch outward from the center in a pretty rosette that gets wider as the plant grows. Harvest the older (that is, outermost) leaves to retain the soft mounded shape.

Arranged in a circle around the mizuna, plant several **radicchio** plants with their red and white swirls. Search out one of the varieties that do not require cutting back (see pages 114 to 115), so that you can plant these gorgeous red globes at the same time as the rest of your winter garden.

The next circle contains two types of greens, planted alternately: **arugula** and **winter purslane.** Their textures and leaf shapes make a nice contrast with each other, and their bright green color is a terrific foil between two rings of red: the radicchio on the inner circle, and the burgundy lettuce on the outside. Arugula, with its strong bite, gives a real punch to a mixed-green salad. Winter purslane, less well known in the United States, has a milder taste, a juicy texture, and unusual, very attractive leaves.

The outermost circle is planted thickly with Lollo Rossa **lettuce.** The leaves of this type of lettuce are very unusual; all the outer edges are very tightly frilled and dramatically colored, green overlaid with bronze. A new cultivar called Impuls is bright cranberry red rather than bronze. Placed around the edge of the container as a border, they create the effect of a frilly crinoline petticoat or a ruffle on a tablecloth. As the weather turns cool, the coloration gets stronger and brighter, making this lovely lettuce the perfect finishing touch for a wintertime salad garden.

Vegetables

Onion Family:

Scallions, Leeks, and Green Garlic

GROW AS: **annuals, mostly**

PLANT SIZE: **10 to 12 inches**

START WITH: **seeds, transplants, or sets**

HARVEST SEASON: **summer, fall**

SUN REQUIREMENTS: **full sun**

MINIMUM SOIL DEPTH: **6 inches for scallions and green garlic, 8 inches for leeks**

This chapter is not about growing those big fat whoppers that make you cry when you slice them. Buy those at the store. In a home garden, onions take a very long time in ideal conditions to reach that mature size, and then you have to cure them, and then you wonder why you bothered because they're just like what you could have bought for pennies at the supermarket. In containers the question is even more dicey, since that space cries out to be filled with something more special, more appropriate.

This is not to say, however, that your container garden must go onion-less. With scallions, leeks, and green garlic, you can achieve, in just a speck of growing space and within a reasonable time frame, that wonderful tingling taste for which there is no substitute. And you get a bonus: a green and pungent garnish for your mashed potatoes.

Basics. All three plants described in this section are members of the greater onion family, the alliums. (Chives belong to that same family, but since most people think of chives as an herb, we placed them in the Herbs chapter.) The various alliums are similar in some ways and different in others. One similarity is the way they grow: a young plant, grown from a seed, sends up long, slender spears of green foliage (you wouldn't really think of them as leaves). Then, after enough time has passed, the part underground begins to develop into a rounded bulb and the green tops stop growing. Eventually the tops turn yellow and die down, and the underground part is ready to be harvested and dried; and then you have a full-fledged onion or a head of garlic.

All well and good, except that the full cycle takes a very long time. Essentially what we are doing in this section is interrupting that cycle midway through—when the plants still have succulent, flavorful green tops.

Planting. Since the planting techniques for the three vegetables are different, they will be described individually below.

Success with Onion Family Members.

These are among the easiest vegetables to grow in containers, with little chance of serious diseases or plant pests. In fact, many organic gardeners plant garlic and onions in with pest-prone vegetables, for there is some evidence that the strong aroma repels harmful insects. Regular watering is important, and you need to be careful not to disturb the shallow-rooted plants by yanking out neighboring weeds or other vegetables planted alongside them. Otherwise, these plants are pretty undemanding.

Harvesting. Specifics are described below, but basically all three vegetables can be harvested whenever you're ready for them.

SCALLIONS

First, some terminology. A scallion, often called a green onion or a spring onion, can be either (1) an immature regular onion or (2) a specific type known as a bunching onion. If you plant seeds or sets of regular onions and harvest them while they're very young and haven't yet formed a big fat bulb, you'll have what most people call scallions. Bunching onions have long, graceful green tops and slender white bottoms that never develop into a wide bulb—again, most people's idea of scallions. Many seed catalogs list these varieties together under "Bunching Onions or Scallions."

Because of their growth pattern, true bunching onions are actually perennials. Each seed produces a cluster of seedlings that eventually grow into a bunch of green onions that can be harvested all at once by the handful or one at a time. If you leave some in the ground, each one will divide at the base and new onions will grow to replace the ones you removed—ergo, a perennial.

Planting. For bunching onions, plant seeds indoors a month before the spring frost date, or direct-seed in very early spring. The seeded area needs to be kept lightly moist and otherwise undisturbed. The sprouts are very tiny, like green threads reaching upward. When transplanting seedlings into your container, think about whether you might want to keep some through the winter for next spring; if so, winter care will be easier if you put them in their own pot.

The traditional way that bunching onions are grown accentuates their long white shanks, and this is easy to do in your container. As the seedlings grow, mound soil up around the base, blocking out the sunlight. Continue this process as long as it is practical.

To get scallions from regular onions, you have three planting choices: you can grow onions from

Recipe: Green Garlic Soup

Jan Roberts-Dominguez, food writer and illustrator, writes a syndicated column and is author of *The Onion Book* and *The Mustard Book*. Jan says: "This is the perfect recipe to introduce the uninitiated to the wonders of green garlic. The white pepper and dry sherry are integral components of the flavor structure, so be sure they make it into the soup."

12 green garlic plants, each measuring about ½ inch in diameter at the root end, and including all the white part and some of the pale green

1 tablespoon butter

1 tablespoon olive oil

3½ cups chicken broth

4 or 5 small red potatoes, peeled and quartered

⅓ cup half-and-half

¾ teaspoon salt, or more to taste

¼ teaspoon white pepper, or more to taste

2 tablespoons dry sherry

1. Trim away the roots and most of the green portion from each garlic plant, then halve each stalk lengthwise and chop into 1-inch lengths.

2. Heat the butter and oil over medium heat in a large, heavy pot.

3. Place the garlic in the pot and sauté briefly, then add the chicken broth and potatoes. Bring to a boil, reduce the heat, and simmer, covered, until the potatoes are very tender, about 30 minutes.

4. Remove the soup from the heat and let cool briefly, then puree in batches in a blender or food processor until very smooth.

5. Return the soup to the pot, stir in the half-and-half, salt, and white pepper, then place over a gentle heat. As the soup is reheating, stir in the sherry. Adjust the seasonings before serving.

Serves 4 to 5

Reprinted with permission from The Onion Book.

seeds (treat just as described above for bunching onion seeds), from baby plants (which you can buy via mail-order as well as at garden centers), or from onion sets (which are very small onions, about the diameter of a dime, grown last year and harvested at this small size specifically for this purpose). You'll have faster results from transplants or sets, and with sets there's the extra advantage of being able to space out the planting over several weeks for a staggered harvest.

Harvesting. You can start harvesting either bunching onions or young onions whenever they reach the size you want. And since the part you're interested in is above ground, it's not hard to keep track. Left growing long enough, regular onions will eventually start to form small round bulbs, which may suit your purposes just fine.

Varieties. Just about any kind of regular onion will do a fine job of producing scallions. For bunching onions, we like two varieties: **Evergreen Hardy White** (60 days), a very hardy variety that will keep through the winter, and **Deep Purple** (60 days), which has exquisitely colored red shanks, very beautiful on a relish tray. (Be forewarned: only the outermost layer is red, so don't strip off too much during cleaning if the color is what you want to accentuate.)

LEEKS

The humongous leeks that you find for sale in the supermarket, looking like wildly overgrown scallions with white shanks as big around as the handle of a baseball bat, are mild-flavored and surprisingly sweet, especially when slow-roasted with a little butter or olive oil. The trouble is, it takes a long time to reach that size, and you may not find it practical in a container garden. But even at a smaller size, which is definitely doable, leeks are delicious, with a gentle and unique taste. And they keep on growing through light frost, reaching a larger size just in time for wonderful winter soups.

Planting. Start seeds indoors two months before the spring frost date; after a month, transplant to larger intermediate pots. When seedlings are about 6 inches high, plant in your outdoor containers. Alternatively, buy transplants at the garden center at about this same time.

Use a chopstick or a dibble to make deep narrow holes, and insert one transplant per hole; leave just a bit of green showing. As the plants grow, mound up soil around the base; this process of blanching makes the white stems longer.

Harvesting. After a couple of months you can begin harvesting small leeks. The longer you leave them, the larger the white stems become and the tougher the leaves.

Varieties. If your climate supports a long growing season, the heirloom **Giant Musselburg** (100 days from transplants) is wonderfully sweet. **King Richard** (75 days from transplants) will give you baby leeks by summer. Developed specially for direct sowing, **Kilima** (70 days from transplants) is another fast-growing summer leek.

GREEN GARLIC

Traditional gardeners, aiming to grow full heads of garlic for drying and storage, plant in the fall and harvest their jewels some nine or ten months later. Container gardeners do better with a different strategy and a different goal: not bothering with the bulb, but growing the plants for the green tops. Green garlic isn't a separate species; it's just regular garlic that hasn't been growing long enough to form a full head underground. It's "green" in the sense that an unripe apple is green, and also in the sense that it's the green part that you harvest.

We think there's very little reason to attempt to grow full-size garlic bulbs, which are readily available year-round, but every reason to grow green garlic, a gourmet treat generally available only to home gardeners. Green garlic has that unique garlic taste but in a milder version, and a bonus of bright green color. Another advantage: it is so simple to plant. You don't have to study catalogs, choose varieties, order seeds, count back to planting time, or any of that. Just break off a few cloves from a head of garlic, which you may already have in your kitchen, poke a hole into any container wherever there's an empty spot, and plant. You can do this whenever you think of it, starting in early spring, for a continuous supply of delicious green garlic.

Planting. At the market, buy a whole head of garlic; pick the fattest, firmest one you can find. At home, separate it into individual cloves; do not peel. Notice that the cloves have a squared-off base end and a pointy tip. Poke holes into your container soil about 2 inches deep, and put one clove into each hole, pointy end up; cover with soil, and water thoroughly.

Harvesting. Begin harvesting the baby garlic plants as soon as they form green leaves, starting about four to five weeks after planting the cloves. After trimming away the roots, you eat the whole plant: stem, leaves, and any small bulb that has begun to form at the base—and that's green garlic. Those left to get a bit larger, with a bulb forming, are perfect for grilling.

You can also treat this as a cut-and-come-again plant (see box on page 112). Slice off some green shoots with a knife—just the amount you need for tonight—and they'll grow back. You can do this up to five times. The plant grows fast, so keep up the fertilizing with a complete fertilizer (see page 67).

Rose Marie says: I love cooking with green garlic. It goes well in soups, casseroles, stir-fry dishes, sautéed greens, salsa, pesto—in fact, in any dish that would be complemented by a hint of garlic. But my favorite way to cook it is on the grill with a little dab of olive oil. Along with other grilled vegetables, this is a very wonderful dish with steak or grilled chicken.

Vegetables

Peas

GROW AS: **annuals**

PLANT SIZE: **18 to 30 inches (bush types); 5 to 6 feet (vines)**

START WITH: **seeds, direct-sown**

HARVEST SEASON: **primarily late spring to early summer; secondary fall crops**

SUN REQUIREMENTS: **full sun**

MINIMUM SOIL DEPTH: **8 inches**

In 1823 the British essayist Charles Lamb wrote about how the accumulation of wealth changes a person's life, especially one who originally had very little and was forced to live simply: "There was pleasure in eating strawberries before they became quite common, in the first dish of peas while they were yet dear." People with great wealth, he suggested, had the wherewithal to purchase peas and strawberries whenever they wished, shipped in at great expense. But when those foods became everyday items, they ceased to be special, and so those privileged members of society were denied one experience enjoyed only by those of modest means: the exquisitely sweet taste of the first peas of the season.

Today purchasing fresh peas out of season, flown in from another climate, is not so much an issue of class or wealth as it is a question of flavor. Fresh peas are imbued with a natural sugar that gives a hint of sweetness to their taste—and begins to turn to starch as soon as they are picked. No commercially harvested pea can match the taste of one you picked five minutes ago.

In this chapter we have grouped together three different kinds of peas: regular garden peas, sometimes called English peas or shelling peas (because you shell them and discard the pods); edible-pod peas, often called snow peas, which are picked and eaten before they make peas inside; and snap peas, which combine the best of both—plump peas *and* sweet crunchy pods. The tastes of these three kinds of peas are different, but the growing conditions are pretty much the same.

Pea Basics. Peas are cool-season vegetables. They grow on vines that send out curly tendrils that attach themselves ferociously to any nearby support—even the stem of another pea plant. In Asia the tender shoots (the newest leaves and tendrils at the tip) are prized as a vegetable delicacy, but Americans seem content to wait for the peas to form. If for some reason you should decide you've had enough fresh peas for one year, you might want to try snipping off some shoots for a salad or stir-fry. The pretty little flowers are also edible, if you can bear to sacrifice the peas that would otherwise follow.

Many of today's varieties are dwarfs—that is, with very short vines, often described in catalogs as "bush type." Don't make the mistake, though, of thinking they grow like bush beans. Many types of dwarf peas easily reach 24 to 30 inches and more, and they all grow much better with some sort of support for the tendrils to cling to. Good catalogs provide information on height so you can be prepared.

Planting. Peas germinate when the soil is still cool, around 40°F, grow vigorously during cool weather, and start to shut down when the thermometer consistently hits 80°F. This means that you need to plant your peas as early as possible. Gardening books and catalogs frequently use the phrase "as soon as ground can be worked." That means when it is no longer frozen or totally waterlogged.

Container gardeners have something of an edge here, for often you can position a container in a warmer or more sheltered spot, where the soil won't freeze and where it will absorb sunlight for a quick winter warm-up. In that case, you could conceivably start your peas in January; in any case, try to plant them by early March. Container gardeners can expect to have a crop of peas two weeks earlier than traditional gardeners.

Peas should be direct-seeded, for they don't transplant well. You

Nitrogen Converters

Peas, beans, and other legumes have the ability to pull nitrogen from the air and "fix" it into nodules on their roots, providing a source of this important nutrient for their own growth and also enriching the soil for the future.

But for this conversion to occur, certain beneficial soil bacteria must be present. Maybe they're already in the soil, maybe not—there's no way for us to know. To be on the safe side, therefore, it's a good idea to add those critical bacteria at the time you plant the seeds, by treating the seeds with what is known as **inoculant.** Inoculant comes in the form of dust, which you coat the seeds with before planting, or granules, which you mix into the soil along with the seeds. One application is enough; the packet will tell you the correct amount. Inoculant is available at most garden centers and by mail order.

can, however, speed up the process through presprouting (see page 128). And don't forget to add inoculant (see box above); it's inexpensive, completely safe, and without question promotes superior growth.

Before you do anything, however, decide what kind of pea support you will use. Pole peas need a tall trellis of string or plastic grid, something with a small diameter. Dwarf or bush peas can survive without any support but do much better with some kind of help (see page 40 for a few suggestions). Whatever you decide to use, have it in place *before* you plant, to avoid tearing into the roots.

The roots of peas grow laterally, so a wide, shallow container is perfect. Plant peas twice the depth of the seed (or 1 inch deep if the weather is still very cold), spaced an inch or so apart. It always seems to take a long time before new growth shows itself (maybe because it's the start of the season and we're eager), but once up the plants grow fast.

Success with Peas. Peas, like all other legumes, are nitrogen factories (see box at left), but they are also heavy feeders and will benefit from a regular program of fertilizing. Once the first flowers appear, begin adding a liquid fertilizer with a ratio of 1:2:1 (that is, a higher middle number for more phosphorus) once a week or so. Liquid seaweed is very effective with peas.

If you ever grew peas in a traditional garden, you may have experienced some problems because they are susceptible to several diseases. Some come from pathogens that exist in infected soil, and therefore container gardens are usually spared. But others are spread by insects or travel through the air. Your best course is to choose disease-resistant varieties; catalogs will tell you which they are. One of the nastiest diseases, at present limited to the western United States, is pea enation virus, which blocks the plant's vascular system. Infected plants simply collapse. The virus is spread by aphids, which is another reason peas do better in the cool spring, before aphids come around.

Because they thrive in cool weather, peas are also at risk of mildew. You can help by selecting resistant varieties and by watering carefully. Add the water to the soil; don't spray the leaves. Check leaves frequently for mildew, and spray with baking soda solution (see page 76) at the first sign of trouble.

Harvesting and Varieties. The specific point at which the peas are perfectly ready for harvest varies among the three types, and is described below. For all of them, however, the ideal technique is the same. Grasp the main stem with one hand and the pea pod with the other; lift upward until the pod separates from the vine. Or use clippers or scissors to cut them off neatly. Do *not* yank; peas are very shallow rooted, and you'd be surprised how easy it is to pull the whole plant out of the soil.

This, too, is true for all three: once they start producing, check your plants every single day and keep them picked. Peas left too long on the vine are tough and bitter, but that's not even the worst of it: the plant, having achieved its inbred goal of making seeds to reproduce itself, will simply stop producing.

As a rough guide, plan on harvesting one gallon of pea pods from each plant of the bush varieties during the season, and one to two gallons from pole types. For English peas, which you'll shell, your edible harvest will of course be smaller.

■ **Garden peas.** These little green jewels are ready when they have completely filled the pod. It's easy to check: break one open and taste the peas inside; then you'll know what to look for—just how fat and shiny the pod should be. Two favorites are **Oregon Pioneer** (61 days) and **Green Arrow** (70 days); both are dwarf types, reaching 2 feet in height. Both are strong producers with good disease resistance; the principal difference is that one begins producing earlier. A brand-new dwarf variety that won the All-America award for 2000 is **Mr. Big** (58 days). The AAS judges reportedly admired its high yields, disease resistance, and giant size: almost 5 inches long.

■ **Snow peas.** A staple of Chinese stir-fries, these crunchy peas are also very delicious raw in salads (slice cross-wise into chunks and use a sesame-oil dressing). It is the outer green pod that we eat; the little peas inside are either nonexistent or so small they're insignif-icant, depending on how mature the pea is when you pick it. You can begin harvesting these peas whenever they reach the size you want, but they are most flavorful when mature enough that you can just begin to see the

bumpy outline of the peas inside. Don't let them go much beyond that, or the pods will become tough and bitter.

Two of the best varieties were developed in our home state by Dr. James Baggett, professor emeritus at Oregon State University, but that's not the reason we recommend them: they're simply the best. **Oregon Sugar Pod II** (68 days) is a 2-foot bush with stringless pods. **Oregon Giant Sugar Pod** (70 days) is a larger plant (up to 3 feet) and makes larger peas. Both are resistant to several viral diseases and also to mildew, making them good choices for fall planting if you have a yen to try that.

■ **Snap peas.** **Sugarsnap,** the origi-nal snap pea, is an All-America Gold Medal plant, and if anything ever deserved it more, we can't imagine what it would be. When it was introduced, Sugarsnap was some-thing the plant world had never seen: both the outer pod and also the plump peas inside were edible, and wondrously so, extremely crisp and crunchy, extremely sweet. It was an instant hit.

That was 20 years ago. Today, the name of the original plant has passed into general usage as the term for an entire category, although technically Sugarsnap refers to just that one cultivar. New varieties have been introduced, including some fine bush types.

These peas can be harvested and enjoyed while they are still somewhat immature, but wait at least until the sides have started to plump out. They are at their sweet best, many think, when the peas inside are fully formed

Fast-Track Peas

Here's a trick to speed up pea production: presprout them indoors.

In a small plastic bag, place your seeds and the appropriate amount of inoculant (see page 126); shake the bag to coat the seeds. Then spritz the seeds lightly with water, and close the bag. In about three days, the seed coat will open up, and you'll see the beginning of a root "tail." Handling them very gently, plant those seeds in your out-door container, ½ to 1 inch deep.

Trellises for Bush Peas

If you're growing pole peas, you need a tall trellis, for the vines can reach 8 feet or more. But even bush peas, which still have the vining habit deep in their genes, do better with a bit of support. Adding a short version of a trellis will make a real difference in your crop.

A good all-purpose height is 30 inches; that allows you to sink the legs to a depth of 6 inches and leaves 2 feet of support, sufficient for most dwarf plants. Here are five possibilities. In all cases, set the trellis up first, then plant the seeds right up against its bottom.

1. Using light fencing material such as chicken wire or concrete-reinforcing wire, make a circle approximately half the diameter of your container. Set it into the middle, and plant peas on both sides of the wire.

2. Plastic grids designed for trellises can be used the same way but may not be stiff enough to stand upright on their own. Thread four or five dowels or tree branches through the grid, and sink the bottoms into the soil.

3. In your garden center you'll find a selection of short, decorative wire fences, usually in rectangular sections hinged together for folding and storing. If your container is large enough, you can shape five fence sections into a pentagon and treat it like a circle. Or take three hinged sections and set them up in the shape of a "Z."

4. Purchase a small tower-style trellis and set it inside a container.

5. Perhaps easiest of all, providing you have access to the materials: use a series of twiggy branches from trees or shrubs. Choose narrow branches with lots of tiny twigs at the top, strip off any leaves, and jam the twigs into the soil, thickly and in no particular pattern. As the peas grow, they will grab onto these twigs and cover the bare bark; quite a charming effect.

and the pods are really fat, completely round in cross section. But if they stay on the vine past that point, the pea kernels begin to turn starchy. Just as you do with garden peas, pick one or two and sample them until you teach yourself what the perfect stage of ripeness looks like. They are delicious raw in salads or with dips, or as a cooked side dish, lightly sautéed or steamed.

Let us all pity poor Mr. Lamb, born 200 years too soon.

Super Sugar Snap (68 days), an improved, mildew-resistant version of the original Sugarsnap, is our recommendation for a vining type. It may reach 5 to 6 feet, and needs a strong trellis to support its heavy crop of peas. Two very fine bush types are **Cascadia** (62 days), an enation-resistant variety that does extremely well in the Pacific Northwest and northern California; and **Sugar Sprint** (62 days), brand-new but quickly becoming everyone's favorite. It is resistant to multiple diseases, including mildew, so it works well for both spring and fall plantings. Both are 24 inches tall and could manage without extra support, but do considerably better with it.

Younger generations of Americans, accustomed to buying foodstuffs like precut, shrink-wrapped vegetables and 67 kinds of breakfast cereal in suburban mega-supermarkets the size of airplane factories, would be astonished at the shopping habits of homemakers in small European towns, where the ingredients of each night's dinner are purchased fresh that day. What these suburbanites may not realize is that in our largest cities, in neighborhoods originally settled by immigrants, something of that same tradition still exists in the tiny sidewalk markets selling the vegetables, herbs, and fruits familiar and dear to the newcomers and their descendants. From these fresh ethnic ingredients, wonderful meals are made in America's kitchens.

Theme Garden

The Ethnic Market at Your Doorstep

If you had the good luck to be born into the right family or the good sense to choose your friends well, you may have had the great pleasure of being invited to share a holiday dinner with your friend's Vietnamese family or magnificent pasta feasts prepared by your Italian-speaking grandma. If so, you already understand the essence of good food—made from fresh, authenic ingredients and cooked with love. Second best, but still wonderful, is a meal at a local ethnic restaurant whose owners are proud to serve the foods of their homeland.

Our lives have been immeasurably enriched by our exposure to the exquisite tastes of the world's cuisines, and today many good cooks are eager to duplicate those foods in their own kitchens. Cookbook publishers have matched our interest by bringing out many terrific new books teaching us how to prepare these dishes, but a key problem remains: where do we get the ingredients? If you don't already live where the ingredients are everyday fare at the neighborhood greengrocer, you're stymied.

Unless, of course, you grow them yourself.

Here we suggest five different container gardens that will provide you with the ingredients for your favorite ethnic dishes. With these gardens, it's almost like having a small ethnic market right at your doorstep.

THE SALSA BOWL

Once known only to patrons of Mexican restaurants, the cool/hot/spicy blend of tomatoes and herbs we call salsa is now the first or second most popular condiment in the United States, sometimes outranking even ketchup. Every year or so a "new" style of salsa emerges, made from different vegetables or even from fruit, but the classic tomato version remains the standard.

Here, in one large container or two smaller ones, you can grow all you need to make your favorite salsa recipe. For the aesthetics of it, we like the idea of putting everything in one container, but it will have to be a good size, preferably 3 feet in diameter, and you will need to add a trellis or some support for the tomato. Otherwise, you can put the tomato in its own pot, smaller but still deep, and everything else together in a medium-size container. To enhance the Mexican theme, you might wish to use all terra-cotta pots, or one of the new lightweight molded pots that mimic Mexican styles.

Starting very early in spring, and continuing throughout the growing season, sow seeds of **cilantro** directly into the container. Harvest the leaves when they are young and tender, then pull out plants when they get too gangly or start to go to seed. About every three weeks, tuck in a few replacement seeds to keep a fresh supply going all through summer into fall.

For the **tomato,** choose any nice red one with medium-size fruit from the varieties listed in the Tomatoes section (see page 159). A small **hot pepper** gives you the fire; the traditional pepper is of course jalapeño, but other, smaller varieties may work better in your limited space. We like Super Chile pepper for this reason. To represent the onion taste, plant one or two clumps of **chives** near the edge of your container. Most salsa recipes call for fresh chopped onion, and certainly you may add that as well, but the onions will have to come from the grocery store because growing bulb onions is not practical in containers. If you like fresh garlic in your salsa, you can grow it in one of two forms: **garlic chives,** which give you a hint of onion and garlic together, or **green garlic,** which adds a nice contrasting touch of green when chopped into the mix.

A TASTE OF ITALY

All the ingredients for a rich pasta sauce at your fingertips. Here again you have a choice of putting everything together in one large container, or grouping three smaller ones. The decision depends on your space and the containers you have available.

Let's envision using one large container first. To support the tomato, you would be smart to install some kind of semicircular trellis before planting anything. It could be a section of heavy-duty wire grid fitted into the curve of the container, or several wooden or bamboo stakes positioned around half of the rim, braced together with crosspieces at several levels.

Within this semicircle, plant one Italian **plum tomato** close to the trellis. Near the opposite edge, put two Giant Marconi roasting **peppers.** These three plants, which form the main elements of the garden, should be positioned so that from a bird's-eye view they form a triangle; this will allow all three room to grow. Fill in the spaces around the three main plants with Italian herbs: **oregano** (or **marjoram**), **parsley,** and **basil.** Choose from the many wonderful basil varieties not normally available at the supermarket. Oregano is a perennial in all but the coldest climates, but many gardeners treat marjoram as an annual. If you're in doubt about your weather, or not sure whether you will want to repeat the Italian garden next year, marjoram is probably the better choice because it gives you the greatest flexibility.

Most of these plants will reach their full size and their harvest peak in mid to late summer; to begin your harvest sooner, you may want to plant Black Tuscan **kale,** a favorite green of many Italian cooks. As a cool-season vegetable, kale is at its best in late spring and early summer, and begins to fade out just about the time the hot-weather plants are bursting into their full glory. Alternatively, you can put in some small kale plants in late summer, just as the basil and the peppers are winding down, and enjoy a fall harvest.

This garden can also be assembled easily in three smaller containers, grouped together. One should hold the tomato (you still need some kind of support) and possibly the basil; both need the same rich soil and hot, bright sun. In the second container, the peppers and the parsley (and maybe more basil if, like us, you can't get enough). A third can contain the oregano (in a small separate pot, it is much easier to keep your oregano through the winter if you decide you can't live without it).

A CHINATOWN GREENGROCER

Many adults who now consider their palates very sophisticated had their first non-American meal in a Chinese restaurant, often Cantonese. As we have been exposed to wider circles of international influence, there has been an occasional tendency to discount this style of cooking in favor of other, supposedly more exotic foods. As everyone who has enjoyed an authentic Chinese meal knows, this is decidedly unfair to one of the world's greatest cuisines. For all lovers of good food, and for all styles of Asian cooking, we suggest this garden of Chinese vegetables.

Use a large container with a tall trellis. If the trellis is made of strips of wood or bamboo, cover it with either fine wire mesh or a string trellis; peas need something very thin to grab onto. In very early spring, plant lots of seeds of **edible-pod peas** at the feet of the trellis. These can be either the familiar flat peas we know as snow peas or the more recent snap peas; snow peas are more common in Chinese dishes. In one section of the container, put one or two clumps of **garlic chives.**

At the same time, plant seeds or, better yet, young transplants of several Asian greens: **spinach,** the upright **bok choy,** the pretty flat rosette of **tat soi,** and the richly colored Osaka Purple **mustard.** We suggest transplants rather than seeds simply for convenience; these four greens have very different looks, and you will find it easier to arrange them in a pleasing pattern if you have plants to work with. In any event, put in lots of plants; don't leave any bare soil.

All these are cool-season plants, at their best in late spring. By the time summer's heat arrives, the greens will be ready to bolt and the peas will be shriveling. At that point, yank everything out (except the chives) and put some heat lovers into the container—perhaps a rich tapestry of several basils.

MEDITERRANEAN MEDLEY

The countries of the Mediterranean region have long histories of bitter political conflict and fierce warfare, but they are also alike in many ways, not the least of which is their table. This region is the native habitat of most of our familiar culinary herbs, and the soil and climate are just right for a rich bounty of vegetables and fruits. In honor of Rose Marie's grandmother, we think of this as a Greek garden, but in truth it represents the entire area.

This is another container garden that could work either in one large container or as a grouping of three smaller ones. Figure out which physical format your space will accommodate, and what containers you have on hand. It may be slightly easier to manage as a three-pot garden, so we'll describe it that way, but the other approach is certainly possible.

The main container is fairly large and deep, about 18 inches. In the springtime, cover the entire surface of this container with seeds of fast-growing **spinach** and **mustard greens;** resow all through the spring as you harvest these early-season favorites. In early summer, plant a **cherry tomato** of your choice; you'll need some sort of trellis or other support structure, to tie it to as it grows. At the base of the tomato, add one or more **basil** plants; take advantage of the room in this large pot and put in several basils. Then, at the end of summer, before a cool night turns the basil plants black, remove them and put in more small mustard plants; they thrive in cool fall weather, right up to a hard freeze.

In a second and somewhat smaller container, plant one or more **eggplants.** This vegetable is used often in Greek cuisine, and if you like it you'll want several plants. In a third pot, smallest of all, one Greek **oregano** plant. If your winters are severe, you will need to move the oregano to a more protected location, and this is easier to do if it is in its own pot.

BANGKOK BANQUET

One of the most delicious trends in ethnic cooking of late has been the great interest in the foods of Southeast Asia, principally Thailand and Vietnam. The taste is complex—recognizably Asian, but with layers of other subtle flavors that make the whole far more than the sum of the parts.

Here we suggest a garden with some of the vegetables and herbs that are important in Southeast Asian cooking. In combination with the Chinatown Greengrocer garden described above, it will provide almost everything you need for a banquet.

For various practical considerations, you'll have better results if you put this garden in a cluster of separate containers. If you are purchasing new pots this year, try to find some with an Asian theme or design, and arrange them on small pedestals of varying heights. A beautiful addition to this garden would be a small outdoor Japanese lantern, set on its own pedestal in a place of honor near the front of the garden.

One container will hold one or more **Thai peppers** and two herbs at different seasons: **cilantro** in the spring and **Thai basil** in the summer. As soon as the cilantro starts to bolt, remove it and plant the basil in its place. This will probably be your largest container.

In a second container, plant one or more **Japanese eggplants.** These varieties of eggplant, with their long, slender, satin-smooth fruits, are particularly appropriate for containers and very beautiful to look at. You might want to plant several, to take advantage of their beautiful colors: the deep glowing purple of Neon, the soft ivory of Asian Bride, and the bright chartreuse of Green Goddess. Susceptible to damage from flea beetles, eggplants seem to do better if raised off the floor a bit.

A third container holds a **Kaffir lime,** whose aromatic leaves are essential in several Thai dishes. The lime plant is not frost-hardy and so needs to be moved indoors in winter, a chore made simpler by its being in its own pot.

Finally, plant a container of **lemongrass,** another Thai and Vietnamese flavoring for which there is no good substitute. It's also extremely tender, and needs an indoor spot for the winter.

Vegetables

Peppers

ÁROW AS: **annuals**

PLANT SIZE: **12 to 16 inches**

START WITH: **transplants**

HARVEST SEASON: **late summer**

SUN REQUIREMENTS: **full sun**

MINIMUM SOIL DEPTH: **8 inches**

Pepper plants are among the most decorative of vegetables, so pretty that we might grow them just for looks if we didn't know that the fruits were edible. Small hot-pepper plants with upright fruits are as ornamental as many flowers. They're so attractive that some of the small-fruited types, greenhouse-forced to yield red peppers in December, are labeled "Christmas peppers" and marketed as holiday gift plants. (And the peppers are edible, unless the plant is really a Jerusalem cherry, which is not a pepper.) In your container garden you can display bright orange peppers that look like fingerling carrots, small round peppers that look like colored beads, tiny red or yellow arrow points that sit sassily on top of the leaves, and the familiar square bell-pepper shape in luminous shades of red, yellow, orange, lavender, ivory, and chocolate brown.

As if that color bonanza weren't enough, the foliage is handsome enough on its own to pass for a houseplant even before the fruits put on their show. Other advantages: the plants stay at a manageable size through the entire season, and as a group, peppers suffer relatively few problems. The principal cultural concern is getting the soil and the plants warm enough, a task that is far simpler to achieve in containers, which can be moved into the sun, than in an open garden. All told, peppers are extremely successful in containers, in many ways superior to traditional gardens. Container pepper plants maintain a smaller size but often produce fruit earlier.

Pepper Basics.

Peppers give us an interesting lesson in one important botanical fact of life: you can't always distinguish one species from another just by looking. Sometimes things that appear to be the same are different, and vice versa. It comes as a surprise to some people that sweet peppers—the gentle, harmless, mild-flavored green bell pepper—and many of the fiery hot peppers that blister the tongue are the very same species. It also is news to some

Recipe: Lecso (Hungarian Pepper Salsa)

Peter Kopcinski of Berkop Seeds, a grower and breeder specializing in peppers, says: "The Hungarians have their own version of salsa, which they call Lecso. It is eaten with hot or cold cooked meats or spread on good Hungarian bread. Sometimes eggs are scrambled with Lecso, which turns it into a quick meal. And sometimes sour cream is also added. When visiting in village farmhouses, you must clean your bowl with your last piece of bread or risk offending the cook."

Serve Lecso with crusty bread or cooked meats.

2 red bell peppers
1 medium onion
1 medium tomato
2 tablespoons olive oil
Salt and freshly ground black pepper, to taste

1. Remove and discard the stems and seeds from the peppers. Cut the peppers into chunks. Peel and chop the onion. Core and dice the tomato, reserving the juice.

2. Heat the oil in a large skillet over medium heat. Add the peppers and onion and sauté until the onion has softened, 5 to 10 minutes.

3. Add the tomato to the pepper mixture and continue to cook until the peppers are just fork-tender, about 10 minutes more. Add a little water if necessary to keep mixture from drying out. Season with salt and black pepper to taste.

4. Serve hot, at room temperature, or cold.

Makes about 1½ cups

that a red pepper is *not* a separate variety but simply a green pepper left on the plant long enough to reach maturity.

All peppers start out green and gradually, through a long, hot growing season, turn the color that is programmed into their genes. The key to growing peppers is hot weather. It's only a guess, but we think it possible that Americans got used to eating sweet peppers in their green stage because for a long time that was all most of us could manage to grow. The red, yellow, and orange sweet peppers that are found in supermarkets in the off-season are usually imported from tropical and semitropical parts of the world, where hot weather lasts long enough to do the job. Now, responding to consumer demand, resourceful plant breeders have been hard at work developing varieties that mature early.

Planting. The trickiest part about growing peppers is timing. If they're planted too soon in the spring, cool temperatures do them in. If planted too late in the summer, they'll still be trying to produce fruits when the weather starts to turn cool in the fall, and all you'll get is a crop of pitifully immature peppers. So unless you live in the tropics, you have to start your plants indoors, where you can give them the warmth they demand. Pepper seeds need about two weeks at high temperatures (80°F) to germinate, and six to eight more weeks to reach transplanting size. Wait till nighttime temperatures are consistently above 55°F and daytime temperatures are at least 70°F before transplanting them into the container, and don't forget to harden them off first (see page 60).

Even though it could mean lim-

Powerful Peppers

Three important micronutrients have a very beneficial effect on peppers, and all of them are contained in common household items you may already have in your cupboards.

Sulfur—in matches. Before you transplant your baby pepper plants into the container, tear the cardboard cover from a book of matches, leaving the bunch of matches intact. Dig the hole for the plants, lay in one match bunch per hole, cover with an inch or so of potting soil, then pop in the peppers. By the time the roots grow down to the matches, the matches' sulfur will have dissolved into the surrounding soil. Sulfur is also found in Epsom salts; see magnesium, below.

Calcium—in eggshells. Save a few eggshells and leave them out on the counter a few days until they are thoroughly dry, then crush them (place the shells inside a plastic bag and run over it with a rolling pin). Place a spoonful in the bottom of each pepper's planting hole.

Magnesium—in Epsom salts (which is magnesium sulfate, and therefore also a source of sulfur). Mix a bit of salts into plain water and spray the solution on the plants when blossoms begin to appear.

iting your choice of varieties, you may decide it's simpler to buy transplants than to start your own. But even then, keep an eye on the weather. Don't forget that the transplants were grown in commercial greenhouses, under controlled conditions, and may show up at the garden center while the weather is still too cool for them. If that's the case, be sure to provide some kind of nighttime protection (see page 55 for suggestions) until the weather warms up.

At the garden center choose the healthiest, strongest young plants—not tall and leggy, but dense and compact. And don't allow yourself to be seduced by large pepper plants in gallon containers, with several flowers or even tiny fruits already showing. Logic would tell us that those are the best because they have a head start, but Mother Nature does not always operate on principles of human logic. If you transplant a young pepper that is already showing tiny fruit, the growth curve hits a kind of dead end from which the plant may never recover. Research by growers has consistently shown that these never develop into vigorous, productive plants. Preventing this stunted condition is a simple matter of nipping off flowers and fruits before you transplant.

Success with Peppers.

Concentrate on keeping peppers warm: while the plants are getting established, position the containers where they get the most sun, and move them as needed when the sun's path changes. If your season is so short that you have to plant pep-

pers when the weather is marginal, cover the plants with row cover, which acts like a blanket, until they start to flower. Just to keep us humble, Mother Nature has also thrown us a curve in the opposite direction: it is possible for pepper plants to be *too* hot. In a heat wave (mid to upper 90s), move into the shade any pepper plants that already have fruit.

Peppers respond well to fertilizer that is rich in phosphorus (the middle number of the fertilizer trinity). If you happen to have some superphosphate, bone meal, or bulb food available, mix a bit into the soil at planting time; all are proportionately high in phosphorus. Three other important nutrients are calcium, which helps prevent blossom end rot (the fruits develop a round black area at the tip); magnesium, which helps fruits develop from the flowers and so promotes high production; and sulfur, which promotes plant protein and enriches the nutritional content of the peppers. All three may be present in your potting soil if it contains a full complement of micronutrients, but adding more won't hurt. See box at left for common household sources. The one thing you don't want to do is give them extra nitrogen, or you'll produce plants with lots of beautiful foliage and very few fruits.

Two insect problems to be on guard against are aphids and flea beetles (see pages 73 to 75 for controls). The main disease problem that sometimes affects peppers is tomato mosaic virus, or TMV. (Peppers and tomatoes are in the same family, as is tobacco.) Stick to varieties that are

TMV resistant, and don't let smokers handle the plants.

Harvesting. Early in the season, harvest green peppers when they reach a good size, and enjoy their crisp texture in salads and vegetable sautées. The more you pick from the plants, the more production you will get. Then, later in the summer, let the peppers stay on the plant until they are fully ripe—that is, until they reach their mature color—to enjoy their full-bodied flavor. Harvest by snipping the peppers off with scissors or garden clippers, taking a bit of the stem.

Most cooks know to use gloves when working with hot peppers, to protect their skin from burns. But when simply harvesting the peppers, you are in no danger; the outer skin of the peppers won't hurt you. The fiery oils are located in the seeds and, even more so, in the ribs that the seeds are attached to. If you burn yourself when cooking with hot peppers, pat milk on the area; water won't do any good because it can't dissolve the fiery oil.

If you end up with a bumper crop of hot peppers, string them together and hang them to dry in the sun, southwestern style.

Varieties. For several years now, peppers have been one of the hottest items for home gardeners, and have attracted the greatest attention of plant breeders and commercial growers. New varieties are being introduced every season, and "new" heirlooms are being reintroduced.

Any pepper, including your ethnic favorites, should do very well in containers.

Note: The maturity times given here are counted from transplanting, not seeding, and designate the time when peppers are ready at the green stage. Add another 15 to 20 days for full color.

SWEET PEPPERS

■ **Red.** Ace (50 days) is a strong producer and quite early; peppers are small to medium size. **North Star** (62 days) is another reliable early choice. **Gypsy** (70 days), an All-America winner, is a pretty yellow-green at its immature stage. **Giant Marconi** (72 days), an All-America Selection, is our choice for a roasting pepper; roasting peppers have completely smooth sides (not indented), which make it much easier to remove the charred skin after roasting.

■ **Red miniatures.** Jingle Bells (58 days) is fun for the novel shape. The mature peppers are small, about 1½ inches square, which means they mature more quickly than larger fruits. They are also prolific; in summer, the plants are covered with red and green minis. For perfectly round peppers about the size of a golf ball, try **Cherrytime** (53 days) or **Sweet Red Cherry** (70 days).

■ **Orange.** Valencia (70 days) ultimately produces peppers in a lustrous orange color.

■ **Yellow.** As a class, yellow peppers have gorgeous color and wonderful flavor, and thus have become very popular. To meet demand, growers are introducing new varieties at a fast clip. One we like is **Golden Summer** (70 days); others are sure to come on the market soon. Speaking only in terms of looks, yellow peppers have one advantage over reds: when a green pepper is turning red, at the intermediate stage the pepper shows blotches of a muddy dark gray where the two colors overlap. In yellow peppers, the overlaps are a very pretty lime green.

Purple. Purple Beauty (65 days) and **Lilac** (70 days) will give you showstopping purple peppers—but only for a while. Both have purple skins at an intermediate stage, and ultimately turn bright red. But if you catch them at the right time, you'll have a real conversation piece for a salad or vegetable tray. Just be aware that the purple color turns to green when you cook them.

Chocolate. It tastes like a pepper, not like candy, but the outer color will certainly remind you of chocolate: a rich shiny brown at maturity, with red inner flesh. **Chocolate Beauty** (70 days) is a well-known variety; **Sweet Chocolate** (58 days), also fine, is remarkably early.

HOT PEPPERS

Hotness in peppers is a matter of the concentration of capsaicin, the active constituent. This concentration is measured in Scoville units, named for Wilbur Scoville, who developed the system. To give you a scale of relativity,

jalapeños, which you have no doubt eaten at some point, measure between 2,500 and 5,000 Scoville units, depending on the cultivar and how and where it was grown. It's not possible to tell how hot a hot pepper is simply by looking at it. Size is not an indicator; some of the tiniest ones are hot enough to take the top of your head off.

When you begin perusing catalogs, you'll find lots of intriguing types of hot peppers. We suggest a few of our favorites:

Señorita Jalapeño (60 days) has the flavor of regular jalapeño but less of its fire—300 Scoville units rather than 3,000—for great versatility in the kitchen. Produces large quantities of 3-inch-long peppers with the familiar jalapeño shape.

Super Cayenne II (70 days) peppers are the long, slender shape that is typical of the cayenne type, and they are *hot:* 55,000 Scoville units. Selected as an All-America winner for their high yields, even in northern states. This one has a particularly lovely shape: a 2-foot plant, compact, rounded, and spreading, it fills a medium-size container like a bouquet of peppers.

Thai Dragon (50 days) produces short (2- to 3-inch), slender peppers for all your spicy Asian dishes. They are ferociously hot—60,000 Scovilles—but the plant is very pretty, a nice choice for containers.

Super Chile (50 days), an All-America winner, is an especially fine choice for containers: the plants stay short and wide, with handsome leaves, and the tiny peppers sit up on top of the foliage like birthday candles on a cake. Very hot: 37,500 Scovilles.

Vegetables

Potatoes

GROW AS: **annuals**

PLANT SIZE: **2 feet**

START WITH: **seed potatoes**

HARVEST SEASON: **summer, fall**

SUN REQUIREMENTS: **full sun**

MINIMUM SOIL DEPTH: **start with 10 inches of soil in a 30-inch-deep container**

Forget those big baking potatoes with the rough brown skin; you need lots of land to grow them, and besides, they come under the heading of "available year-round at the market at a very reasonable price, and I'd rather use the garden space for something else." Instead, try some of the intriguing types not always available at the supermaket.

Gardeners have a marvelous menu of potato colors to choose from: pink, red, blue, lavender, and gold. But the real delight of potatoes for home gardeners is ready access to those choice morsels known as new potatoes. By definition, "new" potatoes are the ones eaten as soon as they are harvested, as opposed to the ones that are cured (toughened up) for storage. New potatoes aren't necessarily tiny in size, but most are small simply because we don't want to wait for them to get big. With their thin skin and tender flesh, new potatoes are a real treasure.

Rose Marie says: Fresh baby potatoes are one of the great delicacies of the home garden, and if you think they can't be grown in containers—think again!

Potatoes are native to the cool mountain regions of South America. With that sort of climate in their genes, it's no wonder that most commercial potato operations are in colder areas like Idaho, Maine, Canada, and even Alaska.

Potato Basics.

Potatoes are part of the nightshade family, which makes them close cousins of tomatoes, eggplant, and peppers. Once you grow potatoes and have the opportunity to observe their pretty little flowers, you'll see the family resemblance.

The tuber, the part we eat, is not a root even though it grows underground; a potato plant has ordinary roots like other plants. The tubers grow on short runners called stolons, which develop from nodules on the underground part of the stem; the longer that stem, the more tubers there are to harvest. Keep that visual image in mind, and you'll understand how to grow potatoes for maximum success.

Planting. Have you ever forgotten some store-bought potatoes, tucked away in the back of the cupboard, and had them sprout on you, the potato itself becoming shriveled and spongy? If so, you understand exactly how potatoes reproduce. The eyes—those small indentations in the skin—hold the tiny buds for new growth; as they sprout, they draw nutrients from the adjacent flesh, and so the potato gradually shrinks and shrivels as the sprout gets larger and stronger. All this happens in the dark, and in your cupboard it happens accidentally. But if you took those sprouted spuds, cut them into segments, and put them into the garden, before long you'd have bushy green plants and a whole new supply of tubers underneath. And if you then saved a few of those, you could start the whole process over again next year. (That's an explanation of the basic concept. We're not suggesting that you do this with your cupboard renegades for the simple reason that there's a better way.)

Field-grown potatoes are susceptible to many diseases, some of which are capable of wiping out the entire crop, especially if descendants of the same type are grown in the same place year after year. This is exactly what happened in Ireland in the 1840s, with devastating consequences. To counteract this, modern plant breeders have developed ways of producing disease-resistant miniatures specifically for use in reproduction. They are called seed potatoes,

but they aren't seeds in the usual sense; they are very small tubers, grown under conditions as disease-free as possible. An even newer technology has produced what are known as minitubers, grown from tissue cultured in the controlled environment of a laboratory. Mail-order sources will tell you whether their seed potatoes and minitubers are certified disease-free, and that's what you want.

This possibility of disease is the reason most experts caution against using supermarket potatoes as seed. There's another reason too: often they have been treated with a chemical to inhibit sprouting (sprouting is not a good thing in supermarket bins), so even if you did cut them up and plant them, they would never grow well. Besides, it's much more fun to grow some of the nifty varieties that are best when harvested at salad size.

If, in spite of our caution, you decided to try growing potatoes from supermarket spuds, do *not* use that soil to grow potatoes, tomatoes, eggplant, or peppers next season.

Maggie says: When I had my big garden, I used to save kitchen scraps in a small bucket and dump them directly into bucket-size holes in the vegetable beds (the lazy gardener's approach to composting). If potato peelings were in the bucket, I'd always get potato plants in the "dump site" later on, and some pretty nice tubers. Of course that's not practical in container gardens, but I'm telling you this so you'll know that growing potatoes is actually a piece of cake. If a scrap of peeling with just a bit of potato flesh is sufficient to produce a fair-to-middling plant, think how much more vigorous will be plants grown from good seed potatoes.

When you order seed potatoes or minitubers from a mail-order catalog, they'll be shipped to you at the proper planting time for your climate—sometime in early spring. If you are not in a position to plant them immediately, store them in the vegetable drawer of your refrigerator. In any case, seed potatoes benefit from

a process of presprouting; you get potatoes sooner, and more of them. If you order minitubers, you can skip the presprouting step.

Presprouting. Place seed potatoes one layer deep in a shallow pan or tray, even an egg carton, and set that container in a bright, warm indoor spot. Spritz them with liquid seaweed. In about two weeks, sturdy sprouts will form. When the sprouts are about an inch tall, the seed potatoes are ready for planting. Start this process about two weeks ahead of your spring frost date, so they're ready to go outdoors when the outside environment is ready for them. Seed potatoes can range in size from that of a robin's egg to a chicken's egg. Just before planting, you might want to cut the larger seed potatoes into smaller chunks; be *very* careful not to break off the sprouts.

What you do next depends on how you plan to grow the potatoes.

Two Ways to Grow. Remember that the tubers grow out from the underground stem; the goal for maximum production is to elongate that stem. Traditional home gardeners and commercial potato farmers accomplish this through a process known as hilling up. They plant the seed potatoes in a trench, then gradually fill in the trench with more soil as the plants grow; even after the trench has been filled in, they continue to mound up soil around the stems, so that it appears the plants are growing on top of a small hill. The tubers grow out from the entire length of the underground stem, starting at the

A New-Potato Bin

Here's an easy way to grow lots of wonderful potatoes in a small space.

Start with a new 20-gallon plastic garbage can. Drill holes in the bottom for drainage. Fill it one-third full with potting mix, and plant your potatoes following the directions in this chapter.

To pretty this up, drill 2-inch holes at various spots on the sides of the garbage can, and plant bright summer flowers to camouflage the plastic.

At the end of the season, when you've pulled out all the wonderful new potatoes you want, chances are good there are still some potatoes inside that you couldn't reach. Spread out a thick layer of newspaper or some kind of drop cloth, and dump out the entire contents. Sift through for all the potatoes. Then return the soil to the garbage can, first closing up any side holes with duct tape. This may become the beginning of your soil-mixing bin next year.

bottom of the trench all the way up to the top of the hill.

It's a simple matter to use this technique in containers. The only drawback is aesthetic: until the plants reach full size, the pots will not be pretty. But for the pleasure of harvesting your own new potatoes, you may decide it's worth it.

Start with a large container, approximately 30 inches deep and 20 inches across. Fill it about one-third full with potting soil. Lay the sprouted potato segments on top, 5 to 6 inches apart and 4 inches in from the edge of the container, with the sprouts facing up. Cover with another 2 inches of soil. When the plants are about 6 inches tall, add another 3 inches of potting soil (yes, cover up the lower leaves). Continue this process—letting the plants grow, then covering half the leaves with soil—until the soil level is about 1 inch below the rim of the pot, leaving room for watering. Let the plants grow some more, then mound up soil around them, remembering to leave a lower perimeter for watering.

A modified version of this technique, described in box at left, combines potatoes and flowers for a more attractive look.

The second technique is in some ways easier but depends on your having access to a supply of hay, straw, or lots of dried leaves. If you do, here's the procedure. Start with a large container (20 inches wide or more), fill it nearly full with potting soil, and lay the presprouted potatoes on top.

Next, make a cage about 1 foot high around the inside edge of the container, using plastic grid or wire fencing. Cover the sprouts with an inch of straw (or hay or leaves), and wait for the plants to grow. Continue to add the material as the plants get taller, just as in the scenario above, covering about half the foliage growth with straw each time.

One extra advantage to this technique: the organic material will make the soil acidic, which potatoes like.

Success with Potatoes. By using disease-resistant seed potatoes and growing them in containers, you automatically avoid many of the soil-borne problems that plague traditional gardeners. The most common insect pest is the Colorado potato beetle, a ferocious-looking little twerp that will defoliate potato plants in nothing flat. If they are a problem in your area (ask your county extension office, see box on page 74), block them out with row covers; if you're too late, pick them or their egg clusters off by hand (look under the leaves). At night, look over the plants with a flashlight. Whenever you see anything nasty, pick it off and drop it into a small bucket of soapy water. When that's full of bug corpses, or when you can't stand it anymore, just dump the contents of the bucket down the toilet.

It's very important to keep the plants well watered. Uneven watering—dry soil, then lots of moisture—produces lumpy, misshapen potatoes with a mealy texture.

If you use the straw method for growing, make sure your cover material does in fact cover thoroughly; when young tubers are exposed to sun, they develop the alkaloid solanin, which is toxic. You can tell when this has happened: the skin turns green. Soil-grown potatoes are less likely to show this problem, although it does happen—the potatoes push their way to the surface—so check that no part of the potato tuber is exposed to sunlight.

Harvesting. The first tubers are ready for harvesting after about two months. One sure signal is that the plants have started to flower, except that some types of potatoes don't make flowers at all, so this is not foolproof. The nice thing is, you can check without damaging the plant: just reach down close to the stem as far as you can reach, scrabble around with your fingers, and see if you feel anything round.

At this point, those who use the straw/cage method have a huge advantage over the soil/hill method. Just by reaching in through the cage, they can easily get to the base of the plant, where the earliest tubers will form. The other folks have to dig down up to their elbows to make the same test.

Use your fingers to feel around the potato and gauge its size. If it seems too small, simply leave it to continue growing. But if it's the size you want, just pull. Whenever you find one potato of eating size, there will be several others nearby; keep scrabbling.

Plan on harvesting a season-long total of two to four pounds from each plant.

By the way, digging for potatoes is great fun for children (grown-ups too, if the truth be known). It's a bit like going after buried treasure, with that irresistible feeling that you're going to come up with something terrific.

Varieties. If you're trying to make selections from a catalog with a long list of varieties, remember these general guidelines: russets are good for baked and mashed potatoes, but require a very long growing season—not the best choice for containers. Any of the red-skinned types make superb baby potatoes, and even the larger ones hold their texture well when cooked. Potatoes described as "waxy" are excellent as small boiled and buttered potatoes, and for salads. Yellow-skinned and fingerling types (see below) tend to have this waxy texture, and are often very hard to find in the produce sections of supermarkets.

The heirloom potato **All Blue** is a rosy purple on the outside, but it really is blue on the inside. To maintain the color, add a tablespoon of vinegar to the cooking water and don't overcook. Make a stunning potato salad from blue potatoes, red sweet peppers, and green onions.

Yukon Gold has yellow flesh and a rich, buttery taste. **Yellow Finn** is another excellent yellow variety with a smooth texture and rich flavor.

For red-skinned potatoes, try **Dark Red Norland** or **Red Pontiac;** both are delicious. **Rose Finn Apple,** with pink skin and yellow flesh, is a fine example of a type of potato called fingerling, distinguished by its shape: like a short, fat, untapered carrot. Because they are the same diameter all the way down, fingerlings slice into perfect rounds of the same size, which makes for extremely attractive potato salads.

Vegetables

Radishes

GROW AS: **annuals**

PLANT SIZE: **4 to 6 inches above ground**

START WITH: **seeds**

HARVEST SEASON: **spring, fall**

SUN REQUIREMENTS: **full sun to light shade**

MINIMUM SOIL DEPTH: **4 inches**

Radishes have won a permanent spot in the hearts of gardeners for two reasons: (1) they are the earliest, fastest vegetables you can grow, providing reassurance that again this year spring has actually arrived and the growing season can begin; and (2) on a more prosaic level, these superfast germinators, mixed with slower seeds, serve to mark the rows and keep the soil loose.

Oh, and they taste good too.

Radish Basics. We really should speak of radishes in two separate categories: (1) the familiar round ball or icicle types usually grown in spring; and (2) the Asian daikon, the long, fat, very robust radishes of fall. Those in the first group are planted very early in spring and are ready to eat in less than a month. Most Asian types are planted in late summer for fall or winter eating, because they have a longer growing period and will bolt in summer if spring-planted. With one irresistibly pretty exception, we will leave the daikon type to traditional gardeners who have the room for them.

Planting. Radish seeds are tiny, and should be direct-sowed about ¼ inch deep. Sowing them is simplicity itself: with a garden fork or small cultivator, scratch the soil surface to loosen it (if you're reusing a container from last year), sprinkle the seeds around, push some soil over them, give them a pat and a drink, and you're done. We find it useful to have several seed packets of different varieties on hand at the beginning of the season; then, whenever you think of it, plant a few seeds just to get yourself in the gardening mode.

To use radish seeds as a ground breaker, you'll find it simpler to premix them with the slower seeds in a small cup and then plant the mixture.

147

In both cases, be assiduous about thinning the seedlings to a spacing of about an inch.

Success with Radishes. Lots of water—that's what keeps radishes growing quickly, and growing quickly is what keeps them from becoming too hot. Do not let the container soil dry out.

Few diseases bother radishes, but you may encounter two common insect pests: flea beetles or cabbage root maggots; see Chapter 6 for controls. Overall, though, radishes are very carefree plants.

Harvesting. If we make any mistake with radishes, it is leaving them in the soil too long; they become tough and bitter, and sometimes develop a hollow core. The round types are at their best when they are the size of large marbles (the shooters, remember?). The icicle and French types should also be pulled when they are young and tender; if you're not sure whether they're ready, just pull one up and sample it.

Varieties. The most familiar radish is the small red, round type, and it is a very satisfying vegetable to grow. **Cherry Belle** (30 days), an All-America winner, is a classic. **Easter Egg** (25 days) is a kid's delight. In each packet is a mixture of seeds of radishes of different colors: pink, red, white, lavender. When you pull one up, you never know what color you'll get (although all the insides are white), and that's the fun of it.

French radishes are long and slender, more like a fingerling carrot in shape than what most people think of as a radish. The heirloom **White Icicle** (28 days), white inside and out, is crisp and refreshing; it will reach 4 to 5 inches but is better when harvested young.

French Breakfast is the name of a specific heirloom variety, and the term has also been extended to mean a group of varieties with a similar look: short and cylindrical, red except for a bright white tip that looks for all the world as if it had been dipped in cream. **Early French Breakfast** (25 days) is an improved, earlier variety, and **D'Avignon** (21 days) is earliest of all.

Now the one fall radish we couldn't resist: **Misato Rose.** It's shaped like a large radish or a small turnip, from 2 to 4 inches in diameter, and because of this larger size needs a deeper container, with a minimum 8 inches of potting soil. The outside coloration is mediocre: a bland green at the top, gradually blending down to white at the tip. But the inside color is something else: clear, pure pink.

Slice them crosswise and toss in a light dressing of white wine or rice vinegar, and the pink color becomes electric. The fine British garden writer Joy Larkcom, an expert on Asian vegetables, tells us that in China they are carved into many-petaled radish roses and sold as winter street snacks.

Vegetables

Spinach
and Spinach Substitutes

GROW AS: **annuals**

PLANT SIZE: **6 inches; more for vining plants**

START WITH: **seeds or transplants**

HARVEST SEASON: **spring, summer, fall**

SUN REQUIREMENTS: **full sun to partial shade**

MINIMUM SOIL DEPTH: **6 inches**

Somehow spinach has come to be the ultimate "because it's good for you" vegetable, and all children in America knows what that means: if it's good for you, it doesn't taste good. With any luck, eventually they'll have the chance to enjoy a dish made from fresh spinach prepared with skill and respect, and they'll realize what they've been missing.

Maggie says: I used to detest spinach, mostly because I grew up in a part of the country where everything green is (or was then) cooked to mush. Ironically, with all the vitamins and minerals cooked out of it, not only did it not taste good, it wasn't even good for you.

And then, revelation. As a young adult, trying my darnedest to be sophisticated like the other guests at my first big-city dinner party, I forced myself to try the wilted-spinach salad, and life was never the same.

Spinach Basics. Spinach is a cool-season crop that quickly fizzles out and bolts when the weather turns hot. It grows well in spring, medium well in fall, and rarely in summer. To fill in the gap, we also suggest several warm-season plants with a spinachlike look and taste, which can be used as respectable substitutes. Any specific information you need about growing them successfully is included in their individual sections below.

Planting. As early in the spring as you can manage, plant seeds directly in your containers about ½ inch deep and 1 inch apart. (Spinach germinates so well in cool weather that there's little reason to start seeds indoors, although you can certainly do so.) Thin the seedlings, spacing about 3 inches apart as plants grow. For a fall crop, replant by the first of August. Fewer seeds will germinate than in spring, but they'll come up at a faster rate.

Success with Spinach. Like other cool-season vegetables, spinach is tastiest when it grows rapidly, so

149

water thoroughly and give a light application of a balanced fertilizer a couple of times during the season.

Spinach has few insect or disease problems. Its biggest enemy is the sun: if hot weather doesn't make the plant bolt, the sun will scorch the leaves. If you still have healthy plants growing when the summer heat arrives, move your containers into some shade; that will buy you extra time.

Eventually, though, any remaining plants will bolt. When you see that about to happen (flower buds start forming), cut off the tops of the plants down to some good-looking lower leaves, and you can delay the inevitable by a few days.

Spinach planted in late summer for a fall crop is susceptible to mildew; your best bet is to choose a mildew-resistant variety.

The summer substitutes have the same needs as most other warm-season vegetables: keep them well watered and fertilized, watch for aphids, and harvest regularly.

Harvesting. You can slice off an entire plant, if that's what you need, or pick individual leaves. The former gives you a large volume of spinach in a hurry; the latter leaves you with an ongoing source of more spinach. Large seedlings that you remove for purposes of thinning are very tasty in mixed salads.

Varieties. Two types of spinach are to be found in seed catalogs, although you sometimes have to read the descriptions carefully to distinguish them. One has deeply crinkled leaves (called "savoy" or "savoyed"); the other has relatively smooth leaves. This differentiation is primarily important to market gardeners, for the crinkled leaves collect garden soil more easily than smooth ones and thus require more washing. Otherwise, the two types are almost identical in flavor and growing conditions.

In an effort to help us have spinach for a longer season, plant breeders have been developing varieties that are slow to bolt and resistant to mildew; fortunately, they have had great success. All the varieties we suggest here will do well for spring, early summer, and fall: **Melody** (42 days), lightly crinkled, large leaves; **Indian Summer** (39 days), semi-savoyed leaves and an upright growth pattern; **Bloomsdale Long Standing** (46 days), an heirloom with deeply crinkled leaves. For superfast production, we like **Razzle Dazzle,** which is ready to harvest in only 30 days. It's a good variety to have on hand very early in the season; plant a few seeds whenever you think about it, and you'll be eating fresh spinach a month later. This is only an early-season variety, though, for it is not heat-tolerant.

SPINACH SUBSTITUTES

Even though "spinach" is found in their common names, none of these is true spinach in a botanical sense. All, however, produce dark green, nutritious leaves that taste close to spinach and can be used like it in the kitchen. And all of them are able to endure the heat of summer without bolting.

Recipe: Spinach with Lemon Thyme

The flavors of olive oil and lemon are wonderful complements to the slightly bitter, earthy flavor of spinach. This recipe adds another lemony note with fresh lemon thyme.

1 pound spinach, or a combination of spinach and Malabar spinach

2 teaspoons olive oil

1 garlic clove, peeled and crushed

2 teaspoons chopped fresh lemon thyme

Salt to taste

Juice of ½ lemon

1. Rinse the spinach thoroughly and remove any tough stems. Dry the spinach well in a salad spinner or with paper towels.

2. Heat the oil in a large, heavy skillet over low heat. Add the garlic and sauté until it begins to turn golden, then remove; do not let the garlic burn. Immediately add the spinach and thyme and sauté until the spinach turns bright green, about 5 minutes, then drain.

3. Season the spinach lightly with salt, and place in a hot serving dish. Sprinkle with the lemon juice and serve at once.

Serves 4

■ **New Zealand spinach** (70 days) is essentially a vine with tasty leaves all along its stem. To keep it in bounds in your container, keep the tips pinched out or run it up a trellis. Its vining habit also makes it a good choice for hanging baskets. New Zealand spinach positively thrives in hot weather, and in appearance and taste is very close to true spinach. The only drawback is that it takes a long time to germinate—as much as a month. You can speed up the process somewhat if you soak the seeds overnight before planting, and give them a head start indoors.

■ **Malabar spinach** (35 days) is another vine, and a very vigorous, fast-growing one. If your summers are hot, this definitely should be grown on a trellis, where it can reach 6 feet or more. In cooler climates, the vines stay shorter and would work well in a hanging basket. The leaves, which are attached directly to the ropelike stem, are larger and fleshier than those of spinach.

Two types are available, red and green. Green Malabar spinach is a rich green all over, including the stems. The red version is particularly attractive, with a bright red stem and green leaves tinged with red or copper.

Rose Marie says: To show that sometimes unusual combinations work wonderfully, I have a very pretty container planting that consists of a columnar apple tree and two plants of red Malabar spinach that twine around the trunk and climb up into the limbs. We love the gorgeous magenta spinach leaves in salads and stir-fry dishes.

In late spring start seeds indoors, where you can give them the heat they need; presoak seeds overnight. When seedlings are 3 to 4 inches tall, harden them off and plant outside when nighttime temperatures are no lower than 50°F. If you want plants with thick, bushy growth rather than long vines, keep the tips pinched off. This will cause side shoots to develop off the main stem, and you can either harvest the entire shoot, with its tender young leaves, or allow it to become a new stem with more leaves.

The leaves contain a natural mucilage (like okra's) that is released with long cooking. If you don't want that quality, cook the leaves lightly and quickly, just as you would spinach. With slow cooking, the leaves serve as a thickening agent, which is an advantage in dishes such as soups and stews.

■ **Spinach beet,** also commonly called perpetual spinach (60 days), is neither a spinach nor a beet, although it is a beet cousin. It's actually a variation of chard, with smaller leaves and less prominent stems and ribs. It does have the upright growth that will remind you of chard, but the taste is gentler, more like that of true spinach.

Spinach beets provide a continuous harvest from summer to early winter, as long as you keep cutting it. It survives the heat nicely, and also will tolerate light shade.

■ **Orach,** sometimes called mountain spinach (50 days), is very popular in Europe but not yet well known in the United States. It's a tall, handsome plant, reaching 6 feet or more, and gardeners with lots of space frequently grow it just for its looks. The leaves are small, triangular, and have a mild-flavor. As with Malabar spinach, both green and red varieties are available. We prefer the red for its magnificent color. Lit by the sun, the entire plant turns a brilliant magenta, and individual ruby red leaves do wonders for a green salad.

Direct-sow seeds in spring or early summer; cover with ¼ inch of soil. The first harvest of tender leaves is ready in about six weeks. To keep the plants at the height you want, snip off the growing tips; this will force new growth of tender leaves. Keep cutting and watering, and the plants will produce most of the summer.

Vegetables

Squash

GROW AS: **annuals**

PLANT SIZE: **3 to 4 feet**

START WITH: **seeds or transplants**

HARVEST SEASON: **summer, early fall**

SUN REQUIREMENTS: **full sun**

MINIMUM SOIL DEPTH: **10 inches**

If you ever had a regular in-the-ground garden, or ever lived next door to, worked with, or were related to someone who did, or had even the remotest second-, third-, or fourthhand connection to anyone with a vegetable garden, you know all the jokes about zucchini. How it's so prolific that people run out of friends to give the squashes to and start leaving them on the doorsteps of total strangers in the dead of night. How it grows so vigorously that one hidden under leaves gets large enough you could make a doghouse out of it. How whole cookbooks have been written about ways to disguise it.

This reputation is unfair. Zucchinis are perfectly fine vegetables, attractive in the garden and very versatile in the kitchen. Italians, who know good food when they see it, have enjoyed a long love affair with zucchini, and we could do far worse than to follow their lead.

In all the commotion about zucchini, we sometimes forget its squash siblings: the crooknecks, the yellow straightnecks, the cute little pattypans. All these are collectively known as summer squashes, and for many reasons they are excellent candidates for your container garden.

Summer squashes have been bred to grow in bush form, rather than in vines as most winter squashes do, so their basic architecture is compatible with containers. The plants themselves are very handsome, with large, imposing leaves and voluptuous flowers; even a single plant will make a strong statement in your garden. And perhaps best of all, growing them in your garden is the best way (maybe the only way) to have a supply of blossoms for fritters, and of tiny squashes with the blossoms still attached for show-stopping side dishes.

Squash Basics. Squashes fit into one of two worlds: summer and winter. Summer squashes are small and fast growing, and have soft skins; winter squashes tend to be larger, take longer to develop, and have very tough skins, which makes it possible to store them for the winter.

The truth of the matter is that the so-called summer squashes are species that we humans have decided taste better when they are eaten at the immature stage of development. Winter squashes start out with soft skins too, but we let them stay on the vine until the rind becomes very stiff because we prefer the taste of those types when they are older. We could let summer squashes get much more mature, but we would not like the taste or the texture; we could eat immature winter squashes (and in fact people sometimes do at the end of the season), but most of us would think they don't taste quite right.

In any case, in this book we concentrate on summer squashes for the simple reason that their bush shape works best in containers. Winter squashes grow on vines that have an irritating tendency to sprawl to kingdom come. The only winter squashes we include are the miniature pumpkins (yes, pumpkins are a winter squash) that are so delightful to children; and some of them have the extra virtue of a bush growth habit.

Planting. In all probability you will want only one plant of each of the squashes you choose to grow, so it makes good sense to buy small plants at the garden center. Set them out in your containers when nighttime low temperatures are 55°F. But if the variety you have your heart set on is not available as commercial transplants, you will have to plant seeds.

Start seeds indoors two to three weeks ahead of the spring frost date, or direct-seed around about the time of that date. You'll have a lot of seeds left over; save them till next year, or give them away to other gardeners or to a school for a science class project.

To get your baby plants off to a vigorous start, put them into containers in which you have prewarmed the potting soil by wrapping the empty pot in black plastic and setting it in your sunniest spot for several days. You can push the season by a week or more if you set the transplants into warm soil *and* cover them with row cover, which acts like a blanket and also protects the young plants from harmful insects.

Success with Squashes.

Squashes are in the same botanical family as cucumbers, and like them are fast-growing, heavy-feeding, hard-drinking heat lovers. Don't let the potting mix dry out, and add a fertilizer rich in phosphorus several times: about a week after transplanting, at first flowering, and when the squash fruits begin to form.

Disease and insect pests are usually only a minor problem with summer squashes. Keep the foliage washed free of aphids, and use an insecticidal soap if you get a severe infestation. Spotted cucumber beetles or any other bad guys can be picked off by hand and dropped into a little bucket of soapy water. Slugs meet the same fate. In the fall you may get some powdery mildew; control it by not watering leaves directly, or by spraying with baking soda mixture, or both. See Chapter 6 for more details.

Don't panic if some of the early flowers fall off without producing anything. They are probably male flowers. It's also fairly common for the first few squashes to turn black or just stop growing; this is because they weren't pollinated, a problem that Mother Nature remedies with a burst of new flowers to attract the bees.

Harvesting. As is true with all vegetables that contain seeds inside, squash plants will cease producing once a fruit gets old enough that its seeds begin to mature. Then, no more squash. Prevent that by faithfully picking the squash when they are small and succulent. You want to do that anyway—why else are you growing them? Anyone can buy full-size squash at the store; only gardeners can harvest the oh-so-delicious baby squashes, perhaps with the flowers still attached.

Use a knife or your garden clippers to cut the squash from the plant, taking about 1 inch of stem. Clippers work best for removing the flowers.

You'll probably be using your

squash the same day you harvest them, but they will keep in the crisper drawer for a day or so if need be. However, if you harvest just the flowers, or baby squashes with blossoms attached, cook and serve them that same day.

Wash the blossoms (or squash-cum-blossom) in tepid tap water, shake them dry, then spread them out in a single layer on damp paper towels and cover with another layer of damp paper towels. Healthy garden plants attract lots of beneficial insects, and we know they're friendly so we don't shriek when we see them. At the same time, we'd just as soon not eat them. During this resting period on the paper towels, most of the critters that may be hiding inside the blossoms will simply walk away. Then do one more visual inspection before cooking or stuffing the flowers.

Varieties. Here are some of our favorite squashes:

■ **Zucchini.** Spacemiser (45 days) is tailor-made for container gardens: small and compact, and only 18 to 24 inches across, yet it produces normal-size zucchini. **Seneca** (42 days) handles cool weather better than any other zucchini, and so is a good choice for those with short summers.

Eight Ball (42 days) is a very compact plant (12 to 18 inches) that produces an amazing number of zucchini, which appear to be stacked up around the center stem. The squashes are perfectly round, perfect for stuffing.

Recipe:  Stuffed Squash Blossoms with Fresh Tomato Sauce

Squash blossoms are a rare treat because they're so delicate and perishable. We love this recipe from Renée Shepherd, owner of Renée's Garden Seeds, and a widely respected seedswoman known for introducing many unusual varieties to American cooks. She's the author of *Recipes from a Kitchen Garden* and *More Recipes from a Kitchen Garden*.

For tips on harvesting squash blossoms and preparing them for eating, see page 155.

FILLING AND SQUASH BLOSSOMS

½ cup grated Jack cheese

1 cup ricotta cheese

1 jalapeño pepper, seeded and finely chopped

½ cup chopped prosciutto or other ham

1 teaspoon ground cumin

1 teaspoon chopped fresh oregano

2 tablespoons chopped fresh parsley

1 medium tomato, peeled, seeded, diced, and drained

Salt and freshly ground pepper to taste

16 to 18 fresh squash blossoms, stamens removed

2 tablespoons olive oil

SAUCE

2 tablespoons olive oil

1 medium onion, chopped

4 large tomatoes, peeled, seeded, and chopped

1 cup dry white wine

1 tablespoon tomato paste

1. Preheat the oven to 325°F. Oil or butter a casserole or baking dish thoroughly.

2. To make the filling, mix together the cheeses, jalapeño, prosciutto, cumin, oregano, parsley, and tomato in a medium-size bowl. Season with the salt and pepper to taste. Stuff each squash blossom carefully with about 1 tablespoon of the cheese mixture, and press the edges together; don't overfill. Place the filled squash blossoms in the prepared casserole or baking dish, drizzle the oil over them, and cover the dish with aluminum foil. Place in the preheated oven and bake for 15 minutes, then remove the foil and bake for 15 minutes more.

3. While the squash blossoms are baking, prepare the sauce. Heat the olive oil in a skillet over medium heat and add the onion. Sauté until it has softened, 5 to 10 minutes. Add the tomatoes, wine, and tomato paste and let the mixture cook, uncovered, until it has reduced and thickened slightly, 5 to 8 minutes more, stirring occasionally.

4. Remove the casserole from the oven, spoon the tomato sauce over the squash blossoms, and serve hot or at room temperature.

Serves 4 to 6

Reprinted with permission from More Recipes from a Kitchen Garden.

Eight Ball was an All-America winner in 1999, and it's a real conversation piece.

Finally, **Gold Rush** (52 days), also an All-America Selection, has the recognizable zucchini shape but is a brilliant golden yellow. It holds its color nicely when cooked, and has a fine flavor.

■ **Crookneck/Straightneck.** Many people consider the flavor of these yellow squashes far superior to that of zucchini; they tend to use descriptors like "buttery," "sweet," and "nutty." We concur.

Yellow Crookneck is the name of an heirloom variety that has also become the name of a type: squashes with a bulbous bottom and a narrow, curved neck like the top of a question mark. Crooknecks are a longtime favorite, and many gardeners still prefer this old-fashioned type.

Newer varieties of crooknecks include **Sundance** (50 days), **Horn of Plenty** (50 days), and **Fancycrook** (43 days). Be sure to remove these from the plants with a knife, not a hand twist; the necks snap easily.

Straightneck squash are just

what you would think: like crooknecks in color and taste, but the
curved neck has been bred out of
them. You can tell straightneck yellow squash from yellow zucchini by
their fat bottoms; zucchini are the
same diameter for their whole
length, and usually have slightly
raised vertical ribs. **Seneca Prolific**
(50 days) is a good one.

For the sheer fun of it, you might
want to grow **Zephyr** (54 days), a yellow straightneck with a green base. It
looks for all the world like someone
took each squash and dipped it about
a third of way in green paint, giving it
a novelty appearance in addition to its
fine taste.

■ **Pattypan.** The shape of pattypan
squash is distinctive and unforgettable:
small, flattened rounds with scalloped
equators. The flavor is rich and buttery, the texture creamy but firm.
They are delicious stuffed, steamed
whole (especially the baby size), or
sliced vertically to show
off their pretty pro-
file. The original pat-
typans were green, but
a new yellow one has
won every gar-
deners' heart:
Sunburst (50
days), a
strong, rich
golden yellow
with a round
circle of bright green at
the base. For elegant baby squash, pick
them when very young, about 1 inch
in diameter.

■ **Pumpkins.** You *know* you can't
grow a full-size jack-o'-lantern in
your containers; don't even try. But
you may not be aware of the cute-as-
a-button miniatures that will thrive
in containers and are certainly worth
growing for the children in your
life. Several varieties are available.

Jack-Be-Little (90 days) is a
pumpkin for fairies, with a flattened
top and bottom and deeply ribbed
sides, but only 3 inches across.
Wee-B-Little (85 days), an All-
America winner in 1999, is a total
charmer. The 5-foot bush-type plant
yields an average of 6 to 8 small
pumpkins, about 3 to 4 inches in
diameter, with a more rounded shape
and smoother sides than Jack-Be-
Little. The plants are short, productive vines that do better with trellis
support.

Baby Bear (100 days) pumpkins are bigger than these two
miniatures but are still much smaller
than full-size pumpkins; they run
about 6 inches in diameter and 4
inches in height. This All-America
winner needs room to spread (a 24-
inch container with an extra foot
of tumbling room all
around), but it's worth the
space. The sweet flesh
makes wonderful pies,
and the semi-hull-less
seeds make a nutritious
snack. These show an attractive strong orange color early
in the season.

Vegetables

Tomatoes

GROW AS: **annuals**

PLANT SIZE: **2 to 5 feet**

START WITH: **transplants**

HARVEST SEASON: **late summer, fall**

SUN REQUIREMENTS: **full sun**

MINIMUM SOIL DEPTH: **12 inches**

I f you could take the soft, warm air of a summer afternoon and turn it into a taste, it would be the taste of a thoroughly ripe tomato, warm from the sun—tangy on the tongue and sweet at the same time, simultaneously juicy and velvet-firm. Compare that to the cardboard flavor of supermarket produce, and it's no wonder tomatoes are the number one favorite vegetable of all home gardeners.

Tomato Basics. Tomatoes are heat lovers, and they belong to the nightshade family along with potatoes, peppers, and eggplant. Like peppers and potatoes, they are native to Central and South America, where European explorers "discovered" them and brought them home. As you probably know, for a long time it was thought that tomatoes were poisonous. The nightshade family contains one very toxic plant, aptly named deadly nightshade; wary Europeans, undoubtedly recognizing the nightshade flower on the new import, were afraid to try tomatoes, growing them instead as ornamentals. Did you ever wonder who was the brave soul who first tried eating one? Whoever that was, we are profoundly grateful.

Today, tomato lovers have an incredible range of tastes, colors, shapes, and sizes to choose from. Plant hybridizers have developed new varieties that stand up well to numerous diseases, harmful insects, and short growing seasons. At the same time, heirloom types with scrumptious old-fashioned flavor are being rigorously and lovingly preserved.

In seed catalogs you are apt to find tomatoes categorized in various ways (by size, by length of growing season, by growth habit, by color, by most common use) and described with varying terminology. Most of these descriptive terms are self-evident, but the most important of all may be new to you: **determinate** and **indeterminate.** Those two little words have a huge impact on gardeners who aspire to grow tomatoes. You'll find them in the fine print of seed catalogs and maybe (or maybe not) on the label sticks in garden-center transplants.

Determinate tomatoes grow to a certain height and then get no taller. (You can think of them as having a "predetermined" size.) The plants are usually 2 to 3 feet tall, and can stand on their own without staking, although they do better with it. Flowers and fruits form only at the tips of stems, and the plants yield their entire crop of tomatoes in a concentrated span of time.

Indeterminate tomatoes just keep going until frost kills them. Rather than setting flowers, the tip ends continue with new growth—more stem, more leaves, more flowers. Flowers form from short branches all along the stems, starting near the bottom, and the tomatoes ripen over a long period of time. It's important that you realize how rambunctious an indeterminate tomato can be, and plan appropriately (see the Providing Support section on page 163).

Planting. So many varieties of tomato are available today, you stand a very good chance of finding the perfect choice at your garden center—both the type of tomato you want and a variety well suited to your climate. If so, go ahead and get it; you'll save yourself some work. Only one caution: don't buy the first one you see. Young tomato transplants often show up in the store well ahead of the proper planting season.

On the other hand, you may fall in love with a particularly seductive catalog description of a special type that you just know will not be grown in a local nursery. Your only choice then is to order seeds.

You may have noticed a small timing dilemma: the catalogs arrive in December or January; the garden center starts selling tomato seedlings in March, April, or May, depending on where you live. Should you order seeds or wait for the plants? If you wait and the exact one you want never appears, you're sunk. Our advice is, make your best guess and then don't worry. If you don't find your heart's desire in the garden center, you'll just have to choose something else wonderful. Or if you do order seeds and the garden center later carries plants of the same variety, that's not so terrible. Plant both, and you can consider it a controlled experiment: how do your seedlings compare to the nursery's?

Starting Seeds Indoors. In the warmest spot you can manage, plant seeds in sterile seed-starting mix six to eight weeks ahead of the spring frost date. When they have two or three sets of true leaves, move the seedlings to a larger temporary pot. Bury them deeper in the starting mix, so that just one set of leaves shows. You may have to move them to a larger indoor pot before the weather is warm enough for outside planting; again, bury the stem and half the leaves. Keep the seedlings in good light; the goal is to produce

Recipe: Fresh Tomato Soup

Bruce Naftaly is the chef-owner of Seattle's Le Gourmand restaurant and a champion of using fresh, seasonal foods. He has cultivated a network of local growers to supply him with heirloom vegetables, exotic greens, and fresh herbs, some of which he uses in this delicious soup.

2 pounds ripe tomatoes
2 small carrots
1/2 onion
2 cups chicken stock
1 bay leaf
1/2 teaspoon chopped fresh thyme
1/2 teaspoon chopped fresh marjoram
1 sprig chervil
Salt, to taste
Cream (optional)
Snipped chives

1. Remove the stems and cores from the tomatoes; slice them in half and squeeze out the seeds. Peel the carrots and slice them into 1/4-inch rounds. Peel and chop the onion.

2. Place the chicken stock in a heavy, nonreactive pot over medium heat. Add the tomatoes, carrots, onion, bay leaf, thyme, marjoram, and chervil and cook until the onion and carrots are soft, about 20 minutes. Remove and discard the bay leaf.

3. Puree the tomato mixture in a blender, then strain through a mesh sieve back into the saucepan. You may have to do this in batches. Season with salt and add a large splash of cream, if desired. Garnish with snipped chives before serving.

Serves 4

plants that are vigorous but not leggy (with long sections of stretched-out stem between the leaves).

Choosing at the Garden Center. At the garden center, look for stocky plants with rich green leaves and not a lot of stem. Once the weather is warm enough, a small, vigorous plant in a 4-inch pot will catch up to a larger 1-gallon plant in no time, and may eventually surpass it because the smaller plants recover more vigorously from the shock of transplanting than do larger ones. Avoid if you can plants that are leggy.

Planting Transplants. The tomato seedlings (either from your windowsill or the nursery) are ready to go into outdoor containers when warm weather has really arrived—when nighttime temperatures stay above 55°F. Fill the containers completely with potting mix, using no foam or soda can spacers (see box on page 62). Tomatoes are heavy feeders and drinkers with a large root system, and for that they need lots of soil. An indeterminate plant that produces large tomatoes needs at least a 5-gallon container.

Dig a deep hole and sink each young plant deeper than it was in the small pot, covering up the lowest sets of leaves just as you did with the indoor repotting. All your deep planting has a very important goal: making lots of roots. The points on the stem where the leaves are attached (called nodes) are where the growth hormones are concentrated, and so they're also the points from which

roots will grow. By burying the nodes, you're encouraging the plant to set lots of roots, and in tomatoes that is a very good thing. After all your tomatoes are planted, add a weak solution of complete fertilizer or fish emulsion to the soil around them.

Plant tomatoes deep in the soil to promote lots of root growth.

Getting an Early Start. The first ripe tomato is a signal event in a gardener's summer, and the source of serious bragging rights. If you want to join that party, here is one way to get a jump on the season. Start two weeks earlier than you normally would; nighttime lows of 45° to 50°F are okay.

1. Prewarm your soil by wrapping the unplanted container in black plastic and setting it in direct sunlight several days ahead.

2. Move your transplant into the container (ignore the earlier warning not to buy the very first arrivals at the garden center).

3. Partially cover the top of the container with clear plastic, leaving breathing room around the stem of the plant.

4. At night, cover the plants with something to protect against cold temperatures: a cloche, a hotcap (a pyramid made of specially treated paper), a bottomless milk jug, or plastic sheets propped up on short stakes. Uncover in the morning.

You are creating a semi-artificial environment in which the temperatures are higher than the surrounding air, and babying the plants through cool nights. When warmer weather arrives, you can discontinue your overnight protection.

Providing Support. Tomatoes are essentially vines (hence the term "vine-ripened tomatoes"), and in their natural state will scoot along the ground in all directions. Even in traditional gardens, that creates a slew of problems; in containers it becomes physically unmanageable. Unless you are growing only determinate types, you'll need to provide some support for the tomato plants, and even determinates do better with some assistance.

The classic device, and it works just fine, is a stout stake. As the tomato grows, keep tying the main stem loosely to the stake. A modern version is a gently spiraled corkscrew of aluminum; the main stem of the plant twists into the corkscrew curves.

Another excellent system is a wide circle made of heavy-duty wire, such as concrete-reinforcing wire, with grid openings large enough to get your hand through. This wire cage catches and holds up the plant as it grows.

The demicage described for cucumbers (see page 96) would be another way to go, but make it tall—3 to 4 feet above the top of the container. The tomato cages sold in garden centers are adequate for determinate tomatoes but too short and too flimsy for most indeterminate types. You can even use a flat trellis, tying the tomato branches to the horizontal supports as they grow.

Decide what you will use for support, and install it at the same time as you transplant the tomato. If you're using a stake or trellis, insert it

Most tomato plants need some kind of support; here are several possibilities.

at least a foot deep and right next to the plant.

Success with Tomatoes.

Tomatoes need a lot of water. This will be your main challenge with containers. Because the heavy watering will also wash away soil nutrients, you'll also need to provide additional fertilizer. Use liquid complete fertilizer every two weeks, or add a new application of timed-release fertilizer (sprinkle it right on top of the soil) about midway through the season. Make sure that the fertilizer you use is not heavy in nitrogen; you're interested in growing fruits, not pretty foliage. An application of liquid seaweed every two weeks will give wonderful results.

One optional but very useful tomato task is pruning. If you are growing determinate tomatoes, you don't need to prune at all. In fact, you should definitely *not* do it; Mother Nature has already done the work for you genetically. For indeterminates, the process is not as scary as it sounds; you don't even need pruning shears, just your fingertips.

Look for new leaves beginning to grow in the "V" where a leaf or a short branch joins the main stem; that new growth is called a sucker. If you leave it there, it will grow into lots of foliage (which you don't want) and will pull energy away from production of flower-bearing stems (which you do want).

Remove all suckers; just pinch them off with your fingers. The tricky part is keeping up with them. When the weather is warm and the soil is rich and moist, tomatoes grow amazingly fast, and that unwanted new growth can appear seemingly overnight; the larger your plant gets, the more "Vs" there are. Also, if your indeterminate tomatoes start outgrowing their cages, pinch off the growing tip from the tallest stems to keep them under control.

If you're using a stake or trellis, keep tying the main stems as they grow. Use something soft like strips of an old T-shirt or ribbons cut from old panty hose. With a wire cage, continual tying is not necessary, but you would do well to help the stems find an upright position while they are still young.

Tomatoes are subject to certain diseases and pests, but nothing you can't handle. One is blossom-end rot, in which the blossom end (where the

Remove suckers that grow in the notches; they're all leaf and no fruit.

flower used to be, not the end that is attached to a stem) gradually turns into a sunken dark-colored mess. One good preventive measure is steady, even watering; alternating wet and dry conditions seem to encourage this rot. Never let the soil dry out completely. Many experts believe that blossom-end rot is related to a lack of calcium in the soil; as a preventive, they work in a small amount of agricultural lime or some crushed eggshells at the bottom of the planting hole.

A fungal disease called early blight seems to occur when water splashes infected garden soil onto the leaves; this is seldom a problem in containers. More problematic is late blight, which hits tomatoes late in the season, when the weather is hot and humid. The leaves develop brownish spots and quickly rot, and soon the entire plant is dead. While this disease is relatively rare, it is, unfortunately, almost impossible to eradicate; tomato lovers have to proceed with a certain amount of faith.

Another problem you may encounter with tomatoes is cracking, in which the skin splits open. This is the result of uneven watering; if the plant gets a large amount of water one day, after several days of dryness, the sudden infusion of water makes the fruits crack open. Obviously you can't control the rain, but as a container gardener, you are in complete control of keeping the soil evenly moist.

Two critters may show up uninvited: cutworms and tomato hornworms (see Chapter 6 for descriptions). Your best defense is a careful eye; when you see one, pick it off by hand and dump it into your trusty bucket of soapy water.

Harvesting. Tomatoes of indeterminate types start ripening from the bottom of the plant. Determinate tomatoes ripen pretty much all at once. For that incomparable ripe-tomato flavor, let them stay on the vine until they are truly ripe. Color is your best indicator.

As summer draws to a close and the nights begin to turn cool, gardeners know with a sad sinking feeling that there will not be time for all the green tomatoes still on the plant to ripen, and they begin a cat-and-mouse game with the weather forecaster. Totally green tomatoes will not ripen off the vine, but once they have matured past that stage, even if only to the point that the green has started to lighten to the faintest tinge of color, they will continue to ripen inside your home. So the game is to check the tomato color every day, and watch the weather forecast every night.

Anything lower than 40°F is dangerous, but as long as the forecast is for 40°F or above, you can risk it for one more night and give the tomatoes one more day of vine-ripening. If you can cover the entire plant with protective plastic, or even haul it inside for what is predicted to be just a short cold snap, you can push back the cold nights for a while longer. Then, on the last possible day, pick all the remaining tomatoes and invite a few friends over for fried green tomatoes.

Tomatoes at a Glance

Name	Determinate or Indeterminate	Category	Fruit Color	Fruit Size (diameter in inches)	Days to Maturity (from transplants)	Grow In*
Big Beef	indeterminate	full size	red	5–6	73	1
Brandywine	indeterminate	full size, heirloom	pinkish red	4–5	85	1
Champion	indeterminate	full size	red	4–5	65	1
Early Girl	indeterminate	full size	red	3	66	1
First Lady II	indeterminate	full size	red	3	66	1
Green Grape	indeterminate	cherry	green	1	75	1
Jet Setter	indeterminate	full size	red	4–5	64	1
Lemon Boy	indeterminate	full size	yellow	3–4	72	1
Sun Gold	indeterminate	cherry	orange	1	62	1
Sweet Cluster	indeterminate	salad size	red	2	72	2
Celebrity	determinate	full size	red	4–5	72	1, 2
Gold Nugget	determinate	cherry	yellow	1	60	2
Italian Gold	determinate	plum	yellow	2	70	2
Oregon Spring	determinate	full size	red	3–4	60	2
Tiny Tim	determinate	cherry	red	1	60	4
Tumbler	determinate	salad size	red	1–2	55	3, 4
Viva Italia	determinate	plum	red	2	76	2

* Grow in:

    1 = a large container, at least 18 inches wide and 2 feet deep, with a serious stake or trellis/cage

    2 = a medium container, at least 12 inches wide and 18 inches deep; stake or cage optional but recommended

    3 = a hanging container, at least 12 inches deep

    4 = a small container, 8 to 10 inches deep

Varieties. Perhaps because tomatoes are everyone's favorite garden vegetable, there is a greater breadth of choices than with any other. Browse through several catalogs, and you'll find that invariably the tomato selection takes up more space than anything else. We've tried to help you sort it out by zeroing in on a few choices in each category, and assembling the key information in the chart above.

As a general rule of thumb:

1. The smaller the fruits, the sooner you'll have your first ripe tomatoes.

2. Determinate tomatoes produce earlier and over a shorter period of time. Indeterminates show their first ripe tomatoes later but continue to produce over a much longer time span.

Rose Marie says: After helping gardeners find satisfaction with tomatoes for some 20 years, I offer this advice for people with limited space: choose one highly reliable "mainstay" variety, such as Big Beef or Celebrity, and then try one or more others, as much as your space will permit, just for the fun of it.

Note that here, days to maturity given here are counted from time of transplanting, *not* time of starting seeds.

■ Full-size Tomatoes (3 inches or more in diameter).

Big Beef (indeterminate, 73 days) is a strong new hybrid of the classic beefsteak type—those big whoppers that you can barely hold in one hand. It has broad disease resistance, matures earlier than other beefsteaks, is very productive, and has a fabulous flavor—no wonder it's an All-America winner.

Celebrity (determinate, 72 days) is a medium-large tomato with a nice flavor; another All-America winner. **Oregon Spring** (determinate, 60 days) has medium-size tomatoes, often seedless or nearly so. This variety handles cool temperatures better than most.

Jet Setter (indeterminate, 64 days) produces lots of good-size, good-tasting fruits. It is remarkably early for a full-size tomato, and has multiple disease resistance. This is a relatively new variety that is destined to be around for a very long time.

Early Girl (indeterminate, 66 days) and **First Lady II** (indeterminate, 66 days) are similar to each other: rich red, midsize tomatoes that are ready early.

Champion (indeterminate, 65 days) has large, tasty tomatoes and good disease-resistance. **Lemon Boy** (indeterminate, 72 days) produces midsize tomatoes that are a beautiful lemon yellow in color and have a pleasant, mild taste.

Brandywine (indeterminate, 85 days) is currently the best-known and most popular heirloom tomato. The tomatoes are large, pink-tinged in color, and may be a bit lumpy in shape, but with a powerful, honest-to-gosh tomato flavor that will curl your toes. This is a large plant that needs serious staking. You will get fewer tomatoes than from modern hybrids of similar size, but once you taste the tomatoes, you won't care.

■ **Salad-size Tomatoes** (1½ to 3 inches in diameter). **Tumbler** (determinate, 55 days) was specifically bred for hanging baskets. The plants are bushy rather than lanky, and nicely fill a large hanging container. The tomatoes are small, salad size (approximately 1½ inches in diameter), with a very nice flavor.

Sweet Cluster (indeterminate, 72 days) produces clusters of 2-inch tomatoes in a long spray of six to eight fruits. Commercial growers harvest them in clusters, and ship to retailers with the tomatoes still attached to the stems. These are the elegant and pricey "ripe on the vine" tomatoes that you have no doubt admired in the produce market.

■ **Plum Tomatoes** (oval shape). These tomatoes are sometimes known as Romas, after an early variety named Roma that is, incidentally, still available and popular with many gardeners. Because they have a greater proportion of flesh to juice than other categories, cooks prefer them for tomato sauces, and so they're also sometimes called sauce or paste tomatoes. But don't let that nomenclature deter you; they are terrific for fresh eating.

Plum tomatoes may be as small as 1½ inches in length, on up to 3 inches, and nearly cylindrical, with almost the same diameter for their whole length. When sliced crosswise, they make circles of a consistent size, which are very attractive for an arranged salad or vegetable tray.

Italian Gold (determinate, 70 days) tomatoes are a deep yellow in color, almost orange; good yield, good disease resistance, and a very rich taste.

Viva Italia (determinate, 76 days), a red Roma type, has an unusually high sugar content, making it as nice for fresh eating as it is for your favorite homemade tomato sauce recipe.

■ **Cherry Tomatoes.** **Gold Nugget** (determinate, 60 days) is a delight: compact plants (2 feet high) produce scads of bright golden cherry tomatoes in a relatively short time frame. This variety is just about perfect for a container tomato.

Sun Gold (indeterminate, 62 days) tomatoes are not really gold, but more of a red-orange. High sugar content gives them a sweet taste.

Green Grape (indeterminate, 75 days) tomatoes are fun to grow because of their unique color: at the eating stage they're still green, with just a tinge of yellow showing. Sample a few to test for ripeness. The vine is a rambler, and needs pinching back now and again; fruits are the size of a very large green grape.

Tiny Tim (determinate, 60 days) plants are real dwarfs, just about a foot tall, with small red fruits. If you're planning a large combination container and need a "tomato garnish," this is it.

CHAPTER 8

HERBS

Ask either of us to name our favorite plant, and you might as well ask a parent which child he or she loves more. It's an impossible question. However, there's no denying we both have a special feeling for herbs. Rose Marie comes by her passion naturally, for her parents began their herb business, Nichols Garden Nursery, when she was a small child, and it's been the center of her professional life ever since. Maggie is much more of an amateur, with only the experience that a small personal garden can contribute, but her delight in these wonderful plants is increased by a lifelong interest in popular history. Some of the most intriguing threads in the story of humankind start with our understanding (or misunderstanding) of the plants around us, and the legends, lore, and botanical history associated with the plants we call herbs are especially intriguing.

In the broadest sense, herbs are usually defined as plants that have a strong utilitarian focus; they may be used as flavoring for food, as medicine, as dyes, for household products or personal cosmetics, or for floral crafts. In earlier days they were the only medicines available, but today most of the interest is on culinary herbs, and certainly that is the focus in this book.

You have only to try a small container of rosemary or a collection of basils to realize how magical these plants are. When herbs are growing right by your elbow, you come to know and admire them in a way that simply isn't possible when your exposure is limited to commercial versions. As the gardener, the steward, you get to watch each plant as it changes with the seasons, from sassy little shoots or bright new growth appearing in spring through robust, full-flavored leaves in summer to fading foliage as frost arrives. With your own hands you help the plant pass through these phases, and that gives you a tremendous feeling of accomplishment.

Herbs touch all our senses. Walk around your patio garden, lightly fondle the leaves of nutmeg thyme or lavender, and then inhale the wonderful

Drying Herbs

Your herbs are so successful, you have more than you know what to do with. You prune the thyme and the rosemary to keep it in shape, and end up with more snippings than you can immediately use. Your basil is going along like gangbusters at the end of summer, when suddenly the weather forecast calls for an early cold snap and you know you have to cut all the basil *now*.

What to do with all the excess? Do what gardeners and cooks have done for thousands of years: dry it, and store it for use later on.

Drying removes from the plant the moisture that is naturally contained in its cells, thereby making it impossible for the leaves to decay. It's a preserving process, pure and simple. In theory, fully dried material will last forever; but with herbs, the chemicals that make the herb aromatic and flavorful gradually dissipate with time, so dried herbs lose much of their potency after about a year—by which time you'll have another garden crop on hand.

The process of drying is not at all complicated—you can do just fine by tossing a few snippings on a paper towel and letting them stay there until you remember to check—but it helps to keep a few things in mind.

1. Unless the leaves have mud splatters from a recent rain, you need only the lightest rinsing to remove air pollutants. Careful consumers thoroughly wash produce from the market to remove any trace of pesticides, but you haven't used any toxic sprays on your edible plants.

2. Find a spot indoors that is warm and has good air circulation. An attic is perfect, if you have one. If not, look up: anyplace near the ceiling is a bit warmer than the rest of the room. A great spot is the top of the refrigerator.

3. Next, decide how you will place the herbs in that spot. This is primarily a question of volume. If you're drying just a small amount at any one time, you can simply lay the branches out flat on a paper towel or paper plate. For larger quantities, you'll get better efficiency of space if you bundle them together and hang them upside down from something, such as a curtain rod or wooden dowel temporarily hung from the ceiling, or high up on the wall spanning a cor-

fragrance that your fingers now hold. There's nothing like it, and only those wise enough to grow their own herbs can experience it.

You may, if you need additional inspiration, think in terms of convenience. With a container herb garden, you're much less likely to be in the position of not having the herbs you need for a certain recipe. You will also, it's worth pointing out, have them fresh, which is almost always superior.

Herbs may well be the perfect plants for container gardens. They tend to be small, good looking, not particularly fussy (most of them, anyway), and well behaved. In this book we include only the herb plants that ner. Even a broomstick laid across the backs of two chairs will work.

To fasten the bundles to the dowel, use a rubber band, which will hold tightly even when the stems dry and shrink. Wrap the band around the stems once or twice, leaving some slack. Hold the bundle along one side of the dowel, then pull the slack part of the rubber band underneath the dowel, up over the top, and loop it over the stems on the other side.

4. Leave everything where it is until it's dry, which will take anywhere from a few days for small leaves to a couple of weeks for larger ones. They're ready when they crumble as you scrunch them. It's counterproductive to leave them longer than that; all they'll do is collect dust.

5. Strip the leaves from the stems. If the leaves are large (such as with some basils), you can either leave them whole, in which case they retain their flavor better, or crumble them now, in which case they take up less storage space.

6. Store away from direct sunlight in glass containers with a tight-fitting lid; avoid plastic, which often imparts a hint of "eau de plastic" to whatever it contains.

7. Label the jars. All little dried green things look alike, and even though you think you'll remember which is which, chances are you won't.

Drying *seeds* (from fennel, for example) is a slightly different process. The traditionalist's method is to let them dry on the plant, and hope you can catch them just at the right point before they fall to the ground. An easier way is to use your oven.

When the plant has formed a seed head and it has started to dry out (it will be brown and brittle), snip off the entire seed head with clippers. Working over a large bowl, scrunch the seed head in your hand to dislodge the seeds; discard the dried stems and other plant parts.

Set the oven at the very lowest temperature, which if you are lucky is less than 200°F. Spread the seeds in one layer on a cookie sheet or pie tin, and dry them in the oven until all the moisture is gone. To check, remove the cookie sheet and let the seeds cool, then try to bend one in half. If it's still flexible, it's not ready yet.

are appropriate for containers, and where applicable we suggest the specific varieties that will work best for your container garden.

Although we've included a separate chapter on edible flowers, don't forget that *all the flowers of herb plants are edible*. They are usually not especially showy in size or color, but as dainty garnishes they add both a nice taste and a tender charm to many dishes. Finally, just in case you were wondering how the word is pronounced: Rose Marie says "herb," like the man's name. Maggie says "erb," with a silent "h." Whichever you prefer is fine with us.

Herbs

Basil

GROW AS: **annual**

PLANT SIZE: **1 to 2 feet**

START WITH: **seeds or transplants**

HARVEST SEASON: **summer**

SUN REQUIREMENTS: **full sun**

MINIMUM SOIL DEPTH: **8 inches**

Of all the so-called sweet herbs, basil is probably *the* all-time favorite. It's the one that grabs you with its aroma when you walk past it in the garden, enticing you to find it, rub its leaves, and smell its goodness in long, wonderful inhalations. It's also a pretty plant and one of the most versatile of all herbs, for it goes with almost any dish, from fresh vegetables and salads to fish and meat to rice and pastas and even fruits. But of all the foods it enhances, basil has a special affinity for tomatoes. The two go together in a way that is absolutely magical. Fresh minced basil, fresh tomatoes, diced onion, a little olive oil or balsamic vinegar, and you've created a masterpiece.

People whose only access to herbs begins and ends with those little bottles of dried green flakes at the supermarket may assume that basil is basil. But gardeners have an amazing world of basils waiting to be discovered: flavored or scented types, and varieties with different colors and shapes. As we become more attuned to good nutrition, and as our palates become more adventurous, growers have responded with wonderful new varieties of many herbs, including basil. Scanning two or three seed catalogs will generally turn up a good 18 to 20 different kinds.

We encourage you to read the catalog descriptions and keep an eye out for the unusual. Be bold. A few leaves of cinnamon basil may be just the right note for a fruit compote or cheesecake. A citrusy lemon basil or the new lime basil is a very sophisticated addition to teas and cold summer drinks. Clove basil adds a spicy warmth to peach cobbler, and the hint of anise in licorice basil perks up homemade tomato soup.

Basil Basics. In all but the most tropical parts of the country, basil is considered an annual. It craves heat, and simply will not start growing vigorously until hot weather settles in to stay. But if you can provide the warmth, you'll find basil easy and rewarding to grow in containers. The plants mix well with other herbs and flowers, and some make nice little borders at the edges of large containers of taller plants. Basil is the ideal herb to grow around your tomato plant.

Planting. Basil presents a perfect example of the classic seeds-or-plants dilemma that gardeners so often face. Starting with the premise that you will want to try several different varieties and that you'll probably want just one plant of each, we believe it's easier to purchase small plants at the garden center in late spring. Unfortunately, some of the newest and most interesting varieties won't be available at your garden center, so you will have no choice but to buy seeds and start them yourself, which means that ultimately you'll have about a million little seedlings to deal with. At that point you have two choices: select the best-looking ones for yourself and send the others off to the garden gods with silent thanks, or put the extras in small temporary containers and share them with friends.

Starting seeds yourself means reading the catalog or seed packet description about the germination period, and then back-timing from the date your true summer usually arrives. To give you a rough idea, it takes about 90 days from the time you plant seeds of the common variety called Sweet Basil until you can begin harvesting the leaves. Review the general directions for seed starting on pages 54 to 60, and remember: don't start the process too early or you'll have seedlings that are ready to go outside before the weather is warm enough.

When it comes time to plant the basil in your big container (either your own seedlings or ones from the nursery), start with an all-purpose potting mix with a bit of sand and dolomite lime added. There's nothing particu-larly special about planting basil. Set it into a planting hole in the container at the same level it was in the starter pot. Firm it in, water just enough to settle the new soil, and it's on its way.

Success with Basil. Like many of our most popular herbs, basil is a Mediterranean plant and develops its best flavor when the temperature is sizzling hot and it is allowed to go slightly dry between waterings. Big, lush plants with soft leaves and stems may be pretty, but they are *not* the most flavorful.

To ensure strong, healthy basil plants, don't plant them too early. Wait until the nighttime temperatures do not dip below 50°F. If the weather is not cooperative and you simply cannot wait, you can cheat a bit by covering the young plants with a protective cover (see page 55) on those nights when the weather is iffy.

Feed once when first planted, then again about mid summer, with a high-nitrogen plant food. Also, take a light hand with watering. Water the young plants very sparingly until they start to show signs of new growth. Then water enough so that the plants don't wilt, but be on guard against overwatering.

Keep an eye on the weather conditions as summer draws to an end. Cold temperatures just stop basil in its tracks, and even the merest hint of frost, so light it wouldn't harm other plants, can be fatal. The first time you come outside in early September and see that your erstwhile beautiful basil has turned black overnight, you'll never forget it and you'll be very watchful thereafter.

Harvesting. To harvest enough basil for tonight's supper, simply snip off a few leaves. To keep the plant bushy for the season, pinch off an inch or so of the growing tips as each new branch develops. This forces the plant to grow side branches, which will give you even more tips to harvest. Eventually the plant will flower, and the pretty flowers are also useful, but the most flavorful part of the plant is the growing tips, and you can keep them coming until cold weather arrives by regular harvesting.

This continuous harvesting honors the basic rule of plant growth: when you remove the growing tip, buds lower down on the stem are stimulated to open. However, new research has shown that with basil there comes a point of diminishing returns. Regular pinching keeps the plant looking tidy and well shaped, but eventually it seems to have the effect of stimulating flowers rather than the foliage that most cooks are interested in.

Decide what you want to achieve. If looks are as important to you as utility, keep up the pinching and you'll have handsome plants that produce both lovely flowers and an adequate supply of leaves. But if your goal is maximum production of leaves, you can turn your plants into little basil factories with the following technique. It may seem drastic, but it works.

As soon as you see flower buds forming, cut the main stem all the way back to the point where just four leaves are left. Then give the plant a light dose of fish fertilizer, and it will quickly grow new leaves. Use the leaves you cut off to make a nice batch of pesto or basil vinegar (see page 257). Any extra leaves that you don't use fresh can be dried.

In the late summer or fall, as weather becomes a problem, you can dig up a couple of basil plants and repot them into smaller containers for indoor use. On a sunny windowsill or under grow lights, they will continue to provide that luscious flavor for which there is really no substitute.

Varieties. The variety called **Sweet Basil** is the standard, and probably the easiest to grow. **Red Rubin,** a softly colored purple version of Largeleaf Italian, is ornamental and very sturdy. Another handsome purple-leaved basil is **Purple Ruffles,** an All-America winner in 1987. As its name implies, it has gorgeous foliage, deeply fringed and ruffled, and soft rosy lavender flowers; use this as a salad garnish. The purple basils frequently have a flavor that edges toward bitterness; many people look on them as more decorative than culinary, and there is no doubt they make absolutely stunning rose red vinegar.

Several varieties grow into small, round globe shapes that stay tidy and compact; two names to look for are **Globe** and **Spicy Globe. Siam Queen,** an All-America winner, is the one to use for authentic Thai flavor; it's also quite good looking, with large green leaves nicely set off by rich purple stems. **Lemon Sweet Dani,** another All-America winner, is a robust plant with an intense lemon fragrance, ideal for seasoning fish and salads. And of course, don't forget the two favorites for making pesto, **Largeleaf Italian** and **Genovese.**

Herbs

Bay

GROW AS: **small tree**

PLANT SIZE: **to 5 feet**

START WITH: **plant**

HARVEST SEASON: **continuous**

SUN REQUIREMENTS: **full sun with afternoon shade**

MINIMUM SOIL DEPTH: **10 to 12 inches**

Homemade soup or stew gets that extra aroma and distinctive taste from simmering a couple of bay leaves in it, and a pot roast just wouldn't be the same without the flavor of bay. Unlike other herbs, whose flavorful oils are quickly dissipated by heat and thus are added at the very end of the cooking process, bay leaves need more time—30 minutes or more—to release their flavor. Dried bay leaves are readily available in the spice section of every supermarket, but fresh ones give you the best flavor. However, if you need to prune your bay tree to control its size—and eventually you will—by all means dry the leaves you remove, and share them.

As an ornamental plant on a big-city high-rise balcony or a suburban ground-level patio, a bay tree is the perfect focal point around which you can arrange a collection of potted herbs to create a visually pleasing container garden. Decorative pots of thyme, rosemary, winter savory, or winter pansies all make excellent companion plants to the dark green foliage of bay.

Bay Basics. The first thing you need to realize is that, unlike other herbs, most of which are small in size and modest in demeanor, bay is a *tree*. Grown in the ground, it can easily reach 10 or 15 feet. In your container, with regular pruning, you can keep it at whatever size works best for your space; 5 feet is a good workable height, allowing you to reach all the branches. Bay is a slow-grower and will need five years to reach 5 feet.

A bay tree is a very handsome plant, and one you might well choose for a container garden just on the basis of looks, even if the leaves were not so wonderful as a seasoning. It is evergreen, so you can pick leaves fresh from the plant as you need them year-round; it also lends itself well to pruning, shaping, even topiary. And it has other uses besides cooking. A few leaves placed in the pantry with the flour, pasta, rice, and

Root Pruning

Most trees grown in containers will eventually get too large for their pots. When that happens, you have two choices: move the tree to a larger container, or trim the roots. Root pruning will control the size of the tree, and if you do it every three or four years, you can keep the tree growing in the same pot almost indefinitely. It seems brutal, but actually it's good for the roots and hence the tree. This is how you do it.

First, take the bay tree out of its pot. This can be a tricky operation if the tree is large. If you were terribly clever you could have built a special wooden container with removable sides. But if you didn't, recruit a buddy to help. Lay down a protective plastic sheet, carefully tip the container on its side, grasp the trunk at the soil line, and gently pull. One of you should hold the pot steady while the other pulls out the tree. Try to keep the root ball as intact as possible.

You'll likely see a lot of roots growing around the sides of the pot, and may find the center of the root ball very dry. This means the roots are so tightly packed that water isn't able to penetrate. With a large, sharp knife, slice off about 2 inches of the bottom of the root ball and slice an inch or so of soil and roots from around the sides. Next, cut three or four long slashes down the length of the root ball, going about 1 inch deep. This technique will help the plant to grow healthy new roots. Just add some fresh potting soil to the bottom of

the pot, set the trimmed root ball back in, and fill in with fresh soil around the edges.

This is also the time to do some pruning and shaping at the top of the plant. Remove any branches that are broken, rubbing against another branch, or growing in a direction you don't want. Then, to compensate for the root loss, trim the remaining branches so they are somewhat shorter, about two-thirds to three-fourths of the original length. This pruning is not absolutely necessary, but in the long run the tree will be better for it, and in the meantime you can dry the leaves from the pruned-off parts.

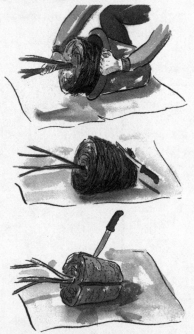

Root pruning is needed when a large plant is rootbound and no larger container is available. First remove the plant and intact soil ball. Cut away the mat of roots at the bottom, and slice the sides vertically to promote new roots.

beans will help to ward off meal moths and grain weevils. Toss a few leaves in your pet's bed to discourage fleas and mites. Or simmer a few leaves in a pan of water and inhale the steam to clear a stuffy nose.

Planting. You can buy young bay plants in most nurseries: anything from a small starter plant in a 6-inch pot in the herb section to a 3-gallon plant in the shrub section. It's probably a good idea to start with a pretty good size, at least a 1-gallon pot. This way you can harvest leaves the first year without denuding your young tree.

A basic potting soil will do just fine, but add about a teaspoon of dolomite lime per 5 gallons of soil to the container in the second year, and every couple of years thereafter. Don't cover the top of the root ball with more than ½ inch of soil.

The bay tree will be perfectly happy in a 3- to 5-gallon pot for about three years before it needs to be moved to a larger container or be root-pruned (see box at left). You can save yourself the chore of repotting if you start it off in a large pot, perhaps filling in with annual herbs or flowers in the first few years. Also, think about your climate as you choose your permanent container. Keep in mind that this is a plant you will have year after year, and that means some long-range planning. If your winters are very cold, you'll need to move the tree and its container into a sheltered location, so start off with a container that is portable, either with casters or on a wheeled dolly.

Success with Bay. There are only a couple of things you can do wrong with a bay tree, and one is to let it freeze. Most nursery professionals say 20°F is the lowest recommended temperature, but that's for trees in the ground. Remember that a plant is much more susceptible to cold damage when grown in a pot, where all sides are exposed to the weather. So when the temperatures start to drop in early winter, gradually begin moving the plant to a protected area, such as a sunporch, where it won't freeze. Give the bay plant as much light as possible through the winter before you move it back outside in late spring.

The other error gardeners succumb to is the dual temptation of overfeeding and overwatering, which can cause root rot and can lead to soft, weak leaves with little flavor. Since the bay tree is very slow growing, it needs to be fertilized only once in the spring, when new growth starts, and again about mid summer. Bay is fairly drought-tolerant, so don't be too eager with the watering. The soil should drain well and not be soggy.

Occasionally you'll find two leaves of your bay stuck together by what looks like thick, cottony webbing. Actually, it's the larva of a moth, and there will be a small green worm between the leaves if you pull them apart. If left alone, the worm will chew holes in the leaves, so grit your teeth, close your eyes, and pinch the leaves together to squish the intruder. Pick the affected leaves off and throw them away; new ones will grow.

Another problem you might encounter with bay is scale. These are the same waxy oval spots you find on citrus trees; remove them with a cotton swab dipped in alcohol. Because we live in a world with a lot of air pollution, it's a good idea to give the entire plant a good shower once in a while. This will keep the leaves clean and fresh and the plant looking healthy.

Harvesting. You can pick or cut the leaves off your bay tree all year long. Select mature leaves, which will have the best flavor. They're the dark green and slightly leathery ones farthest from the tip of the branch.

Bay leaves should be used whole during cooking but removed before serving. This is very important. Sometimes you'll see cookbook instructions to crumble a bay leaf into a dish as it is cooking. Do *not* do this. Whether fresh or dried, bay leaves are very stiff, with sharp edges that do not soften with cooking. There have actually been reports of people sustaining cuts in the throat and esophagus from the sharp edges of a bit of bay leaf they did not see. If you leave the leaves whole in cooking, it's easy to remove them before serving.

Varieties. This is perhaps an excellent time to remind you about botanical names. The one and only sweet bay is *Laurus nobilis*. Be on guard against other plants that may be called bay but are not acceptable for culinary use. For example, there is *Umbellularia californica,* known as

The Noble Herb of Apollo

In the legends and folklore of herbs, the herb most associated with nobility is bay. Even its name—*Laurus nobilis*—attests to its honored status, which can be traced back to Greek mythology.

Apollo, one of the primary Greek gods, was smitten with the beautiful young maiden Daphne, but she spurned his affections. The more he pursued her, the more she resisted. Finally, she turned for help to her father, the river god Peneos; to make her unavailable, Peneos turned Daphne into a tree—the bay.

Ever after, Apollo claimed the bay as his personal favorite, and decreed that its leaves would be used to honor excellence or great courage. That is the origin of the Greek tradition of crowning heroes (including Olympic athletes) with garlands of bay leaves. In our day, this symbol of excellence is perpetuated in the terms *poet laureate* and *baccalaureate*.

California bay and sometimes marketed as the herb. It's a handsome shrubby tree, but has a strong, rank flavor you'd never want in your food.

The true bay, known as sweet bay, has some charming cultivars. One is the very pretty **Willow Leaf Bay,** with twisty leaves and droopy foliage like a willow. **Golden Bay** is much like the standard bay, but the leaves, when they first appear, have a very pretty golden cast that diminishes as the season progresses.

Herbs

Borage

GROW AS: **annual**

PLANT SIZE: **2 to 3 feet or more**

START WITH: **seeds or plants**

HARVEST SEASON: **spring through fall**

SUN REQUIREMENTS: **full sun**

MINIMUM SOIL DEPTH: **8 inches**

Borage is an aggressive, self-sowing annual native to the Mediterranean. In open ground it can become a very large, multibranched plant, with big hollow stems covered with bristly hairs, and thick, juicy walls. Confined to a container, it's much better behaved. The leaves are large, coarse, gray-green, and bristly; in fact, the whole plant appears to be covered in some kind of coarse silvery hair. Borage is a lovely sight when backlit by the early-morning sun. But the real glory of this herb is its flowers.

The flowers grow in airy clusters from stalks that originate in the "V" where a leaf joins the stem, and then continue to form until frost. The star-shaped blossoms are an astonishing blue color. In the center of each flower is a raised crown of pure white, and out of that rises a tiny star-shaped cluster of jet black, whiskerlike stamens. Each flower measures slightly less than an inch across. Nothing else adds that sparkling blue color to your containers.

The exquisite flowers are edible, and can be used in many ways by creative cooks. Crystallized (see page 180), they become "candy stars" to decorate a cake or delight a child. They will keep in the refrigerator for several days. Make lots of extra candy stars and store them in airtight containers to serve as a garnish for ice cream at winter birthday parties. Freeze some in ice cubes to serve in cold drinks. Fresh flowers can be strewn over a salad; they have a cucumber-like taste. The tender new leaves also taste like cucumber, and can be used in salad before their bristles develop.

Crystallized Flowers

Fresh flowers that have been pre-served with a coating of sugar are not only a delightful sweet treat but a very beautiful decoration. Small, dainty flowers such as borage and violets, and pretty leaves such as spearmint or sweet woodruff, are exquisite additions to cakes, petits fours, and other small pastries.

The tricky part is getting the sugar to stick. For many years the classic method of crystallizing flowers began with a dip in beaten egg white, and you'll still find this instruction in many cookbooks. But in recent years, concern over salmonella poisoning from raw eggs has made many people hesitate, and rightly so.

Rose Marie has developed another technique that does not use egg but produces wonderful results. Here is her recipe:

Sprinkle one envelope (¼ ounce) gelatin over ¼ cup cold water in a medium-size bowl, and let it soften for about 3 minutes. Add ¾ cup boiling water and stir until the gelatin is completely dis-solved. Chill until the mixture is slightly thickened (about the con-sistency of egg white). Whip the cooled mixture with a fork or whisk until it is foamy. Dip the flowers into this mixture, or use a small brush to apply it to individual flowers. Immediately sprinkle a thorough coating of sugar over the flowers, and set them aside to dry on waxed paper. Store candied flowers in an airtight tin, using sheets of waxed paper to separate the layers.

The late herbalist and edible wild plant specialist Euell Gibbons counted borage as one of his most useful and tastiest plants. Use the leaves in moderation, though, as some people have a reaction to the alkaloids they contain; the flowers do not have the same effect.

It must be said that borage is not a plant for the timid gardener or the very small garden. In the words of more than one experi-enced gardener, it can be a garden thug, hogging all the space. But growing borage in a pot will stunt its growth quite a bit, so there is a place for it in a container garden if you have some "tall" space to give it, and if you're willing to do a little trimming now and then. Remember: the gardener is the boss.

Borage Basics. Unlike many of the herbs in this book, borage is an annual. Its mandate is to perpetuate itself, which it does by flowering and making seeds. Once the first flowers begin to set seed, the plant is heading downhill. You can delay the inevitable for a time by carefully removing all the remaining flowers, or you can simply let nature take her course, giv-ing you the last flush of flowers and then scads of seed to save for next year or for sharing with friends.

Planting. Plants grown from seed perform best, and it's a snap to plant them. In early spring, about a month before the last frost, sprinkle the seeds right into the container where they will be growing. Seeds germinate very quickly, and the small plants grow quite fast.

You may find small plants at the nursery, and you may be tempted to think this would be an easier course. However, because borage forms a large taproot, it doesn't take to transplanting very well. If a nursery plant is your only option, handle it carefully and try not to disturb the root ball as you transfer it from nursery pot to container.

A large container is best, to accommodate the eventual size of the plant. You can grow other things around the base of your borage, such as parsley, basil, or pretty leaf lettuce. Nasturtiums would also be a good choice; they are a pretty color complement to the borage flowers, and will clamber up through the borage plant and give you edible flowers and leaves.

Success with Borage.
Growing borage is about as easy as it gets. The main problem is that it actually grows too well, and will need cutting back regularly.

Because this plant normally grows in rather poor soil, it's not necessary to give it anything special. Use any basic, all-purpose potting soil and minimal fertilizing. Other than one feeding to get it started, it won't need any more fertilizer during the growing season unless it really seems to be struggling. Be a bit stingy on the water, too, or your borage plant (you'll need only one!)

A Colorful Combination

For a sensational mixed planter, put these three together in a large container:

1. Borage, one plant

2. Bronze fennel, in the center

3. Soft yellow flowers around the edges: Moongleam nasturtiums or Lemon Gem marigolds

The wispy, smoky foliage of the fennel is a year-round jewel in moderate climates. The blue flowers of the borage look sensational against flittering bronze fennel, and the shot of clear yellow from the other flowers makes the whole planter sparkle.

To enhance the color scheme, start with a large container that you have painted a rich royal blue in the same shade as borage flowers.

---

could easily get out of bounds. If it does, don't be afraid to whack it back to size; it will recover with some fresh new growth for you. Keep the flowers picked to keep the plant thriving.

Harvesting.
Borage is a robust grower, so just snip off a few leaves for salads. Pick and use the flowers as soon as they start to appear; more will come along almost immediately. Once the plant begins to bloom profusely in mid summer, harvest all the flowers you can for those pretty crystallized confections.

Varieties.
Just one species, *Borago officinalis*.

Herbs

Chamomile

GROW AS: **annual or perennial**

PLANT SIZE: **3 to 9 inches tall, 10 to 12 inches wide (perennial); 1 to 2 feet tall (annual)**

START WITH: **seeds or transplants**

HARVEST SEASON: **late summer, early autumn**

SUN REQUIREMENTS: **full sun to part shade**

MINIMUM SOIL DEPTH: **8 inches**

There's nothing quite as soothing as a hot mug of golden-hued chamomile tea on a frosty evening. The fragrant steam drifting upward has a gentle, lilting aroma, reminiscent of ripe apples. Chamomile tea is valued as a natural sleep aid, as well as a way to ease indigestion or menstrual cramps. A small amount steeped in a hot bath is also wonderfully relaxing, to make yourself sleepy or to ease aching muscles. Shampoos and rinses containing chamomile enhance blond highlights, and you sometimes see this herb listed as an ingredient in mild hand lotions and face creams. Some gardeners value the dried flowers in potpourris because they hold their fragrance and color, and they don't disintegrate.

All you need to indulge in this herbal pleasure is a handful of dried flowers, and homegrown ones have much more body and richness than the dusty fragments in a store-bought box or the powdered contents of a commercial teabag. This delight is well within the reach of container gardeners because the plant is on the small side and naturally sprawls. Tuck a few plants into a pot with other herbs or flowers, or add some to a window box, where they can spread out even more. If the plant thrives, you can get a surprisingly good harvest from even a single specimen.

Chamomile Basics.

There are two kinds of chamomile: the so-called German chamomile (*Matricaria recutita*), which is an annual, and the one known as Roman chamomile (*Chamaemelum nobile*), which is a perennial. They are similar in many respects, but also different in significant ways. German chamomile grows into a small, upright shrub with tiny, daisylike flowers sitting atop the feathery stems. Roman chamomile grows in a completely different fashion—small, spreading mounds stay low to the ground—but the foliage and the flowers resemble the German. The German type is far better for tea; although the Roman has a sweeter fragrance while it is growing, tea made from its dried flowers has a bitter taste. It is also the German that is most commonly used for hair rinses and other cosmetics. And of course a critical distinction for gardeners is that the German chamomile, an annual, has to be replanted each year (although Mother Nature often lends a hand, for this is a faithful self-sower).

Which of the two you plant is a question of what you want to end up with. For the best-tasting tea, choose German. For a pretty, frilly plant that makes a sweet-smelling blanket underneath other plants, choose Roman. Considering aesthetics and garden design, remember that German chamomile is a tall, upright plant and Roman chamomile is a low, spreading mat. Pay attention when ordering or purchasing seeds, and take special care when buying small plants at the garden center; as young plants, the chamomiles are virtually indistinguishable.

Planting. Both German and Roman chamomile are found in garden centers as small transplants, but can easily be started from seed; follow the general directions in Chapter 5. The seeds are tiny, so you must take care not to sow them too deeply or to let the seed-starting mix dry out while you're waiting for them to germinate.

Seeds of Roman chamomile germinate best in warm soil (70°F); those of German chamomile can get started in cooler soil (55°F). In either case, seedlings will emerge in about 10 days. Keep the pots out of direct light until the plants are a few inches high. At that point you'll probably need to thin them; crowded plants will not prosper.

When you start with transplants, no special treatment is required. Containers of the tougher Roman chamomile can go outdoors in late spring with no trauma, or camp on a windowsill before warm weather fully arrives. Wait for warmer, frost-free weather before putting pots of German chamomile outdoors.

Success with Chamomile. Not only is chamomile completely safe to use, but it is a pretty plant and a cinch to grow.

Although chamomile plants are fairly tough once they're established, they do not prosper if watering is neglected. When they are still young and have not developed a strong root system, they can also be damaged by too much sun. Once they are growing strong, they're practically indestructible.

Harvesting. For tea and for personal cosmetics, it is the flowers you're interested in. Chamomile belongs to the same family as daisies and, like daisies, has flowers that are technically made up of two parts. The yellow centers are actually many tiny, densely packed flowers; this is where

Windowsill Herb Garden

A pretty window garden filled with favorite herbs is a sight guaranteed to warm the heart of everyone who loves to cook.

Start with a narrow planter box, as close to the width of your windowsill as you can find. Choose a window with a southern or western exposure; if it's your kitchen window, so much the better. Check the planter for drainage holes and drill some if need be, then add a tray to protect the windowsill from drips. Fill with potting mix, stir in some granular fertilizer, and plant young herbs.

As they grow, try to keep the leaves away from direct contact with the window glass, which may get too hot in summer and too cool at night.

Recommended plants: chives, basil, rosemary, thyme, sage, chervil, and Fernleaf dill.

the pollen resides and is the useful, beneficial part that you want to harvest. The white petals are technically called "ray flowers"; they make the flowers pretty but have no beneficial properties and should really be removed if you're drying chamomile for tea.

Try not to be impatient and pick off the petals before their time. Chamomile flowers are ripe when the petals begin to curl back toward the center, in late summer or early fall.

You can either pull off all the petals before drying, which is more tedious but less apt to damage the yellow centers, or wait until the flowers are dry. The petals rub off more easily when they are dry, but take care not to scrunch the yellow buttons while you're at it.

Spread the individual flowers on a flat surface and set them in a warm, ventilated spot (see box on pages 170 to 171). After a few days, you'll have a pile of little yellow buttons, ready to be turned into tea or natural cosmetics.

If your goal is to preserve the entire flower for use in potpourri, then naturally you wouldn't remove the petals. Dry entire stems by hanging them upside down, and carefully snip off the dried flower heads.

Varieties. For German chamomile there's just one basic species, *Matricaria recutita*. This is largely true of the Roman kind *(Chamaemelum nobile)* as well, but occasionally in large nurseries you may find varieties of Roman chamomile with special characteristics. One kind, intended as a grass substitute for lawns, doesn't form flowers. Another type has flowers with yellow rather than white petals; it is favored by people who create natural dyes.

For our purposes, the most intriguing Roman varieties are those with double flowers (which means that there are at least twice as many petals, making for a bigger, fluffier-looking blossom). These are often grown solely for their beauty, and are thus a good choice for potpourri ingredients. Look for cultivars named **Pleno, Flore-Pleno,** or **Flora-Pleno.**

Herbs

Chervil

GROW AS: **annual**

PLANT SIZE: **1 to 2 feet tall, 6 to 12 inches wide**

START WITH: **seeds**

HARVEST SEASON: **late summer into winter**

SUN REQUIREMENTS: **partial sun**

MINIMUM SOIL DEPTH: **8 inches**

One of the joys of growing your own herbs is that you can cultivate plants you are unlikely to find in the local market. Chervil is one of these unsung treats, a plant that is not only simple to raise but redolent with wonderful flavor that will enhance all sorts of dishes. It looks a bit like very delicate parsley (indeed, it is a relative), with its frilly leaflets and tiny white umbrella-like flowers.

But its flavor is a world away from parsley's sharp presence. Instead, a tender, lingering aniselike fragrance pervades the tasty leaves and stems, reminding many people of tarragon. Fresh or dried, but especially when just picked, chervil brings a warm yet zesty flavor to salads and soups. (It's a fragrant and delicious constituent of mesclun.) It can also be minced over broiled fish, savory casseroles, egg dishes, and steamed vegetables, or used in place of tarragon in béarnaise sauce. It is a traditional part of the popular French herb mixture known as *fines herbes* (along with dried parsley, thyme, and chives), which many chefs seem to add to almost anything they cook.

For best flavor and texture, add chervil at the very end of cooking. Fresh sprigs also make a novel scented garnish that visitors will exclaim over.

In the past, chervil was touted as a healing herb, useful for aiding digestion and even for lowering high blood pressure. It was also once believed that chervil-infused vinegar would cure hiccups. These claims have not been validated by modern medicine, but certainly the herb is perfectly harmless.

Because chervil is not a big plant—it rarely reaches more than a foot tall, even planted in a traditional in-the-ground garden—it makes a wonderful potted plant. The lacy little flowers are quite pretty as they toss lightly in a breeze. A container perched on a windowsill near a lace curtain is a fetching sight.

Chervil Basics. Unlike most of our popular culinary herbs, chervil is an annual. It will live through a complete life cycle in one year, and nothing you can do will change that. So the best way to enjoy this delightful herb is to start it early, grow it fast, and say farewell at the end of the year.

You know an annual plant is getting close to its demise when, toward the end of the growing season, it suddenly changes from the shape it has had all along into a tall, stretched-out thing with lots of stem between leaves, and a tall flower stalk shoots up above it all. It looks as if someone reached down into the center of the plant and pulled the whole thing upward. This is called bolting, and it seems to happen overnight. Bolting is a necessary part of the life cycle because it is the plant's device for creating seeds and thus ensuring its continued existence. But it is a nuisance for gardeners who are interested in eating the leaves, as most herb lovers are, because quality begins to deteriorate once flowers form.

If bolting really becomes a problem with your chervil, you can always make continuous sowings, starting over in other pots or discarding plants that have gone to seed and reusing the same pot. Fortunately, the young plants grow rapidly, giving you a fresh supply up through late autumn. Even if you somehow manage to save it over the winter, chervil will go to seed in the spring, and you will have lost precious growing time for a new crop.

Chervil tolerates cool weather well, so you can put pots outside early in the year and leave them there well into fall. It does not need as much light as some herbs, so it's a good candidate for a windowsill that gets only part-day sun, perhaps an eastern or western exposure. Outside, it will appreciate some shelter from the blazing midday sun.

Planting. Chervil plants are rarely seen in local nurseries, no doubt because they resent transplanting (they form a long but delicate root). So when you raise them from seed—not a difficult process—keep this in mind and sow them in the pot you want them to stay in all season.

Chervil seeds are fairly easy to come by on seed racks or in catalogs. If there is no herb section in your favorite catalog, check the vegetable section; sometimes chervil gets slotted there.

Chervil seeds need light to germinate. Sow the seeds lightly on top of the soil or in a shallow depression; do not cover them over, or, if you must, sprinkle only the lightest dusting of potting soil over them. Watering at this stage can be tricky because you don't want to flood or dislodge the seeds. Try watering from the bottom (add the water to a drip pan) or spritz from above with a spray bottle set to a fine mist.

Seeds should sprout in about 10 days to two weeks and take hold quickly. When the seedlings are a few inches high, thin so they are about 6 to 9 inches apart.

To grow well in a container, chervil needs a good, well-drained potting mixture. Because the plant can reach 2 feet and stands more or less upright, you'll want to choose a large container that can allow it to grow to its potential; it will look better and you'll get a bigger harvest.

Success with Chervil. For best results, use a good-quality potting mixture that contains a high proportion of organic matter such as peat moss. Keep it moist.

To prevent the plant from bolting (and thus bringing a halt to the tasty harvest) clip off and use the leaves continually throughout the growing season.

Don't set this herb in a hot or exposed location; it really prefers cooler conditions to look its freshest, to produce a good yield, and to avoid bolting.

For the most succulent, delicious harvest of leaves and stems, never neglect watering.

Harvesting. Once your chervil plants reach a decent size (generally six weeks to two months after sowing), harvest the leaves continually so the plant concentrates on producing more foliage. Younger leaves have better flavor, anyway. Note that the outer leaves are the oldest ones. As you remove these, new ones are generated from the interior. New leaves will continue to grow until a flowering stalk begins to rise.

When harvesting, snip off leaves at their base with scissors or a sharp knife. For maximum flavor, use them immediately or store them in the refrigerator, loosely gathered in an open plastic bag, until you are ready.

If you have such a bountiful harvest that you can't use all the leaves at once, you have two choices. You can freeze the fresh leaves and stems; you might mince them first so they're ready to go upon thawing, perhaps on some chilly winter's day when you want to add them to a hearty soup or frittata. Alternatively, you can dry your chervil harvest. Just be advised that the flavor will dissipate somewhat. Oven drying is a good idea because it's fast; then crumble and store everything in an airtight bag or jar.

Varieties. Though they are not always distinguished in catalogs or books, or even on seed packets, chervil does come in two forms. One is plain-leaved and the other is more curly. They do not have separate varietal names, but the difference is apparent even when the plants are very young. Both grow to the same height and are equally tasty.

In Shakespeare's day, most illnesses were treated with home remedies made from herbs, and few doubted that many plants had special, even mystical powers.

In his childhood in Stratford-on-Avon, young Will surely learned about the plants around him by osmosis, as all youngsters do. Later he would incorporate this folk knowledge about plants into his work, turning it sometimes into ribald humor and often into beautiful, lyrical poetry. In his plays people speak of sweet-smelling roses and shy violets, of cowslips, gillyflowers, and cuckoo buds. No one who has watched the haunting scene of the beautiful, mad Ophelia singing and solemnly passing out flowers and herbs to the innocent and the guilty can ever forget that rosemary is for remembrance, that pansies are for thoughts, and that sweet violets, symbol of faithfulness, wither when a loved one is murdered.

Theme Garden

Romeo and Juliet

Shakespeare's audience needed no reference guide to help them decode the symbols and subtle messages; they understood the language of flowers as well as the playwright did. And so they completely understood the joke when the young maiden Perdita, in *The Winter's Tale,* says to Polixenes, father of her beloved:

> Here's flowers for you,
> Hot lavender, mints, savory, marjoram,
> The marigold that goes to bed wi' the sun
> And with him rises weeping. These are flowers
> Of middle summer, and I think they are given
> To men of middle age. You're very welcome.

All the herbs mentioned were commonly used at that time to brew remedies for middle-aged men anxious to regain the physical strength and sexual prowess of their youth. As to the marigolds, Perdita is commenting on their habit of closing up at night and opening in the morning, cupped with dew.

The garden here is designed to honor the Bard, one of his best-loved plays, and all the good people of that era who so cherished their familiar herbs and flowers that they incorporated them into daily life and ritual.

Start with a large, deep container, at least 2 feet wide. Add the most attractive trellis you can find; it should be at least 3 feet tall.

For details on growing the plants in this garden, see

Basil, page 172

Calendula, page 360

Chervil, page 185

Marjoram, page 221

Rosemary, page 242

Tagetes marigolds, page 374

Tomatoes, page 159

The centerpiece of this garden is a new small-fruited **tomato** variety named Juliet. It is an indeterminate type, usually grouped with the cherry tomatoes in seed catalogs, even though the tomatoes are not cherry-round but more oval in shape. They are red when ripe, with a mild, sweet flavor. Juliet was an All-America Selection for 1998, always a good indication of quality.

Set out the tomato transplant once summer weather has really arrived. (If you want to use the container for a spring salad garden in the meantime, be our guest.) Tie the tomato plant loosely to the trellis as it grows.

Underneath the tomato vine, plant two kinds of marigold: Lemon Gem **Tagetes marigold** and **calendula.** In the language of flowers, marigolds symbolize grief, and thus are the perfect complement for a tomato named Juliet. On a more practical level, marigolds are also a beneficial companion plant for tomatoes, helping to repel harmful insects.

But why two? For one thing, we are not completely sure which plant Shakespeare meant by "marigold." The flowering herb we today generally call calendula is also known as pot marigold, and may well have been the marigold of the Elizabethan era. For another, with two different plants you'll have multiple colors (a bright lemon yellow and a deep yellow-orange), multiple textures (frilly, fragrant foliage and larger, dark green leaves), multiple shapes (upright and rounded, sometimes even sprawling), and multiple seasons (flowers from early summer through late autumn).

Be generous with the marigolds. Set the tagetes type close up against the tomato, and position the calendula near the rim so it can more easily tumble over the sides.

You can, if you like, tuck a few herbs in among the flowers. **Rosemary** is closely identified with Shakespeare and would be a fine addition; just remember that it is a perennial, whereas everything else you have planted is an annual. In a mixed container, it's a bit easier to manage all annuals; some nice herbal possibilities include one of the **dwarf basils, marjoram** (the golden variety would look good with your color scheme), or **chervil.**

As a final touch, add two or three hurricane lamps with candles, either nestled in among the flowers or suspended from the trellis. Flickering candlelight is a lovely addition to a summer evening on the patio.

Herbs

Chives

GROW AS: **perennial**

PLANT SIZE: **12 inches**

START AS: **seeds or plants**

HARVEST SEASON: **spring through fall**

SUN REQUIREMENTS: **full sun**

MINIMUM SOIL DEPTH: **6 inches**

Chives are probably the smallest member of the edible and highly aromatic onion family, and in fact resemble miniature scallions. They have small bulbs; narrow, hollow, round stems of bright green with a bluish gray cast; and a taste like very mild onions. They are well adapted to container growing because of their small size and the fact that they grow in tight clumps rather than as a single bulb. Chives are very hardy and quite prolific, multiplying by self-sowing their seeds or making new bulbs.

In the Pacific Northwest, where filberts (hazelnuts) are grown commercially, chives were planted some years ago under the trees to help ward off pests. As the orchards were tilled, the small bulbs were carried along on the tines of the tiller; at the same time, wind and rain scattered the seeds from unharvested seed heads. In some places, the filbert orchards are now completely carpeted with chives—quite a pretty sight in late autumn when the tree leaves are all brown and the dew glistens on the foliage of the chives.

All parts of the chive plant are edible, even the pretty lavender pompom flowers. No matter how small your garden is, even if it's just a kitchen windowsill, you can grow chives. With their spiky upright look, they make a nice visual contrast when grown in a mixed pot with herbs such as sage, thyme, parsley, or basil and some pretty leaf lettuce or spinach. You could plant a border of chives around the edge of a large container of vegetables or a tomato plant. For an indoor garden, a wide, flat ceramic bowl full of chives will look like a small lawn.

Chive Basics. Like the other members of the onion family, chives grow from an underground bulb, but the edible part of chives is the green tops, not the bulb below. The bulbs are left in place to multiply themselves and grow new green foliage. They will do this year after year more or less indefinitely, with only a little attention from us now and then, which is why we consider them perennials.

Be aware, however, that in extremely cold regions, the foliage will die down to the ground for the winter. The bulbs hold the plant energy underground through the coldest weather, and push up new green shoots come springtime.

Planting Chives. Chives are very easy to grow from seed, and you can find packets on any seed rack. But it's even easier, and much more practical, to buy a small pot of them. You can find chives in the herb section of your garden center, and frequently they're also available in the produce section of the supermarket.

All-purpose potting mixture suits chives fine. Plant them in a pot by themselves or in a mixed container, setting them in the soil so just the bulb and about half of the white part of the lower stem are covered. Water to settle them in, and you're done.

Success with Chives. Chives are easy to grow in containers because they need very little fussing to keep them going. Regular watering and light fertilizing are about all you need to do. Chives are not heavy feeders; give them a dose of balanced fertilizer once a month if you are harvesting

them regularly, less often if you don't cut the foliage.

It is okay to leave chives outside in all but the harshest climates; they'll simply go dormant for a few months. You can also dig up a small section of the main clump and put it in a temporary pot for indoors; on a sunny windowsill or under lights, the chives will grow nicely. And if you live in a mild-winter area, chances are your chives will continue growing all year outside. It's probably a good idea to divide clumps of chives after a couple of years anyway, just to keep them growing well and to prevent them from becoming rootbound or crowding other plants in a mixed container.

On occasion you might find an invasion of aphids on your chives, in which case you can simply take the pot to the sink and wash them off. Traditional garden folklore holds that members of the onion family will actually repel insects, but that's not always true. Check your plants regularly so you can catch any possible pest problems early.

Harvesting. To harvest the foliage and flowers of the chive plant, use a pair of clean scissors and clip off the grasslike foliage as you need it, taking a few stems at a time. Cut the stems clear to the base, cutting only what you can use fresh. Then, in the kitchen, snip them up finely and sprinkle over foods, or mix into dips and salad dressings.

Each time you cut off some stems, new ones will grow to replace them, giving you an almost continuous harvest. It's sort of like mowing

The Ancient Chive

Chives were well known in the kitchens of ancient Greece and Rome. It is said that in the English countryside today, clumps of chives grow wherever Roman soldiers camped.

Recipe: *Pasta with Fresh Herbs*

Garden photographer and writer Walter Chandoha has a beautiful garden each year at his home in New Jersey. Walt says: "My Italian son-in-law, Flavio Valentino, gave me this recipe. It is unbelievably quick yet tasty. When I asked him if it should be topped with Romano or Parmesan cheese, he answered very emphatically, 'Absolutely not. Never!' But frankly, when he's not around I not only top it with some cheese but I also add a clove of crushed garlic to the herbs."

1 pound pasta, preferably thin spaghetti
¼ cup chopped fresh parsley
¼ cup chopped fresh basil
½ cup chopped other fresh herbs, such as chives
½ cup extra-virgin olive oil
Salt and pepper, to taste

1. Bring a large pot of water to a boil. Add the pasta and cook until al dente.

2. While the pasta is cooking, sprinkle the chopped herbs over the bottom of a large serving bowl. Heat the olive oil in a heavy saucepan over medium heat. As soon as it reaches the smoking point, remove the pan from the heat and pour the oil over the herbs in the serving bowl.

3. Drain the pasta, pour it into the serving bowl, and mix thoroughly with the oil and herbs. Add salt and pepper to taste. Serve immediately.

Serves 4

the lawn: each time you cut it, it grows back. If you find you're using your chives faster than they can regrow, buy more plants.

If flowers do form on the plant, you can leave them either for their ornamental effect or to make seeds, which you can plant or give to friends. Or you can cut the flowers before they are completely spent and toss them into salads as a garnish. They're very pretty and perfectly good to eat, with a very light oniony taste. Either use the entire blossom, or break it apart into individual florets. The flowers also make a very beautiful flavored vinegar with a luscious pink color.

Varieties. All chives have lavender flowers with the exception of **Forescate,** which has bright rose-colored flowers. (Sometimes you'll see the variant spelling Forsegate; it's the same thing.)

In addition to true chives, you have the option of growing a couple of wonderful but less common alternatives, garlic chives and society garlic. Both provide a nice hint of garlic.

■ **Garlic chives,** also known as Chinese chives. Garlic chives are similar to regular chives but with a few differences. They have a pleasant, mild, but distinct garlic taste. The leaves are flat, with a faint ridged vein down the center. The leaves curve downward in a slight fountain shape, so garlic chives look somewhat like an ornamental grass. The flowers are white and smaller than those of regular chives, and grow in an open cluster at the end of a long stalk.

Garlic chives don't seem to be quite as robust as regular chives; they benefit from more frequent feeding and watering and a warmer, sunnier location. But they are harvested in the same way, by clipping the foliage and snipping it into fine pieces to sprinkle over salads, meats, and vegetables. Don't harvest the bulbs; you need them to keep growing and producing new foliage.

Garlic chives contribute a noticeable garlic taste to whatever they're added to, but they do not tolerate long cooking very well—they turn slimy. Use them in cold dishes or, for hot foods, add at the very last minute, just long enough for the snipped chives to get heated through.

■ **Society garlic.** It's not in the allium family, but it's close enough. The foliage of society garlic has the garlic-chive taste, but the primary reason for growing this plant is its very pretty flowers. The star-shaped lilac pink blossoms are formed in clusters on long stems that sit well above the foliage. The flowers make a good garnish, and the foliage can be chopped and used like chives. In mild climates, the plant is evergreen and blooms year-round. Frost kills the foliage, but it comes back in spring. Typically the leaves are flat and green, but there is a strain with variegated foliage that makes a fine container plant.

Herbs
Cilantro

GROW AS: **annual**

PLANT SIZE: **12 to 36 inches tall, 8 to 12 inches wide**

START WITH: **seeds or transplants**

HARVEST SEASON: **early summer**

SUN REQUIREMENTS: **full sun**

MINIMUM SOIL DEPTH: **8 inches**

This handsome herb has many uses, so it more than earns its keep. The lush, bright green foliage looks a lot like flat-leaf parsley (in fact, one of its common names is Chinese parsley), but the taste is quite different. Cilantro has a unique lemony tang that makes it ideal for many recipes. It is especially popular in Mexican cooking, chopped into salsas or sprinkled atop various dishes as a piquant flavoring and garnish. It appears often in Southeast Asian cuisine as well, including coconut milk–based soups and stir-fries. The trick is to use it often and liberally, because the plant grows quickly and thus goes to seed quickly.

Cilantro Basics. This annual herb gives us two harvests. Cilantro is the name we give to the leafy part of the plant. At the end of the season, the plant flowers and makes seeds that we call coriander. Many people consider coriander a spice rather than an herb, thus complicating the old debate over the difference between the two. The plant does very well in the cooler parts of the growing season (late spring and early summer); in hot weather the lush, leafy growth fizzles out as the plant moves into seed-making mode, eager to reproduce itself before the season ends.

If you wish, of course, you can allow a plant or two to produce flowers. They are indeed lovely—little soft pink- or white-hued clusters that wave atop graceful stalks.

Planting. Cilantro is best grown from seed because a maturing plant forms a significant taproot that doesn't like to be transplanted. Out in a garden, the taproot anchors the plant and helps it survive periods of dry weather. But in an under-size pot, the taproot can hit bottom and result in a struggling or stunted plant; be sure to sow cilantro in a fairly deep container to avoid this problem.

You can certainly start seeds indoors to get a jump on the season, but transplanting takes careful handling, especially of the taproot. So all things considered, you're probably better off starting seeds directly in the container where they will grow, as long as your winters are not so severe that the potting soil is completely frozen at planting time.

Sow the seeds in early spring in a shallow furrow or hole, and cover them lightly but firmly with about half an inch of the potting mix. They will germinate in about two weeks in cool soil (60°F or so). When they are a few inches high, thin out the little seedlings so the ones remaining have room to grow. Or if you started your seeds indoors, move them to permanent quarters at this time; just be sure to handle them gingerly so the developing roots are not harmed.

If you're purchasing plants, your best bet is to go for the ones that are still quite small, that show no signs of flowers or flower bud development. One way to avoid transplant shock is simply to keep them in the pot you bought them in *if* it is deep enough; just sink it into a slightly bigger or more attractive pot if you wish. Or if you want to transplant into your larger containers, do so as early as possible and with great care.

Success with Cilantro. For best flavor and lush, attractive foliage, cilantro must have plenty of sun. Set it on a bright windowsill indoors, or place it in a sunny location on your deck or patio. Because the plants are loose growing and thus somewhat floppy, they appreciate a little shelter from tossing breezes, which can also dry out the plants. As for water, make sure there is always enough. Cilantro is a greedy drinker but rewards the gardener with succulent, delicious leaves.

If you're growing this plant so you can harvest the leaves, you will have to be especially vigilant. Cilantro grows quickly and bolts, or goes to seed, quickly. (Plants that have been transplanted bolt even faster, it seems.) Keep up with watering, and harvest often.

Harvesting. To gather the leaves for use in the kitchen, cut leafy stalks right at the base, at the soil level. Young leaves are tastiest. Older leaves can veer toward a bitter or sharp taste; they look different, anyway, with a feathery appearance that may remind you of dill foliage. Note that dried leaves are virtually flavorless.

For a continuous harvest of tasty leaves, you'll want to make small, repeated sowings every few weeks. Tear out spent plants and reuse the same pot, or start new ones.

If you've had enough cilantro, or want coriander seeds, allow the flowers to bloom and fade naturally. Clip off the seed heads just as they are turning brown; gathered too early, they don't smell or taste good (a bit musty or bitter), and if you wait too long, the plant will dump the entire crop onto the soil. Dry them before using (for instructions on drying harvested edible seeds, see box on pages 170 to 171), and store them in an airtight jar.

Varieties. Today, most seed companies offer varieties that are slower to flower and set seed, and thus the best choice for leafy cilantro. The key word to look for in catalog descriptions is "nonbolting." **Santo** is one such variety, but there are many others.

Herbs

Dill

GROW AS: **annual**

PLANT SIZE: **1 to 5 feet, depending on variety**

START WITH: **seeds**

HARVEST SEASON: **summer into fall**

SUN REQUIREMENTS: **full sun**

MINIMUM SOIL DEPTH: **12 inches**

The pickle industry could not survive without dill seeds, but this refreshing herb plant has much more to offer us than pickle flavoring.

Dill is featured in many dishes from Scandinavia and eastern Europe. The seeds are used in breads, gravies, and sauces, salad dressings, fish soups, and lamb and beef stews. The leaves have the same taste as the seeds, to a lighter degree. Snip them into sauces for fish (dill is a classic with salmon), into light cream soups, into potato salads. Add leaves to cauliflower, green beans, carrots, squash, scrambled eggs, and omelets. Combine with cottage cheese and cream cheese and spread on crackers. Give extra zip to a summer salad of sliced tomatoes and cucumbers by tucking in snippets of dill.

The commercial product labeled "dill weed" is actually dried dill leaves. You can dry your own, but they're much better fresh. This is one of the main reasons to grow dill: to enjoy the fresh leaves, for both cooking and a beautiful garnish.

Dill has several beneficial chemical ingredients that have earned it a place in herbal medicine and home remedies. It has been safely used for centuries as a mild sedative (in the form of a tea) to calm colicky babies and help them fall asleep. In fact the name comes from the Saxon word *dilla,* which means "to lull."

Dill also has the property of easing intestinal gas and promoting good digestion, which may account for its long association with pickles. Many people have difficulty digesting cucumbers (the development of "burpless" strains is a fairly new phenomenon), and dill has constituents that ease that difficulty. Without benefit of modern scientific analysis, the first homemakers who combined cucumbers and dill managed to both solve a culinary dilemma and create a delectable taste combination that endures to this day.

Dill Basics. Dill is in the same family as chervil, cilantro, fennel, and parsley. This is the umbellifer family, characterized by its distinctive flowers: like an open parasol held handle side up. The flower head, which appears at the top of the stem, is actually multiple clusters of tiny yellow-green flowers that ripen into the familiar seeds.

Speaking generally, dill tends to be a tall plant, and even gardeners with a large traditional garden place it near the back of the beds so it doesn't overwhelm its neighbors. It has long, hollow stems and feathery, very pretty foliage that gives the plant an airy, open look.

Planting. Keep in mind that like their umbellifer cousins, dill plants have a long taproot and don't like to be moved. That means they'll be much happier if you direct-sow the seeds in the spot in the container where you want plants to grow. You may find transplants at your local nursery and they will work reasonably well, but starting seeds is so easy,

there's little reason not to do it; also, plants that are direct-seeded are less likely to bolt prematurely.

Traditionally, home gardeners plant dill at the same time they plant cucumber seeds so that the two are ready for pickling at the same time. But container gardeners are not confined to tradition. Plant the first seeds in late April, and more every few weeks for a continual harvest through October, especially if you find yourself snipping lots of the pretty foliage.

In any case, remember that dill is an annual, which means planting new seeds each year—unless you let the seeds ripen on the plant and some happen to fall to the soil, in which case you're quite likely to have dill babies popping up the next spring.

Dill will appreciate being in a container that gives it plenty of room to form a substantial taproot, so start your seeds in a pot at least 12 inches deep.

Success with Dill. Dill is not especially demanding. With lots of sun and regular watering, it will perform happily for you all the way through summer, especially if you remember to sow a few new seeds every three weeks or so.

The taller varieties are vulnerable to wind damage, so add a stake near the main stem or position the container where it has some shelter from the prevailing winds.

If you have your heart set on growing dill, and the only variety you can find is one of the full-size ones, you can keep its height down to a

Dill Doth Make Good Pickles

The association of dill with cucumbers is not a modern invention. John Parkinson, the English herbalist who served as royal apothecary to King James I, wrote about dill in *Paradisus* (1629), the book for which he is best known today, "It is also put among pickled cucumber, where it doth very well agree, giving to the cold fruit a pretty spicie taste or relish."

manageable size if you keep cutting back the main stem.

Harvesting. The pretty, frilly foliage is utterly charming, and we suspect you'll find yourself snipping off bits frequently, to add to many dishes or simply for an intriguing garnish. Once the young plant is about 5 inches high, you can start trimming whenever you like as long as you take care not to completely denude the plant.

Dill will reach full maturity, with flower heads blossoming, about two months after you sow the seeds. An entire flower head makes a spectacular garnish, and adds a unique touch to an arrangement of cut flowers. Or you can add the whole thing to the dish you're cooking, which has the advantage of being easy to remove when the dish is ready.

If you leave the flower head on the plant, the seeds will start to form a week or so later. At this point you can remove the entire seed head and use the still-green seeds in your cooking. Or you can wait until the seeds have turned brown and dry, collect them, and store them in your spice cabinet. (For details on collecting and drying herb seeds, see box on pages 170 to 171.)

Varieties. Most dill plants reach a height that is difficult to manage in a container, unless you have an extremely large pot and want to put together a large, dramatic garden. Specialty herb nurseries and mail-order companies that specialize in herbs sometimes carry varieties they

Dill on Sunday

Dill traveled from Europe to the New World with the English colonists, where it became one of the "meeting house seeds." Every Sunday, some churchgoers prepared themselves and their children for the long sermons by tucking dried dill seeds into their pockets. Whenever the children became restless, parents gave them a few seeds to chew on, and the natural sedative in the seeds would calm the children.

describe as "dwarf," and that's what you want.

Fernleaf is the only dill that is truly a dwarf; at full size it will be at most 18 inches tall. If you want to harvest very small plants, like the baby dill in the produce section at a gourmet market, this is the variety to choose. It is even small enough to work satisfactorily in a windowsill herb garden. The flowers are attractive to butterflies, as well as to humans.

Fernleaf is very aptly named, because it produces a mass of delicate, feathery foliage. Several plants together will give you a beautiful green backdrop for smaller plants with bright colors (red or orange begonias, for example).

Taller than Fernleaf, **Dukat** is still, relatively speaking, on the dwarf side, with a full height of about 3 feet. This variety is an especially good choice if your main interest is in harvesting the seeds, for its seeds are particularly high in essential oil and therefore have more flavor and aroma.

Herbs

Fennel

GROW AS: **tender perennial**

PLANT SIZE: **2 feet tall, 1 foot wide**

START WITH: **seeds**

HARVEST SEASON: **late summer**

SUN REQUIREMENTS: **full sun**

MINIMUM SOIL DEPTH: **12 inches**

In an open garden, fennel is a beast of a plant—tall as a person, lush with sweet, licorice-scented, feathery foliage, and topped with a bounty of flower heads that eventually bear delicious edible seeds. But container gardeners need not be deprived of the glories of this wonderful herb. There's no reason you can't raise a plant or two in a pot, so long as it is deep enough to accommodate the taproot. Your fennel plant will be about half as tall, but there will still be much to admire and plenty to harvest.

Fennel lives a double life as a vegetable and an herb. The stems are as crisp as celery but more flavorful. Though they are anise-scented, they're softer and nuttier than you might expect. Try the stems raw as a finger snack or diced into a summer salad. Or steam them lightly to serve as a side dish; they're terrific with salmon or roast chicken. The lacy leaves are also edible and have the same soft, aniselike taste. They're too thin and frail to survive cooking well, but make a nice last-minute sprinkling atop grilled fish and cold soups.

As for the seeds, they are produced in profusion late in the season and sport a distinctive fresh flavor. You sometimes see them in a bowl on the counter at Indian restaurants, for patrons to nibble on as a breath freshener after a spicy or heavy meal. There's even a fennel toothpaste. In cooking, fennel seeds are popular in holiday breads, Italian sausages, and tomato-based sauces.

Fennel Basics. Some confusion persists about the two types of fennel. The one we have described here is most commonly called sweet fennel, or just plain fennel. We grow it for the delicate foliage, the sweet seeds, and perhaps the edible stalks. The other is usually called Florence fennel, or finocchio, by the Italian cooks who prize its unusual flavor. Finocchio is usually considered a vegetable rather than an herb because you eat the substantial bulb. You may have seen it in produce markets: a broadened, fat base of overlapping stalks that have been trimmed off. It looks a bit like a pregnant celery, and sometimes is mislabeled "sweet anise." Finocchio can be grown in containers, but unlike sweet fennel, it is considered an annual.

Planting. If you plan to harvest the delicious seeds and you have a short growing season, you'd be wise to get an early start indoors. Fennel can take up to 70 days or more to mature.

Press the seeds lightly into the soil mixture and cover them with a half inch or so of soil. They'll sprout in about two weeks and develop steadily. Don't wait too long to move them into their permanent home; remember, this herb forms a taproot.

In a permanent container, a good potting mix that drains well and is not overly acidic is key. Fennel prefers soil on the neutral or even slightly sweet side. Play it safe and add a dash of powdered lime to the pot.

Success with Fennel. The trick to growing this naturally big, bold herb in a container is providing ample space. Choose a big pot and set it in a sunny area with plenty of elbow room so the plant can reach its maximum potential in height and girth.

In the wild this plant and its relatives are drought-tolerant and tenacious. For the home gardener, this means that fennel does not need coddling. In particular you should not be too zealous with water once the plant is established. Your fennel will do just fine with only occasional drinks, unless it is subjected to a period of especially hot, dry weather.

Harvesting. The frilly foliage can be snipped off anytime you need some. The stalks can also be harvested at any time, although younger ones are more tender. Cut them right at the base to inspire the plants to regenerate more.

If it's fennel seeds you want, watch carefully and make your move at the right moment. Seeds are at their most delicious just as they begin to turn from green to brown, right before they are fully mature. Because the flower heads may spill their bounty, clip them off and quickly slip them into a paper bag. Wait a week or two, then shake off the seeds. If you aren't going to cook with them right away, store the seeds in an airtight container in a dry place.

Varieties. The regular sweet fennel has soft green foliage but there is a very beautiful type called **bronze fennel,** which is increasingly available and justly popular. Its stems and foliage are a gorgeous bronze color that glows in sunshine and is especially appealing in combination with other plants.

Florence fennel is not as weather-resistant as regular fennel, so it must be treated like an annual, but it is otherwise identical.

Herbs

Feverfew

GROW AS: **perennial**

PLANT SIZE: **2 to 3 feet**

START WITH: **seeds or transplants**

HARVEST SEASON: **summer**

SUN REQUIREMENTS: **full sun to partial shade**

MINIMUM SOIL DEPTH: **8 inches**

Most herbs are grown for their foliage, but here's one that's full of flowers all summer long. Lovely feverfew is a small, compact plant that literally covers itself in little white or yellow daisies for months. It's tough, too, withstanding all sorts of weather, blazingly hot to cool and misty. Even drought (as when you forget to water it or go on a weeklong vacation) seems not to dismay it.

Because feverfew is so pretty, and because the flowers are so petite (about a half inch in diameter), feverfew makes a wonderful container plant. Grow it all by itself in a ceramic pot, or let it skirt taller herbs or flowers in a bigger container. It's also terrific in a window box—picture it foaming out below a lacy curtain in a white or green house.

Feverfew has one odd quality that is worth mentioning. You may notice, at close range or when you rub the foliage between your fingers, that the plant emanates a sharp, unpleasant scent. This is apparently more noticeable to insects, including bees, which avoid the plant. In fact, if you want bees to come around (for pollination of nearby vegetable plants), you'd be wise to isolate feverfew so it doesn't repel them.

Feverfew Basics. Few herbs are as simple to grow, and grow as well, as feverfew. Just give it some decent, well-drained soil and a sunny spot (it will be okay in part-day sun). Water it as needed; this is an easygoing, thrifty plant that can take a lot of neglect before wilting. Because it is a perennial, and a pretty tough one at that, you'll get to enjoy its pleasures for many years.

Planting. You can sow the seeds indoors in early spring, and move the plants into a pot on a windowsill or outdoors later. Cover them lightly with a dusting of potting soil, and expect seedlings in about two weeks. Be forewarned that feverfew is a lusty germinator, so it's quite possible you'll end up

Feverfew as Medicine

Feverfew was given its common name centuries ago, when it was believed to help reduce fevers. That belief dates from the time, before antibiotics and over-the-counter painkillers, when people depended on herbal remedies created and dispensed by monks from their monastery gardens, and later passed down to apothecaries and pharmacists.

The effectiveness of many of those ancient herbal formulations has been scientifically verified as modern laboratory research has isolated individual chemicals in the plants, while the curative abilities of others have been shown to be total poppycock. Feverfew is somewhere in between.

The potency of this herb as a fever inhibitor has not been documented, but there is new evidence that it can help ease headaches. Recent research has revealed that the leaves contain an anti-inflammatory chemical (parthenolide) that is effective in treating migraines. Demand for feverfew remedies has leapt, and capsules containing its powdered leaves are now available over the counter in health-food stores.

Does it work? The medical jury is still out, but many people believe that feverfew is soothing when they have a headache. And any physician will acknowledge that a condition will sometimes improve if the patient has faith in his or her treatment.

It is not advisable to eat the lacy leaves of feverfew straight from the garden (they have a very bitter taste, anyway). But a tea made from its dried leaves and flowers, sweetened with honey and perhaps perked up with a bit of mint, may be just the thing for your headache. Use it in moderation (think of it as medicine), and while you sip, remember with gratitude those long-ago monks who cared for the people of their villages the best way they knew how.

with too many seedlings. Thin them when they reach 2 or 3 inches high. When they're ready, the seedlings will transplant to new quarters with ease.

Alternatively, buy young plants in late spring. They'll adapt quickly to their new home and be blooming in short order.

If you wish to grow a variety of feverfew that has double flowers, you might have to order seed because most nurseries seem to have only the standard species with single flowers.

Success with Feverfew.

Although feverfew is considered a cinch to grow, it is not a no-maintenance plant. In particular, it will need supplemental water if grown in a small or shallow pot in full sun. In such conditions, a little afternoon shade is also good.

If you raise feverfew from seed, you must thin it at some point. Crowded plants just don't thrive.

Sometimes the plants, though not large, get a bit leggy. To keep them compact and encourage bushy growth, simply pinch off the ends every now and then.

Harvesting. The flowers produce scads of seeds, some of which may fall into the pot but others of which might invade nearby pots or fertile ground; it's wise to clip off the flower heads before they go to seed. Some gardeners are so charmed by the little daisies that they pick them for petite bouquets—which heads the encroachment problem off at the pass.

The fresh flowers make delightful garnishes for many dishes. Dried leaves and flowers can be added to your own personal blend of herbal tea.

Varieties. The basic plant, with single white flowers, is sometimes labeled with the cultivar name **White Single.** A very pretty variation is **Aurea,** also sold as **Aureum.** It has the regular, single daisy flowers but unusual foliage of bright lime green; it looks fabulous in a pot with yellow or yellow-green flowers.

For double flowers, look for **Snowball, White Double, Flora-plena,** and **Flora-pleno;** as you can perhaps guess from the names, all have fluffy white flowers and dark green foliage. **Golden Ball,** sometimes called **Butterball,** has double flowers that are completely yellow, petals as well as centers.

Golden Moss is a dwarf, mat-forming variety with yellow leaves and very full, ball-like white flowers.

Herbs

Lavender

GROW AS: **perennial**

PLANT SIZE: **18 inches to 4 feet tall, 1 to 2 feet wide**

START WITH: **transplants**

HARVEST SEASON: **summer**

SUN REQUIREMENTS: **full sun**

MINIMUM SOIL DEPTH: **8 inches**

Lavender is one of the most enduringly romantic and evocative fragrances in the world. Fresh or dried, its seductive scent conjures up visions of sun-drenched fields in Provence, quaint English cottage plots, and classic herbal knot gardens. It hints of soap and lace and sachets in linen cupboards, of sunlight slanting into windows, of dried bundles in a crafter's studio.

The good news is that even container gardeners can know the pleasure of growing their own lavender. The trick is to grow the right kind, a species or cultivar that stays compact. There are literally dozens to choose from, and we give a few suggestions here. Ideally your choice is also a lavender that repeat-blooms, so you can enjoy it for practically the whole summer—even, depending on where you live, right up through the first frost. You must also give the lavender of your choice the growing conditions that it needs to thrive, but fortunately, this is not difficult.

A handsome container, with or without complementary plants, can make your small but lovely lavender crop a showpiece. Because lavender flowers are not flashy in appearance, you can indulge in a decorative pot, perhaps a ceramic one with a hand-painted design. A generous carpet of, say, creeping thyme at the base of a sturdy lavender plant creates a richly fragrant and attractive sight.

Alternatively, fill a larger pot with several lavender plants of varying heights along with something in golden yellow tones, such as variegated sage or golden marjoram, and you've got a "cottage garden in a pot." (Yellow and purple, which are complementary colors, look especially attractive together.)

Maggie says: I think lavender qualifies as the eighth wonder of the world. I have heard that there are people who don't care for the fragrance, but I simply do not believe it.

So you won't be surprised to learn that the first thing I planted in my new patio garden was several

Recipe: Quick Herb Jelly

Rose Marie says: "Commercial apple jelly, a microwave oven, and fresh herbs are all you need to make delicious herb jelly. Use whatever fresh herbs you have on hand, to make the jelly as intensely or subtly flavored as you like. I make this one jar at a time."

Herbs that we think make good jelly include rosemary, lavender, basil, scented geraniums, sage, thyme, lemon balm, lemon verbena, and mint.

> **2 sprigs (3 inches each) of rosemary or basil, or 5 sprays of blooming lavender, or 4 scented geranium leaves, or comparable amounts of any other fresh herb**
>
> **1 glass jar (10 to 12 ounces) apple jelly**

1. Rinse the herbs carefully, keeping them in large pieces for easy removal. Pat them dry with paper towels.

2. Remove 2 tablespoons of the jelly from the jar and set it aside.

3. Place the opened jar of jelly in a microwave oven, and heat on high for 30 seconds. Add the herbs to the softened jelly and microwave on high until the jelly is just beginning to bubble, about 1 minute. Stir the jelly with a chopstick, heat for 1 minute more, and let cool for 2 minutes.

4. Remove the herbs from the jelly and return the 2 tablespoons of reserved jelly to the jar. Reheat in the microwave on high for 30 seconds, remove from the microwave, and reseal with the original lid. Invert the jar for 10 seconds (the lid will usually reseal itself). Cool, then store in the refrigerator.

Makes 1 jar

lavenders. Then I quickly added other plants, to make lavender/lavender combinations. Did you know there is a lavender thyme? It really is a thyme, and it really does also smell like lavender. Or how about lavender mint, which combines both lavender and mint fragrances in one plant?

Do you think that gives me enough lavender to satisfy my cravings? Of course not. But life is not always fair, and we make do.

Lavender Basics. Lavender is a smallish shrubby plant with long, thin gray-green leaves and spires of tiny flowers at the end of long stalks that reach up above the foliage. All parts of the plant have that marvelous scent. The leaves resemble needles of fir trees except for their lighter color, and they also look very much like the foliage of rosemary, except that the leaves of some lavender varieties are longer than rosemary's.

Most of the flowers are some shade of purple, from dark to pale lavender in color, although a few are pastel pink or even white. Individually, the fully opened flowers look like tiny orchids, the perfect size for garden fairies, but the general sense that you get is not of the individual flowers but of a tall, slender wand covered at the end with a short mass of blossoms. The unopened flower buds have the most intense fragrance, and they retain their heavenly aroma for a very long

time after drying, which makes them a popular ingredient in potpourri mixes; they look like purple grains of rice. Most people consider the flowers the main reason for growing this plant, and if you are among them you'll be glad to know that some varieties have especially long bloom periods, and others put on a second flush of flowers later in the season.

Lavender is a perennial, but not as long-lived as you might wish, especially if you fall in love with it. You'll probably notice after a few years that it is becoming threadbare down in the center of the plant. Careful pruning (explained below) will help, but there comes a point when the plant is just not as lush as you would like and cannot be restored.

In nature and out in the garden proper, lavender loves warmth and a well-drained, somewhat alkaline soil. Such conditions are easy for a container gardener to provide. Indeed, after planting you would be wise to give your lavender plant minimal care; in particular, do not overwater or the roots will rot and the plant will languish. Be aware, too, that in really hot climates it is possible for lavenders to get too much sun.

Planting. It is not advisable to grow lavender from seed because most cultivars do not come true from seed and you'll likely end up with a mongrel plant. Also, these

I n ancient Greece and Rome, the herb lavender was considered precious and was often used to symbolize luxury or to recognize outstanding achievement. Its flower stalks were woven into crowns bestowed on high-ranking citizens during celebrations. It was believed that the asp, a highly poisonous snake for whose venom there was no known antidote, lived in shallow nests at the foot of lavender plants; it took a brave soul indeed to approach and harvest the flowers, which made them all the more precious.

Theme Garden

Lavender Lady

Centuries later, we know we don't have to worry about the snakes, but lavender flowers are no less special. In fact, the entire plant, leaves as well as flower stalks, is suffused with that delicious, haunting fragrance that is like no other, and that many people (Maggie is one) adore. For them, we created this small garden to honor the loveliest of floral herbs.

In the center, in the place of honor, one fabulous **lavender** plant. Surrounding it, two surprising herbs: **lavender mint** and **lavender thyme.** Both of them have the basic herb fragrance and taste you would expect, but both also have an overlay of lavender. The mint will want to take over the pot, so you'll need to keep plucking it out. And the thyme will, with a bit of help from you, spill over the sides of the container, a very pretty look.

To fill in any bare spots and to continue your lavender theme, two edible flowers: lavender-colored **tulips** for the spring, and lavender-colored **pansies** for fall and early winter.

You have two choices of physical arrangement. All the ingredients of this garden can go into one medium-size container (18 to 24 inches); this is less than ideal but workable for a few years. Eventually, the mint, with its invasive roots, will attempt to strangle the others and you'll have to keep yanking it out. Also, you'll have more success with tulips if you plant new bulbs each fall (or lift the old ones in summer and replant them in fall), and this is easier to manage if they are in a separate pot. You can either sink a nursery pot planted with tulip bulbs down into your large container, whence it is easily removed, or put the tulips in their own fancy pot set beside the larger container. Alternatively, you can group several smaller containers together: one with the lavender, pansies, and thyme; one with the mint; and one with the tulips.

Consider painting the outsides of the container a pretty lavender color. And if at all possible, position it near your front door, where visitors will brush against the lavender and release its wonderful fragrance. We can think of no sweeter way to welcome your friends.

For details on growing the plants in this garden, see

Lavender, page 205
Mint, page 223
Pansies, page 382
Thyme, page 278
Tulips, page 405

seeds take a month or more to germinate and even then have a low survival rate.

Instead, go shopping in late spring at a large garden center, or better yet an herb nursery, and let yourself be swept away by the many wonderful choices. Choose plants that are still small. Or browse through the pages of catalogs that feature broad selections of herbs, paying careful attention to the descriptions about the ultimate size of the plants.

If you have access to a greenhouse or a cold frame, or can duplicate those conditions inside your home, you can take cuttings from a lavender plant you admire. All you need is a healthy shoot or two, cut so that a bit of old wood at the base is retained. Dip the stem lightly in a rooting powder (available at garden centers), and set the cutting in evenly moist, sandy potting mix. Cuttings generally root in a few weeks and may be moved into their own pots the following year.

No matter where you obtain your lavender plants, make sure you prepare an appropriate potting mix that drains well, perhaps a traditional potting soil to which some sand has been added. Some gardeners include a spoonful or two of powdered lime to provide alkalinity, and the plants seem to appreciate this. Water well on planting day, and thereafter only occasionally.

Success with Lavender. A warm spot in the sun and alkaline soil on the dry side—that's what make lavender happy. One thing it does not like is muggy conditions. One way around this humidity problem is to keep the plants pruned for good air circulation. Some determined southern gardeners have succeeded by simply covering the base of the planter with white stone gravel; white reflects light and also helps to keep air moving through the plant. If these tiny stones are hard to locate, you can use crushed eggshells instead.

Moderate climates are ideal—not too hot, not too cold. If your winters are mild, with only an occasional cold snap, you can safely leave your containers outside. Simply cover the plant with plastic to protect it from below-freezing temperatures. In areas with more severe winters, you have two choices for keeping lavender over the winter. Start by clipping them back as cool weather approaches. Then either temporarily sink them into the ground and mulch well, or, if outdoor space is not available, bring them indoors. Set them in a spot where they will not be exposed to freezing air or drafts (around 50°F is best) and keep an eye on them, watering very sparingly until spring returns and growth is renewed.

In any climate, the one thing you really ought to do for pot-grown lavender is keep it clipped. Even the compact dwarf varieties will eventually attempt to outgrow their space and begin to look scraggly. Snip the tops lightly and often to encourage bushier growth lower down on the plant.

To do this without sacrificing flowers, prune in very early spring

What's in a Name?

The herb we call lavender is not named for the color, even though most of its flowers are lavender-hued. Rather, it's the other way around: the color is named for the plant.

The genus name, *Lavandula,* is derived from the Latin verb *lavare,* meaning "to wash." Through many centuries, starting with the ancient Greeks and Romans, homemakers have included lavender in the rinse water to impart a clean fragrance to household linens; they didn't know it, but they were also disinfecting.

Lavender was used in medieval times to clean the air in musty sickrooms, and was one of the most popular "strewing herbs" (scattered over the floor and allowed to dry, for an air freshener).

Initially it was the clean fragrance that appealed, and there was also a general sense that the presence of lavender in a sickroom was healthful. Until the beginning of the twentieth century, lavender was even used to dress battlefield wounds.

Now modern science has verified that the herb does indeed have antiseptic properties, and so those long-ago homemakers had the right instinct.

---

when the worst of the winter cold is past. The tips of the branches may be looking a bit greener, but new growth has not really started in earnest. Once your plant is three or four years old and shows signs of dying out in the center, this early-spring pruning needs to be a more serious operation than just tip pruning. Cut each stem back to about half its original length, and you'll be rewarded with vigorous new growth.

You can also do a touch-up pruning in summer when the peak flower production is winding down. Clip the flower stems all the way back into the branches to shape and prune. If you're doing this in very hot weather, we suggest moving the planter into light shade for a few days; newly exposed areas can actually sunburn with sudden ultraviolet exposure. Some types of lavender will put on a new flush of flowers later in the summer.

Harvesting. Both the leaves and flowers are fragrant and worth harvesting. The leaves can be taken at any time, including, of course, when pruning the plants. In some lavenders, they smell almost like rosemary. Lay leaves flat until they are fully dry, a matter of a day or two, then store in an airtight jar.

For optimum fragrance—for making potpourri, sachets, and even cooking—pick the flower spikes early, just before the flowers open. Their fragrance fades quickly if you wait till they are fully open. Harvest early in the day, when the oil is at its peak and before the sun bakes some of it away. Immediately lay the spikes flat on paper in a cool, dry, windless spot out of the sun.

Strip the individual flowers off when they are fully dry (after about a week) and store them in an airtight container; or leave the spikes intact if you are making bundles, tussie-mussies, wreaths, or other decorations. Over time, exposed flower spikes will lose their color and fragrance.

Varieties. Two species of lavender are our choice for container gardeners: *Lavandula angustifolia* and *L. heterophylla*. Fortunately, both of them have many interesting and lovely cultivars, so you should have no problem finding several that will steal your heart.

As a container gardener, you'll also be concerned about size. Both recommended species also include a range of sizes, from dwarf forms, which are a good choice for gardeners with limited space, to medium-size and larger varieties, which make a bigger splash for those who have the room to accommodate them.

English lavenders (*L. angustifolia*) are the most sweetly fragrant of all, and take well to container life. In a well-equipped herb nursery or catalog you'll find numerous cultivars, including several that rebloom; just remember to take into account the height and girth information and choose ones that will fit into your containers.

Two excellent choices are **Sharon Roberts** and **Buena Vista,** both of which bloom strongly in late spring and early summer, then rebloom from fall to frost.

Cultivars of *L. heterophylla* are also superb in pots and are particularly good for warmer climates. These have the added advantage of blooming all summer long.

For maximum drama if you have the space, try **Sweet Lavender,** which has a real presence, reaching 3 or 4 feet tall. It blooms nearly year-round in milder climates, and is hardy to about 15°F.

Herbs

Lemongrass

GROW AS: **annual**

PLANT SIZE: **2 feet tall and wide**

START WITH: **transplants**

HARVEST SEASON: **late summer**

SUN REQUIREMENTS: **full sun**

MINIMUM SOIL DEPTH: **6 inches**

A few years ago, it seems, lemongrass was all but unknown in the United States. Nowadays, with the increasing popularity of Southeast Asian cuisines, this tangy, delicious herb has become more familiar and more widely available.

The name is apt. It is indeed a true grass whose fresh-cut blades waft an appealing lemon scent. Lemongrass is a relative of the sharper-scented citronella and, like that plant, is reputed to repel bugs, including pesky mosquitoes. Our chief interest, however, is the magical flavor it imparts to so many dishes. The tastiest part is not the top grassy portion of the leaves but rather the base of mature stems. Cut and trimmed, they are yellowish and crisp, superficially resembling a blanched asparagus spear or the white part of a scallion. A homegrown plant yields enough stems to flavor at least several savory meals.

A lemongrass plant is unremarkable looking, just a clump of broad, flat grassy leaves, light to medium green in color. Thanks to its origins in the Asian tropics, this is not a hardy plant and thus must be grown in a container in temperate climates. It can get quite large in the ground in its native habitat, but container culture keeps it to a manageable size with lots of branching.

Lemongrass is well adapted to container life, but because it is a tropical plant, it is a bit more demanding than some other pot-grown herbs. In particular, it must be watered often and well, and fertilized frequently throughout the growing season. This plant also likes warm, humid conditions. It is much too tender to survive cold weather, so if you want to keep it going from one year to the next, you need to move it to a greenhouse or greenhouse-like setting and coddle it through the winter months.

In home gardens, lemongrass generally does not flower or set seed, but a happy potted plant will pump out plenty of long blades of grass. To make the display more attractive, grow it in a pretty pot or tuck it in with flowering plants.

Lemongrass Basics. Two species of lemongrass have found their way to the West. *Cymbopogon flexuosis,* with origins in Indonesia, is grown principally for the essential oil that is distilled from it; the intensely aromatic oil is used commercially in soaps, perfumes, and lemon-scented household products, and is also sold for aromatherapy treatments and other herbal remedies. It is not, however, the most satisfying herb for cooking. For culinary use, the preferred lemongrass is *C. citratus,* from Southeast Asia. This is the one that consistently produces the tender white hearts that are added to foods.

Unfortunately, if you're looking at two small nursery plants, you can't always tell one species from the other. To make sure you're getting what you want, order from a mail-order nursery that specializes in herbs and that has proved itself reliable in the past. Two other effective strategies: ask a gardening friend to let you take a chunk when he or she is dividing a plant in the springtime; or look closely at the offerings in the produce section of an Asian market. Sometimes among the bundles of lemongrass stalks you'll find one that still has healthy roots attached (just as we often see with scallions), and you can use that as a starter for your own plant. The one thing you do *not* want to do is buy seeds. The best lemongrass is propagated only by division; any seeds you see are sure to be the inferior Indonesian type.

Don't forget that unless you are up to the challenge of overwintering a tender plant, lemongrass will be an annual. So lavish lots of care on it from the start, and enjoy it while you can.

Planting. Remember, transplants only; don't plant seeds. Lemongrass doesn't require a very big pot; 6 inches deep is adequate.

Success with Lemongrass. Water! This tropical plant soaks up plenty of water and must not be neglected. It is also a greedy feeder, so fertilize every other week with a water-soluble, balanced plant food (but cease feeding as winter approaches).

Put the pot in a warm or even hot spot. Deck and balcony gardeners should not hesitate to give lemongrass a bright, sheltered corner where the summer sun will blaze. Increase local humidity by spritzing the leaves from time to time.

Harvesting. The blades themselves are too tough to eat, as you might expect from a grass. Instead, harvest mature stems, and trim away greenery from above and any roots from below. Peel away the outer layers on the remaining base until you get to the tender white heart, which is the part used in cooking. Slice it and add to a stir-fry, or simmer in a coconut milk–based soup. The warm, rich, lemony tang is truly unique.

Varieties. For culinary lemongrass there's only one basic species, ***Cymbopogon citratus.*** To be sure you get that one, buy labeled transplants from a reputable nursery.

Herbal Gifts from Your Garden

You know how much pleasure you get from the herbs in your container garden; imagine how delighted your friends will be with a gift that enables them to share in that pleasure.

Homemade gifts from your garden and kitchen can be as fancy as you wish, and you'll find many excellent resources for creative ideas at the library or bookstore. Here are a few extremely simple gift items that you can quickly put together from your herb containers. We're not talking about elaborate projects; you don't have to be the Queen of Crafts to manage them.

■ The next time you're invited to a friend's home for dinner, take along a nosegay of fresh herbs. Snip off a few sprigs of whatever is especially gorgeous at the time, and tie them into a bundle with pretty ribbon. It is simple, elegant, and sure to be appreciated by anyone who enjoys cooking.

Maggie says: I keep a spool of thin ribbon, in a pale dusty rose color, by my back door (the one that opens to my patio). It takes at the most two minutes to collect enough herbs for a tiny bouquet. Tying it with ribbon makes it seem more special, more like a gift, and when the ribbon is right there at hand, it's no extra trouble. The rose color seems to go well with everything.

■ From your store of dried herbs, put together a *bouquet garni:* several different herbs tied into a small bundle of cheesecloth, for long simmering in stews and cassoulets. Cheesecloth is sold in fabric stores, cooking stores, variety stores, and hardware stores. Cut squares about 6 by 6 inches, layer several together for extra strength, and pile a small stack of herbs in the center. Bring the edges together, and tie with undyed string. Whole herbs work best (that is, avoid tiny bits that would leak through the cheesecloth). Add a tag listing the ingredients; be sure to make it clear that the tag should be removed before cooking. If the *bouquet garni* is going to be used immediately, you can make it from fresh herbs. Otherwise, use dried herbs. Make a slew of these when you have lots of dried herbs on hand, and store them in an airtight container until needed.

A classic French *bouquet garni* includes parsley, thyme, and a bay leaf. Other good herbs for *bouquets garnis* include basil, fennel seeds, lemongrass, lemon verbena, oregano, rosemary, sage, and tarragon. You can create any combination you like from what you have on hand, perhaps a special blend geared toward fish or one for chicken; include these suggestions on your gift tag.

■ Tea herbs from your garden are guaranteed to warm the heart of any tea drinker. They can be either from one plant, such as spearmint, a combination of several tea plants, or a special blend meant to be added to brewed black tea as a flavorful extra— perhaps mint and lemon verbena, or chamomile and stevia. Present in a small jar with an explanatory gift tag. Even better, make up your own teabags. Several mail-order catalogs listed in the Appendix sell small bags that you fill and seal shut with an iron; they are used just like teabags from commercial tea companies.

■ Herbal vinegar is delicious, versatile, and gorgeous to look at. For directions, see box on pages 257 to 259.

Herbs

Lemon Verbena

GROW AS: **annual or tender perennial**

PLANT SIZE: **3 to 4 feet tall, 2 to 3 feet wide**

START WITH: **transplants**

HARVEST SEASON: **summer**

SUN REQUIREMENTS: **full sun**

MINIMUM SOIL DEPTH: **8 inches**

A wonderfully fragrant plant, lemon verbena has a distinctly old-fashioned appeal. Back when formal meals included a finger bowl at each place setting, it was customary to set a refreshing single sprig in each bowl. Even the O'Hara women in *Gone with the Wind* considered it a favorite scent.

The willowy leaves, even when brushed ever so lightly, whisper a delicate perfume. If you pause to crush or rub them, the lemon fragrance is downright intense. Except for lemons themselves, lemon verbena provides the most lemony fragrance in nature. Not surprisingly, it has been used in years past in colognes and toilet waters. It also makes an intriguing contribution to festive wreaths and pretty little tussie-mussies. (The frail white flowers, tiny and carried in loose sprays, are insignificant and don't last long anyway.)

Lemon verbena is a handsome, shrubby plant that hails from the hot, sunny slopes of Chile and Argentina. As such, it is not hardy in much of North America, and really must be grown in a container. A large, substantial terra-cotta pot or a half whiskey barrel would allow the plant to reach maximum potential, although it will do fine in something smaller. When autumn's cool weather comes and the verbena's leaves begin to fall, you'll have to decide whether this plant you've become so fond of is worth overwintering indoors.

South Americans have a long history of using the dried leaves in teas to treat various ailments, particularly digestive distress, but the taste is so refreshing we don't have to think of it only as medicine. Either by themselves or in combination with other herbs, leaves of lemon verbena brew up into a delicious and refreshing tea.

Lemon Verbena Basics. The shrubby, unassuming looks of this plant can be misleading. It does require regular attention and sometimes careful handling. Feed it often throughout the growing season, slowing down only as winter approaches. Do not water too zealously or the roots will rot.

Remember that unless you live in the south of Florida or southern California, lemon verbena is one of those plants that change with the seasons. When the leaves turn yellow and start to fall each autumn, this does not indicate the plant is dying. It is going dormant and, with proper care over the winter, will return in all its glory the following spring.

There is no way to stop lemon verbena from going dormant, but if you have invested in a large pot, or if the plant has won your heart, do overwinter it. Let it rest in a cool place where it still gets some sun but is not at risk of freezing. Water very lightly during the winter, just enough to keep the soil from completely drying out.

Planting. The plant doesn't often produce seeds, so you're unlikely to encounter them in catalogs or even in a friend's garden. It is, however, easily propagated by cuttings—just coddle the mother plant following the operation. Or purchase small plants from a specialty nursery in spring or early summer.

Make sure your potting mix drains well, because you don't want the roots ever to be sodden. Water the new plant well and start a fertilizing regimen once you can see that it is becoming established.

Success with Lemon Verbena. Even with regular water and feeding, and a good sunny spot, lemon verbena gets attacked by pests. Whiteflies and spider mites are the most common villains. Inspect the leaves every few days, undersides as well as tops; and if you spot signs of either, act immediately. Quarantine the plant, wash the leaves clean, and resort to insecticidal soap sprays if you are really worried.

As with any containerized plant, you want to guard against legginess. Make sure it has sufficient sun, and trim it back to keep it bushy (you'll relish getting these sprigs for your own use, anyway).

Harvesting. Snip off leaves or small sprigs at any time during the growing season. They retain their wonderful scent even when dried. Use them in herbal tea blends, or set a small open basket of dried leaves in the powder room as an air freshener.

Varieties. Just one species: *Aloysia triphylla*.

Picture this: a big shady front porch with a ceiling painted sky blue, and several hanging flower baskets spilling red geraniums. Three people sit side by side in Adirondack chairs, their feet up on the wide rails that surround the porch. On a small table nearby is a plate of oatmeal cookies, and in the spot of honor, where everyone can reach, is homemade lemonade in a huge glass pitcher, the kind with the wide round bottom. Ice cubes clunk when someone pours a refill, and bright slices of lemon bob against the pitcher's fat belly. On the lawn, several children are playing Red Rover. At the end of each round, they thunder up the steps to grab another cookie and slug down half a glass of lemonade. When the game is over and the pitcher is empty, the smallest child reaches in for the last lemon slice, its skin soft and sweet from absorbed sugar.

Theme Garden

The Lemonade Party

It may seem a nostalgic fantasy, but if you had a lawn, a front porch, and the right chairs, you could duplicate that scene tomorrow. But even if you have only a balcony or small patio, you can still create a container garden that pays homage to the memory of that sweet summer afternoon, and not incidentally provides you with the ingredients for a wonderful lemonade party.

This garden celebrates the luscious lemon in both taste and color. It features an actual lemon plant, several lemon-sharp herbs, and edible flowers in bright shades of yellow.

The backbone of this garden is three rather large plants, each in its own pot: **Meyer lemon, lemon verbena,** and Mabel Gray **scented geranium,** whose leaves have the fragrance of lemon. They are all tender plants, and in all parts of the country except the Sun Belt will need to be moved to a protected area for the winter; this is easier to accomplish if they're in separate pots. A good size is 18 to 24 inches in diameter; this gives the plants room to grow but is not too large to move around. To create a visually pleasing collection, use pots of all the same material, size, and color.

Then fill in underneath each large plant with edible flowers. Remember, one of your goals is to have no bare spots in any container. All around the lemon verbena and the young lemon tree, sow seeds of Moon Gleam **nasturtiums,** which have a soft yellow blossom. Underneath the scented geranium, plant tubers of a yellow-flowered **begonia,** with its lemon-tart petals.

Now arrange these three main pots in a pleasing pattern. Variation in height is achieved naturally, as some plants are taller than others, but it would be even better if you could place some of the pots on risers, creating a tiered effect of continuous foliage. If you are setting them against the wall, put the center one on a small riser so it is taller than the others, and place the other two beside it and slightly forward. If your space more readily accommodates a garden-in-the-round, put one container

For details on growing the plants in this garden, see

Begonias, page 352

Basil, page 172

Thyme, page 278

Lemon verbena, page 216

Lemons, page 312

Nasturtiums, page 376

Scented geraniums, page 262

Violas, page 382

in the center, elevated on a short pedestal, and the other two on opposite sides.

Next fill up several smaller containers and tuck them in among the larger ones. In one you could start the spring with yellow **violas;** if you feel like adding another color for accent, include some Johnny-jump-ups, bright purple and yellow. In that same container or another, add **lemon basil** when the summer heat comes on. The violas may survive through the winter, but the basil definitely will not.

Another small container holds **lemon thyme,** which really does have the taste its name implies, and which is quite lovely to look at with its tiny leaves edged in yellow. Raise this one slightly so that the maturing thyme has room to spill over the sides, and so you can more easily approach its sweet-smelling leaves.

Each of the three main plants is (with some wintertime pampering) a perennial. The flowers growing underneath are not; you will plant anew each spring. As time passes and the three perennials get larger, you may find yourself switching their position in the grouping so that whatever plant is tallest that year is in the center. Stagger the heights of the smaller containers so that the trailing plants always have room to drape and the bare sides of the containers don't fill up the eye space. The goal is to put the spotlight on the plants themselves, not on the containers.

Then, when you're ready to celebrate summertime with an old-fashioned lemonade party, look what you can do:

- Use some of your Meyer lemons for the lemonade.
- Make lemon verbena simple syrup. Mix 1 cup of sugar in 1 cup of boiling water, and add several leaves from the lemon verbena to steep. When cool, strain out the leaves, then use the syrup to sweeten the lemonade.
- Make flower-filled ice cubes from the violas; see page 372 for directions.
- Chop the thyme and mix with softened cream cheese for hors d'oeuvres.
- Make tea sandwiches with lemon-basil mayonnaise and Lemon Boy tomato (see page 167).
- Line the sandwich plates with nasturtium leaves, and garnish with the flowers.
- For dessert, serve lemon sorbet made from the begonias; see page 358 for the recipe.

Herbs

Marjoram

GROW AS: **annual**

SIZE: **6 to 12 inches**

START WITH: **seeds or transplants**

HARVEST SEASON: **summer**

SUN REQUIREMENTS: **full sun**

MINIMUM SOIL DEPTH: **6 inches**

Picture a Mediterranean hillside, perhaps in Greece, dotted with small, dark green clumps of marjoram. On a warm day under a big blue sky a tangy, almost sweet, balsamlike fragrance wafts in with the breeze. You hike out to the site and pinch off some sprigs, then stroll back to your village to prepare tonight's supper of a succulent lamb roast and some roasted vegetables, rich with the heavenly aroma and taste of marjoram. You can re-create this tantalizing dream in your home garden, for marjoram is easy to grow. It takes to life in a container beautifully, growing strong and lush and spilling attractively over the lip of the pot. It is a joy to harvest and immediately transport to your kitchen.

But surplus leaves can be dried and used later, including in the winter months, when they'll make a welcome contribution to stews, soups, and sauces. You might even tuck them into a culinary wreath. For unlike many other herbs, marjoram retains all its unique fragrance and flavor when dried.

Marjoram Basics. If you can approximate the conditions found on the herb's native Mediterranean hillsides, your marjoram plant will thrive. This means, first and foremost, plenty of sunshine. So reserve a spot on a bright windowsill, in a south-facing window box, or on a sunny patio, deck, or balcony. Marjoram is not overly fussy about soil and will do fine in your basic potting mix. Water lightly; it can tolerate dry spells and doesn't like wet feet.

Alas, marjoram is a bit too tender to make it through most North American winters, so most gardeners treat it as an annual, discarding it each fall and starting over the following spring.

We grow marjoram for the leaves, but it also puts on a mid-summer show of dainty flowers. They're generally white or pink and are initially clasped in a ball of tiny leaves on the ends of the stems. Their appearance is your cue to start harvesting, if you haven't already.

Planting. You can raise marjoram from seed easily; get started indoors in late winter. Be light-handed with the seeds because they're quite tiny and it's easy to overdo them, which means you'll have to do more thinning later. Cover them lightly with moist seed-starting mix. Seedlings will be up in a matter of days and begin to grow quickly. It will be a month or two before they're ready to be moved into individual permanent pots. They should not go outside too early, as they are vulnerable to frost. This plant has a rather shallow root system, so it's safe to grow it in a smaller or shallower pot.

Alternatively, buy young plants later in the spring. Make your selection by sniffing the leaves at the nursery to make sure you get the sweet-bitey fragrance you'd like to cook with.

You can leave the plants in the nursery pots if they are large enough, but eventually you'll want to move them into a more permanent container, especially if you want to include marjoram as part of a mixed planting. And if that's the case, you're better off moving the plant while it is still young. Handle the shallow root system with care, retaining as much of it as you possibly can.

Success with Marjoram.

Plenty of sun is key. A marjoram plant that is not getting enough sun will broadcast its displeasure by growing poorly, with leggy stems. A happy plant will grow thickly, carpeting the soil surface and spilling down the sides of the pot. Although you don't need to be lavish with water, this herb requires good-quality potting soil.

Harvesting. The best time to pick the fragrant leaves is when they are young, before the small flower heads develop fully. To dry the cuttings, array them on a paper towel in a warm, shady area. In a few days, you can strip off and crumble the leaves if you wish (discard the stems), or store them as is. Remember, unlike some other fragrant herbs, marjoram keeps its flavor when dried. Store the bounty in an airtight jar away from heat and light.

If you have a mild climate and a long growing season, you might try forcing your marjoram to generate a second harvest. When the ball-like flower buds first appear, cut the leaves you need. Then chop the entire plant down to within an inch or two of the soil surface. A second, lusher crop will develop over the coming weeks. Again, harvest just as more flower buds start.

Varieties. In addition to the basic species, *Origanum majorana,* there are several worthy variations. Prostrate, creeping marjorams are particularly nice in containers because of their lovely effect of spilling over the sides. Some gardeners have had fun clipping these into topiaries.

The crinkled golden-leaved variety **Aureum Crispum** is a novel addition to a mixed container, thanks to its bright color. The color tends to revert back to green late in the season if it is not receiving enough sunlight. This one makes a particularly attractive topiary.

Herbs

Mint

GROW AS: **short-lived perennial**

PLANT SIZE: **varies from ½ inch (Corsican mint) to 2 feet high (peppermint)**

START WITH: **plants**

HARVEST SEASON: **spring through fall**

SUN REQUIREMENTS: **full sun to partial shade**

MINIMUM SOIL DEPTH: **6 to 8 inches**

O f all the garden herbs, there are probably more varieties of mint than any other (except perhaps for the equally wonderful thyme). You'll no doubt find more than one or two that you simply can't live without and that you cannot buy in any market. They come in sizes from tiny little scented mats of Corsican mint—which makes pungent emerald trails between stepping-stones, but is not considered an edible—to the graceful, 2-foot stalks of spearmint and peppermint that most of us know. Maybe your favorite will be lavender mint, or chocolate mint, or maybe lemon balm. One of the great pleasures of having a garden is sharing its bounty with friends, and so far we haven't found a single person who isn't enchanted with a spur-of-the-moment snipping from a mint plant. If it's one of the more unusual varieties, your gift is all the more special.

We tend to think of mint in terms of beverages, especially mint tea, but it actually has many culinary uses. Numerous ethnic dishes are seasoned with mints of different kinds. Spearmint and peppermint are grown commercially in great fields and harvested to extract the essential oils that flavor gum, candy, toothpaste, soaps, lotions, medicines, tea, and other drinks. To be anywhere near a field of mint when it is being harvested is a genuine delight as the wonderful scent saturates the air.

In your container garden, we suggest you grow mint where you can brush against it as you walk past, where you can reach out and touch the plant and smell the scent it leaves on your fingers.

Position a container near your favorite sitting nook so you can pick a few leaves to drop into your tea or lemonade, or just pick a sprig to brush

The Many Uses of Mint

Wise men and women have since ancient times used herbal remedies to treat illnesses and other afflictions. Some of those treatments were strange indeed, and in many cases the patient got well in spite of them. But others have been verified by modern science, and today many medicines are derived from herbal formulas or based on their synthetic counterparts.

Mint is a good example. Here's what our modern laboratories have confirmed:

■ Mint leaves, rubbed on itchy skin, are cooling and have a slight numbing effect. They have the same soothing effect on toothaches if rubbed on the gums.

■ All mints aid digestion. Our tradition of after-dinner mints grows from this, and the soothing habit of drinking mint tea at bedtime all but guarantees no indigestion.

■ Peppermint contains an ingredient that works on the body as an antispasmodic, so peppermint tea is very soothing for menstrual cramps, diarrhea, and tummyaches of all kinds.

■ Mint is also a natural pesticide. Dried or fresh leaves in your pantry will deter mice. Grow pennyroyal mint in a pot, indoors or out, to keep the mosquito population down; and put dried leaves in the dog's bed to help with fleas.

---

against your face. It calms the nerves and soothes the body after a busy day.

Mint Basics. You can always tell if a plant is in the mint family because it has square stems. Most mints are hardy perennial plants that spread by underground stems, which root all along their length and send up new growth from buds along the stems. In winter the plants often die back to the ground, and if you're not expecting this you may think they're dead. The underground stems are still vigorous, however, and come spring you'll see hundreds of tiny leaves popping up.

Many mints also self-sow if they are allowed to flower and make seeds. (Lemon balm is notorious for this.)

In moist, fertile conditions mints can be quite invasive; with no effort at all, they'll grow underneath a sidewalk and come out the other side. Gardeners are often advised to confine them to containers, even in a traditional in-the-ground garden.

Mints grow very happily in pots and make a desirable addition to your container garden. And because of the many leaf shapes, colors, and textures, a grouping of three or four plants can almost be a garden in itself. Mints are easy to grow, and as long as they get plenty of moisture and regular haircuts, they are excellent compact foliage plants. They tend to die out in the middle after about two years. At that point it's a good idea to unpot them, cut out and discard the old roots, and start new plants from the youngest roots, which collect around the edges of the pot. This way you can keep mint plants going for years.

Planting. Start with small plants, because seeds are too slow. Choose an interesting container and fill it with an all-purpose potting mixture. It's best not to grow mint in a mixed container with other plants, as the roots tend to take over and can crowd out less vigorous neighbors. But mints are very acceptable specimen plants grown individually in their own pots. For a mixed garden, group individual pots together in a larger container. Just remember to label each plant; many of them look so much alike that after a few years you can't tell which is which.

Success with Mints. There's an old story about an elderly English noblewoman and her equally elderly gardener. As they strolled around her estate debating what to plant for the coming season, the duchess murmured something about wanting to add a new mint but worried that it would entail too much work for her frail employee. "You know how we grow mint, don't you, madam," the gardener replied with a straight face. "We just plunk it in the ground and step back out of the way."

And we container gardeners do the same: plunk it in a pot and step back. There are no magic tricks needed to grow good mint. With

Mint for the Gods

The Greek god Pluto was already married when he fell in love with a beautiful nymph named Minthe. His jealous wife got rid of her rival by changing the maiden into a plant. Pluto was unable to save her life, but he did give her everlasting sweetness that could not be destroyed, even when crushed underfoot.

plenty of moisture and some shade during the hot part of the day if temperatures really soar, mint will generally do well. Mints aren't heavy feeders; in fact, the leaves have more intense flavor if they aren't so vigorously fertilized that they grow big and lush. Get the plants started in the spring with a drink of a balanced fertilizer, then again in mid summer. This is usually enough, but if you see the plants beginning to slow down or fade in color, go ahead and feed them again.

Left to their own devices, mint plants have a tendency to get lanky and threadbare, especially at the bottom. This doesn't interfere with their utility, but it is unattractive. The solution is simple: cut them back, heavily if need be. They will quickly put out new growth, restoring a tidy, compact look.

Most mints are hardy, and can be left outside in a moderately protected place throughout the year. A few are more tender, so check with your nursery expert or read catalog descriptions to find out if yours should be brought in for the winter.

C at lovers will especially appreciate this garden designed to celebrate their passion. Even if circumstances prevent you from having a cat at the moment, a Cheshire Cat garden will remind you of why you love them. And those with only a passing feline interest will find it appealing for another reason: it's a tiny garden that works very well in a small space. It will do nicely in one medium-size container, say 18 to 24 inches wide.

Begin with a treasure just for the cat: **catnip.** Sometimes people are

Theme Garden

The Cheshire Cat

surprised that catnip starts out as a living green entity, but in fact it's nothing more, or less, than the leaves of a pretty plant in the mint family. And with its upright growth form, it will make a nice centerpiece for your garden. Catnip has the typical square stems of all mints, and grayish green leaves that are slightly fuzzy to the touch and fun to caress—just like your cat. Starting in late spring and lasting all through the summer, it produces tall spikes of small white or lavender flowers. Catnip is grown just like the other mints, and like them will die to the ground in winter and resurface in the spring. Dry the leaves for your cat's wintertime pleasure. Then, if you're handy with a needle, sew up a small sack and stuff it with your own dried catnip.

Did you know that catnip also makes a soothing tea for the cat's owner? It has a pleasant, lemony flavor and contains a very mild, very safe sedative; adults can enjoy it just before bedtime to help them fall asleep.

A word of caution: if you have a cat and this container garden is anywhere within leaping range, the cat will find the catnip and wallow around in it in cat-ecstacy, seriously scrunching the garden in the process. It might be prudent to start a separate container of catnip to entice kitty away from your garden. Or you may decide it was all for the cat's benefit anyway, and let her have it.

Another alternative is to substitute **catmint.** It's a close cousin to catnip, which it resembles in many ways, but catmint is somewhat less attractive to cats. With soft purple flowers in tall spikes that stay on the plant a long time, it's a favorite border plant in traditional gardens and will look equally lovely in your container garden. It, too, makes a delightful tea.

For details on growing the plants in this garden, see

Marjoram, page 221
Mint, page 223
Pansies, page 382

To balance the upright habit of the catmint or catnip, put several small plants of Curly Golden **marjoram** along the edges of the container and allow them to trail over the sides. This marjoram has crinkled round leaves that will remind you of a cat's fur, and its golden color is a fine complement to the purple flowers.

Here and there among the marjoram and beneath the catnip, plant as many **pansies** as you can fit in. Choose the ones whose flowers look like kittycat faces.

As a final touch, for sheer whimsy and to remind you of what this garden is all about, place a wooden or ceramic figure of a cat in your container. It will make you smile all winter when the garden is resting.

Harvesting. Harvesting mint is a simple matter of picking a few leaves whenever you need them. Pinch off new tips and use them to garnish a salad or drink as needed; the stem will send out new branches at the pinch point. A few leaves steeped in a pot of black tea are wonderful; fresh leaves skewered to a slice of fruit make a jaunty garnish for a cold drink.

If you are going to dry mints, pick them just before they flower. You can use the mint flowers, too, but the flavor and essential oils are best before the flowers open fully. If your plants get ahead of you and grow lots of tall stalks, which some are likely to do, just cut them and use them in bouquets to scent the room, or set a basket of mint in the bathroom as an air freshener. Lemon balm is especially pleasing for this last use. New growth will almost immediately come up from the roots to replace anything you cut off.

Varieties. Among the best for flavoring drinks or making tea are the old standards: **spearmint, peppermint,** and **lemon balm. Lavender mint** is delightful: its flavor is lavender and mint mixed together. **Chocolate mint,** actually a form of peppermint, will send chocolate lovers into ecstasy. **Bergamot mint,** also known as orange mint, tastes like Earl Grey tea. **Apple mint** has large, fuzzy leaves and a soft flavor that will remind you of apples. It blends very well with spearmint or peppermint, whose sharpness it pleasantly dilutes. Cut stems are often used in floral arrangements. **Pineapple mint** really does taste and smell like pineapple, and with its creamy variegation, it is one of the prettiest. Check out herb farms and specialty nurseries for these and other delightful mints.

Herbs

Monarda

GROW AS: **perennial**

PLANT SIZE: **1 to 3 feet**

START WITH: **plants**

HARVEST SEASON: **summer through fall**

SUN REQUIREMENTS: **sun to partial shade**

MINIMUM SOIL DEPTH: **8 to 10 inches**

Bergamot, bee balm, Oswego tea, horsemint—monarda is one of those plants with so many names you wonder what to call it. It is native to the eastern and central parts of the United States and was long used as both beverage and medicine by the Oswego Indians. They introduced it to the early European settlers for making a delicious and fragrant tea, and so it became known as Oswego tea, an essential plant in the colonial kitchen garden. One of its other names comes from its resemblance to the scent of bergamot, a citrus fruit very similar to oranges, which grows in the Mediterranean; and another from the attraction it holds for bees.

The original native plant has brilliant scarlet flowers, and hybridizers have developed many other strains so that there is now a wide range of colors, from deep burgundy to several shades of red, pink, violet, and white. The fragrance is almost as complicated as its many names. To some monarda smells citrusy, to others it hints of basil and mint. If you think it smells like Earl Grey tea, you'd be absolutely right, as this herb has much the same aroma and taste as the bergamot fruit that flavors the famous tea blend.

Aside from the fragrant tea, the chief delight of growing monarda is its flowers, which are larger than those of most herbs and add a strong note of color, especially the bright red variety. The blooms have a shaggy, unkempt appearance that has its own funky charm. When you look closely, you see that the flower head is actually a mass of narrow, tube-shaped flowers that hang loosely from around the

Tea for the Revolution

Can you imagine, as you settle down in the evening to enjoy a quiet cup of herbal tea, that you're committing an act of political protest? More than 200 years ago, that's exactly what the American colonists did.

They had loved tea in their homeland and depended on shipments from England, but the Crown, attempting to control the economy of its colonies, levied taxes on tea imports, making it too expensive for many colonists. As the forces of revolution began to build, the tea and its tax became a symbol of all that the colonists were struggling against, and they decided to boycott it.

From the Native Americans the colonists had learned to enjoy tea brewed from the plants that grew around them. Of these, an especially delicious beverage was made from the plant that the colonists called Oswego tea and we today call monarda. Soon the colonists were blending their own herbal teas from the plants that grew in their backyard gardens: thyme, red clover, hyssop, chamomile, and raspberry. These became known as Liberty teas, and creating them and sharing the recipes was a bold act of defiance among pre-Revolutionary housewives.

In December 1773 a group of colonists, disguised as Indians, climbed aboard three British ships lying in Boston Harbor and threw 342 chests of tea into the water. The Boston Tea Party served to accelerate the movement toward American independence.

---

oversize center. They are handsome in fresh bouquets, and dried flowers retain their fragrance nicely, making them a good additive to potpourri or dried flower crafts. Monarda is a wonderful hummingbird and bee plant, and will likely be one of the most interesting-looking plants in your garden.

Monarda Basics. Monarda is a hardy perennial that thrives in moist, fertile soil and warm temperatures. It starts out in spring with a low mat of what look like little individual plants with a reddish tinge and a soft velvety look. But it soon sends up square stalks similar to mint, sometimes 2 to 3 feet tall. The pointy, fragrant leaves have just a hint of downy fuzz to them; the varieties with dark red flowers often also have a reddish cast to the leaves, which is very attractive. It's the leaves that you steep in hot black tea to make your own herbal version of Earl Grey tea. Most varieties of monarda bloom in July and August; if you clip off the flowers, sometimes you'll be rewarded with side branching and a second bloom.

Planting. We wholeheartedly recommend that you start with young plants, to be sure you get flowers right away. You might even want to buy your plants later in the season, when they're in bloom, so you can choose the color you like best.

Monarda can be grown as an individual plant in its own container, or it can be put in with other plants in a large tub or pot. Since it is fairly tall, give it a place at the back of a container, or use it as the tall focal point in a round one that will be viewed from all sides.

By mid summer, monarda will likely have lost its bottom leaves, giving it a skinny, bare-legged look. Hide the bare legs by tucking in some smaller plants at the base. Sweet woodruff is a good choice.

Success with Monarda. Give monarda plenty of water, and feed it with an all-purpose fertilizer such as 16–16–16 about once a month, beginning when the first new leaves start growing in the spring and continuing until the end of summer. The monarda root system isn't very deep but it is spreading, so you'll need to keep an eye on your plant after the second year and divide it so it doesn't crowd out other plants you may have planted with it.

The only problem you are likely to have with monarda is that late in the season it is prone to powdery mildew. Use the baking soda solution described in Chapter 6.

Harvesting. Pick off leaves to use in tea as you need them. Cutting the whole stalk back will stimulate new foliage to grow. When the flowers are just at their peak, cut them for use in salads; and cut those just over their peak for drying.

Varieties. If you're hoping to attract hummingbirds, choose the monardas with scarlet or red flowers. **Cambridge Scarlet** is a reliable older variety, with scarlet flowers on extra-leafy spikes. **Adam** is another good scarlet, and **Jacob Kline** is a newer scarlet type with good mildew resistance.

Pink varieties include **Croftway Pink** and **Granite Pink; Marshall's Delight,** another good pink variety, has the extra advantage of being more mildew-resistant than the others.

Violet Queen, also mildew resistant, is a good strong violet hue.

Not much bigger than your thumb from head to tail, hummingbirds are one of nature's small miracles. Because they are so tiny, they must feed almost continually, and so their entire existence is a never-ending search for the flower nectar that is their sustenance. They zip from one spot to the next so fast we humans can't follow with our eyes, and then, when they find a likely blossom, they hover in midair to dip their long beaks down into the honey-rich heart of the flower.

Theme Garden

A Hummingbird Garden

Their tongues flick into the nectar an average of 13 times a second. While feeding, they keep themselves in position by rapidly beating their little wings; 60 beats per second is common, and some species hit 80 without even trying. The wings beat so fast that all we humans can see is a blur, but we can definitely hear the high-pitched humming sound it creates.

Hummingbirds' beaks are long in relation to the birds' overall size, and so they are instinctively drawn to flowers that have a deep, narrow throat with the nectar concentrated at the base. They have no sense of smell and find the flowers only by color; in one of those quirks of nature we may never fully understand, they are especially attracted to the color red, for it is the only color they see clearly.

This garden is filled with plants that attract hummers, as they are affectionately called. All have the deep-throated flowers that the birds need, and it is not by accident that all the flowers are in shades of red.

To prime the pump, so to speak, we suggest that you suspend a commercial hummingbird feeder from the trellis late in spring, when the birds are building nests and establishing their feeding pattern. Look for a feeder that has a wasp screen and lots of red color so you don't need to dye the sugar water. Fill it with syrup made of one part sugar to four parts water, and replace with a fresh batch every three or four days.

Growing up the trellis are **scarlet runner beans.** This old-fashioned favorite produces masses of bright red-orange blossoms; many people grow them just for the flower show. But when the flowers fade, the long, fat bean pods begin to form. You can either pick them when very small, which keeps the flowers coming, or leave them on the vine to reach mature size. If you let them dry on the vine, the pods become mottled gray and papery, and inside this wrinkled exterior you'll find a glorious surprise: the beans themselves are large, meaty, and beautifully colored, shiny black with magenta swirls.

Planted with the beans are several plants of **monarda,** commonly known as bee balm. These herb plants, with their sassy, funky flowers, will fill in the bottom few feet of the bean vines, which tend to look bare-legged and straggly by midseason. The leaves make a nice tea, and the flowers are great fun as a garnish. Start with plants instead of seeds so you'll have flowers the first year. These perennials are quite hardy.

For details on growing the plants in this garden, see

Beans, page 81
Begonias, page 352
Monarda, page 229
Pineapple sage, page 255

In recent years breeders have developed monardas with flowers in several shades of pink, but bright red is the standard color and that is what you want here. The flowers are quite distinctive. From a few feet away the flower head looks like a shaggy puffball, but if you examine it more closely you'll see that it is composed of masses of long, thin individual flowers—just the shape that hummingbirds love.

By the way, monarda is known as bee balm because it's very attractive to honeybees as well as hummingbirds. Bees are well-trained, industrious pollinators, and anything you do to encourage them to spend time in your vegetable garden is a good thing. Don't panic when you see them, and for heaven's sake don't kill them.

Alongside the monarda, put several plants of **pineapple sage.** The leaves are intriguing, with tastes of both sage and pineapple, but our chief interest here is the remarkable flowers. Long, slender, and an astonishing scarlet color, they are perfect for hummingbirds. This variety of sage blooms quite late in the year and is atypically tender, so gardeners in colder climates seldom get to see the flowers. But if your weather is cooperative, or if you have a gambler's soul, pineapple sage is definitely worth a try; worst case, you'll get to enjoy the delightful leaves.

Providing the third tier for this arrangement are **tuberous begonias.** The flowers are flat (rather like camellias) and so not good for nectar as far as the hummingbirds are concerned. But if you choose begonias with flowers in shades of red, deep pink, and red-orange, the birds will be attracted to your garden by their incandescent color. For your own pleasure, look for the hanging-basket types rather than the upright form, so their showstopping colors will spill over the edge of the container. Begonias do well in filtered shade, which will be graciously provided by the beans and the monarda.

At the end of the season you'll have to remove the dead bean vines (clip them at ground level) and, in many regions, the bare sage plants as well. Depending on your climate, you may also have to dig up the begonia tubers for storage. Try not to disturb the roots of the monarda, which will stay in place through the winter.

Even if hummingbirds don't come calling, your garden will produce a wonderful bounty: delicious dried beans (great for winter soup), delicately beautiful edible flowers for a surprising sorbet (see page 358), a wonderful cooking herb, and the makings of a soothing herbal tea. But if you do succeed in tempting the birds, you will have a front-row seat at one of nature's most entertaining shows.

Herbs

Oregano

GROW AS: **perennial**

PLANT SIZE: **8 to 12 inches tall and wide**

START WITH: **transplants**

HARVEST SEASON: **summer into fall**

SUN REQUIREMENTS: **full sun**

MINIMUM SOIL DEPTH: **8 inches**

Anyone of Italian or Greek descent, or anyone who loves Italian or Greek cooking, immediately associates these cuisines with oregano. Pungent, peppery, savory oregano is essential in everything from spaghetti and pizza sauce to zucchini and eggplant dishes. It's a natural in any recipe that includes tomatoes.

Oregano has been in cultivation so long, both in the ancient world and in this country, and passed around so often by gardeners and cooks, that a deeply tangled taxonomic thicket has developed. Is *Origanum vulgare* the "true" oregano?

What is the best oregano: so-called Sicilian oregano, or Greek, or some other species, or a cross with the similar-tasting marjoram? These are questions that may cause purists and botanists to furrow their brows, but don't let the debate bother you. Let your nose be your guide at the garden center. Run your hand along the foliage of the various choices and buy the one you love best.

Though a favorite of chefs, oregano can also be appreciated as an ornamental plant. It's a member of the mint family ("family" in botanical terms is the equivalent of "extended family" in human terms), so expect a lush plant with substantial, attractive leaves on all sides of the characteristic square stems. In addition to the plain green type, there are varieties with especially colorful leaves: a soft golden shade, or green rimmed in white. These are handsome in combination containers with other herbs and flowering plants.

Even the flowers are showy. If you grow the plants outdoors, bees as well as butterflies may be drawn to them. Several types are favored for their fascinating blooms. Although grown primarily as ornamentals, they can still be used in cooking; try their flowers as a garnish.

First Cousins and Look-Alikes

Oregano (botanical name *Origanum vulgare* is a close cousin to another well-known herb: marjoram (botanical name *Origanum majorana*). Somewhere along the line, the species name *majorana* became marjoram.

Most people think that oregano has a stronger, sharper flavor than marjoram, but in fact the two are so similar in taste that in a pinch, good cooks freely substitute one for the other. Gardeners should also realize that marjoram is more vulnerable to cold weather.

Oregano Basics. Oregano does beautifully in containers, staying relatively compact (the trimmings you take for the kitchen will also help keep it that way) and requiring little fuss. It must have well-drained soil and should never be overwatered. Place it in full sun for best appearance and flavor.

Gardeners in dry, mild climates have the best luck with this splendid herb. It struggles in long periods of cool and rainy weather, and in areas with high humidity (humid weather or poor air circulation around the containers encourages disfiguring fungal disease). Although oregano is fairly hardy, it will not survive bitter cold. You should probably play it safe and either mulch the containers well when the weather turns frosty or bring the plant inside to a bright windowsill for the winter months.

Planting. Oregano is seldom raised from seed, not because it is a poor germinator but because it is so variable. It hybridizes readily, and there's no telling exactly what the resulting seed will produce (in addition, some seed is sterile). So start with a small plant, from either a mail-order nursery or a well-herbed garden center.

Shop for plants in the spring, and don't worry if they seem small; they are fast growers, and spread out quickly.

To distribute plants of your favorite varieties to friends, divide mature specimens or take cuttings, which is what professional nurserymen do.

Success with Oregano. The best fragrance and flavor, and the richest foliage color, occur when pots of oregano receive plenty of warm sunshine. For brand-new plants, fertilize when you transplant them into the permanent container; for established plants, fertilize once early in the growing season. Don't overwater, and don't let the pots stand in saucers of water; that's a sure route to root rot. Early in the season, take a look at the overall shape of the plant and do a light pruning to tighten it up, if needed.

Unhappy plants sometimes get attacked by spider mites, aphids, or other insect pests. The best course of treatment is prevention—that is, raising healthy plants. As you snip bits of oregano for cooking, check the leaves for any sign of damage. Review Chapter 6 for controls.

Harvesting. Liberal harvesting doesn't set oregano back. In fact, the more sprigs you snip, the bushier the plant grows. Use the leaves dried or fresh. The famous cookbook author Craig Claiborne said he found that dried oregano actually had "more character" than fresh.

Varieties. Warning: in the nursery trade, oreganos are frequently confused, so it's not easy for us ordinary folks to know if a particular plant is correctly labeled or accurately described. Our best advice is to sample anything that intrigues you in a catalog description, or visit a well-stocked garden center and choose on the basis of your own impressions.

The basic oregano, the common wild plant, is *Origanum vulgare.* Aficionados say it is not as flavorful as some of its subspecies, notably *O. vulgare hirtum,* sometimes also labeled *O. heracleoticum.* This is the one that nursery people usually mean when they speak of Greek oregano. It has superlative flavor, and is indeed the favorite of Greek cooks, but it's also the classic choice in Italy.

Another outstanding variety for culinary use is the one known as Sicilian oregano, which is actually a cross between an oregano and a marjoram. It has white flowers and very good flavor.

Ornamental oreganos are less fragrant but still edible. Of those that do well in containers, two are especially beautiful. The cultivar **Herrenhausen** has masses of tiny purple blossoms clustered along the stems. The long-lasting flowers are deep and rich in color but with a brightness that is especially appealing. They look lovely in fresh flower bouquets, and dry beautifully. The stems of this plant are essentially upright, rather than trailing, but they form a graceful spray that is lovely in containers.

The other charmer is **Kent Beauty,** a cultivar of *O. rotundifolium.* Its primary appeal is its unique soft pink flowers, which form at the very end of the stems and look very much like the flowers of hops. Because of these lovely blooms and the trailing foliage, this one is very popular for hanging baskets. It is not, however, hardy enough to stay outside in winter in most of the country. Bring it indoors, and keep it on the dry side.

Herbs

Parsley

GROW AS: **annual**

PLANT SIZE: **6 to 12 inches,**
   with seed heads reaching 3 feet

START WITH: **plants**

HARVEST SEASON: **summer through fall**

SUN REQUIREMENTS: **morning sun,**
   light afternoon shade

MINIMUM SOIL DEPTH: **8 inches**

D ried parsley flakes are a common item on many a spice rack, but they are a very poor substitute for the fresh version. The flavor and texture of fresh parsley make it seem like a completely different herb, aromatic and sharp. Modern cooks are using it by the handful. When a dish needs a little something, many of us try chopped fresh parsley as a flavor booster instead of salt. Plant enough so you can really use it.

If you're one of those people who think of fresh parsley in one way only—as that green frilly thing perched on the edge of the plate at sandwich shops, usually returned untouched at the end of the meal—you owe it to yourself to try it as a cooking herb. It is full of flavor (not to mention vitamins and breath-sweetening chlorophyll), and if not overcooked retains its bright green, perking up many dishes with color as well as taste.

In the garden, parsley is a handsome and versatile plant that works well in many combinations. The rich green foliage is a nice foil for many other colors, and the small, tidy shape makes it a good choice for tucking in wherever a spot suddenly becomes empty. Use it freely to help tie together the look of a mixed pot, or plant it as a border around the edges of a large container. It's almost like garnishing your containers with parsley.

Parsley Basics.
Parsley belongs to the plant family known as Umbelliferae. It's a valuable family for cooks to become acquainted with because it comprises so many herb plants: anise, chervil, cilantro, dill, fennel, and sweet cicely. Carrots are also umbellifers, and so is a wildflower you have doubtless seen many times: Queen Anne's lace. Think of the flower of Queen Anne's lace, like an umbrella opened up but held upside down so that it would catch water rather than repel it, and you have

the key distinguishing trait of this family.

In addition to the curly parsley that you push around on your plate at the diner, there are several other types, interesting to know about and interesting to try in your garden. One type is called flat-leaf or Italian parsley. It looks very much like a large, dark green version of cilantro, but with the distinctive parsley taste. Many people consider the flavor of flat-leaf parsley superior to that of the curly type.

You may also enjoy experimenting with the so-called double-curled and triple-curled types. These are not as tightly frilled as curly parsley, but they're also not totally flat. The flavor is approximately the same, so the main appeal is visual. For your mixed container you might simply prefer the look of one over the other. All these types have the same basic growing requirements and uses as the curly varieties.

Although we grow it as an annual, parsley is botanically a true biennial, meaning that it takes two years to go through a full life cycle. In the first year from seed, it is a small, leafy plant, and this is the foliage we cut and use. As long as a small amount of foliage in the very center of the plant is left in place and the long, carrotlike taproot is not disturbed, the plant lives over the winter. The following spring a tall flower stalk shoots up from the center of the foliage, and ultimately produces seeds. At the end of the second growing season the plant dies, first scattering its seeds to begin a new cycle next year. In the second year, the foliage is coarse and

Showtime

The larvae of swallowtail butterflies are sometimes found on parsley. They are usually yellow and green, and seen most often on plants that are blooming or about to bloom. Your first reaction may be to smash them, especially if you are squeamish about worms, but *resist*. Encourage them to stay and dine (they don't eat much). Soon they will form cocoons, which you can watch for that magical moment when full-grown butterflies emerge.

unappetizing, so gardeners who are also cooks tend to start anew with first-year plants each spring.

Planting. Parsley seed is slow and erratic to germinate, and even commercial greenhouse managers have to soak the seeds overnight before planting. We suggest you take the easy route and buy plants at the garden center.

Select young plants that are small and appear to be growing vigorously (the color will be bright green and healthy looking). Plants that are large or crowded in the nursery pot are difficult to transplant; in your container they will simply sit and sulk, unhappy about their root disturbance.

Parsley is a good cool-season grower, so often the plants appear at the garden center early in spring. Go ahead and transplant them into your container whenever it's convenient; they can even take a light frost without damage. Parsley isn't particularly fussy about the soil it grows in, as long as it isn't waterlogged, and will

239

Recipe: Focaccia

Rose Marie says: "Focaccia is an Italian flatbread, traditionally topped with herbs, olive oil, and coarse salt. Serve warm in wedges or thin slices, or cut in half horizontally for a spectacular sandwich large enough to serve several people.

"You have two options for getting herbs into your bread: either bake them in, or spread them on top in the form of a flavored oil, some pesto, or a few sprigs pressed into the dough. You can also do both—but adjust the amounts accordingly. One of my favorite versions is plain focaccia spread with rosemary pesto (see page 243) during the last 10 minutes of baking."

> 4 teaspoons active dry yeast
>
> 8½ cups unbleached all-purpose flour
>
> 1 teaspoon salt
>
> 2 tablespoons chopped fresh herbs (optional)
>
> Olive oil, for coating bowl, pan, and dough
>
> Coarse (kosher) salt (optional)
>
> 1 tablespoon rosemary pesto (optional; see page 243)

1. Mix the yeast with ¼ cup of the flour in a large mixing bowl. Add ½ cup lukewarm water and stir until the yeast has dissolved. Set aside for about 10 minutes, until the yeast mixture is bubbly.

2. Add 2½ cups of water to the yeast mixture and gradually stir in the remaining flour and the 1 teaspoon salt to make a dough. Mix in 1 tablespoon of the chopped herbs, if desired. Knead the dough until it is elastic, 2 to 3 minutes. Place the dough in a well-oiled large bowl, turn the dough once to coat completely with oil, then cover the bowl with plastic wrap or a clean, damp kitchen towel. Set aside in a warm spot until the dough has doubled in size, about 1 hour.

3. Punch down the dough and knead a few times. Oil 2 baking sheets. Divide the dough into the desired number of loaves and shape them into flattened rounds. Place the loaves on the prepared baking

sheets and use your fingertips to make numerous shallow indentations across the top surfaces. Lightly coat the tops with the olive oil and sprinkle with coarse salt if desired. Lightly cover the loaves with a clean, damp kitchen towel and set aside to rise again until doubled in size, about 45 minutes.

4. Preheat the oven to 450°F.

5. When the loaves are ready, bake for 10 minutes. Reduce the heat to 400°F and continue baking for 15 to 20 minutes more. During the last 10 minutes of baking, sprinkle with all the chopped herbs (the remaining 1 tablespoon) or spread the pesto over the top, if desired.

6. Remove from the oven and transfer the focaccia to a wire rack. Let cool completely before serving.

Makes two 12-inch rounds, or several smaller loaves

usually do just fine with whatever conditions are available. It's one of the least demanding plants you can grow.

Success with Parsley. Give parsley a sunny to partially shady spot, and it will be happy. In fact, it's one of the herbs that will take more shade than most and still give lots of nice foliage. Again, the most serious error you can make is creating waterlogged conditions (a combination of too much watering and soil that drains poorly).

Harvesting. Parsley can be harvested anytime there are enough leaves on the plant to give you what you need without cutting off all the foliage. It's a good idea to have several plants to cut from so one doesn't get overharvested.

Parsley is a cut-and-come-again herb, and will continue to produce leaves all season. Cut the oldest leaves first, leaving the center leaves to grow. Fresh parsley, chopped or minced, is wonderful in salad dressings, dips, soups, potato dishes, baked fish, or chicken—in fact, it is one of the most versatile cooking herbs we have.

Varieties. **Green River** is an extra-hardy curly type that doesn't lose its curl even in heat; it's one of the most flavorful and one of the best for drying, if you have more than you can use fresh. **Gigante d'Italia,** a very large, old variety from northern Italy, is a good choice for flat parsley. It has a more robust flavor than some, and is especially good in salads and when teamed up with fresh tomatoes. It's taller than most parsleys, a foot or more in height, and so probably should go in the center of your container.

Herbs

Rosemary

GROW AS: **perennial**

PLANT SIZE: **1 to 2 feet**

START WITH: **transplants**

HARVEST SEASON: **summer**

SUN REQUIREMENTS: **full sun**

MINIMUM SOIL DEPTH: **8 inches**

Few plants are as easy to grow in containers, or as satisfying, as rosemary. Herb lovers have dozens of varieties to choose from; some sprawl and drape, some form jaunty little bushes, and certain upright ones lend themselves to training into fun or elegant topiary displays (see page 245). Rosemary's pliable stems are always thickly lined with fragrant, needle-like leaves, and the flowers, though small, are quite pretty, usually in shades of blue but occasionally white or soft pink.

That evocative, almost piney fragrance is the reason this herb is so beloved. You will discover, if you visit a well-stocked nursery, that there is some variation in scent. Gently run your hand along different branches and smell your fingers, then pick the variety you like best.

Although rosemary leaves dry and freeze well, the flavor they impart to certain dishes when fresh is incomparable. Add them to roasted meats, game, and poultry. Simmer them in tomato-based sauces. Toss rosemary into ratatouille or steamed squash or beans, or sprinkle it, finely chopped, over a fruit salad. You can even bake it into bread; it's wonderful in foccacia.

Rosemary Basics. In nature rosemary favors dry, sunny locations. Put your pot in full sun, and don't worry if it gets lots of reflected heat from your patio or courtyard walls; rosemary loves such conditions.

Don't, however, neglect water. One of the main causes of death is drying out, and the plant will not recover if you discover your error too late. And when you water, include a little liquid seaweed fertilizer. Rosemary plants adore this food and respond with lush, beautiful growth.

Rosemary is a perennial herb, and will last for many years as long as you can give it some assistance during the winter. This is not a cold-tolerant plant. It can remain outdoors to about 25°F; below that, it's at risk. So unless you live in a mild climate, your best bet is to bring the rosemary indoors when temperatures dip, and keep it there until well into the following spring. Many varieties of rosemary are winter

Recipe: Rosemary Pesto

Rose Marie says: "Because pesto is traditionally made with basil leaves, we tend to think that's the only option. But the word *pesto* simply means 'crushed,' and any herb can be turned into a richly flavored paste."

This rosemary pesto is wonderful with potatoes. Swirl a generous scoop into mashed potatoes, or use it to coat oven-roasted potatoes.

½ cup fresh rosemary leaves

1½ cups chopped fresh parsley

2 large garlic cloves, minced

½ cup freshly grated Parmesan cheese

½ cup extra-virgin olive oil, plus extra for covering

½ cup toasted pine nuts, almonds, or walnuts (see Note)

Salt and freshly ground pepper, to taste

1. Place the rosemary, parsley, garlic, Parmesan, and ½ cup olive oil in a food processor or blender, and process until very well blended.

2. Add the nuts and process again until they are finely chopped. Season to taste with salt and pepper.

3. Place the pesto in a small jar with a tight-fitting lid and cover with a thin layer of olive oil to prevent discoloration. For short-term storage, refrigerate. For longer storage, freeze the pesto; you can later remove small amounts as needed.

NOTE: To toast pine nuts, place in a low (250°F) oven in an ungreased pan for about 5 minutes.

Makes about 1 cup

bloomers, so that's a nice indoor bonus.

When you bring rosemary indoors, be extra conservative with water. Growth naturally slackens at this time of year, and the plant's needs will change in its new environment. So keep an eye out for the first few weeks, until you get a sense of what the plant needs. Also, hold off on the fertilizing until early spring.

Planting. Rosemary is rarely raised from seed. For one thing, it takes forever and a day to grow; for another, the many different varieties are best propagated by cuttings. If someone you know has one you covet, ask to take a cutting or two in early summer from fresh growth. Once it has rooted, transfer it carefully to its permanent container and don't move it again. Rosemary doesn't enjoy being transplanted. If you buy small plants from a nursery in the springtime, move them—gently—into a permanent pot as soon as you can.

This herb isn't especially fussy about soil quality, but your potting mix should drain well to head off the potential for root rot. Add a touch of lime; in nature rosemary grows in slightly alkaline conditions.

Success with Rosemary. The real challenge with raising rosemary in containers is watering. Neglect it and the plant, unforgivingly, dies. Overwater, and the roots rot; again, the plant dies. Here are a few tips. Choose a clay pot, which is porous and wicks water away from the root system. Fill it with a well-draining mix, one that includes some sand or a high proportion of perlite. Then, after you water, remove the dish under the pot and toss away any excess liquid. If the plant is in a very hot, sunny spot, spritz the foliage every now and then.

It's not common for rosemary to experience pest problems, but you should check the plant occasionally, particularly if other potted plants in your collection have problems.

Powdery mildew occasionally appears; see Chapter 6 for controls.

Harvesting. You can snip off foliage bits at any time. The newer, younger growth at the tips is softer and tastier. As a rule of thumb, try not to remove more than one-fourth of a branch's length at any given trimming.

To dry, simply lay out the stems—not touching one another—on paper or a screen in a warm dry place. After a few days or a week, store them as is, or strip off the leaves. To retain maximum pungency, keep your harvest in an airtight container in a dry place.

Varieties. Browse the pages of any good herb catalog, or if you can, visit a nursery that is known for a broad selection. You can try different ones in different years, or combine two or more in the same container, all in the name of finding your favorites.

If you want plants that drape over a pot's side, look for **Severn Sea** or **Mrs. Howard's.** Both are robust trailing varieties, with medium blue flowers, and grow rather rapidly. They are also good for topiary because of their lanky, flexible stems. **Lockwood de Forest** is another fine trailing variety with lavender blue flowers and especially dark green foliage. For an upright-growing rosemary, **Tuscan Blue** is the classic choice, though there are many others. **Arp,** a medium-size rosemary with a mostly upright habit, has light blue flowers and gray-green foliage. Many experts believe it is more cold-tolerant than most others.

Topiaries

At their ultimate, topiaries are large landscape shrubs that have been trained and pruned into very unshrublike shapes—geometric forms or fanciful animals or sometimes even green versions of statuary. You've probably seen them in the large formal gardens that seem to be the setting of so many romantic movies that take place in nineteenth-century England.

At the level of container gardens, topiaries are of necessity smaller and usually simpler. Whether or not you find the idea appealing is a matter of personal preference, but if you should want to try your hand at it, here's the basic process.

1. It is much easier to train a plant that naturally produces long, rambling, flexible stems. Rosemary stems, when they are young, are just about perfect. Marjoram is another good choice.

2. Decide on the shape you want. In large garden centers it is possible to purchase wire forms designed specially for topiary, either abstract shapes or small animals. Insert the form in the container, and plant several very small plants at well-spaced points around it. As they begin to grow, help them catch onto the wire and wrap around it, with a bit of string or fine wire if need be.

3. If that's too cute for you, you can also do a very nice topiary without the forms. One classic look is patterned after a basket. Take a large container and insert a length of stout wire or thin bamboo; shape it into an arch, like the handle of a basket.

Position a small plant at each end, and train them to grow around the handle. You can make a very handsome mixed planter with herbs on three levels: rosemary handles; sage, tarragon, or dwarf lavender upright in the basket; and several varieties of thyme spilling over the sides. This would be a wonderful gift for a friend who enjoys cooking with fresh herbs.

4. Another popular technique is to train one sturdy plant into what is known as a standard: a single specimen shaped like a miniature tree. The lower branches are completely removed to create a bare lower stem that mimics a tree trunk. Then the upper part of the plant is allowed to grow, but shaped into a round ball or a more free-form tree shape. Sometimes you see roses done this way and marketed as tree roses. A pair of matched pots containing the same variety of plant, flanking a front doorway, is a classic look.

Rosemary is easily trained into a topiary or a standard, as shown here.

Herbs

Saffron Crocus

GROW AS: **perennial**

PLANT SIZE: **6 inches**

START WITH: **bulbs**

HARVEST SEASON: **fall**

SUN REQUIREMENTS: **sun to partial shade**

MINIMUM SOIL DEPTH: **8 inches**

With most culinary herbs, we're primarily interested in the leaves, sometimes the seeds, and occasionally, as a bonus, the flowers. Other plants used to flavor foods are harvested for their roots, bark, flower buds, berries, seedpods—the spices of the world. But in only one case that we can think of is the raison d'être such a tiny element: one specific part of the plant's flower.

It's time for a short detour into the sex life of plants.

All flowering plants have a sophisticated reproductive system, with male and female organs built into their flowers. The male parts, called stamens, produce pollen. The female organ is called a pistil, and it is composed of three separate elements: the ovary, tucked away in the base of the flower; the stigma, the very top part of the pistil, which catches the pollen; and the style, the thin stalk connecting the stigma and the ovary.

When the pollen (the male seed) is ripe, it becomes loose so that when a visiting bee, attracted by the bright flowers of the petals, brushes against it, some pollen is transferred to its legs. Then, as it crawls around in search of nectar, it transfers some of the pollen to the sticky stigma, whence it travels down the style to the ovary, fertilizing the ovary for the production of viable seeds. Thus life goes on.

That's the basic process, and an extraordinarily clever design it is. In the case of saffron crocus, however, there is one minor twist. The very unusual structure of this flower's stamens and pistil inhibits the transfer of pollen, and so the plant does not set seed. The crocuses are propagated from bulbs that naturally divide underground.

Fortunately, though, the crocus flowers still contain the reproductive parts. The pistil of the saffron crocus flower has one style that branches into three separate stigmas. They are bright orange, relatively large in comparison to those of most plants, and droop downward outside the flower petals. It is those stigmas that we call saffron.

Commercial saffron is the world's most expensive spice because of what it takes to grow and harvest it. Each plant makes one or occasionally two flowers a season; that's three or maybe six stigmas per plant. The flowers are picked by hand (backbreaking work) and the stigmas plucked out, again by hand, and dried. It takes 75,000 flowers to make one pound of dried saffron.

So is it worth growing a few flowers for the small amount of saffron you would harvest? Actually, yes. For one thing, it takes only a few threads of saffron to flavor a dish of paella or bouillabaisse. For another, you get to enjoy the pretty lavender-colored flowers that bloom in late fall.

And think of how smug you'll feel.

Almost everyone is familiar with crocus flowers. In the early springtime they're among the very first splashes of color in an otherwise bleak landscape, sometimes bursting through the snow with a yellow or purple hello. But not everyone realizes that there are also fall-blooming crocuses, and the saffron crocus is one of these (see the important box on page 249). Except for the characteristic bright orange stigmas, it looks very much like a soft purple spring crocus, both flower and foliage. So when you choose to grow the crocus for the saffron, you have the bonus of beautiful flowers during a part of the year when most other flowers have passed.

The saffron crocus is native to the areas around the central and eastern Mediterranean that we now call

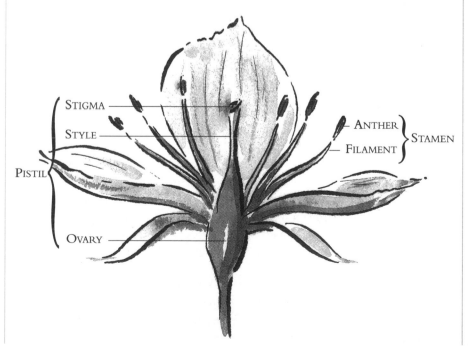

STIGMA

STYLE

PISTIL

OVARY

ANTHER
FILAMENT } STAMEN

the Middle East, where its main commercial growing areas still exist. From there it spread westward to the ancient cultures of Greece and Rome, and eastward to India and China as part of the spice trade. The plant was brought to Spain in the eighth century by the Arabs; from Spain it spread across continental Europe, and eventually to England.

In 1699 the English botanist John Evelyn wrote of saffron: "Those of Spain and Italy generally make use of this flower, mingling its golden tincture with almost everything they eat." This is still largely true today, for saffron is best known in dishes that we associate with Mediterranean countries: paella and arroz con pollo from Spain, bouillabaisse from France, and risotto Milanese from Italy. (Notice the special affinity between saffron and rice.) All those dishes get both a "golden tincture" and a very distinctive, exotic flavor from just a few threads of saffron. Luckily, a few threads is all you need.

Note: be very sure that you are buying *Crocus sativus* and not *Colchicum autumnalis,* a flower called the autumn crocus, which is *extremely* poisonous (see box, opposite page).

Saffron Basics. Saffron crocus, like all crocuses, grows from a bulb. It blooms in October and November, with flowers in shades of lilac or purple. Like their springtime namesakes, these crocuses open in the sun and close on wet and cloudy days. When the blossoms fade, that's the time to gather the stigmas. Once the flowers

are past, the plant sends up its foliage: spiky, narrow dark green leaves.

This is one of Mother Nature's contrary plants: it goes dormant in summer and grows its foliage in winter. Where winters are mild, the crocus has no problem. But a heavy snow would totally cover the new foliage, preventing the production of chlorophyll, and the plants would die. Solution: if you live in a very cold climate, bring the container inside in the fall and let the plants finish their flowering on a windowsill. Move them back outside as soon as you can in the spring.

When the foliage dies back in summer, stop watering. Your goal is to let the plants move into dormancy naturally. In the fall, when moisture and cooler temperatures return, a new season of flowering begins.

Planting. Bulbs are easy to plant. Use a basic potting mix and fill the pot half full. Sprinkle about a tablespoon of bulb food or bonemeal over the soil for every three bulbs you plant. Cover the bulb food with an inch or two of potting mix, then set in your bulbs, spacing them an inch or so apart with the pointed end up. Cover them with 3 to 4 inches of the potting mix, and water to settle it all in. Add a little more soil if the tips of the bulbs are exposed.

Because saffron crocus bulbs, like other bulbs, will multiply, you may not want to put them in with other plants if the container is small. Also, don't forget that you will want a container that you can move inside if you live in a very cold climate.

A Word of Warning

Not all purple crocuses that bloom in the fall are saffron crocuses. Much more commonly available in garden centers are bulbs of *Colchicum autumnalis,* which is **extremely poisonous.** They go by the common name autumn crocus, and they make pretty lavender flowers, but they are deadly!

If you saw them side by side, you could easily tell the difference between colchicum and saffron crocus. The saffron is a small, tidy plant very much resembling spring crocus, with perky flowers on upright stems. Colchicum is a larger plant, with big, floppy leaves and large, blowsy flowers that tend to droop over from their own weight, especially when they've been rained on. Also, only the saffron crocus has the orange stigmas. Even the bulbs are quite different: the colchicum bulb is large (more than 2 inches in diameter), brown, and scraggly; the saffron bulb is smaller (about 1 inch), tight, and with a silvery tan sheath.

These plants should be clearly marked with their botanical names. Because colchicum is so very dangerous, growers are very careful to differentiate and label their products correctly. So check before you buy, and if you don't see botanical names on the label, shop somewhere else.

Whatever you do, don't assume that any fall-blooming purple crocus you happen to come across is saffron, and decide to take a bite.

In any case, you'll need to unpot the bulbs every year or two and divide them; as the bulbs multiply, the pot can get overcrowded and the plants will stop blooming. Do this in mid to late July, when the plants are dormant. Simply plant the new bulbs in another pot and have that much more delicious saffron to harvest.

Success with Saffron. As long as you switch your mind over to the plant's timing—blooming in autumn, growing new foliage in winter, going dormant in summer—you'll find this an easy plant to grow.

Each year in summer add some bulb food and fresh potting soil, even if you don't think it's time to divide and repot the bulbs.

Harvesting. When the stigmas of the crocus flower are fully ripe and bright colored, pick them carefully. Use a small tweezers to hold them while you clip off each one with small scissors, and lay them on a glass dish or paper plate to dry. Saffron can be used fresh, but the flavor is best and more concentrated when the stigmas are dried. Store dried saffron in a closed container that is clean and odorless (most plastic has an odor). Dried saffron is adversely affected by sunlight, so store it in a dark glass jar or keep it in a cupboard.

Varieties. There is just one species, the inimitable *Crocus sativus.*

I n ancient times, when all diseases and their cures were mysteries, it was believed that evil spirits hovered over the cradles of newborns, ready to take them away when the parents' attention was diverted. To protect baby boys from death, they were swaddled in blue clothes; blue, the color of the sky, was thought to shield the baby from the evil spirits. Girls, considered the less valuable of the species, were given no special protection. At some later time, perhaps reflecting a more balanced view of humanity, a new childbirth legend developed:

Theme Garden

Pretty in Pink

baby boys were born in a cabbage patch (think of the blue-green foliage of many cabbages), and the more delicate baby girls were born tucked inside the petals of beautiful pink roses.

Pastel colors are comparatively uncommon in a vegetable garden. But those who love them should not be shortchanged, as girl babies of long ago were, and so we put together herbs, flowers, and vegetables in this container garden that celebrates the color pink.

We want to achieve a sense of lush beauty: a container garden spilling over with beautiful plants, showing at least some pink in every season. This is the place for your prettiest container, perhaps one of the new molded foam types that are so wonderfully lightweight but look like elegant stoneware or antique terra-cotta.

In the center, the beautiful Marshall's Delight **monarda;** unlike the more common red flower, this monarda has soft pink blossoms. A perennial, it blooms in summer and gives you both interesting flowers and leaves for a refreshing tea. For best results, plant it in a smaller pot and sink that pot inside the larger container; the hidden pot will help contain the plant's vigorous root growth, leaving room for other plants.

In a circle at the base of the monarda, alternate clumps of Forescate **chives** and seedlings of Ruby **Swiss chard.** The stems of the chard are a deep magenta color that glows like neon when the sun hits it, and this variety of chives has bright pink flowers. The chard will be at its peak in late spring; when it starts to bolt in hot weather, pull it out, giving the chives more room. By mid summer the monarda gets bare at the ankles, and the pretty arching spray of the chives will cover them nicely.

Just outside the circle of chard and chives, put several small plants of tricolor **sage** and pink-flowered **dianthus.** The sage has green leaves boldly streaked with creamy white and rich pink. The dianthus, also known as pinks, couldn't be a better choice for this all-pink garden. As they grow during the season, the two plants seem to blend into one—a very lovely plant with richly colored foliage and bright flowers.

In the outermost circle, close to the rim of the container, start the season with as many pink-flowered **pansies** as you can fit in. They will wilt with the heat of summer, and you'll want to either take them out or cut them back severely. This opens up room for the sage and dianthus, which will be coming into full growth about that same time. With a bit of luck, the pruned-back pansies will flourish again in the fall, giving you one last blush of color before the season ends.

If you still don't have enough pink, think about adding scented geraniums for next year. And of course roses, for all the new baby girls.

For details on growing the plants in this garden, see

Chives, page 191

Dianthus, page 370

Monarda, page 229

Pansies, page 382

Sage, page 252

Swiss chard, page 106

Herbs

Sage

GROW AS: **perennial**

PLANT SIZE: **1 to 3 feet**

START WITH: **transplants**

HARVEST SEASON: **summer and fall**

SUN REQUIREMENTS: **full sun**

MINIMUM SOIL DEPTH: **8 inches**

Attractive and fragrant, sage gives you the best of both worlds. The plain species (*Salvia officinalis*) sports handsome silver-green leaves, but there are lots of cultivars and some of them provide splashes of color from apple green to gold to deep purple. These add cheer to any container when planted with each other or as a complement to other herbs or flowers. Draw near and rub the soft, textured leaves, and a warm, rich, almost lemony, almost minty scent envelops and seduces you.

If you love to cook, home-grown sage is a must. Its unique flavor enhances so many dishes, particularly the foods of autumn. Mix it into your Thanksgiving turkey stuffing, stir it into beef-and-carrot stew, or sprinkle it over mushroom risotto. Its flavor enriches marinades, omelets, steamed vegetables, even apple pie. Sage holds up pretty well in cold weather, so you should be able to slip outside and cut what you need right on the spot. If you dry the leaves, their flavor changes slightly and becomes a touch more pungent.

Rose Marie says: For a long time I never cooked with sage because the dried herb has a certain mustiness that always put me off. But in spite of that I found myself repeatedly planting it because I like the look of the plants, especially those with purple or golden leaves. Then I became curious about sage tea, which was once so highly regarded by the Chinese that they traded their own fine China tea for it. Sage tea is really quite delicious. To try some, place two or three golden sage leaves in a white china cup and let them steep for two or three minutes. Enjoy the fragrant tea and the pretty patterned leaves in the cup. Of course, now I often cook with sage—but only with the fresh leaves, which I can harvest a few steps from my kitchen door.

Sage Basics. All the sages are a cinch to grow, asking only for a good potting mix that drains well. Water when the mix looks dry, and don't let it get soggy.

Midway through summer or toward the end of it, sage plants may send up flower stalks. The color varies from pink to white to purple to blue, depending on the cultivar. If you like the way the flowers look, of course, let them be. Sage flowers are a favorite of honeybees (which are cherished by all vegetable gardeners) and make an incredible herb vinegar, turning white wine vinegar a glorious magenta. But if you're growing sage mainly for your kitchen, snip off the flowers so the plants can't go to seed and foliage production can continue unabated. Also, as you harvest or prune leaves throughout the growing season, you'll be forcing the plant to grow more compactly, which looks better.

Unless your winters are severe, you can usually keep pots of sage outdoors (when in doubt, bring them in). Prune plants low each spring when warm weather returns, and a flush of new growth should follow. Be forewarned that sage does not have a long life span. You'll likely get only two or three seasons out of a plant before it becomes woody at the base and produces fewer and fewer leaves. So be prepared to start over with cuttings or new plants every few years.

Planting. Sage is not often raised from seed, partly because most gardeners want the interesting cultivars, which are best grown from cuttings. Also, sage seed tends to germinate poorly and the plants that finally appear grow slowly.

Your best course, then, is to buy young plants in the spring. If your local nursery has a disappointing selection, check out mail-order nurseries or take cuttings in the fall from varieties you like.

Sage is not fussy about soil, though you shouldn't subject it to a heavy mix that drains poorly. Instead, add a handful of sand or extra perlite or vermiculite to a commercial potting mixture. Sage thrives and looks great in clay pots, which also wick moisture away from the roots.

Success with Sage. Sage is a dry-land plant; it does best with plenty of sunshine and in well-drained soil. The leaves of some kinds are so pretty that you might be tempted to include one or more in a combination planter built around a color theme. Be careful, though, not to combine sage with water-loving plants, or you may not be able to keep everyone happy.

Pests never seem to trouble sage; they're no doubt repelled by the strong fragrance we find so appealing.

Harvesting. Clip off a few branches strategically around the plant so it doesn't look butchered or lopsided. Pinch off the leaves and discard the stems. To use fresh, mince leaves with a very sharp knife, or use them whole. Add midway through a recipe, so they have time to release their flavor but don't completely lose their texture.

To dry the leaves, put them in a warm, dark spot on paper or a screen. Their color will fade and they'll curl a bit and become brittle, so when you gather them up to put in jars, handle them gingerly. Or go ahead and pulverize them between your fingers. Fully dried leaves when crumbled become a fluffy mass that can be measured out by teaspoonfuls in the kitchen. The flavor of dried sage leaves is a touch more pungent or bitter than that of fresh ones.

Varieties. A classic variety, the one used by commercial producers

Recipe: Herbed Roast Pork

G arden photographer and writer Walter Chandoha says: "This rosemary and sage mixture can also be used to coat veal or lamb roasts, and it is especially good on grilled chicken."

Note that the amount of sage and garlic you use depends on the size of your roast. Serve the pork with rice or mashed potatoes.

1 boneless pork loin, 3 to 5 pounds

5 sprigs (6 inches each) of fresh rosemary

10 to 20 fresh sage leaves

3 to 4 garlic cloves

2 tablespoons salt

1/2 teaspoon freshly ground black pepper

1 to 2 tablespoons olive oil

1 1/2 cups chicken stock, or more

Splash of white wine

2 tablespoons flour

10 ounces mushrooms, sliced

1. Preheat the oven to 400°F.

2. Score the fat side of the pork with crisscross gashes about 1 inch apart, penetrating through the fat and just barely cutting into the flesh.

3. Strip the leaves from the rosemary stems, chop the sage leaves, mince the garlic, and mix them together in a small bowl. Add the salt and pepper, and blend with enough olive oil to make a thick paste. Rub the herb paste all over the pork, working it into the crisscross cuts.

4. Place the pork in a metal (not glass) roasting pan. Place the pan in the preheated oven. After 30 minutes, pour 1/2 cup of the chicken stock into the pan, lower the heat to 325°F, and continue roasting for another 30 minutes for a 3-pound roast, and a total of 20 minutes per pound for a larger roast. Add more chicken stock as needed; the bot-

tom of the pan should never become completely dry. Place the pork on a serving platter and allow it to rest for about 15 minutes.

5. While the pork roast is resting, deglaze the roasting pan. Place the pan over medium heat, add the flour, and stir to blend, 1 minute. Add the wine and the remaining 1 cup chicken stock to the roasting pan and stir to mix. Cook until the sauce thickens. Add half of the mushrooms to the sauce and cook until the sauce is reduced by half, about 10 minutes. Add the remaining mushrooms, and cook for 3 minutes more.

6. Slice the pork into ½- to 1-inch slices, and cover with the mushroom sauce before serving.

Serves 6 to 8

of packaged dried sage, is **Holt's Mammoth.** It has large gray-green leaves with a clean, noncamphorous flavor, and produces masses of soft blue flowers in late spring. As for the colorful-leaved cultivars, some of the best are purple sage (**Purpurascens**), golden sage (**Icterina**), and the justly popular **Tricolor,** splashed with green, cream, and pink. Unfortunately, Tricolor tends to be shorter-lived than other varieties, but it's so lovely you won't mind replanting it.

In addition, there is one very special type so unique that we give it special billing here: pineapple sage.

PINEAPPLE SAGE

GROW AS: tender perennial

PLANT SIZE: 2 to 3 feet tall, 1 to 2 feet wide

START WITH: transplants

HARVEST SEASON: fall

SUN REQUIREMENTS: full sun

MINIMUM SOIL DEPTH: 8 inches

Something of a novelty in the world of sages, pineapple sage takes no special trouble to grow and promises a range of culinary treats. The plant emits an irresistible sweet-ripe-pineapple aroma that you and visitors to your garden will enjoy from a foot or two away. Both the leaves (which are light green and a little bit fuzzy) and the amazing red flowers (long, thin, and shaped like a medieval trumpet) are fragrant and edible. And they really do taste and smell like pineapple.

The entire plant is beautiful with a reddish theme: the stems have a red hue, the leaves are rimmed in red, and the flowers, when they finally appear, are a dazzling scarlet. Leaves and flowers contribute their novel, sweet flavor to everything from fruit salads, pork, chicken, and rice dishes to jams and jellies. Add a few sprigs to lemonade, iced tea, or homemade piña coladas. Or dry some for use in sachets or potpourri.

Pineapple Sage Basics. Even though its appearance is so different from the other sages', pineapple sage needs much the same growing conditions. Like other sages, it prefers well-drained soil, but it does require more water than its cousins and should never be allowed to go completely dry. On the other hand, look out for root rot caused by overwatering.

The chief delight of this plant is its astonishing flowers, but a minor catch-22 is at work here. Pineapple sage sets flowers in response to short day length, so in the north it is a late bloomer, sometimes so late that cold weather threatens the tender plant by the time it comes into bloom.

This is not a problem for gardeners in mild climates, who can leave the pots out on their patio or deck and may get to see late-browsing bees, butterflies, and even hummingbirds stop by to sample the sweet nectar. But since pineapple sage cannot tolerate freezing weather, it will have to be brought indoors in climates where a winter freeze is inevitable. Make sure it gets a sunny spot on a windowsill or in a heated sunroom. It makes a gorgeous houseplant; the scarlet flowers, coupled with the pineapple fragrance, are wonderful to enjoy while the snow flies outside. In a heated room the pot may dry out faster than it did when outside, so keep an eye on soil moisture.

Inside or out, it is good practice to cut the plant down to several inches after blooming is over so it will greet spring with fresh growth.

Planting. Seeds are not widely available, so you probably will have no choice but to start with young plants. Even then you may have to search specialty nurseries to find them, but it's a worthwhile search. Plan ahead for moving the containers indoors in cold-winter areas.

Success with Pineapple Sage. This is not a sage you can plant and neglect. You'll need to hover over it year-round. In addition to plenty of sunshine, pineapple sage requires regular watering but should never be left in standing water or the roots will rot. However, it seems to tolerate dry weather more than most plants. When it begins setting flower buds, keep up with the watering, both to maintain good flowering and because plants are especially thirsty when blooming.

Harvesting. Like other sages, pineapple sage benefits from a little pruning to keep it shapely, and this is your opportunity to harvest some of those tasty scented leaves. They make a novel garnish for drinks or salads, and are best consumed fresh, as dried leaves lose most of their potency.

The fragrant flowers are also edible. Pinch them and use immediately so their scarlet color can be appreciated. Sprinkle them into a holiday punch bowl, press them into cake frosting, or add them to soft cheese as an appetizer.

Varieties. The basic species, *Salvia elegans,* has scarlet flowers. The cultivar **Frieda Dixon** has blossoms in softer colors: coral red to salmon.

Herbal Vinegars

Having fresh herbs just a few steps away from the kitchen is the delight of all cooks. But what to do if your bounty overwhelms, and you grow more than you can use in fresh form? The traditional answer is to dry the herbs and store them for later use, and that's a fine, time-honored solution (see box on pages 170 to 171). But there is another way to preserve the pleasures of your wonderful home-grown herbs so they can be savored later in the season: turn them into flavored vinegar.

Vinegar itself is a preservative. And when you use vinegar to preserve herbs, you get herb-suffused vinegar, a wonderful elixir that can be used as a delicious cooking condiment or as the basis of several old-fashioned beauty treatments.

Making the Vinegar. The process is unbelievably simple. Take all your excess herb snippings, stuff them loosely into a glass jar with a tight-fitting lid, and pour in enough vinegar to cover all the foliage. Leave the jar on the counter for a while (a few days to a week or more), during which time the vinegar extracts the flavor, aroma, and color from the herbs. When it has reached the flavor level you want (test by tasting), strain off and discard the sodden mass of herbs. All the herbal essence that used to be held in the plant is now in the vinegar, ready for you to use in marvelous ways.

You can use any kind of vinegar you have on hand, but for a really perfect product, keep these points in mind:

■ Plain white distilled vinegar has the harshest taste, and is therefore not our first choice for an herbal vinegar you intend to use in cooking. As the basis of a cosmetic vinegar, it's fine.

■ White wine vinegar provides the best way to enjoy the gorgeous colors that some herbs and flowers release. For example, purple basil produces a rich magenta, and so does sage when it is in flower. Nasturtium vinegar captures the neon orange of the original flowers, and lavender vinegar is a sumptuous rose red.

■ Red wine vinegar is a flavor complement for basil, thyme, oregano, marjoram, and other robust herbs.

■ Apple cider vinegar, with its slightly fruity undertones, is especially nice with milder-tasting herbs and with herb-flower combinations. Mint vinegar, made with apple cider vinegar, is wonderful in dressings for fruit salads.

■ Rice vinegar is a good choice for flavored vinegars with herbs we associate with Asian cuisines, such as lemongrass, garlic chives, or cilantro.

Herbal Vinegar in the Kitchen. Using the herbal vinegars in cooking is a matter of creativity combined with common sense. The common-sense part is to understand what you're starting with: the taste of vinegar plus the taste of whatever herb you used. The creative part is letting your imagination loose: in what foods would that combination of tastes be an asset? Any herbal vinegar makes sensational salad dressing, of course, but also can be a flavorful addition to pot roasts and stews,

(continued on next page)

(continued from previous page)

sauces for chicken or fish, and can add a welcomed zing to steamed vegetables.

Herbal Vinegar in the Bath.
You're probably aware that many herbs have constituent ingredients that are beneficial to the human body in various ways. This is the basis of herbal medicine, a subject that is far too complex for this book, and also of herb-based natural cosmetics. Here we want to introduce you to the notion of using the essence of various herbs, preserved in vinegar, in the bath. In particular, two ideas that are both modern and old-fashioned: refreshing and relaxing herbal soaks, and herbal beauty treatments for your hair.

Herbal baths. A long soak in a hot tub is such a restorative experience that modern science has given it a name: hydrotherapy. Even better than bathing in plain water is a leisurely soak in an herbal bath. For a short time, the entire room is turned into a magical cloud of fragrance, and your only task is to enjoy it. The aroma released by some herbs is reported to have beneficial effects on the body (this is the basis of aromatherapy); in addition, many herbs are good for your skin, and so is the vinegar itself—it cleanses the pores and restores skin pH to the proper level. For all these reasons, then, an herbal bath would be a decidedly healthful thing to do even if it weren't such a pleasure.

The general process is this: add about a cup of herbal vinegar to the bathwater. Slip into the tub, close your eyes, deeply inhale the fragrant air, forget the world.

The type of herbal vinegar you use is often a matter of what you have on hand, but here are some suggestions based on the salutary properties of various herbs:

■ Chamomile is considered soothing and relaxing, and it is excellent for chapped skin.

■ Bay, oregano, and sage are good for sore muscles.

■ Because they stimulate blood circulation, basil, bay, fennel, lavender, mint, rosemary, sage, and thyme are both invigorating and relaxing.

■ Calendula and spearmint, in addition to chamomile, are soothing to rough or damaged skin.

■ The foliage and flowers of bay, nasturtiums, rosemary, sage, and salad burnet have astringent properties, and will tighten the pores of the skin.

Herbal hair rinse. Take about half a cup of herbal vinegar, dilute it with about a pint of warm water, and pour it over your hair as a final rinse. The vinegary smell dissipates quickly, and you're left with a gentle herbal fragrance on your hair. The vinegar itself is good for your scalp (helps reduce dandruff) and helps give your hair a good pH balance. The herbs add their own magic:

■ Calendula and chamomile lighten the color; blonds get blonder, auburn redheads get brighter.

■ Sage darkens the color, giving rich highlights to brunettes.

Calendula, parsley, rosemary, and sage add shine and body, and help control dandruff.

Chamomile makes hair softer.

Calendula, lavender, mint, and rosemary are good conditioners for oily hair.

Parsley and sage are good for dry hair.

Safety Precautions. Herbal cosmetic preparations are generally very safe; that is, in fact, one of their appeals. However, it's impossible to say they are totally safe for everyone, because someone, somewhere, is going to be allergic to something. To be on the safe side, test herbal vinegars on your skin; dab some on with a cotton ball and wait an hour or so for any reaction. If nothing happens, you can enjoy your herbal bath to your heart's content.

Gifts of Herbal Vinegar. Once you experience the pleasures and versatility of vinegars flavored with your own herbs, you'll no doubt enjoy sharing them with friends. A pretty bottle of lavender vinegar, with a handmade tag explaining how to use it, is sure to delight. To turn your herbal vinegars into extra-special gifts, make a large batch and then add a few refinements:

Strain the finished vinegar through a coffee filter to remove all flecks and traces of sediment. Even though the commercial herbal vinegars that you may have admired in gourmet food shops often have a sprig of the herb in the bottle, we discourage this. Human nature being what it is, your friends will tend to save your gift for a special occasion, and in time the vinegar will cause the piece of herb to disintegrate, creating an unattractive layer of sludge at the bottom of the jar. If you wish, you can tie on a decorative sprig of the dried herb to the *outside* of the bottle.

All year long, save pretty bottles and jars that pass through your life. A salad cruet, the kind with a removable stopper, is wonderful for bath vinegars. Either present your gift in the cruet, if it doesn't have to be mailed, or include the empty cruet along with a tightly sealed bottle and a note of explanation.

Create a large gift tag that describes several ways to use the vinegar, both in cooking and cosmetically. Add a recipe card.

Explore craft shops and stationery stores for stick-on labels with floral or herbal designs. Use them to make or embellish the labels or gift tags you will add to the bottles.

Herbs

Salad Burnet

GROW AS: **perennial**

PLANT SIZE: **6 to 12 inches**

START WITH: **seeds or transplants**

HARVEST SEASON: **spring to early summer**

SUN REQUIREMENTS: **full sun to partial shade**

MINIMUM SOIL DEPTH: **12 inches**

I n a world of herbs intended as seasonings, salad burnet is something different. Although it looks like an herb, grows as easily as many other herbs, and is fragrant and delicious, it almost seems to belong to the vegetable tribe. Why? Because its leaves—the young ones, especially—taste uncannily like cool, crisp cucumber. And they are ready to enjoy well before your vegetable garden will have any ripe cucumbers to offer.

Salad burnet, or burnet, as it is also known, is a natural for salads, of course. Strew fresh-picked, loosely chopped leaves over an ordinary lettuce and tomato salad, and surprise and delight everyone at the table. Creative cooks also like to add it to coleslaw, plain yogurt (as a dip or side dish), and herb butters. It also enhances cold summer soups; imagine how delicious it would be garnishing vichyssoise or added to gazpacho. If you're making Bloody Marys or Virgin Marys a sprig of salad burnet would be an intriguing garnish and conversation piece (granted, it's floppier than the traditional celery stick).

This is a charming little plant, with delicate, lacy leaves on short stems that grow in a rosette shape. The flowers are small but adorable: little lime green globes that spray out tiny pink pistils at all angles.

Salad burnet is an early-season herb, best used while young. In any case, it can be enjoyed only by those who grow it, for this is definitely a fresh-only herb. Dried leaves are a disappointment; they lose all color and flavor. The only way to preserve salad burnet's wonderful taste beyond the season is to steep the foliage in vinegar to make a cucumber-flavored infusion. Use it in salad dressing, and save a few bottles for holiday gifts.

Salad Burnet Basics. A perennial that keeps its leaves in all but the coldest months, burnet is an easy-going plant. It thrives in sunshine, likes its soil slightly alkaline, and doesn't require much water or coddling.

To keep a steady supply of young leaves coming on, you'll want to clip the plant regularly. Once it goes to flower, the flavor diminishes.

This plant has been in cultivation for a long time. Its wonderful flavor accounts for at least some of its enduring popularity, but the fact that it is widely adaptable certainly doesn't hurt. It grows in almost any soil except heavy clay or acidic ones. It likes full sun best, but tolerates some shade, and is never troubled by pests or diseases. Burnet withstands periods of neglect and is extremely hardy; in fact, it can stay outdoors all year long in all but the harshest climates, so long as the container itself is frost-hardy. In short, it is a low-maintenance perennial plant.

One caution: salad burnet does not like to be moved around because it develops a taproot that gets longer with age. So choose a deep pot.

Planting. This plant is no trouble to raise from seed, either purchased from a catalog or gathered from someone else's plant in autumn. You can start the seeds in either autumn or spring. Sow seeds in a seed-starting mix, cover with a light dusting of the mix, then set in a warm spot (70°F or so). Germination generally occurs in a week to 10 days. Move the seedlings into their permanent pot as soon as it's practical, so you won't disturb the developing taproot.

Or avoid the issue from the outset by sowing directly into the chosen pot; the seedlings may look dwarfed at first, but will be overflowing their bounds by summer's end. And be fore-warned that if you allow your plant to develop those little flowers and go to seed, you'll have volunteer seedlings in the pot next year, as well as in adjacent pots and any nearby dirt.

If you buy seedlings from a nursery, go for the smallest ones you can find (so long as they are well rooted, of course). At home, transplant promptly so they can develop that taproot without inhibition.

Success with Salad Burnet. Despite its wispy, fernlike foliage and delicate little flowers, salad burnet is a pretty tough plant, able to survive drought and neglect. Again, to get the most attractive plant, not to mention the tastiest harvest, you should grow it in soil that is neutral or even a touch alkaline. It really doesn't like acidic soils.

Make sure your potting soil drains well, and water sparingly. A soggy salad burnet plant develops crown rot and struggles or even dies.

Harvesting. The younger the leaves, the more pronounced and delicious the cucumber flavor. So begin clipping in early summer. When you notice the plant sending up flower stalks, pinch them off to force the plant to concentrate on making more foliage instead. Despite your best efforts, however, the foliage does coarsen and the flavor diminishes as the season goes on.

This is an herb you must use fresh. Dried leaves curl up, turn brown, and lose all flavor.

Varieties. Just one basic species: *Sanguisorba minor.*

Herbs

Scented Geraniums

GROW AS: **annual or tender perennial**

PLANT SIZE: **1 to 3 feet**

START WITH: **plants**

HARVEST SEASON: **spring through fall**

SUN REQUIREMENTS: **full sun**

MINIMUM SOIL DEPTH: **6 inches**

You can find scented geraniums with the aroma of rose, lemon, lime, apple, orange, apricot, peppermint, lemon balm, nutmeg, coconut, ginger, eucalyptus, and camphor—to name a few. The array of possibilities is staggering, and plant breeders are continually introducing new cultivars to feed the demand from enthusiasts.

Scented geraniums, rich with spicy, fruity, and floral fragrances, have been around for hundreds of years. It's likely your grandmother grew some on her front porch. In the winter she would prune them back and bring them into the house to grow on a windowsill or in a sunroom, as they would be killed by a hard frost. You'll have to do the same with yours if you live in zone 8 or colder.

But these plants smell so good you'll be glad to have them inside with you, placed where you can brush against them to release their intriguing scents.

If you enjoy reading old cookbooks, you may know that at one time the leaves of rose-scented geraniums were used to line cake pans to impart their flavor to the cake. The leaves were often steeped in tea as well, so that when you sipped from your cup you could actually taste the scent of roses. And jellies flavored with scented geraniums were a real treat. All these old-

W e're not talking here about the familiar window box "geraniums" (which are actually pelargoniums), the ones with large flower heads in assertive colors, although they are relatives. We're also not talking about true geraniums, the fluffy bedding plant gardeners call hardy geranium. Scented geraniums are something else entirely, and they are wonderful indeed. The flowers are dainty and pretty but not especially noteworthy. The real joy of these plants, and the whole reason for growing them, is the amazingly aromatic leaves.

fashioned delights are possible today for gardeners who discover the joy of growing scented geraniums. Do remember, however, to remove the leaves before eating or drinking.

The fragrance is in the foliage, and the best way to experience it is to rub the leaves between your fingers. When you do that, you also become aware of the great variety in shape, color, and texture of the foliage. One geranium may have downy soft, velvety leaves as big as your hand, while another has such finely divided foliage it reminds you of a fern. Some leaves are shaped like a child's hand, others like a maple or oak leaf, and quite a few have brownish or burgundy patterns in the center. One lemon-scented variety has small, nickel-size leaves with ruffles around the edges.

All scented geraniums have blooms, but they are usually small and pale-colored, not of much significance. Occasionally you may run across one that has a really gorgeous little flower, and then you have a plant with a double bonus. One example is Snowflake, named for the creamy white splotches on the leaves that make the plant look as if it had been snowed upon, and bearing large clusters of light mauve flowers.

Scented Geranium Basics.

These are perfect for that hot, dry spot where other plants seem to shrivel. They have fairly small root systems and do well in smaller pots than you'd think; even when root-bound, they just seem to keep on going. Geraniums are also drought-tolerant and can be revived from a wilted state with a good soaking.

On the opposite end, they will not survive a hard freeze and must be brought inside in freezing weather. Since they are quite leggy growers, you'll need to do some drastic pruning at summer's end or they may become too large to fit in your space. If space is really limited, a better alternative is to take cuttings and root them in damp soil or a glass of water, and discard the old plant.

Planting. Soil requirements are simple; a basic potting mix with a little sand added is fine. The soil should be slightly on the alkaline side, rather than acidic. For small plants, a 6- or 8-inch pot is probably adequate, but larger specimens such as Chocolate Mint need a larger pot, the problem is not so much the roots but the fact that the pot will become so top-heavy it will tip over. A mulch of pretty stones or small pieces of lava rock spread over the soil will help give weight and balance to a large plant.

The smaller scented geraniums can be grown in mixed containers with other plants. Plant them with other herbs that like the same growing conditions, such as lavender, rosemary, sage, and thyme.

Success with Scented

Geraniums. Heat, sun, and water is the combination needed to grow these plants: heavy on the heat, moderate on the sun, and light on the water. Let the containers dry out slightly between waterings, to help flavors and scents develop. Overwatering is about the worst thing you can do, as scented

Recipe:  Rose Geranium
Tea Cake

Rose Marie says: "Scented geranium leaves lend their fragrance to the entire cake when baked into the batter. The leaf pattern and whipped cream filling make this a very pretty tea cake. You can also make it with other scented geraniums (lemon, perhaps) for an equally delightful taste."

FOR THE CAKE
20 rose-scented geranium leaves
1½ cups all-purpose flour
½ teaspoon baking powder
8 tablespoons (1 stick) butter
1¼ cups sugar
4 large eggs

FOR THE FILLING
¼ cup rose geranium jelly (see page 206)
1 cup heavy cream

GARNISH
Confectioners' sugar
Crystallized violas, geranium blossoms, or rose petals (optional)

1. Preheat the oven to 375°F. Lightly butter two 9-inch cake pans and arrange 10 geranium leaves in a pleasing pattern on the bottom of each pan. Set them aside.

2. Sift the flour and baking powder together in a medium-size bowl and set aside.

3. In a large mixing bowl, cream the butter until light. Add the sugar and continue beating until the texture is light and fluffy. Add the eggs,

one at a time, beating after every addition until the mixture resembles mayonnaise. Fold in the flour mixture, just until well combined.

4. Divide the batter between the cake pans and bake until the surface is golden and the edges begin to pull away from the sides of the pans, 18 to 20 minutes. Remove the cakes from the pans and let them cool on wire racks, covered with a clean kitchen towel.

5. To make the filling, soften the jelly slightly in the microwave and stir until very creamy. Whip the cream until it stands in soft peaks, then carefully fold the jelly into the whipped cream.

6. Remove the geranium leaves from one of the cake layers and cover the layer with the filling. Place the second layer on top, leaves facing up. Sift confectioners' sugar over the top, covering it completely, then carefully peel away the geranium leaves, allowing their pattern to remain. For a special occasion, decorate the cake with crystallized violas, geranium blossoms, or rose petals (see box on page 180).

Serves 8 to 10

geraniums don't like to have wet feet.

If during the course of the summer your plant needs pruning to keep it to a manageable size, cut back one or more of the stems all the way to the base. Then remove all but the top leaves (keep the leaves you remove for tea or whatever), and push the almost-denuded stem into a pot of moist soil to root for a new plant. Be sure to label your plants, especially the cuttings you take, as sometimes the scents are similar and the plants often look alike.

Harvesting. Just pick the leaves as you need them for tea, for baking, for jelly, or for the sheer pleasure of having one to rub against your cheek. Leaves can be dried and stored for later use, or added to potpourri. A few tossed into a drawer of linens will give them a lovely scent.

Varieties. The three most popular types are the mint, lemon, and rose varieties, and there are quite a few cultivars of each. **Chocolate Mint** is a large plant with velvety leaves and a hint of chocolate in its fragrance. **Snowflake,** mentioned above, has the fragrance of both rose and mint. **Mabel Gray** is the best of the lemon types. **Prince Rupert** is a large, sturdy plant with an intense lemon fragrance; very nice for teas and jellies.

But probably the all-time favorites of nostalgic gardeners are the rose-scented geraniums. Two suggestions, among many: **Attar of Roses** and **Old-Fashioned Rose.** These make heavenly herbal tea.

Herbs

Stevia

GROW AS: **annual or tender perennial**

PLANT SIZE: **2 feet**

START WITH: **plants**

HARVEST SEASON: **year-round**

SUN REQUIREMENTS: **full sun**

MINIMUM SOIL DEPTH: **8 inches**

Shorter than sugar cane and prettier than a sugar beet, the plant called stevia (also known as sugar plant or sweet herb of Paraguay) has a sweetening agent that is many times sweeter than sugar, with zero calories. This is why stevia has gained such popularity in the diet-conscious United States in the last few years.

Stevia is native to the mountains of Brazil and Paraguay, and the people who live there have used it as a sweetener for centuries. But it wasn't until the 1800s that it became known in Europe, and during World War II the British used it as a sugar substitute when real sugar was rationed. Japan began growing stevia after the war and is now a major grower; stevia is approved for use as a sweetener in many food products and soft drinks there. It has not yet been approved by the USDA as a tabletop sweetener (the powdered extract) in the United States, but it can be sold in various forms in health-food stores as a "dietary supplement," and you can certainly buy the plants and have your own supply of perfectly legal, completely safe, no-calorie sweetener.

Stevia Basics. In its native habitat, stevia is a perennial plant that grows wild in rather infertile, sandy soil along the edges of streams and marshes, which tells us it isn't very fussy about its growing conditions. Without pruning, it gets to be about 2 feet tall, branching from the main stem into a bushy little plant with small leaves and hairy stems. It's not particularly impressive in appearance, but that's not the point. The first time you nibble a leaf, we guarantee you'll be impressed.

In most climates stevia must be brought inside for the winter, or be grown as an annual, because it won't survive even a light frost. You can take cuttings from the main plant and root them in a glass of water or a pot of damp, sandy soil to grow inside over the winter.

Planting. Plant stevia in a pot by itself, to facilitate moving it indoors for the winter. Any basic potting mix with a neutral to slightly acid pH is fine. Small plants sometimes start slowly, but be patient and they'll soon take off.

Success with Stevia. Once the plant is growing well, set the pot where it will get full sun all day, with a little filtered shade during the peak of the hottest summer days. Otherwise, heat is stevia's friend. Position the container in such a way that the plant can lean on its neighbors for support. Wind and rain can cause the brittle stems to break.

A monthly feeding of a balanced plant food such as 20-20-20 will keep stevia happy all summer. Watering requirements are also basic: water well when the top inch or two of soil feels dry to your fingers. If the plant seems to be wilting, check for moisture. Water with tepid water, not cold, and move the plant to a warm, shady place until it perks up. If the soil feels really wet and the plant is still wilting, you may have a drainage problem. Check that the drainage holes aren't plugged, and move the pot out to a shaded, breezy spot where the excess moisture can evaporate. In winter, reduce watering.

Stevia is no more or less susceptible to insect damage than other plants, but aphids do seem to go after it.

When growing stevia inside, give it lots of bright light and good air circulation. A sunny south-facing window is best, but a west window will do. In short-day climates with less than 12 hours of good strong light, use grow lights. And if your plant suddenly dies, don't despair; it probably wasn't your fault.

Harvesting. Regular harvesting will keep stevia from getting long, lanky growth. Snip off fresh leaves or little sprigs whenever you wish to sweeten your tea or lemonade, or to sprinkle over fresh fruits. The leaves are good and sweet all year round, but the sweetness often becomes even more concentrated in late summer, when small flower buds are just beginning to form. You may think, then, that the flowers are a good thing, but in fact they have the opposite effect: they take the life and vigor out of the plant. When you see a tight cluster of buds in the leaf axils (the axil is that "V" formed where the leaf is attached to the stem), it's your cue to act. Use small scissors or your fingers to pinch out the flower buds.

In early fall, cut back the plant to three or four leaf clusters, and then bring the pruned plant inside for the winter to continue growing. (Of course, you will harvest the leaves from the pruned-off stems.) If indoor growing space is limited, you can pull up the whole plant, pick off the leaves, and dry them all at once for a year's supply of sweetener. To dry stevia, just spread the leaves out on paper plates or newspapers until they're crisp and crumbly. They can then be pulverized into a powder with a mortar and pestle, or in a spice or coffee mill, and stored in a glass container with a tight-fitting lid.

You'll have to experiment with stevia to determine exactly how much to use because the degree of sweetness will vary depending on how or where the plant is grown, but figure that between 1 and 3 teaspoons will equal a full cup of sugar—and with no calories!

Varieties. Just one species: *Stevia rebaudiana.*

Herbs

Sweet Woodruff

GROW AS: **perennial**

PLANT SIZE: **4 to 8 inches high**

START WITH: **plants**

HARVEST SEASON: **late spring through early fall**

SUN REQUIREMENTS: **partial to full shade**

MINIMUM SOIL DEPTH: **6 inches**

S weet woodruff is not usually considered an edible herb, but it is nonetheless a valuable addition to your garden, for it is a very pretty ornamental and the dried leaves have many pleasant household uses.

The plant contains a chemical ingredient that gives it a vanilla fragrance, and this is much more pronounced once the leaves have started to dry. This fresh, sweet smell made woodruff a favorite

strewing herb. In times before modern sanitation, particularly aromatic herbs were strewn on the floor in houses and public meeting halls and allowed to dry before being swept up, to help eliminate unpleasant odors.

Sweet woodruff has a place in the modern herb garden as an endearing ground cover, and is especially valuable because it is one of the few plants that truly thrive in shady conditions. It quickly spreads to become a low carpet of extremely attractive dark green leaves. In late spring it is covered with clusters of tiny white starlike flowers on stems that rise above the foliage, like a layer of lace floating above the green carpet. In Europe these flowers are traditionally added to Riesling wine to make a festive punch called May Wine, sometimes served with a few wild strawberries added to the punch bowl.

With its invasive roots, sweet woodruff can take over a large area in an open garden if not controlled. Confined to a pot, it will drape over the rim and help soften harsh edges. Grow this comely plant as a petticoat under taller plants such as monarda, or as a pretty ground cover under your container fruit trees, where it will be happy in the shade created by the trees.

Recipe: *May Wine*

Rose Marie says: "In Germany, May Wine is traditionally served on the first day of May. It makes a lovely punch, especially when fresh strawberries are floated in it."

1 bottle Riesling wine
3 to 5 sprigs of fresh sweet woodruff

1. Remove and save the cork from the wine bottle.

2. Rinse the woodruff and pat dry with paper towels. Bruise the sprigs gently with the back of a spoon. Insert them into the wine bottle (a chopstick helps) and replace the cork. Set the bottle aside for three days at room temperature, then remove the herbs (use the chopstick to help tease them out) and replace the cork.

3. Refrigerate the wine until serving. For the best flavor, drink within two months.

Makes 1 bottle

Sweet Woodruff Basics.
Woodruff forms a dense mat, spreading in all directions by sending wiry roots under the surface of the soil and also by self-sowing. In mild climates it stays at least partially evergreen all year, but in most areas it dies back to the ground in winter. Fear not; it is a really tough character and will come back with the spring tulips.

Planting.
Buy small pots of sweet woodruff at the garden center in the spring, or get a start from a friend who has a patch of it in his or her garden. Just take a sharp knife and cut out a square or plug, much as you'd lift a square of cornbread out of a pan. Make a shallow depression in the soil of your container and press the plug into place. Keep it moist and shaded until the roots take hold, which usually takes only a few days, and it's on its merry way.

Success with Sweet Woodruff.
This is a native woodland plant in some parts of the country, growing wild on the damp, shady, humusy forest floor. In your container you would do well to strive for the same conditions: a loose, airy potting mix with lots of organic matter and even moisture.

Regular watering is important. If allowed to dry out or get too much sun, sweet woodruff will turn dry and burnt looking. It doesn't seem to need much in the way of fertilizer, but an application of fish emulsion or liquid seaweed in the spring as new growth begins would get it off to a good start.

If your woodruff begins to look a little shopworn late in the summer, just shear it back with scissors and give it plenty of water, and it will reward you with fresh, new growth, although it won't flower again until next spring. If it is really looking peaked and unhappy, feed it with a solution of fish emulsion. Otherwise, you can just sit back and enjoy it.

Harvesting. Sweet woodruff is easy to harvest. All you have to do is give it a haircut with household scissors, leaving only about an inch or two of stem so new foliage will grow.

Dry the foliage and use it in potpourri and sachets, or to stuff a pillow for a sweet-smelling night's sleep. In times past a special woodruff-stuffed pillow was made for a young woman's wedding night. Sprigs of the foliage laid in the linen closet will impart their light vanilla fragrance for a long time, and a friend of ours keeps a few branches in the back window of her car, replacing them every couple of weeks, for a natural deodorizer.

Varieties. There's only one species: *Galium odoratum.*

Herbs

Tarragon

GROW AS: **perennial**

PLANT SIZE: **2 to 3 feet**

START WITH: **plants**

HARVEST SEASON: **spring though fall**

SUN REQUIREMENTS: **full sun**

MINIMUM SOIL DEPTH: **8 inches**

Tarragon is a wonderfully pleasant, great-tasting herb that is best used fresh. It has an elusive flavor that reminds you a little of basil, slightly hinting of fennel, with a little bit of licorice, but in the end it is uniquely tarragon.

The leaves are on the small side, about an inch long and a quarter inch wide, and angle upward from the stems. Older mature leaves are darker and have a faint pearlescent sheen, while new leaves are a bright medium green. This is a small, upright, and fairly delicate looking plant that doesn't take up a lot of above-ground room in a container.

Tarragon is *the* herb for chicken. Try stuffing several good-sized sprigs and a few lemon slices into the cavity of a roasting chicken. Or lay a few sprigs on fish fillets while they bake. Tarragon vinegar is the most popular herbal vinegar for good reason: it's superb. Once you get a taste of this herb in its fresh state, you'll find yourself looking for other ways to use it.

Tarragon Basics. Two different plants are called tarragon, but one of them, Russian tarragon, does not deserve the name. It is harsh and coarse tasting, and if you have tasted only this form of tarragon, you would think we'd lost our minds to be praising it as a culinary herb. True tarragon, or French tarragon (*Artemesia dracunculus*), is the one used for cooking. To make sure you're getting real French tarragon, pinch off a tiny piece of leaf and taste it. You should get a little sizzle on your tongue.

Russian tarragon is grown from seed. French tarragon does not produce viable seeds; you can buy only small plants, propagated in a nursery by cuttings from a mother plant. If you see a packet of seeds marked tarragon, it's certain to be Russian tarragon.

French tarragon is a perennial that goes dormant in winter (for the exception, see box on page 273). The roots spread underground to make good-size clumps up to 2 feet across, sending up new stems to form a small bush with semi-woody stems. You'll probably never see French tarragon flower, as it's usually cut and used before it has a chance to bloom. In any case, the flowers are insignificant.

This is one of the Mediterranean herbs, happiest growing in sunny, dry places. If possible, give tarragon a hot spot where it can get some extra heat reflected from a building or a cement or stone structure. This would be the perfect plant to grow in a stone trough or in a container set on the south side of a building up against a cement foundation.

Planting. Compost and sand added to a basic all-purpose potting mix would make a good combination for tarragon. The soil needs to drain well, as wet soil will cause the roots to rot. (Think of the rocky, dry soil of Mediterranean hillsides.) If possible, use a container that retains heat.

Be a little patient with tarragon, as it takes longer than other herbs for the roots to reestablish and settle in after transplanting. Be sure the soil is gently firmed around the roots, and mulch lightly with a handful of fine peat moss.

Success with Tarragon.

Tarragon does very well in containers. The two keys are to give it a good warm spot in the sun, and not to overwater. Water it lightly after planting to help it get established, then let the soil dry between soakings. Regular snipping will keep the plant neat. Tarragon is a heavy feeder and likes slightly alkaline soil; regular applications of fish meal fertilizer take care of both needs.

Once a year, check to see how much the roots are filling the pot. Tarragon roots tend to intertwine; the species name, *dracunculus,* means "little dragon," a reference to the twisted pattern of the roots. In one season they can fill the pot and will actually choke themselves out in the second season. So repot and divide tarragon once a year. Do this in the spring, after it's been growing inside for the winter (see the box at right), and pass some on to friends.

Harvesting. Cut the top 4 to 6 inches of the stems to use fresh in your kitchen. This will also help stimulate new growth from the sides of the main stem, and will serve to keep the whole plant neat and compact.

Dried tarragon leaves lose most of their really good flavor and fragrance, so it's best to freeze any extra leaves you want to save for future use. Place them on a cookie sheet and freeze them, then put them into plastic bags to store in the freezer.

Tarragon's light flavor is dissipated by long cooking, so generally it is added toward the end of the cooking period. Many cooks stir in the chopped herb when the cooking is finished, and then allow the dish to rest for a few minutes while the tarragon does its magic. (Incidentally, if your recipe calls for adding herbs or other flavorings at a certain point in the cooking process, there is usually a very good reason for those instructions.)

Varieties. As we said, use only French tarragon, *Artemisia dracunculus.* Don't even be tempted to

Tarragon for the Winter

Tarragon dies down to the ground with the first frost, which used to mean we were deprived of its luscious flavor until spring—until a brilliantly simple technique was devised.

In December, when the plant has pretty much died down and you don't see a lot of green growth above the soil line, dig down in the container and pull up about half the plant. (If you feel more secure digging up the whole thing so you can see what you're doing, that's okay; just take half the root cluster and return the rest to the container.)

Don't do this too soon, though; the plant needs a short cold period to return to vigor in the spring.

Now put the roots you dug up into a small container with fresh potting soil, and bring it indoors. In two or three weeks you'll start to see shoots of new foliage. This is the choicest new-growth tarragon, very tender and with lots of flavor. Snip it as needed, and you'll be rewarded with fresh tarragon all winter.

And the half of the root mass that you left in the outdoor container will stay dormant through the winter in the usual way, and start sending up green shoots come springtime.

---

try Russian tarragon. There is, however, another plant that isn't tarragon at all but is actually a very good mimic: *Tagetes lucida,* a type of marigold, sometimes called Mexican tarragon. It is a very acceptable substitute for gardeners in the Deep South, who would otherwise have trouble keeping tarragon through the winter. Because true tarragon needs a resting period of cold weather before the next season's growth develops, it is difficult to grow in truly frost-free areas. Gardeners in hot climates will need to treat French tarragon as an annual, or try *Tagetes lucida,* which is perennial in frost-free areas.

Mexican tarragon gets to be 1½ to 2 feet tall, and produces small, single, deep yellow flowers in clusters rather late in the season. It likes regular, well-drained potting soil, and established plants should be fertilized once a month during the growing season. After a few years, the plant will need dividing; do it in early spring when new growth is showing. Use a sharp knife to cut all the way through the root ball. Replant and keep well watered until you see it begin to grow. The taste is much like that of French tarragon, with a strong scent and flavor of anise. Some people think it is stronger than tarragon, so start with a small amount when cooking, and then adjust for flavor.

Even if your climate is cold enough to be favorable to growing true tarragon, you may decide to grow this marigold as well, for the novelty and for the pleasure of its bright flowers. In that case, you can carry it through the winter by repotting it into an individual container and bringing it inside.

*I*n a small Chinese village some 5,000 years ago, the servants of the village priest were boiling water for the household, as the priest was a very wise man and he believed that water that had been boiled was healthier. The large cauldron was in the courtyard of the residence to minimize the risk of spreading fire to the sleeping quarters, and nearby was a small tree, one of many that grew wild in the area. On this day, some of the leaves from the tree fell into the cauldron. The water changed color, and a pleasing aroma filled the air. The priest, no fool, had one of the servants taste the liquid, and when the servant did not die, he drank a cup himself. That is how man came to discover the pleasures of brewed tea.

Theme Garden

Tea Time

The more frantic our days become, the more we yearn for quiet moments of respite. For many people, one favorite way to steal such a moment is with a cup of steaming tea. Snuggled up on the couch, both hands holding the hot mug up close to our nose, we can literally feel the tensions melting away as we breathe in the haunting aroma. It almost seems as if there is some magical ingredient in those tiny flakes, something soothing and seductive.

Maggie says: A few years ago I wrote a book about tea and tea parties, and in planning what to include I talked to many people about their love of tea. I came away with the strong sense that simply holding a teacup and feeling its warmth begins an automatic process of decompression. All our worries fade into the background, and our minds simply refuse to hold any static; we couldn't solve a problem even if we wanted to. The hectic world will be back soon enough, but for now there is room only for peace.

Imagine how much more satisfying your cup of tea would be if you brewed a pot from your own special blend, made from tea leaves and herbs you grew yourself.

The design of this garden is intended more as an idea starter than a specific plan. It includes an actual tea plant, just like those grown in China and India, plus several tea herbs for you to choose from. Although we suggest a few plants here, we hope you will experiment with others, too, and have fun trying out several combinations of herbs or tea and herbs.

When you come up with a blend that especially pleases you, christen it with a meaningful name (Terry's Tea, Magical Mint Medley, Duke of Earl Grey) and share it with friends.

For details on growing the plants in this garden, see

Chamomile, page 182
Lemon verbena, page 216
Mint, page 223
Monarda, page 229
Stevia, page 266
Thyme, page 278

Several mail-order companies listed in the Appendix of this book sell small bags that you can fill with dried leaves and seal with an ordinary iron. A small basket of your special teabags would be a cherished gift.

Aside from herb teas, all the tea in the world comes from one specific plant: *Camellia sinensis.* This was the small tree growing in the priest's courtyard. It is indeed a camellia, part of the same genus that gives us the beautiful flowers, but its value is in the tiny new leaves, not the blossoms. *C. sinensis* is native to the Far East—China, India, Sri Lanka, Siberia, Indonesia, and other parts of Asia. When tea is grown in different locales, with varying soils, altitudes, and weather patterns, the leaves acquire slight differences in taste; these geographic origins have thus become the names of different types of tea, for example, Assam, Darjeeling, and Ceylon. You are, therefore, completely justified in giving the tea you grow a name that is yours alone.

Don't be surprised that you can grow tea in your container garden. It's a pretty hardy plant, and lends itself nicely to container growing. At tea plantations the plant is a small tree or large shrub, but in your container it will remain a manageable size. You won't get a huge harvest from one plant, but it's fun and satisfying to grow and gives you something special to share with your tea-loving friends.

A **tea** plant is not a common item, but sometimes you can find one at very large garden centers or mail-order nurseries. Purchase a young plant, not seeds. Plant it in its own container, using a potting mix that you have liberally amended with shredded peat moss, commercial compost, or both. These amendments provide two qualities important to tea plants: they hold moisture, and they make the soil acidic. The roots of the plant are close to the surface, so you'd be smart to cover the soil with loose moss or other mulch to hold in moisture. For the same reason, tea is not a good companion plant; it does best in its own pot, where the roots don't have to compete.

Feeding with a basic all-purpose fertilizer once a month is a good idea; if you notice that the plant is not sending out new growth in the spring or flowering in the fall, that's your cue to add fertilizer. Your tea plant is a perennial and moderately hardy, but will need protection when the temperatures drop to about 25°F.

In late fall and early winter, small and very fragrant flowers appear. Most are white, although the cultivar Blushing Maiden has pink flowers; both white and pink flowers have large clusters of attractive, bright yellow stamens. Harvest tea in the spring. The classic instructions are "take two leaves and a bud"—in other words, harvest just the outermost tips with the newest growth. Of course, continual harvesting and tip pruning will encourage new leaves and buds. The harvested leaves can be used as is, in which case what you have is green tea, or they can be spread out to dry for the more familiar black tea.

Herbal tea is something totally different. The term denotes a beverage made from plants other than *C. sinensis,* principally those we normally think of as herbs. Drawing from a long tradition of herbal medicine, many people believe that herbal teas contain various healthful constituents that benefit body and soul. The scientific evidence is mixed, but without doubt caffeine-free herbal tea is delicious and calming, and that's enough for us.

For the rest of your tea garden, select one or more herbs commonly used for beverages. Think about the commercial herbal teas you have enjoyed, and choose plants accordingly. For example, if you like mint teas you have many wonderful varieties to explore, from old favorites like spearmint to new tastes like orange bergamot or chocolate mint. You might enjoy having a collection of several different **mints,** but if you do so, grow each one in its own container.

If you like lemon in your tea, you can get the same taste by adding dried leaves of **lemon verbena.** If you love Earl Grey tea, you may want to grow and dry **monarda,** which adds a similar taste when mixed with regular tea. Or try **German chamomile** for your very own bedtime tea. The leaves of a specialty **thyme** (lemon or lavender thyme, for instance) give a warm spiciness to your tea blend. Finally, be sure to include a small container planted with **stevia,** a plant whose leaves will astound you with their sweetness (400 times sweeter than granulated sugar).

The monarda and the thyme can be planted together, especially if you choose a thyme that will spill over the sides below the more upright monarda. For various practical reasons, all the other herbs work best in separate containers. The stevia and the lemon verbena need to be moved indoors in the winter. The mints have such invasive root systems that they crowd out anything planted alongside them. And the chamomile, an annual, will need to be replanted each spring.

Place the container holding the tea plant in the center, in a place of honor, and arrange the smaller containers around or in front of it in whatever fashion takes best advantage of your space. Use a series of small pedestals to elevate the containers at various heights, creating a staggered effect, so that the plants at the lower levels hide the bare sides of the larger containers. And if in your travels you come across an old tea kettle, plant one of your mints in it and make it a focal point.

Herbs

Thyme

GROW AS: **perennial**

PLANT SIZE: **6 to 12 inches tall and wide**

START WITH: **seeds or transplants**

HARVEST SEASON: **summer**

SUN REQUIREMENTS: **full sun**

MINIMUM SOIL DEPTH: **6 inches**

You undoubtedly know that thyme is an herb that goes with almost anything: from fish and pork to soups, stews, and chowders; in sauces, gravies, and stuffings; and with vegetables fresh or steamed. But if you've never tried it fresh, you haven't lived. Homegrown leaves radiate a memorable, intense aroma that is sweet yet slightly piney. They're equally wonderful freshly snipped or recently dried (provided they're stored in a dry, cool place so they don't lose their punch).

Container gardeners can rejoice in this easygoing herb from springtime well into the fall, for thyme takes eagerly to life in pots, either on a sunny windowsill or outside on a deck or balcony. The roots are relatively shallow, so you don't need a big or deep pot. The common thyme, *Thymus vulgaris,* forms a tidy little shrublet no more than a foot high. If you prefer a thyme that spills attractively over the edge of a pot, perhaps for a hanging basket display, grow a creeping thyme, of which there are many. And there are dozens of other intriguing variations, including thymes that smell like lemons, caraway, and even coconut.

But the common species is terrific in its own right, and utterly dependable. Make sure your potting mix drains well so there is no danger of the roots languishing in standing water; thyme is drought-tolerant and needs only occasional drinks in hot spells. It's hard to imagine an easier herb to grow: you basically won't have to worry about watering, fertilizing, or insect pests. And you can trim off sprigs as needed throughout the growing season, without damage.

One trait all thymes share is their small leaves. If you're looking at a small plant you can't immediately identify beyond knowing it's some kind of herb, and it is covered with masses of teeny-tiny leaves, it's a safe bet that it's a thyme. In the spring many thymes are covered with dainty flowers in white, pink, lavender, or mauve, all lusciously soft pastels. In your outdoor garden, expect lots of honeybees; they adore thyme's blossoms. In fact, thyme is a favorite of beekeepers because the resulting honey is wonderfully aromatic.

Thyme Basics. This ancient herb originally hails from the dry, rocky hills of the Mediterranean countries, so we know it's a sun lover and doesn't need especially rich soil. Water sparingly, and don't fertilize or otherwise fuss over the plants.

Thyme is hardier than some other Mediterranean herbs and can spend the winter outside in most areas with the protection of a light mulch. It does have a tendency to become woody and raggedy over a few seasons, however. You can stave off this natural maturing process for a while by continually harvesting the stems so young ones are always coming on, or by digging out and dividing the plant each spring. But eventually the stems near the base thicken and the interior of the plant becomes open and bare, and it is time for replacement.

Planting. To raise thyme from seed, sow indoors in a light seed-starting mix in early spring, cover with a very light sifting of sand, and keep the flat or pots in a warm spot. Germination will occur in a week or two. Be careful not to plant the tiny seeds too thickly, or you'll have to do a lot of thinning.

Once they're a few inches high and well rooted, the small plants can be moved to the pots that will become their permanent home.

They'll be fine on a windowsill even if chilly winds are still blowing, or you can safely set them outside when the last of the hard frosts is over.

You may, however, find it more convenient and more satisfying to buy small plants from a nursery, especially once you become acquainted with the many wonderful varieties. We bet you'll find yourself wanting many different kinds of thyme, rather than many plants of one kind. When you get your prizes home and are ready to transplant them into their permanent containers, be gentle with the fine, dense roots.

Thymes combine well with other plants and with one another. So start collecting; just remember to label them so you can tell them apart later.

Success with Thyme. Because thyme is a dry-land native, its main vulnerability is too much water. The plant will let you know; watch out for lower leaves blackening and dropping.

Avoid root rot by growing the plants in a well-draining mix that contains a little sand. Avoid crown rot by either watering from the bottom or carefully directing the spout of the watering can to the side of the pot, not right on top of the plant.

Although thyme is fairly hardly and can survive mild to moderate winters with no problems, you will have to take precautions in very cold areas. Wrap the pot, add a layer of mulch, and hope for the best. Or bring the pots indoors, but avoid the temptation to overwater.

Recipe: Mardi Gras Salad

Rosalind Creasy, a leader of the edible landscaping movement, is the author of several gardening books and a passionate cook. She says: "This show-off salad features the colors of Mardi Gras: gold, green, and blue. If your climate allows salad greens and cool-season edible flowers in February, serve this at a Mardi Gras celebration."

FOR THE DRESSING

3 tablespoons balsamic vinegar

Salt and freshly ground black pepper, to taste

5 tablespoons extra-virgin olive oil

1 to 2 tablespoons minced fresh lemon thyme

1 small garlic clove, minced

FOR THE SALAD

1 head butter lettuce

1/2 head romaine

1 handful small, fresh spinach leaves

12 to 20 mixed flowers, such as nasturtiums, calendulas, blue and gold pansies, and violas

1/2 cup whole pecans

1. To make the dressing, combine the vinegar, salt, and pepper in a small bowl. Whisk in the oil and add the thyme and garlic.

2. To make the salad, rinse the greens and dry them well in a salad spinner or with paper towels. Tear the leaves into bite-size pieces. Gently rinse the flowers and remove the petals. Pat them dry with paper towels. Place the petals in a small bowl and set aside.

3. Just before serving, place the greens and pecans in a large salad bowl. Whisk the dressing, pour it over the greens, and toss gently. Adjust the seasonings if necessary. Sprinkle the flower petals over the salad and serve immediately.

Serves 4 to 6

Harvesting. You can harvest stems at almost any time during the growing season, but the natural oils that give thyme its bewitching flavor are at their peak right as the plant is beginning to flower. Pinching off the flowers as they develop prolongs this period.

When cutting off stems, take only a third to half off any given branch. Use this as your opportunity to groom and shape the plant; it will recover quickly from such judicious pruning.

Don't do any drastic harvesting late in the season; this stimulates the plant to put on a flush of soft new growth, which is easily damaged by cold temperatures.

Dry the stems in a warm spot out of direct sunlight. The stems are rather twiggy, so winnow them out by rubbing the dried leaves off with your fingers. Store the leaves in an airtight jar in a cool, dry place, and use dried thyme within a few months; after a year or so, the flavor begins to fade.

Another great way to preserve the harvest is to infuse white wine vinegar with fresh thyme clippings. Let them steep for a few weeks before uncorking and using on green salads, in potato salads, or in marinades (see the box on pages 257 to 259).

Varieties. There are dozens of different thymes, and the most intriguing selections can be found at nurseries that specialize in herbs. If you can't visit and sniff each one, rely on catalog descriptions and experiment with those that entice you. You really can't go wrong. Here is but a handful of what is available.

Bushy French thyme is just a bit sweeter than English thyme and has lovely gray-green foliage (both are varieties of the basic species, *Thymus vulgaris*).

Caraway thyme (*T. herba-barona*) and nutmeg thyme (*T. herba-barona* **Nutmeg**) are similar; some herb specialists consider them the same plant. They have a creeping growth habit. The spicy leaves emit a true caraway or nutmeg scent, and make a delicious flavoring for roast beef or pork, cheese bread, and herbal butter.

Lemon thyme (*T. x citriodorus*) forms a small bush with lemon-infused foliage. Try it with veal or roast chicken, in chicken salad, or sprinkled fresh over lightly steamed and buttered green beans. You might prefer one of the attractive variegated forms: **Lemon Silver** thyme has silvery leaves, and **Golden Lemon** thyme has green leaves edged with yellow.

Creeping thyme, also called mother-of-thyme (*T. praecox arcticus*), forms a low-growing mat of dark green foliage. The similar *T. serpyllum* also comes in an attractive yellow-leaved form called **Aureus.**

Because thyme so readily—some say promiscuously—crosses with other varieties, new strains constantly appear on the market. If you have the good fortune to visit a large herb nursery, be sure to explore the many different varieties. You may find thymes whose fragrance mimics oregano, lavender, orange, coconut, and a slew of other plants, and you are almost guaranteed to find several you can't live without.

Bursting with vegetables, herbs, and edible flowers in golden colors, this garden celebrates the sun, echoing in a small way the extraordinary attention it has received from civilizations past.

Without sunshine, there could be no life on Earth. Remember learning about photosynthesis in high school biology? It's a fairly simple bit of chemistry, with truly profound implications.

Theme Garden

Edible Sunshine

When sunlight touches a plant, a chemical reaction is triggered in which the chlorophyll stored in the plant's leaves, the water in its cells, and the carbon dioxide that the plant has absorbed from the air all interact to convert the energy from the sun into organic energy in the form of simple carbohydrates, or sugars. The plant uses these sugars to nourish its growth; in other words, it manufactures its own food. Happily for us, the plant makes more than it needs, and the rest is converted into more complex carbohydrates and stored in various parts of the plant: roots, stems, and fruits. When we eat those plants (or feed them to our livestock), we're enjoying the end result of a chemical process that began with sunlight.

One by-product of that photosynthetic process is the release of oxygen. Thus green plants give us not only the food we need to sustain our bodies, but the very air we breathe.

This science has been understood only recently, as human history goes. Yet thousands of years ago, people had an intuitive understanding that the sun was the source of all life. That's why the myths of many ancient civilizations designate the sun god as the most powerful of all, and why in some societies the sun itself was worshiped. The classic image of the sun as a powerful god, riding across the sky in a chariot pulled by four white horses and making the corresponding journey across the underworld at night, was as good an explanation as any for the rising and setting of the sun, for sunlight and for darkness. Today we know much more about the star that is our sun, but the magic and majesty of it are no less awesome.

As a token of homage to the sun that gives us everything—food, warmth, light, and a happy disposition—we offer this small garden of sunshine.

**For details on
growing the plants in
this garden, see**

Calendula, page 360
Daylilies, page 367
Marjoram, page 221
Sage, page 252
Thyme, page 278
Tomatoes, page 159

Start with a large container, such as a half wine barrel. Paint it sunshine yellow if you wish. Fill it with rich potting soil, and work in some all-purpose fruit/vegetable fertilizer (in 1:2:1 proportions; see page 67).

The largest plant will be a yellow-fruited **tomato.** Two possibilities are Yellow Pear and Gold Nugget. The pear tomato is hugely popular with children and delightful in salads, but as an indeterminate plant it tends to be big and sprawly and needs attention (and preferably a trellis of some kind) to keep it in bounds. Gold Nugget, a determinate variety, has more restrained growth with sweet-tasting golden yellow cherry-size tomatoes. Put the tomato at the rear of the container if it is to be positioned against a wall, or in the center if you can walk all around it.

In front of the tomato, arrange the other plants by height so that you create tumbling tiers of yellow. The second tier will be a mix of **calendula,** with its bright yellow-orange blossoms that open and close with the sun, and small yellow **daylilies;** you can't go wrong with long-blooming Stella d'Oro. The daylilies are perennial; calendula is a self-sowing annual. Over time, the maturing daylilies will spread and may need dividing to make room for more calendulas. To honor the strong connection that calendula has with the sun, and also to keep the daylilies healthy, it's worth the small effort to do this.

The third tier consists of yellow-tinged herbs, low-growing and spreading, spilling over the sides of the container. Several of the most popular culinary herbs have variegated cultivars, with yellow splashes, stripes, or edges on the green leaves; possibilities include Golden **sage,** Golden Curly **marjoram,** and Golden Lemon **thyme.** Choose the ones that you like to cook with. All these are perennials, so you'll be enjoying them for years.

At the end of the season, the only problem you may have is what to do with the tomato plant. It will have produced a long and sturdy root, and removing it carelessly can damage the roots of the other plants in that same container. Try this: slice off the main stem right at the soil line and discard it. Slowly dig out the root; if it doesn't come easily, leave it in place. Next spring, when the daylilies are beginning to leaf out, the tomato root will have died thoroughly and will probably surrender without a fight.

CHAPTER 9

FRUITS

The first thing to understand about growing fruits is that it's something of a commitment. With the possible exception of strawberries, which some people treat as annuals, plants that produce fruit need several years to become mature enough to bear their crop. Some may yield a few fruits in the second year, or even the first (see table below), but by and large it takes three years to really get the good stuff.

What you have in the meantime are some very handsome plants (some trees, some shrubs) with other virtues: lovely, fragrant flowers, striking fall color, pretty foliage, or all three. And you have a serious plant, something large enough to become the focal point around which you organize other, smaller containers into a coordinated garden design, or to stand regally on its own.

The greatest joy, though, comes with the fruit itself. Ripened to its fullest glory, it is unbelievably superior to anything store-bought. When you and your guests first experience the unique texture of a fresh fig, smooth and slightly crunchy in the same bite, or feel the sweet-tart burst of a fresh gooseberry on your tongue, or melt down to your socks at the honey-sweetness of a tree-ripened peach, you deserve to feel very, very proud of yourself.

It's important to remember, though, that these plants will be around for years. The implications are worth reviewing.

How Many Years to Wait?

With some exceptions, you can expect to harvest your first fruit in the year noted here; "1" means the first fruit-bearing season, the plant's first year of growth. In many cases, the first year of production will be relatively light; as a plant matures, fruit production generally increases.

Fruit	Years
apple, columnar	3
apple, dwarf	2
blueberries	1
citrus	2 or 3 (varies with type)
currants	2
figs	2 (occasionally 1)
gooseberries	2
grapes	3 (occasionally 2)
peaches	2
strawberries	1

First, we're not talking about a petite little pansy here. Many mature fruit trees are large plants, in both height and spread. You need to plan for the future as you're making your original selections, making sure that your space is large enough to do justice to the plant.

Also, the container itself needs to be large enough to hold a plant that will grow in it for years. (Size considerations are discussed in the individual plant sections.) The container should be made of a material that survives freezing weather: wood, plastic, or the new fiberglass material. And because you may need to relocate the container into a more sheltered spot for the winter, you should plan a way to make it easily movable: either add a set of casters, or invest in a heavy-duty plant dolly with wheels.

The second important point to keep in mind: because fruit trees and shrubs live for many years, they have to survive your winters. You need to learn about the climate patterns in your area and match them against the particular needs of the fruits you're interested in growing.

The Crucial Questions About Climate

Two aspects of winter weather are crucial to fruit plants:

1. Exposure to the correct temperature range (32° to 45°F) for the right amount of time to send the plant into dormancy; this is known as winter chill.
2. Protection from prolonged, severe cold that could kill the plant.

These two factors are not interrelated except that they collide on the calendar. Whether either presents a problem for you is a matter of the weather patterns in your region.

WINTER CHILL. All trees and shrubs that produce fruit in the temperate parts of the country (temperate meaning everyplace between the Deep South and the Alaskan tundra) need to go through a period of dormancy in winter. During this time, the tree loses its leaves and its internal systems slow way down; the plant is alive, but resting. In this state, the plant is building the cellular structures that will in spring become flowers, and eventually fruits.

Dormancy is triggered by changes in temperature and in the hours of daylight. In most of the country, it begins in mid autumn and lasts until early to mid spring. This is an important phase in the plant's natural annual cycle, and cannot successfully be either forced or curtailed.

Winter chill is the term used to describe a certain temperature range—between 32° and 45°F—that is necessary for the plant to set next year's blossoms. This period of cold *but not freezing* weather is usually expressed in hours; and different types of fruits, even different varieties of the same fruit, need a different number of hours. For instance, apples (generally speaking) need around 600 hours of winter chill. That sounds like a lot until you realize that 600 hours translates to just 25 days, assuming that each 24-hour period remains within that 32° to 45°F range. Winter chill requirements are cumulative: sometime between when the leaves start to fall in autumn and when the new buds begin to open up in spring, the plant must be exposed to that many hours in total. Temperatures below freezing do not count.

In almost all parts of the country, except the Deep South and southern California, winter chill is not something you even need to think about. As long as you have mild to moderate winters, you will have enough winter chill hours for all the fruits in this section.

The difficulty comes in colder climates, where the dormant period includes bitterly cold months when the plant is in danger of freezing. That takes us to our second concern.

WINTER PROTECTION. Once the thermometer drops below 32°F for any prolonged period, your fruit trees and shrubs move beyond the "good" range that allows for winter chill; now they are in the danger zone where they could be killed.

This is far more of a problem for container gardeners because it is the roots that are at risk. Plants in traditional gardens are surrounded by a large mass of earth that serves to insulate the roots. In containers, the plant's roots have just a few inches of soil, if that, between them and the surrounding air. When the air temperature is, say, 25°F, the soil in the container and the plant roots will freeze, and the plant may die—unless you take action.

We give cold protection special focus here because it's something you have to be aware of for almost all fruits. But keep in mind that the ideas described here apply for *any* plants that you hope to carry through the winter. What you have to be concerned about is severe, unrelenting cold, the kind of weather where it's 15° or 20°F or even colder at night and never gets above 32°F during the day. An occasional night at 25°F will not be fatal to the plant, as long as the temperature warms up to 32°F or above during the day.

If you live in an area that gets that kind of very cold weather in the winter, you surely know it. If your weather patterns are usually warmer than this, but occasional hard freezes are not unknown, then you need to discipline

Cold–Weather Wraps

Several household items can serve as blankets to protect perennial plants from severe winter weather. Here are some ideas, presented in order from lightest to heaviest. Think about your typical winter weather patterns, and choose accordingly.

Winter plant cover. The same people who make the lightweight fabric used as an insect cover, and generically known as floating row cover (one well-known brand name is Reemay), also manufacture a heavier version of the same spun-bonded material. You'll find it in garden centers next to the row cover, labeled "winter cover," "garden blanket," or something similar.

Bubble wrap. The same stuff you use to wrap fragile items for mailing does a fine job of adding an insulating layer around a container. Buy it in wide rolls from a stationery store or shipping center, and tie or tape it in place.

Large foam sheets. At an outdoor store that supplies campers and backpackers, look for lengths of closed-cell or open-cell foam used for sleeping pads. You may be able to find the same thing at an upholstery shop. A 1-inch thickness gives good protection but is still flexible enough to wrap and bend.

Quilt batting. At a fabric store, look for the material that goes inside quilts; it's a fluffy, extremely lightweight spun polyester about 1 inch thick. It's sold by the yard, either 48 or 60 inches wide, and is quite inexpensive.

Household insulation. The same pink stuff that you put in your attic does a fine job insulating containers. It comes in rolls, with a reflective cover on one side; put that side facing outward.

Blankets. Any blanket or quilt or even an old sleeping bag wrapped snugly around the container will do the same for the plant and soil that it does for you.

A combination. For extreme cold, your best protection is a layered approach. Put bubble wrap, foam, batting, or attic insulation next to the container (for the insulating value), and cover tightly with a blanket, to block out the cold air and winds. Best technique: arrange the layers on the floor and move the container into the center; bring the edges of the material up to the top and around the trunk, then fasten tightly with twine or tape.

And if your winters are wet as well as cold, you should add a layer of plastic on top of the insulation, to keep it from getting sodden.

yourself to pay careful attention to the forecast and be ready to take action when needed. In both cases, you have two, maybe three, courses of action:

1. Move the entire container into a location where it will be protected from the worst weather. This may be a garage, an unheated room in your home, an outdoor shed, or something similar. It doesn't matter if the area is dark, as long as the temperature is above freezing. Just be sure not to bring the plant indoors into a room that is heated for human comfort, or it will be too warm. During this time the tree, which is dormant, does not actively take up water, so you do not need to water it as you would outdoors; just check from time to time to be sure the soil has not completely dried out. In spring, when temperatures climb back above freezing, bring the container back outside.

2. If you don't have such a protected space, the tree will have to stay outside, and you'll have to wrap it and the entire container in some kind of insulating material. What you use, and how much of it, will be a function of how low you expect the thermometer to drop. See box at left for several ideas.

3. For double protection, set the wrapped container down onto the ground, if possible. The surrounding soil mass will keep it about 5° warmer.

As we said previously, things will be much easier if you start your fruit trees in containers that are easily moved, either by attaching casters or by setting the containers on plant dollies with wheels. Do this from the get-go, and you'll have no trouble moving your fruit trees during their first winter. You will also find that the gap created by the wheels gives welcome room to maneuver a blanket wrap, if that's the route you take. So in either case—for moving or for easily getting underneath the bottom of the container—a wheeled base makes life much simpler. It all boils down to this:

- Unless you live in a subtropical climate, winter chill happens naturally; you don't have to do anything to provide for it. If you *do* live in a subtropical climate, accept that there are some fruits you simply won't be able to grow. If your climate is marginal in regard to winter chill, look for varieties with significantly lower winter-chill requirements.
- In extremely cold climates you won't have to worry about winter chill, but you will have to worry about freezing. If you're not able to provide protection, you're better off not trying to keep any plant alive through the winter.

Planting Techniques

Another important consideration when growing fruit trees is how to plant them. Most fruit-bearing plants come into a gardener's life in a condition known as bare-root. (Roses are also sold this way, and many landscape plants.) The term means just what you would think: the roots are bare—that is, not planted in soil. They are encased in some material that holds moisture around the roots, and then wrapped with plastic to hold that moisture-retaining material in place.

The first time you buy a bare-root plant and open the package, you may feel your heart sink. The poor thing looks completely dead, especially if there are no leaves or buds showing. But the plant isn't dead, it's merely dormant; it was intentionally harvested by the grower in its dormant state because it can be shipped more safely that way. Planted in soil, watered, and set in the sun, it will soon burst into life.

Most mail-order nurseries time their shipping so that the plant arrives at your door at the correct planting time for your climate. When you receive the plant, whether through the mail or purchased at the garden center, here's what to do:

1. Open the package, pull away the packing material, and inspect the roots. They should look strong and healthy. If they are withered, rotten, or obviously dead, return the plant and ask for a replacement. Experience, however, tells us that most nurseries are extraordinarily careful, and in all probability your new plant will be healthy. Just be sure you proceed to the next step immediately.

2. Either plant the young tree (skip to Step 3) or, if you can't get to it right away, use one of these temporary measures:

   a. Soak the plant in a bucket of water to rehydrate the roots. This will hold it for a day or two.

   b. Resoak the packing material and wrap it loosely around the roots, allowing for some air circulation. This will hold it for three to four days.

   c. Put the plant in a temporary pot and cover the roots with damp potting soil. This will hold it for several weeks.

3. Unless it's already soaking, set the plant in a bucket of water so the roots are submerged while you get your container and all your supplies ready.

4. Prepare your soil mixture: potting mix, hydrogel crystals,

slow-release fertilizer, and any extra soil amendments you might need (review Chapter 5 for details). Fill the container about one-quarter to one-third full. Add more potting mix and shape it into a mound like a volcano, with its top an inch or so below the rim of the pot.

5. Look closely at the roots of your plant, and cut away any that seem dead or mushy. If the roots are a tangled mess, use your fingers to pull them into separate strands. Trim any that are noticeably longer than the others. Your goal is to create a conical shape that will fit down over the "volcano" of soil.

6. Loosely place the roots over the "volcano" and check for fit. The crown of the plant (the spot just above the highest roots where the stem becomes somewhat smaller and darker in color) should be at the ultimate soil line, just below the rim; make the mound larger or smaller if need be.

7. Add more soil over the roots and around the edges, tamping lightly as you go. Water thoroughly and let things settle; add more soil as needed.

If it is not bare-root, a young fruit tree or shrub will be planted in a temporary nursery pot filled with soil. Growers refer to these as "container plants," but don't expect a handsome container that you'd want to use as the plant's permanent home—it will be an ordinary, utilitarian black plastic. Whereas bare-root plants are available for purchase only in the dormant season, from winter to early spring, container plants have no such limitations. Theoretically, they can be sold anytime, and you can plant them whenever you find them at the garden center.

Water the nursery pot thoroughly to loosen the soil and then gently slide out the entire contents of the pot—plant and soil. Try to keep the soil ball intact as much as possible. Fill your permanent container about one-third to one-half full with new potting soil, and set the plant-plus-soil in the center. Fill in around the edges with more potting soil, water thoroughly, and you're set.

Fruits

Apples

GROW AS: **perennials**

PLANT SIZE: **6 to 8 feet**

START WITH: **grafted plants**

HARVEST SEASON: **early to late fall**

SUN REQUIREMENTS: **full sun to partial shade**

MINIMUM SOIL DEPTH: **15 inches**

As you ponder your wish list for your new container garden, you might think you could never include something like apples. It's hard to imagine that the substantial specimens you may have seen in old orchards could grow on a deck or balcony. And in reality, you could never handle those huge trees in a container. Fortunately, apple specialists have developed trees that never get higher than 8 feet, sometimes less. There's also a new form of apple tree, called columnar, that slowly grows to about 8 feet high with little or no branching; this tall, ultraslender shape is very appropriate for small spaces that would not be able to accommodate a wide-spreading tree. With these new types of trees, container growing of apples has become not only possible, but easy. And the fruits you harvest will be fully ripe, rich in flavor, and without the chemical residues found on most commercially grown fruit.

Apple Basics. Most modern fruit trees are a combination of parts of two trees, physically fused together in a process called grafting. The upper portion of one tree, the scion, which produces the fruit, is grafted onto the lower stem of another tree, called the rootstock. This is how the qualities of a particular variety are preserved.

Take the Red Delicious apple, for example. A piece of a branch from an established Red Delicious tree (the scion) is tied to a cut surface on the stem of the rootstock, where they grow together. The resulting tree will produce exactly the same fruit as the original tree from which the scion branch was cut. But if you plant *seeds* from a Red Delicious apple and they eventually grow into trees, those trees may bear fruit, but they won't look or taste like the apple you started with.

The scion, in other words, determines what type of apples the tree will bear. The rootstock, in contrast, determines important growing characteristics; fruit tree growers choose a particular rootstock for the qualities it gives the tree. Some rootstocks are better adapted to wet soils, some are more resistant to certain diseases, some cause a tree to bloom and bear fruit earlier, and so on. Also, most important for our purposes here, it is the rootstock that determines the ultimate size of the tree.

For container growing, then, it is very important to learn what rootstock has been used. Rather than being given colorful names, rootstocks are identified by a code made up of a letter and a number. The letter indicates where the particular stock originated (for example, an M indicates the breeding program at the Malling Research Station in England), and the numbers are assigned in sequence (so M-27 is the one that was developed just after M-26).

Rootstocks that will keep an apple tree to 8 feet, small enough for container growing, are P-22, M-27, M-9, and possibly M-26. Don't bother with anything else. Mail-order catalogs that specialize in fruit trees are usually careful to identify rootstock, but at a retail garden center you may have to do some double-checking. Some garden centers sell trees that have been labeled dwarf or semi-dwarf, terms that are so imprecise they have become meaningless. Before buying a tree labeled in this way, check with staff to *verify the rootstock;* if necessary, ask them to contact the grower and find out what rootstock the tree is on. This will save you many headaches in the future.

Columnar trees will surprise you the first time you see them. They do not have branches in the usual sense, but merely very short stems (called spurs) attached to the main trunk, on which the apples develop, so that in late summer the full-size apples seem to be growing directly from the tree's trunk. Any branches that do form also tend to grow straight up. The trees grow slowly but bear fruit earlier: at two years, compared to three for most others. Because columnar varieties are naturally slow growing, rootstock is not really an issue.

Pollination. Some fruit trees can bear fruit by themselves; these are described as self-fertile. Others need a different variety nearby for cross-pollination, without which they will not bear fruit. Apples are in the second group: they need another variety of apple for pollination. With a few exceptions, any two apple trees that bloom at the same time are pollinators for each other. Ideally, the two varieties should be located within 20 feet of each other. The perfect solution, if you have the room, is to grow two varieties. If that is not possible, you will have to rely on cross-pollination from an apple tree nearby.

You may also find that your tree bears fruit without any obvious pollinator. Jim Gilbert of Northwoods Nursery in Oregon, an extremely knowledgeable grower who has seen just about every possible problem, loves to tell about an old Gravenstein apple tree he once had high in the Cascade Mountains. Growing all alone, without, as far as he could tell, another apple tree for miles around, the tree produced abundant crops of fruit for years.

Hardiness. Most apple varieties are technically hardy to −25°F, which means that almost anywhere in the United States you can have a nice apple tree in your backyard, providing you *have* a backyard. If you're growing your fruit trees in containers, severe cold weather can be more of a challenge.

Bear in mind that the *root system* of an apple tree is hardy to only about 15°F. In the ground, the earth mass keeps the root temperature from falling to dangerous levels. But in a container outdoors, without protection, your apple tree will be killed if the soil temperature drops too low. You have two ways to protect against this: (1) insulate the container and, if possible, set it on the ground, or (2) bring it into a warmer environment. See page 289 for more on both techniques.

The bottom line is this: if your winter temperatures are consistently below 15°F, and you have no way to provide some sort of protection, you will in all likelihood lose your apple tree. Unless you believe this kind of challenge builds character, you're better off not taking the gamble.

Chilling requirements. Like most other fruit trees, apples need to go through a period of winter chill: a certain number of hours between the temperatures of 32° and 45°F. During this dormant period the trees rest, getting ready to bloom and set fruit the following season. (See page 286 for a

more detailed explanation of winter chill, and see specific requirements in the Varieties section below.)

This means that you cannot keep your apple tree at room temperature all winter and expect fruit the following year. It also means that if you live in the Deep South, where temperatures rarely go below 50°F, you should plan on getting your apples at the supermarket. Southerners in marginal climate zones may have success with low-chill varieties (see the special note in the Varieties section).

In more northerly areas, where there is a distinct winter but not horrific cold, just let the tree go dormant naturally (which you will recognize when it begins to lose its leaves). Between November and February, you will undoubtedly accumulate the number of winter-chill hours you need. Remember, though, that if there is a prolonged period of bitter cold in the winter months, the container must be moved into some protected area until the weather is not so severe.

Planting. You can plant your apple tree at almost any time of year, whenever you find a healthy specimen at the garden center. You'll probably find the greatest selection in the spring, and most will be bare-root plants (see page 290). In summer and fall, you're more likely to find small trees in nursery containers. In warmer climates, trees are often available in the winter as well, either bare-root or containerized. If you order from a mail-order nursery specializing in fruit trees, you will in all likelihood receive a bare-root plant.

Choose a large container for your apple tree; a 10- or 15-gallon pot is the minimum for long-term growth. A coarse planting mix that drains well is best.

With a bare-root tree, first trim the roots back to fit the pot without circling, then begin filling the pot with potting mix. As you fill, hold the tree in the pot so that the graft union (the swollen area near the base) is level with the rim of the pot. Fill the pot to within about 2 inches of the top, being careful that the graft union is well above the soil line.

If you are transplanting a containerized plant, remove it from its pot and inspect the root system. If it is quite dense and has circled around the pot, you'll need to break up the root mass somewhat. Pull at larger exposed roots and try to separate them from the main body of roots. Sometimes you may have to beat on the roots with a stick to loosen the snarl. Once you have separated some of the main roots, prune them to fit the pot, and plant as you would for a bare-root tree.

After planting, prune back the branches and the top of the tree to about one-third their length (see details in the Pruning section, below), and water the container very thoroughly, until water runs out the bottom. Now you have one more task: staking.

The dwarfing rootstock that keeps your tree at a small size is, unfortunately, not strong enough to hold up the tree on its own. You need to add some extra support, in the form of a stout stake or trellis. Loosely tie the main stem of the tree to the stake or trellis with thick string or a similar material. Be sure to keep it loose during the life of your tree; tightly tying a tree can disfigure or even kill it.

Columnar apple varieties usually do not need staking.

Success with Apples. Apples are easy trees to grow if you follow a few basic guidelines about watering, fertilizing, pruning, and pest and disease control.

Watering. Proper watering is critical. Your apple tree will not live without water, yet can be damaged or even killed by too much.

When you first plant a bare-root tree in the spring, water it thoroughly as described above. After that it will probably not need water again for several weeks; the root system of a dormant tree is not active, and it cannot use any excess water. Check the potting soil every few days to be sure it is not drying out. Keeping the soil lightly moist is all you need to do until your tree is actively growing.

After your tree begins growing, it will start to use the water in the pot. Check the soil more frequently, and water whenever it shows signs of drying. If your tree is in a large pot, a deep watering every five to seven days should be enough, but be especially vigilant during extremely hot, dry summer days.

Starting in late August or early September, begin holding back on the water, providing just enough to keep the soil very lightly moist. This will slow down the growth rate and

Recipe: Herbed Baked Apples

Maggie says: "The very nice thing about this recipe is that it works so well with so many herbs, even those we don't usually think of as 'dessert' herbs. Don't be afraid to experiment with different herbs. Be bold; try something you don't think will work. Here are some suggestions: lemon verbena (fold leaves lengthwise and stuff into cavity); lavender; fresh bay leaves; any kind of mint, especially apple, orange, or lavender; lemon thyme or nutmeg thyme; cinnamon or lemon basil; and sage. Use your judgment as to amounts, taking into account the relative size of the leaves and the strength of their flavor. And if you don't have geranium leaves to place underneath the apples, just bake the apples without them."

4 cooking apples

Scented geranium leaves

4 tablespoons (¼ cup) butter

¼ cup sugar

Fresh herb leaves or sprigs, plus whole
     herb sprigs for garnish

Lightly sweetened whipped cream

1. Preheat the oven to 350°F.

2. Scrub and dry the apples. Then remove the cores, but leave the bottoms of the apples intact.

3. Lightly butter the bottom of a baking dish and lay 4 geranium leaves in it.

4. Cream the butter and sugar together until light.

5. Set an apple on each geranium leaf, stuff its cavity with fresh herbs of your choice, and place about 1 tablespoon of the butter-sugar mixture on top. Repeat with the remaining apples. Cover the dish tightly

with aluminum foil, place in the oven, and bake until the apples are soft, about 40 minutes.

6. To serve, remove the herbs, place the apples in serving bowls, top each apple with some whipped cream, and garnish with a sprig of the herb used.

Serves 4

allow the tree to prepare for the colder temperatures of winter.

Fertilizing. When you plant a tree in the ground, nature does a pretty good job of providing all the nutrients and minerals necessary for the tree to survive. In a container, however, those essential nutrients must come from you in the form of added fertilizer. This is not an exact science.

Take a moment to review the basics of fertilizer formulas in Chapter 6. Remember, too, that container gardens require more frequent fertilizing than traditional gardens, because the requisite frequent waterings wash away the nutrients that were in the potting mix you started with.

What type of fertilizer you use is a matter of personal choice. Just remember that your goal is the production of flowers and fruit, so select a formulation high in phosphorus (see Chapter 6 for details). Many people report good results from the following program: once a week while the tree is actively growing, give it a drink of soluble synthetic fertilizer such as Miracle-Gro, but dilute it to half strength. Others like the simplicity of a slow-release fertilizer such as Osmocote, described in Chapter 6.

Organic gardeners can choose from a variety of commercial organic fertilizers. You can also apply blood meal and bone meal to the surface of the pot in late spring, for slow-release organic fertilizing. Use one handful of each per foot of height of the tree.

Your apple tree should grow 8 to 12 inches a year, and its leaves should be dark green in color. If this happens, your fertilizer program is working. If you are using homemade organic fertilizers such as manure or compost tea and the leaves turn a pale green or yellowish green, especially the older leaves, you may want to increase the frequency of fertilizing or make a more concentrated solution.

Late in the summer, as you are beginning to cut down on water, you should also gradually stop fertilizing. This allows the tree to harden off and get ready for winter.

Pruning. Let's return to the day you first acquired your tree. After planting, staking, and watering, it is time to think about its form. If you are growing a columnar variety, the tree should be a straight spire with few or no branches. Any branches that do appear should be very short spurs from the main trunk. Basically, columnar varieties do not need pruning. If a columnar tree gets too tall for your space, you can cut it back to about half its height; it will grow back with one or more upright branches that will soon bear fruit.

Apple varieties other than columnar will usually come as a whip (that is, a single slender trunk without branches) or as a young tree with a clearly defined main trunk and a few branches. After planting, check all the branches. First, look for any that are broken and make a cut below the break, discarding the part you cut off. Next, wherever two branches cross and rub together, prune away the weaker one, cutting back to the trunk. It is also a good idea to balance the tree by pruning back any branches that are significantly longer than others.

There is some debate about whether it is useful to do any further pruning. Some growers think it's best to leave the tree alone at this point, while others recommend pruning branches back to about half their length to compensate for the disturbance and shock of transplanting. We advocate the latter approach.

The next thing to think about is how you want to form your tree. Keep this general concept in mind: when you remove the growing tip of a branch, it sends out side branches. If you cut back the central leader of your new tree by about half (the central leader is the shoot growing straight up at the center of the tree, what will eventually become the trunk), you accomplish two things: you control its height, and you also encourage the tree to form side branches, which are generally stronger. Take note, however, that some trees have such a strong urge for a central leader that in a few years another branch will try to grow in that position.

Assuming you started with a dwarf rootstock, cutting back the central leader simply to keep the tree short will not be needed unless you miscalculated your space. You will find, however, that by regularly pruning the leader and the strong branches, you will encourage the tree to grow the short spurs on which fruit is produced. The best time to do this is in the spring; cut away one-third to one-half of the portion of the branches that grew last year.

It is also a good idea to keep branches as horizontal as possible, as this stimulates the formation of flower buds and fruit instead of vegetative buds that simply make longer branches. To accomplish this, you can insert a short piece of wood (a wooden clothespin works well) between the trunk and branch to gently force the branch downward, or you can tie the branch down toward the floor or ground to keep it in a more horizontal position.

As the tree gets older, most of your pruning will entail removing branches that are crossing, or controlling branches or central leaders that are growing too fast and causing the tree to become unbalanced.

Insects and Diseases Probably the worst insect pest of apples is the codling moth. This is a worm that eats the core of the apple and then

Note for Apple Lovers in the South

Your best bet for growing apples is to locate a low-chill variety—that is, one that needs a shorter chilling period than most. Check the wintertime temperature patterns where you live, and choose from these two groups.

■ The following varieties need approximately 300 to 600 chilling hours:

Fuji, a new late-ripening, tasty variety from Japan.

Winter Banana, a large, crisp, juicy yellow apple.

Hudson's Golden Gem, which yields beautiful, light brown fruit with nutty-flavored, crisp, juicy flesh.

■ The following varieties need only 150 to 250 hours of chilling:

Anna, an early-ripening, crisp, tasty green apple with a red blush.

Ein Shemer, a yellow apple from Israel, juicy and crisp.

Beverly Hills, which gives yellow fruit with a red blush fruit; this is a good variety for southern coastal areas where temperatures are not extremely hot.

tunnels out to the surface, leaving a small hole. It leaves a mess at the core, but you can cut around the outside hole and still have apple to eat. This pest is difficult to control. If it becomes a problem for you, purchase a pheromone trap at the garden center, to attract the moth that lays the eggs of the larvae that do the damage.

Two other insects you may encounter are mites and aphids. They don't eat the fruit itself, but can feed on the foliage and severely reduce the vigor of the tree. You may already have experienced aphids if you have a vegetable garden; the best way to control them is to knock them off the plant with a hard spray from the hose, or to apply insecticidal soap, which suffocates them. See Chapter 6 for more details.

Mites are smaller, spiderlike insects that also suck plant juices. They are so tiny that you may see their damage before you see them; you can use a magnifier to identify them. Damage shows as speckling on the leaves or as small webs underneath the leaves. Mites are harder to dislodge with water, but the soap compounds will also work on them. Predatory mites that can help keep the pest mites in check are also available.

Diseases that attack apple trees are a serious concern for commercial orchardists, but represent less of a threat for container gardeners. In the highly controlled environment of one carefully watched container, it is less likely that diseases will get a foothold. The very best advice we can give you is to search out apple varieties that have been bred for resistance to diseases. Apple scab is the biggest problem; read catalog descriptions closely for varieties that are resistant to it.

Harvesting. Now the real fun comes in, the result of all your tender loving care. In the third year, generally speaking (second year for columnar types), you can start picking your own apples. Compared with store-bought fruit, tree-ripened apples are far superior, sweet and delicious. You may find yourself saying, "Now *this* is what apples are supposed to taste like."

All apples must be picked when fully ripe to appreciate their richness and flavor; they do not ripen after being picked. But how do you know when they are ripe? By their color, the ease with which they can be picked, and their firmness and taste. Yellow apples turn from a greenish yellow to a brighter yellow as they ripen; red apples turn a darker red. Apples are also usually ripe when they separate from the tree with just the tiniest tug, or when they begin falling. (However, insect-damaged fruit will sometimes drop prematurely, so you should try tasting one before picking the remainder.) Of course, once you have bitten into a fruit, it will spoil whether it is ripe or not.

Another sign of ripeness is firmness. Try pressing the fruit with your thumb; if it gives a tiny bit, it is probably ripe. Late-ripening varieties are often good keepers and can be stored in a cool room or garage for several months; a month or two of cool storage actually develops better flavor. Early-ripening varieties should be kept in the refrigerator and can usually be stored for a month or two.

Varieties. Apples can be easy trees to grow in containers, and a number of disease-resistant varieties bear delicious fruit. Concentrate on these varieties, and you'll go a long way toward avoiding disease problems.

As you browse through mail-order catalogs, remember to focus first on trees with dwarfing rootstocks (unless you want to try columnar types). The next question is, what variety should you choose for the top of the tree? For container growing, it is best to stick with what are referred to as low- to medium-vigor varieties, meaning that they do not put on a great deal of lush growth but stay relatively small overall.

Here are some recommended varieties, listed in order of ripening. All require a minimum of 600 hours of winter chill.

■ **Dwarf Varieties.** A very early ripening variety, **Wynooche Early** is disease-resistant and easy to grow. Selected by fruit enthusiast Howard Hughes in Aberdeen, Washington, it bears medium-size greenish yellow fruit with a red blush. Very flavorful and juicy, Wynooche Early ripens in early to mid August, and also stores well.

Akane, from Japan, is a disease-resistant variety that bears medium-size bright red fruit with snow white, juicy, flavorful flesh. A low-vigor tree, it is a good choice for container growing. Akane ripens in late August.

Free yourself of worries about apple scab and other diseases; **Liberty** is one of the best disease-resistant varieties. The large red fruit with firm and flavorful flesh is great for both eating out of hand and cooking. The tree has an attractive compact form and dark green glossy foliage. Ripens in mid September.

Spartan bears tasty, large, dark red fruit with flavorful, firm, juicy flesh. Very disease-resistant and of medium vigor, this is a good variety for container growing. Spartan ripens in late September into October and can be stored for several months in a cool room or under refrigeration.

Calville Blanc d'Hiver is a very large, tasty French dessert apple. The fruit is bright yellow with firm, pure white, sweet-tart flesh. It stores very well and is great for both fresh eating and cooking. Calville Blanc is quite disease-resistant and compact in size. The fruit ripens in mid to late October.

■ **Columnar Varieties.** Two very fine new columnar varieties come to us from Canada: **Scarlet Sentinel** and **Golden Sentinel.** Both were bred for their disease resistance and high-quality fruit. Scarlet Sentinel bears attractive red-and-yellow medium-size fruit with sweet, flavorful flesh. Golden Sentinel has large yellow apples with crisp, juicy, flavorful flesh.

Scarlet Sentinel is a low-vigor tree, which makes it an easy plant for container growing. Golden Sentinel is somewhat more vigorous but still a good variety for containers. Both will flower and bear fruit the year after you plant them.

North Pole, also bred in Canada, has a Macintosh-type fruit with dark red, large, juicy apples. It ripens earlier than the Sentinels, but is somewhat more susceptible to apple scab.

■ **Crabapples.** These can also make great container plants and are particularly pretty in bloom. Crabapple varieties to consider are **Dolgo, Callaway,** and **Red Siberian** (which also has red flesh).

Our mental image of lush vegetable gardens always includes a Norman Rockwell sense of hot summertime —the proud gardener wiping away a sheen of well-earned perspiration while lugging baskets spilling over with corn, potatoes, beans, and world-class tomatoes. It's true that summer is the time of greatest bounty, but let's not blindly assume that the other three seasons are barren. With careful planning and reasonable cooperation from the weather, it is possible to harvest home-grown goodies in all four seasons.

Theme Garden

Dinner at the Four Seasons

Everything in this garden will be planted in one large container, at least 2 feet across. In areas of severe winters the plants may require protection; see Chapter 1 for tips.

The centerpiece of this garden is a **columnar apple** tree. (Stop here, take a look at page 287, and decide whether your apple tree needs to be moved for the winter; if so, plan your strategy *before* planting the container.) Columnar apples don't look anything like typical apple trees. They don't have broad branches extending out from the trunk with apples dangling from the branches. In fact, they don't have *any* branches to speak of, just very short stubs sticking out from the trunk; until you look closely, you would think the apples were growing directly from the trunk.

Jim Gilbert, a knowledgeable and generous nurseryman who specializes in fruit trees, once playfully described columnar apple trees as looking like Brussels sprouts. Did you ever see, at a farmers' market or roadside stand, an entire harvested plant of Brussels sprouts? The farmer chops off the roots and removes all the big floppy leaves, and all that remains are the tight little sprouts spiraling around the otherwise bare stem, which looks a lot like a green club with knobby spurs. That's very much what a columnar apple tree looks like, except the "stem" is longer and the "sprouts" are larger.

What's amazing about these trees, though, is that they produce full-size apples, of whatever variety you selected when you purchased your tree. They may look unconventional, but the advantage they offer gardeners with limited space is immediately obvious.

Early in the spring, sow seeds of **Malabar spinach** at the base of the apple tree. This vining type of spinach will climb up into the tree, the better for you to enjoy the rich coloration of its stems and leaves. You'll never get a huge harvest at any one time, but you will be able to take a few leaves of spinach now and then to jazz up your salads for months.

Also in springtime, plant several clumps of **chives** underneath the tree. They help prevent apple scab (a serious disease), provide you with delicious fresh chives practically forever, and in early summer produce endearing little puffball flowers in a soft shade of lavender. Put the chives in as soon as you can; they may die down in very cold winters, but they are a perennial and will come back next spring, stronger than ever.

Beside the chives, plant seeds of regular **spinach,** any variety. The contrast between the emerald green of standard spinach and the rich magenta of the Malabar is gorgeous. Sow the seeds as early in the spring as possible; enjoy fresh spinach all spring and early summer, until the weather gets so hot the plants fizzle out. At that point, yank out the bolted spinach and in its space set out one or more plants of **dwarf basil** and several **Tagetes marigolds.** The basil will do its magic up until the first cool days of fall, and the marigolds will last even longer than that.

When crisp autumn weather kills the basil plants, replace them with cheerful **pansies.** Select pansies in shades of purple and blue and mix them in among the bright yellow marigolds for a beautiful color combination. The pansies will outlast the marigolds, blooming all the way through early winter; if you clip them back and add a layer of mulch before a serious cold snap actually freezes them, they'll sometimes come back with a new burst of blooms in early spring.

The harvest: chives in spring, summer, and fall; spinach in spring and early summer; basil and marigolds in summer; apples in early fall; pansies in autumn and early winter. All in one handsome container, taking up just 2 to 3 feet of floor space. Nice work!

> *Rose Marie says:* A few years back, our friend Jim Gilbert, of Northwoods Nursery, introduced the variety North Pole into this country, and so last year I decided to try it.
>
> Everything went extremely well at first. The young tree looked suspiciously like a buggy whip until it started leafing out, but once that happened it did indeed look like a tree, albeit a very skinny one. I had planted Malabar spinach at the base, and it looked wonderful vining up into the tree.
>
> Then, disaster. One night, a deer from the nearby wooded area found the tree too strong a temptation and ate all the leaves—apple and spinach. A healthy young tree, growing like a champ, was transformed into a buggy whip again. I felt guilty about getting angry at Bambi, but angry I was.
>
> This story has a moderately happy ending. With lots of coddling, the tree lived. It is not as vigorous as it would have been had it not been set back by the deer attack, but it did eventually recover—most plants are a lot tougher than we give them credit for. And we have since moved the container out of Bambi's reach.

Fruits

Blueberries

GROW AS: **hardy perennial shrubs**

PLANT SIZE: **depends on variety**

START WITH: **plants**

HARVEST SEASON: **early to late summer, depending on variety**

SUN REQUIREMENTS: **full sun, except light shade in the heat of the day**

MINIMUM SOIL DEPTH: **18 to 24 inches**

out with reddish tips, then turn dark green with subtle hints of pink and aqua as they mature. They form a canopy over clusters of tiny white or pink flowers shaped like miniature Tiffany lamps. In the fall, the foliage turns a flaming red with brilliant yellows and oranges, a real visual treat. Artists like to paint pictures of blueberries on the bush because there are so many interesting colors intermingled. But the main reason for growing blueberries is because the berries are so delicious: sweet and just slightly tart when ripe, with a distinctive, nothing-like-it taste. One or two plants will provide plenty of berries for eating fresh, making syrup, adding to muffins or pancakes, and even some extra to pop in the freezer for later.

P lump blue beads dusted with a soft, silvery blue powder, hanging in clusters from a neat little shrub, just begging you to pick them. Can you imagine yourself stepping out onto the deck or patio on a summer morning and picking a handful of these sweet, dew-covered berries to plop into your breakfast cereal?

Blueberries are a real joy for container gardeners because they are so easy to grow and produce so well in small spaces. They are striking in appearance, so handsome that many traditional gardeners consider them ornamental plants that also produce delicious fruit. The dainty leaves bud

Blueberry Basics.

Blueberries grow on small to medium-size twiggy bushes, and are grouped into three basic types: highbush, which reach 5 to 6 feet; lowbush, which creep by underground stems and get only a foot or so tall; and rabbiteye, which can top out at a lofty 15 feet. They're all terrific in their place, but a container is not that place. (One exception is a highbush type that can be grown in a container if it's large enough. You might think of it as something between a large shrub and a small tree, providing shade for more tender plants growing in containers beneath it. Highbush blueberries are the ones you'll find in your supermarket.)

Fortunately for us container gardeners, breeders have developed a half-high blueberry (sometimes listed in catalogs as a dwarf blueberry) by crossing the high and low varieties; these are the ones most often chosen for containers.

Planting. If you order from a mail-order catalog, you'll probably receive a bare-root plant. At the retail garden center in early spring, you may find either packaged bare-root plants or potted plants, usually in 1- or 2-gallon containers, that are just beginning to leaf out. Sometimes in early summer you can also find larger plants that actually have fruit on them. Pick bushy plants with multiple stems (if possible) and bright green branches. If a plant has only one main stem but looks really healthy, that's okay; it probably just needs another year in good soil to send up more stems. But if you see a lot of brown or black brittle twigs at the ends of the branches, pass on that plant. Review the general directions on pages 290 to 291 for planting bare-root and container-grown perennials.

Large wooden planter boxes, the kind used for small trees, are excellent choices for blueberries because they drain well, aren't damaged by the weather, and look great. They should be at least 2 feet by 2 feet by 2 feet, and larger wouldn't hurt. Half whiskey barrels also are good choices, but make sure they have several drainage holes in the bottom. Clay pots are not the best choice, as they

may crack in freezing weather.

Blueberries like soil that drains well (so the roots aren't waterlogged) but holds a light, constant moisture level. Finding that delicate balance is not as difficult as you might think: it's only a question of using a planting mix that has a high proportion of organic material such as peat moss or sphagnum moss. Those ingredients also give you something else blueberries require: a soil that is more acidic than alkaline (see the Soil section in Chapter 5 for more on this). Often in garden centers you will find potting soil marked as ideal for rhododendrons, azaleas, and camellias; that's also perfect for blueberries.

Pick the spot for your container carefully, because once it's filled with soil and planted it will be heavy and hard to move around (unless you add casters to your wooden container or set it on a wheeled base). Remove the plant from its nursery pot (if you start with a containerized plant) and fill the container partway with potting mix. Loosen the roots if they are compacted, but try to keep the original soil ball intact as much as possible. Set the plant in position so the top of the soil ball is about 3 to 4 inches below the rim of the new container. Fill in with soil, raising the level of the plant as you go if necessary; the crown of the plant (where the topmost roots end and the stems begin) should never be any deeper than it was in the nursery pot.

Blueberries like their roots right at the surface of the soil but with a light mulch over them. Water thoroughly to settle the plant, then lay 2 to 3 inches of coarse bark, moss, or pine needles over the surface of the soil. This will help hold in moisture and insulate against temperature extremes, while still letting air get to the surface roots.

Success with Blueberries.

Blueberries are, by and large, quite easy to grow. But there are a few things that will help them thrive.

Watering. First, they must have almost constant moisture but not be standing in water. A drip watering system is ideal, if you can provide it; the slowly dripping water moistens, but passes on through, the porous soil. Otherwise, daily watering will be necessary in hot weather. Check the soil with your finger; it should always feel like a damp, wrung-out sponge.

Maggie says: The Pacific Northwest is blueberry heaven. Here in this land of gracious-plenty rainfall and acidic soil, you'd think all anyone would have to do is stick a blue-berry stem in the ground and walk away, then stroll back in the summer to pick the berries. Yet I learned an important lesson from my friend Barbara Ashmun, whose gorgeous garden has several low-lying spots where water doesn't drain. After years of struggling with these mini-bogs, she found that the secret of growing blueberries there was to put them in containers. So here she is, with all the room in the world (nearly an acre), growing 5-foot blueberry bushes in ordinary black plastic nursery containers, with tremendous success.

Soil. Even though blueberry plants love acid soil, it is possible for it to become *too* acidic. When that happens, the plant is unable to take up iron from the soil, creating an unhealthy condition called chlorosis. Fortunately, the plant gives you a very clear clue: the leaves turns yellow except for the veins, which stay dark green. You can correct this condition by adding a small amount of lime. The best is a form known as chelated iron (also called sequestered or micronized iron); it is readily absorbed by the plant and you see results quickly, thus eliminating the temptation to add too much lime, which would make the soil too alkaline.

The best course of all is to prevent this condition from happening by always using a fertilizer with the proper acid balance (such as those recommended for rhododendrons, azaleas, and camellias). Blueberries are heavy feeders, so starting in early spring, feed the plants once a month at the recommended rate. Around mid August, begin tapering off; do not fertilize at all during the fall and winter.

Winter protection is important if you live in a cold climate. Blueberries are naturally very hardy plants, but when grown in a container, their roots are exposed to cold air from all sides. If some of the branches die, new ones will grow; but if the roots die, the plant is gone. When cold weather arrives, move the container into a more sheltered location, or wrap it in some insulating material (see page 288) during the coldest times.

Winter chill is also a factor with blueberries (see page 286). Most blueberries need around 800 hours, although there is one that southern gardeners can grow successfully (see Varieties, below).

Pruning. Your blueberry plants will give you years of berries, especially if you prune the mature plants lightly. The pruning process is not as elaborate or as precise as with some of the tree fruits, and the improvement in production is noticeable. Don't do anything the first two or three years. Each year thereafter, early in the spring, completely remove some of the very oldest branches (with the darkest and scraggliest-looking bark), and clip off any twigs that seem unusually thin and weak. You'll have much larger berries (but fewer of them) if you cut back the remaining stems by about one-third to one-half. This forces new growth, and new growth bears the largest berries.

Harvesting. One of the surest signs that your berries are ripening will be the appearance of visiting birds. Robins, jays, starlings, and a few others love blueberries. When you see the very first berries starting to turn from green to blue, you'll need to protect your crop by covering the whole plant with bird netting. The netting should be raised high enough over the plant that birds can't reach through for a sneak attack, and the bottom should be secured so they can't slip in under the net.

Different varieties of blueberries ripen at different times, but you can tell when they're ripe when most of the berries in a cluster turn dark blue. Pick one of the darkest and taste it. If it's very tart, wait a few days. When fully ripe, they should not make you pucker. The berries do not all ripen at the same time, so you can harvest over a period of two to three weeks for each variety you are growing.

Varieties. All blueberries are self-fertile, but you will get much larger crops if you plant at least two varieties for cross-pollination.

Earliblue, a highbush type, is a vigorous upright plant with good cold-hardiness. It has large fruit that ripens early (June). **Bluecrop,** another highbush, has large, light blue berries in midseason (July); it is very productive, cold-hardy, and more drought-tolerant than most.

Patriot, a half-high type with upright growth, is cold-hardy; it ripens midseason (July), with large, good-flavored fruit. **Northblue,** also a half-high type, is only 20 to 30 inches tall at maturity. For such a small plant it is extremely productive, with masses of large, slightly tart berries in mid summer.

Northsky is a half-high type especially recommended for very cold climates. It grows only about 18 inches high, but spreads to about 3 feet, and ripens in mid summer.

Sunshine Blue, a compact half-high with pretty pink flowers, is the one for southerners. It is less finicky about acid soil than most blueberries, and needs only 150 hours of winter chilling. (Interestingly, it does very well in colder climates, too.) About 3 feet tall, with large berries in July.

Fruits

Citrus

GROW AS: **small trees or shrubs**

PLANT SIZE: **2 to 5 feet**

START WITH: **plants**

HARVEST SEASON: **fall through spring, depending on variety**

SUN REQUIREMENTS: **morning sun, afternoon filtered shade, strong light**

MINIMUM SOIL DEPTH: **18 inches**

Citrus trees are considered almost exotic by those who live where citrus doesn't grow naturally. When oranges were first introduced in Europe, they were so coveted that wealthy families built special glass houses to grow them in. These elaborate and expensive *orangeries* were the forerunners of present-day greenhouses. But you don't need a fancy *orangerie* to grow a citrus tree. With reasonably cooperative weather and good winter stewardship, you can grow one in a pot on the patio.

Citrus trees have handsome foliage and deliciously fragrant flowers. In California and Florida, they are often massed together as hedges. Very small plants are also sold all around the country as houseplants, and those who grow them are happy with their good looks even if they never produce fruit. Somewhere between huge hedges and dainty houseplants are the diminutive citrus trees of container gardens, and they offer the same joys—beautiful foliage, luscious flowers, and, with any luck, wonderful fruit.

Citrus Basics. All citrus fruits grow on small to medium-size trees that thrive in subtropical climates where the days and nights are about equal in length and temperatures stay above freezing. Some of the hardier varieties of citrus will take a light frost of short duration, but none will survive freezing weather.

The fruits that must develop sugars to be palatable—orange, grapefruit, tangerine, tangelo—need longer time in hot weather, and so are questionable for colder areas unless you're interested only in aesthetics. But fruits that are naturally sour, such as lemons and limes, are possible in all but the coldest climates, with some extra attention in winter.

Planting. The citrus trees you'll buy for your container garden are grafted. The top portion is selected for its superior fruit quality, and the bottom portion, the rootstock, is selected for its dwarfing quality. This is what makes these trees small enough to grow in containers. You can see the graft as a diagonal scar on the trunk. If later on you see a vigorous branch suddenly zooming out from the trunk, look at it closely; if it's coming from below the graft, prune it off completely, back to the trunk; any fruit it produces will be undesirable, and it will draw vigor from the "good" branches.

Citrus plants have a shallow, spreading root system with surface roots right at the top of the soil, which don't like to be covered. Whether you start with a bare-root or potted plant, keep this in mind. And review page 290 for the basics of planting both types of perennial plants.

Use a large container that will hold at least 15 gallons of soil, such as a redwood tub, half barrel, or large terra-cotta pot. If you live in a cold climate, it's a good idea to set the container on a plant trolley with wheels, as it will have to be brought inside for winter. Citrus plants like very rich, acid soil with a high content of organic matter. If you can find a commercial potting mix formulated for rhododendrons or camellias, that's perfect. Otherwise, use an all-purpose soil and mix in some extra materials that will increase the organic content: peat moss, sphagnum moss, and commercial bagged compost all will work.

Fill your container about three-quarters full and spread the roots evenly over the top; fill in around them with more soil. When you're done, you want the roots to be just below the surface of the soil. Tamp the soil in around the root ball and water it well to settle the roots. Spread a light, airy mulch such as wood chips over the exposed roots to keep them from drying out.

Success with Citrus. If you live in southern California, the Southwest, or Florida, you already have what citrus needs most: heat, and lots of it. Apartment dwellers in those parts of the country need not envy their friends with large yards; both can grow citrus with equal ease and equal success.

The farther north you live, the more attention you will have to pay to wintertime protection, and here container gardeners have something of an edge because they can move their trees inside for the winter.

Grow citrus outside during the frost-free months; they must have strong light and lots of moving fresh air plus all the heat you can give them. They love to be close to a wall or structure where they will get reflected heat. On the other hand, they need filtered light shade from the harshest summer afternoon sun to prevent sun scald.

Leave the citrus plants outside until the night temperature starts to drop to about 45°F. Then begin to move them gradually into a protected, moderately warm area for the winter. They need as much light as you can manage. Many people grow them inside in a south-facing window and provide supplemental light during stretches of dark, overcast days. Most citrus plants flower around New Year's Day, and if they are indoors you get to enjoy the heavenly fragrance. Then in the spring, after there is no more danger of freezing, move the plants back outside.

These are heavy feeders. Every month (except during the winter) give them an application of fertilizer formulated specifically for citrus (anything labeled "high acid" or "for rhododendrons" will also work). They also respond well to an occasional booster of fish emulsion, two or three times per year.

Water frequently, but be *very* careful that your soil is draining well. Citrus roots are especially vulnerable to being smothered by waterlogged soil. Also, don't wet the trunk while you're watering.

Citrus do have some pest problems that you need to watch for. Red spider mites are one, and if you keep the plant misted and watered regularly you can spot them before they get ahead of you. If mites are present, you'll see the water cling to very fine webbing at the point where a leaf stem is attached to a branch. Washing the plant with a

mild soap-and-water solution will help (you can do this in the shower) but you'll probably need to spray the leaves with an insecticidal soap spray (see Chapter 6) on a regular basis. Remember, never use a systemic insecticide (one that is taken up by the roots) on anything you are going to eat!

The other pest you may encounter is scale, an insect that is very hard to spot. They appear on the stems and underside of the leaves as small oval, translucent spots that look like drops of wax. Use a cotton swab dipped in rubbing alcohol to clean them off. Inspect every leaf, stem, and branch regularly to control scale.

If your tree starts to drop a lot of leaves, it's hungry. Prune lightly and feed it; it should recover quickly.

Pruning is not a major chore with citrus, but since fruit forms on new growth, you want to prune regularly to encourage new branches. Starting about the third year, cut back all new branches by about one-third of their length. Also, check the plants regularly for broken or extremely weak branches, and cut them off.

Harvesting. It takes about a year for citrus fruit to ripen. This is why you often see blooms, green fruit, and ripe fruit all at the same time. Blossoms from last year will have formed ripe fruit just as the plant is beginning to bloom in the present year. Fruit is ripe when it is fully colored and comes away from the branch easily.

Varieties. All citrus are self-fertile; you don't have to worry about planting two varieties for pollination as you do with some fruits.

■ **Grapefruit, Oranges.** Ruby is the small, pink-fleshed grapefruit you see in the supermarket. Remember, if you hope to eat your fruit, all grapefruit varieties need lots of heat to sweeten up and color properly. The same is generally true of oranges, although the navel types take less heat to ripen than juice varieties. **Robertson** is one very productive variety of naval orange, and a fine small-size tree.

■ **Lemons, Limes.** Container gardeners outside the Citrus Belt will probably have more luck with lemons and limes (although of the two, limes are far more tender and easily damaged by cold). **Ponderosa** lemon is a small tree that bears young, with very large fruit. **Pink Lemonade** is a beautiful lemon plant with green-and-white variegated foliage. The rind of the young fruit is striped and the flesh is pink. It does not, alas, make pink juice.

Perhaps the very best choice for marginal climates is the Meyer lemon. While not a true lemon in the botanical sense (it is a cross between a lemon and an orange), it makes a wonderful substitute. The tree is naturally small and thus good for containers; the fruit is rounder than the familiar pointed oval, and a darker golden yellow; and both the flesh and the peel have a somewhat sweeter, mellower taste. It is easy to grow, blooms and fruits almost constantly, and best of all is more cold-hardy than most citrus. The one you are most likely to find is called **Improved Meyer Lemon,** a disease-resistant cultivar.

The Key lime, also called **Mexican lime,** is very vulnerable to cold weather. An interesting alternative and a very good conversation piece is the **Kaffir lime.** This is the one to grow if you enjoy Southeast Asian cuisine. Its fresh leaves are widely used for seasoning, and the fragrant flowers are edible. The fruit itself is not used in cooking, although the peel sometimes is; the tree is grown for the leaves.

Fruits

Currants and Gooseberries

GROW AS: **perennials**

PLANT SIZE: **3 to 4 feet**

START WITH: **young plants, grown from cuttings**

HARVEST SEASON: **mid summer**

SUN REQUIREMENTS: **full sun to partial shade**

MINIMUM SOIL DEPTH: **15 inches**

Bursting with flavor, exquisitely beautiful to look at, and very nutritious, currants and gooseberries are ideal for container gardens because the bushes are small; even when fully mature, they seldom get taller than 4 feet. Both make very attractive plants: handsome shrubs covered in season with small fruits that positively glow in the sunshine. But the real reason for growing them is the incomparable taste of the fruit; sweet and tart at the same time, they are like nothing else you've ever tasted. In fancy markets, you would pay an arm and a leg for a tiny basket of these gems. Imagine the pleasure of having your own supply right at hand.

It's possible you have never tasted either of these fruits in their fresh form. Although they have been a staple in European gardens for centuries, where they are prized for fresh eating and for the wonderful preserves, pies, and other sweets made from them, they are not very well known to most Americans.

If your only experience of gooseberries is a jar of commercial jam from a gourmet shop, and the only currants you've ever tasted are the dried, wrinkled specks sold next to the raisins (which are made from small grapes and are not currants at all), you're in for a delicious surprise. And if you grow the sweeter varieties, you can finish off your next dinner party by presenting a beautiful crystal dish filled with black currants, red currants, and pink and green gooseberries, glistening like jewels. Your guests will have an unforgettable treat.

Besides their exceptional taste, gooseberries and currants are rich in vitamins B and C, calcium, and potassium, and are a good source of dietary fiber. That may not be your primary reason for growing them, but it's a nice extra benefit.

Fruits Follow Flowers

Here's something to ponder: all fruits (and all vegetables that are actually fruits in a botanical sense) are the result of fertilized flowers. This is so fully understood that we seldom think about it, but there was a time in our history when the presence of fruit was considered capricious and magical, a gift from the gods when it appeared, a punishment when it did not. It took a man of science to make the connection.

The Greek philosopher Theophrastus, who lived 300 years before Christ, was intensely interested in botany among other things. A student of Aristotle, he took over as head of Aristotle's Lyceum when his famous teacher retired. Known today as the Father of Botany, Theophrastus wrote a nine-volume work called *An Inquiry into Plants,* wherein he detailed his observation that fruits follow flowers. The lesson for us is simple: if your tree or bush does not flower, you won't get any fruits. Either your plant is still immature, or it needs more fertilizer.

Currant and Gooseberry

Basics. These two fruits are closely related, but there are important differences between them. Currants come in three colors: jet black, red, and white. Gooseberries can be either red or greenish yellow, with distinctive stripes running from top to bottom, like longitude lines on a globe. Gooseberries are bigger, about the size of a marble; currants are tiny, rarely more than ¼ inch in diameter.

Currants are more strongly flavored; gooseberries are often sweeter. These minor differences aside, the two are botanically very similar, and they need the same growing conditions and care.

Size. Even when they reach their full size, currants and gooseberries are relatively small plants, 3 to 4 feet in height and diameter. Gooseberries tend to form round-headed bushes with branches close to the ground. Currants are typically more upright.

Pollination. All gooseberries are self-fertile, and will bear good crops without cross-pollination. So are most—but not all—currants. Read catalog descriptions for currants carefully. If you have a variety that is not self-fertile, you must plant another variety near it (ideally in the same pot) for cross-pollination by bees and other insects. The flowers themselves are small whitish bells, not especially noteworthy in appearance but essential for fruit.

Hardiness and Chilling Requirements. Both types of plants are deciduous, and will lose their leaves with the coming of fall. The autumn coloration is nothing to write home about, but it does serve as a signal that the plant is about to move into dormancy, which in turn is your cue to mobilize wintertime protection.

Currants and gooseberries are much hardier than most fruits. In traditional gardens they can withstand temperatures of −25°F and below, some as low as −40°F. Remember, though, that in containers roots are more vulnerable to damage from freezing than they would be if planted in the ground, and so those numbers need to be adjusted. To be on the safe side, make sure the roots of currants and gooseberries are kept above 20°F.

On the other hand, don't be in too much of a hurry to tuck your plants in for the winter. With gooseberries and currants, which are native to colder regions of the earth, it's a good idea to leave them in a natural environment, complete with hard fall frosts, as long as possible. This ensures they get the 600 to 700 hours of winter chill they need. (See page 286 for a complete explanation of winter chill.) Unfortunately, gardeners in the far southern parts of the country will have a hard time accumulating 600 hours at temperatures between 32° and 45°F.

It's only when the thermometer drops below 20°F and threatens to stay there for a long period that you should swing into action. Complete details on the two basic strategies for winter protection—wrapping and moving the container—are described on page 289. Be sure to remove the insulating wrap, or bring the container back outside, once the danger of severe freezing is past. With the coming of warm weather, your plant will be ready to grow and reward you once again with a bountiful harvest of fruit.

Planting. You can plant your currant or gooseberry at almost any time of year (except the dead of winter),

but the widest selection of varieties is available in the spring. From both mail-order and retail nurseries, what you'll find in the spring will be bare-root plants (see page 290).

Potted plants are often available in summer and fall, usually in gallon-size pots. Before you buy one at the garden center, slip the whole thing out of the pot and inspect the roots. If you see a tangled mass of roots growing in circles, the plant is rootbound; pass on it. Plants that start with such a congested root system are more difficult to get established because the tangled roots have a hard time taking up water.

Because currant and gooseberry plants are smaller overall, you can use a smaller container for them than you would for another fruit tree. They are also shallow rooted, so a container that is proportionally wider rather than deeper is best. Even something as small as a squat 5-gallon size will do for several years; if you start with a 7- or 10-gallon container, the plant can grow even longer before it needs repotting.

Any planting mix that drains well will work. Fill the pot about halfway with soil and then prepare your plant. If you're starting with a potted plant, remove it from the nursery container and loosen the roots by digging your fingers into the root mass and pulling out the larger ones; if any are noticeably longer than the others, trim them back to equal length. Unwrap bare-root plants and spread out the roots; prune back any that are broken or excessively long. Identify the crown of the plant: the point low down on the main stem, just above the topmost roots, where the stem becomes smaller and darker.

Set the plant in the pot, spread the roots out as evenly as possible, and begin filling the pot. When you're done, you want the crown to be about 1 inch below the rim of the container. You may need to lift the plant gently as you add soil, to keep it at the correct height.

If you started with a potted plant, a good rule of thumb is to have the plant in the final container at the same level as it was in the nursery container. Finish by watering the container thoroughly to settle the plant and make sure the potting soil is in good contact with the roots.

For bare-root plants, it's a good idea to cut back the top after planting. This helps balance the top with the root system, part of which was lost when the plant was dug up at the nursery. Cut each branch by about a third to half of its original length. At the same time, remove any branches that are broken or rubbing against other branches.

If you started with a container plant, you won't have to do any pruning other than removing broken or crossing branches. The only exception to this would be if you purchased an older potted plant that was seriously rootbound or had lots of weak growth from the previous season. You should cut back this sort of plant severely, leaving only 2- to 3-inch stubs of the previous growth. This may seem to be harsh treatment, but it will help the plant generate

healthy new growth (see the Pruning section below).

Success with Currants and Gooseberries.

Currants and gooseberries make wonderful container plants. They take up little space, produce good crops of delicious fruit, and are bothered by few pests and diseases. Follow these basic growing practices, and you should enjoy many years of tasty harvests.

Watering. If you're planting a bare-root plant in the spring, it will likely be dormant or just starting growth. Until the roots have begun active growth, they cannot take up much water, and overwatering can cause more harm than good. Check the soil every few days; just poke your finger down an inch or so. If it feels completely dry, give the container a deep watering, and then no more until the soil is dry again.

Within a week or two after planting, if the weather is warm, your plant will begin active growth. When you see buds and new leaves forming and the stems getting longer, you'll know the roots are active, too. At that point, you should begin a regular watering schedule. Deep waterings once a week should be enough, except during the hottest weather, when you will need to keep a vigilant eye. At the first sign of wilting, water heavily.

If you start with a container plant in the spring or summer, you will need to water it more often at first than you would a bare-root plant. Keep in mind that the roots require several weeks to fully grow into the potting soil in the new container. During this time, the soil immediately around the root system (the soil that was in the original nursery container) can dry out while the surrounding oil in the new pot can feel moist. Be sure that you water close to the plant to get water into the root zone. After a few weeks, the roots should have grown into the new potting soil and you can begin the same watering schedule as described for a bare-root plant.

In late summer, begin holding back on water to help your plant harden off and prepare for winter.

Fertilizing. The fertilizer information given in the Apples section also applies to currants and gooseberries; see page 297.

Pruning. To continue looking good and pumping out berries, currants and gooseberries need to be pruned every year. The process is not difficult, but a quick botany review will help you understand why this is necessary.

In some plants, the cellular activity that produces buds for flowers (and ultimately fruit) begins a year in advance. So a branch that forms in year 1 will not actually bear fruit until year 2. The first year nothing of significance happens, at least on the surface; the second year, that same branch will set flowers and fruit.

Gooseberries and currants are of this type; they bear fruit on stems that are two years and three years old. But unlike some other fruit plants, the individual branches do not continue to bear fruit forever. After the third year they lose vigor, and productivity drops way off. To say this a different way, currants and gooseberries form fruits on two- and three-year-old branches—not on one-year-old branches (usually), and not on four-year-old branches. For a continuous supply of fruit, then, you need a continuous supply of new shoots. And that is accomplished by regular pruning. Prune when the plant is dormant, either in winter if your winters are relatively mild, or in early spring before the plant starts growing for the season.

For these two fruits, pruning has three objectives:

1. To shape the plant in the form of an open bush.

2. To maintain equal proportions of one-, two-, and three-year-old shoots.

3. To distribute the fruit-bearing shoots and the current year's growth evenly around the bush.

The difficulty in explaining the process is that we humans tend to think of age in human terms. In a baby's first year of life, we say the baby is so many months old, and doesn't become one year old until the end of the twelfth month. So in its *second* year of life, a baby is one year old. With plants, we calculate differently. The stem or branch that grows in one season is one year old that same season; the following year, that same branch is considered to be two years old. (Gardeners use the term "wood" for all branches and stems; you'll hear them refer, for example, to "two-year-old wood.")

It's obvious, then, that to properly prune these bushes, you need to be able to tell the older from the newer stems. The short answer is that the older they are, the darker and more scaly the bark.

The pruning process is not complicated. With just a bit of practice, you can probably do it in less time than it takes us to explain it. We will describe how to prune, one year at a time, using imaginary colored ribbons to distinguish each year's growth. You could also use ribbons literally, although in bright sun the colors may fade over time. An alternative is to circle each stem with a strip of tape for each year of growth.

1. Early spring, year 1. Plant your new plant; if you started with a bare-root plant, shorten the stems as described in the Planting section above.

2. Summer, year 1. Whether you have planted a bare-root or potted plant, let it grow freely the first year. Mentally (or literally) mark all the new stems that grow this spring as "red" stems. There is a chance of a few fruits being produced the first summer, but primarily this is the year for the plant to get established.

3. Early spring, year 2. Select five or six strong "red" stems that are well spaced around the plant; cut off the rest, down to the base.

4. Summer, year 2. The "red" stems are two years old and bear fruit. Mentally designate the new stems that grow this year as "blue."

5. Early spring, year 3. Prune away several of the "red" stems, leaving three or four good ones. Choose five or six strong "blue" ones, evenly spaced around the bush, and cut out the rest.

6. Summer, year 3. The "red" stems are three years old and the "blue" ones are two years old; both bear fruit. Designate the stems that grow this summer as "yellow."

7. Early spring, year 4. Prune away all the remaining "red" stems; their productive life is over. Also, prune away about half the "blue" stems, leaving the rest for this summer. Select five or six well-spaced "yellow" stems, and remove the others.

8. Summer, year 4. This summer the "blue" stems are three years old and the "yellow" ones are two years old; both will bear fruit. This year's new growth is designated "purple" and will be the source of fruit-bearing stems next year.

And so on.

This is the basic idea. With each year's pruning, you can leave more or fewer shoots than the numbers suggested here, depending on how big you want your plant to be.

To put this entire process in a nutshell: each spring, remove the shoots that are more than three years old, and thin out the others so the plant doesn't get too crowded. What is important is continuous shoot renewal, so that vigorous new growth is always coming on to replace the old.

Insects and Diseases. The most bothersome disease of both gooseberries and currants is powdery mildew, which shows up as a white coating on the leaves (see Chapter 6).

Severe infections can stop shoots from growing, which reduces the crop of fruit for the following year. While it doesn't usually bother the fruit of currants, powdery mildew can seriously damage gooseberries. The best preventive measure is to plant disease-resistant varieties; at the first sign of mildew on your gooseberry bush, begin treatment as described in Chapter 6.

Insects that bother gooseberries and currants include currantworm and aphids. Currantworm is easy to control but hard to see at first. The worm is a green caterpillar that seems to be able to make itself the exact color of the leaves. It starts by eating the edge of the leaves and, if not controlled, can defoliate the plant. Rotenone spray, a natural insecticide, gives excellent control of this pest. Aphids cause discoloring and puckering of the leaves. They are not always easy to control, but insecticidal soaps and simply spraying them off the leaves with your garden hose can be effective; see Chapter 6 for more specifics.

Harvesting. Most varieties of currants and gooseberries ripen in mid summer. Your cue is the change in color. Currants change from the green of young fruit to the color of the variety you have planted: black currants will become jet black, red currants will become beautiful bright red and translucent, and white currants (which are basically a white version of red currants) will become pale white and strikingly translucent, with their tan seeds visible inside the berries.

After the fruit has changed color, the next test of ripeness is taste. When fully ripe, all currants will have a complement of sweet and tart flavors. Ripened currants are easy to pick. Some varieties will be in long clusters called strigs; you can simply pinch off the entire strig. Others will come off easily individually. After harvesting, the berries will keep at room temperature for a day or two, and a week or so in the refrigerator. For longer storage they can be frozen or dried.

Gooseberries also change color when ripe, from green to yellowish green or red, depending on the variety. They also soften a bit when fully ripe. Again, the best way to determine their ripeness is to taste one. Gooseberries are usually sweeter than currants, with a milder flavor. They are picked individually and will keep somewhat longer than currants. They can also be frozen or dried for long-term storage.

Varieties. Because currants and gooseberries have been cultivated for so long, many varieties have been developed. In recent years growers have concentrated on improving disease resistance while maintaining large fruit size and good flavor. The varieties listed here are just a sample of the many available. All varieties listed are self-fertile.

■ **Black currants.** Black Down originated in England. The source of many currant and gooseberry varieties, it is vigorous and disease-resistant, and produces good crops of large, sweet, flavorful berries. The fruits are jet black and come in short strigs that are easy to harvest, ripening in early to mid July.

One of several varieties that originated at a breeding program in Scotland, **Ben Lomond** is a medium-vigor disease-resistant plant. A very productive variety, it bears shiny, jet black, sweet-tart berries that ripen in mid to late July. This is a particularly good variety for making preserves.

Also from England, **Black September** is a medium-vigor, disease-resistant variety that bears abundant crops of sweet, strong-flavored berries. The jet black fruits ripen in mid to late July.

Jostaberry is a unique cross of black currant and gooseberry. The plant is very vigorous and disease-resistant, and quickly grows to a height of 3 to 4 feet. The jet black fruit has an attractive sweet-tart flavor. Berries are larger than black currants, and are harvested individually.

■ **Red and White Currants.** Both red and white currants belong to the same species (*Ribes rubrum*), but they have different-colored berries. With their translucent, bright-colored fruit, they are quite spectacular both in the container and on the table. They all ripen in mid July, and should be picked in clusters as they will leak and spoil if picked individually. They are pruned in the same manner as gooseberries.

Red Jade originated at a breeding program in New York, and is sometimes listed in catalogs as NY 68.

It is very disease-resistant and productive, bearing long strigs of bright red fruit. The delicious sweet-tart berries make a striking sight on the table. This is a good variety for making red currant jam, a rare delicacy.

A new variety from Holland, **Rovada** is disease-resistant and very productive, bearing long and attractive strigs of translucent, bright red berries.

Swedish White is a new disease-resistant variety from Sweden, this attractive small bush bears large crops of very attractive berries. You can actually see the tan-colored seeds through the translucent fruit.

■ **Gooseberries.** An English variety, **Colossal** bears large amounts of very large, sweet berries. The attractive fruits are greenish yellow when ripe, and are very good for fresh eating. Colossal is a medium-vigor plant and grows to about 4 feet in height at maturity.

A new English introduction, **Invicta** features very large, sweet berries and a high degree of disease resistance. The very pretty greenish yellow fruit is good for fresh eating and also makes delicious pies and preserves. Invicta is vigorous and easy to grow, and will reach up to 4 feet in height when mature.

A classic red-fruited English variety, **Whinhams Industry** features large, sweet, delicious fruit on a medium-vigor plant. By itself or with another variety for contrast, the purplish red fruit is very attractive both on the bush and in the serving dish.

Fruits

Figs

GROW AS: **perennials**

PLANT SIZE: **6 to 8 feet**

START WITH: **young plants, grown from cuttings**

HARVEST SEASON: **mid summer and fall**

SUN REQUIREMENTS: **full sun to partial shade**

MINIMUM SOIL DEPTH: **18 inches**

Figs are ideal container plants. Striking in appearance with their large tropical-looking leaves, they grow slowly, are easy to train, and bear abundant, delectable fruit. They have been part of the landscape in southern Europe and the Middle East for centuries—translation: they like hot climates—but now those of us who live in more northerly parts of the world can enjoy this treat by growing them in containers. We can let the plant soak up the warm summer weather it needs, and then move it to a sheltered location for the winter.

A fresh fig is a gourmet's delight, and a far cry from Fig Newtons, which is how most of us have experienced figs. They are as different from each other as a fresh, crisp apple is from dried apple rings, or a fresh grilled tuna steak is from the stuff in the can. Soft and tender when ripe, figs are delicious fresh, especially chilled, and they make wonderful preserves—if you can keep from eating them all first.

Fig Basics. Most fig trees will bear two crops of fruit, the first ripening in mid summer on branches that grew the previous year, and the second crop ripening on the current season's growth in the fall. The ripe fruit can be either yellowish green or dark brown on the outside, with strawberry pink or honey-colored flesh.

Size. When grown in the ground in southern climates, figs develop into trees 15 feet or more in height. In a container they tend to grow more slowly, and with minimal pruning can be kept to 8 feet or less.

Different varieties grow at different rates; the ones we suggest below are low- to medium-vigor types, meaning that they grow slowly and thus are the best choices for containers.

Hardiness. Figs are subtropical plants and when planted in the ground will withstand frost to about 5°F. Temperatures lower than this will freeze the fig back to the soil surface and possibly even kill the plant. Determined Italian Americans in Cleveland and other northern cities have successfully grown figs in their gardens by laying them sideways and covering them with plastic and soil to protect them from cold.

As a container gardener, all you will have to do, once the plant has lost its leaves (signaling the start of dormancy), is move your fig to a warmer location for the winter. Your best bet is something like a sun porch or garage where temperatures are cool but above freezing. This will allow your tree to remain dormant until you move it outside again in the spring. The leaves of a fig tree cannot stand any frost, so don't move the plant outside until you're sure the temperatures will stay above freezing.

If you don't have a coolish storage area like a garage or sun porch, you can *try* bringing your fig indoors for the winter. Kept at room temperature, though, it will likely begin growing in early spring, well before it's warm enough outside to move it back outdoors. In that case, your job is to give it as much light as possible, and keep your fingers crossed.

Pollination. Gorgeous to look at and bearing delicious fruit, fig trees are also interesting botanically. You will never see a fig bloom. The part we eat and call a fruit is actually a modified flower stem; the true flowers are deep inside, invisible to us. Fortunately, most figs are self-fertile and do not need another variety for pollination.

For those varieties that do need pollination, Calimyrna, for example, nature has provided a specialized wasp to do the job. This tiny wasp actually crawls inside the fig and pollinates the flowers with pollen from a wild fig provided by the grower.

Chilling Requirements. As with virtually all fruits that can be grown in temperate climates, figs need a period of time at temperatures between 32° and 45°F after they have gone dormant, to rest and be ready to grow and bear fruit again. (See page 286 for a full explanation of winter chill.) Good news for those who live in the warmer regions of the country: figs require only 100 hours at these temperatures, much less than most other fruits. Figs are also sensitive to light levels and will not start growing until the daylight hours increase in spring. In nature, this protects them from late-spring frosts.

Planting. Young fig trees are available as bare-root plants in the spring and as container-grown plants from spring until fall. The best time to plant your fig is in the spring. You'll likely have a greater choice of varieties then, especially from mail-order nurseries, and spring planting will allow your tree to develop a good root system before going dormant in the fall. If you're purchasing a potted plant, be sure to remove the pot and inspect the root system before buying. If the root system is tight and packed full of roots, avoid that plant; it will have difficulty taking up water.

Choose a good-size container;

the larger it is, the longer you can go without repotting. A fig can stay happily in a 5-gallon container for two or three years, but if you start with a 10-gallon size or larger, both you and your fig will be much better off. A coarse, fast-draining potting soil will work best.

Prepare the young tree for planting as described on page 290. Loosen the root mass and trim away any roots that are broken or excessively long. The root system should fit comfortably in the pot without crowding. Fill the pot partway with potting soil, place the plant in the pot with its roots spread out evenly, and begin filling the pot.

As you fill, pay attention to the height of the plant. On a bare-root plant there will be a place just above the roots where the color of the stem changes from orange to brown. This is the crown of the plant, and when you're finished it should be at soil level. Finish filling the pot to about 1 inch below the rim. With a nursery-potted plant, keep the soil level in the new container the same as it was in the original nursery pot.

The last step is to water the plant well to settle the soil around the roots. It's also a good idea to cut back the top to balance it with the roots lost in transplanting. To prepare your fig for later formation into a vase shape (see Pruning, below), cut the top back to about 2 feet in height and remove any branches below this level.

Success with Figs. The single most important ingredient for growing luscious figs is giving them the heat they crave. All too often this sad scene unfolds: the gardener carefully plants and nurtures the young fig tree, joyfully watches as it leafs out, and proudly counts every single one of the tiny, hard green fruits as they form. But that's as far as it goes, because there isn't enough warm weather for the fruits to reach full size and ripen. The trick is to start with the variety that is best suited for your climate; see the Varieties section below.

You can also help things along by placing the plant on the south side of a building where it will get lots of heat during the day and stay warmer during the night. If the wall is white or light colored and thus will reflect sunlight back toward the plant, so much the better.

Watering. Your fig cannot live without water, and it can die with too much of it. After the deep watering you did on planting day, don't water thoroughly again until you see that the tree is starting to grow. If you started with a plant that was dormant— which is our recommendation— this could be days or even weeks. In the meantime, water only enough to keep the soil from becoming completely dry.

There is, however, one situation where additional watering may be necessary. If you plant a container-grown tree that was already showing signs of new growth in the nursery container, the soil immediately around the root system (what came from the nursery container) may dry out while the surrounding soil in its new container still feels moist. In that case, pay special attention to the soil near the trunk of the tree and water there when it begins to dry out. Eventually, the root system will grow into the new potting soil and regular watering can be done.

Once your fig tree has begun actively growing, it will start to use up the moisture in the potting soil. During cool weather, the tree uses less water and you may need to water the container only every other week, perhaps even less. During hot weather, your fig may need water every four or five days.

The moral is, you must monitor the soil moisture. The easiest monitoring tool is one you always have with you—your finger. Dig down an inch or so; if the soil is damp, don't water. The point is to give the plant adequate water supplies without creating waterlogged soil that will deny the roots oxygen and eventually kill them.

When you water, do so deeply and thoroughly; this helps keep the roots growing toward the bottom of the pot. Frequent shallow waterings can actually encourage the roots to grow upward and weaken your tree.

One other factor to consider is hardening off your plant for the fall and winter. Beginning in mid August, start watering a little less frequently. This will give your fig tree the message to begin slowing down growth. At this time of year, you want the tree to grow more slowly and produce strong sturdy wood capable of withstanding the first frosts of fall.

Fertilizing. Fertilizing is not difficult, nor is it an exact science. Most potting mixes contain enough trace elements and basic fertilizer to help your plant get started and to grow for a couple of months. Your tree will not need any extra fertilizer until it starts growing vigorously. At that point, you can begin fertilizing with an all-purpose, balanced fertilizer formulated for vegetables and fruits (see details in Chapter 6).

Your fig tree should grow 12 to 18 inches a year, and its leaves should be dark green in color. If the lower leaves begin to pale, you may have a deficiency of nitrogen; try using your regular fertilizer more often, or adding a bit of fertilizer high in nitrogen (the first number). Figs also seem to like a little extra phosphorus; mix a handful of bone meal into the top inch of potting soil. Also, as with watering, stop adding fertilizer in mid August. This will help your plant develop strong, frost-hardy branches.

Pruning. Figs are actually fun to prune. Their wood is soft and easy to cut, and they don't develop a thicket of branches as do some other fruit trees. What you want to achieve is a vase shape: open in the center, with branches all around the trunk growing upward and outward at a 30-degree angle. Picture a flower vase that is narrow at the bottom and wide at the top, and you have the idea.

To create the vase shape, first cut off the main stem to about a 2-foot height. This in itself will force the plant to develop side branches. As soon as several young shoots begin to appear, choose three or four that will become the main branches and form the basic vase shape. They should be evenly spaced around the trunk and should be 1½ to 2 inches apart vertically.

The young shoots will naturally grow at an angle from the trunk, but you can help them reach the 30 degrees that is considered ideal by inserting small sticks between the shoots and the trunk, or tying the young branches down to stones or bricks. As your chosen shoots become branches, prune off any competitors back to the trunk. These new branches may even ripen a fig or two in the fall.

As your tree grows, it will continue to develop more and more new branches, to the point that eventually the newest branches will be small and weak. Cut these weak branches back all the way to their base, and new, more vigorous, more fruitful branches will form. As a rule, when a branch has not grown more than 6 inches in a season, it is too weak to produce good fruit and should be removed.

Always keep your main framework branches to maintain the vase shape. If your tree tries to grow new branches from the roots or low down on the trunk, prune them away; they will only weaken the overall tree. And for general good maintenance, always remove any branches that grow into the center of your tree or that cross others, and any broken or dead ones.

Remember that most fig varieties bear two crops, one in summer and one in fall. The summer crop will appear on the branches that grew the previous season, so don't prune last year's growth too heavily or you won't have any summer figs.

Insects and Diseases. Figs are one of the easiest fruit trees to grow. There are no significant diseases that bother them in North America, and only a few insect pests. The biggest insect problem is ants, which are attracted to the sugar in the fruit when it is very ripe. You can prevent ants from climbing the trunk of your tree by applying a coating of sticky material (one familiar brand name is Tanglefoot) around the trunk below the branches. Ants will not cross this barrier. Try to apply the material when the figs are large and close to ripening, as it has the strongest repellent qualities when it is fresh. Birds also are fond of the ripe fruit, and you may have to cover your tree with bird netting to keep some for yourself. If your fig tree is spending a lot of time indoors or in a greenhouse, it may attract mites or aphids. These insects usually disappear or travel to more appealing plants once you put your fig outside, but if they persist, check Chapter 6 for ways to control them.

Harvesting. You'll know the figs are getting ripe when the skin begins to change color, from green to greenish yellow or dark brown. The second sign is that the fruit becomes softer. When fully ripe, a fig is quite soft to the touch and droops downward. To harvest a fig, simply break or clip the fruit away from the branch.

Summer figs ripen from the end of June into August, depending on your location. Fall figs should ripen from late August to late September. Figs do not ripen all at once, so you can usually enjoy them for two weeks or more.

Ripe figs are very perishable. If you don't plan to eat them right away, they'll keep for several days in the refrigerator in a shallow container. Dried figs keep for months and are a great high-energy snack.

Varieties. Choosing just the right fig variety for your area is something of a challenge. On one hand, there are many varieties available. On the other, this is one fruit that is not widely grown, known, or understood. The staff at your local nursery may not know much about figs, and few mail-order catalogs offer complete information about the varieties they sell.

The most important consideration is climate. While most fig varieties will grow satisfactorily where other fruit trees grow, they may or may not *ripen* their fruit. If you live in the Deep South or in central or southern California, you can grow and ripen just about any fig variety. In cooler regions, choose one of the varieties from the list below; they demand less heat.

Lattarulla was developed and named by a nurseryman in Portland, Oregon, in the 1920s. He had experimented with nearly 100 varieties, trying to find ones that would ripen in his cooler climate, and this was one of the best. It is a medium- to low-vigor tree with large, glossy green leaves. It can bear two crops of juicy, large, sweet greenish yellow figs with light honey-colored flesh.

Peter's Honey is a very special variety brought to America by an Italian gardener, Peter Danna of Portland, Oregon, who grew up in Sicily and knew this variety from childhood. Peter's Honey is a medium-vigor tree with large dark green foliage. The fruit, produced in two crops, is large and golden yellow when ripe, and has dark amber, tender, and very sweet flesh. For most successful fig ripening, give Peter's Honey a warm, protected location in cooler regions.

Brown Turkey is a very overused name for figs. It seems that every time a grower found a fig with brown skin, he or she would name it Brown Turkey. **Vern's Brown Turkey** was distinguished from the others by naming it in honor of Vern Nelson, a Portland, Oregon, gardener who was among the first to discover its qualities. A medium-vigor tree, it produces two crops of very large dark brown fruit with honey-colored flesh.

Later-ripening than the figs listed above, **Black Mission** is a familiar variety in California, where it is grown in both backyards and commercial orchards. A medium-vigor tree, it bears abundant crops of dark purple fruit with sweet and flavorful strawberry-colored flesh. This is an excellent fig for drying as well as fresh eating. Black Mission needs a very warm location to ripen its fruit in cooler regions.

Fruits

Grapes

GROW AS: **perennial vines**

PLANT SIZE: **6 feet or more**

START WITH: **young plants, grown from cuttings**

HARVEST SEASON: **late summer to fall**

SUN REQUIREMENTS: **full sun to partial shade**

MINIMUM SOIL DEPTH: **18 inches**

D o you know anyone who doesn't like grapes? Sweet, juicy, flavorful, and attractive, they are a treat for everyone. Beautiful on the vine, the long clusters of translucent fruit are equally spectacular on your table. They're available in many colors, from dark purple to pink, green, and even white, and also offer a multitude of flavors. In fact, grapes have been so popular for so long that they have their own branch of horticultural science: vinology.

Grape Basics. Unlike fruits that grow on trees or bushes, grapes require their own specialized growing system. Grapes are vines, and will scamper up just about any support you give them. Their vining habit is also a gift as they can quickly cover a trellis and form a beautiful curtain or sunscreen. You can put your potted grape by the corner of your patio cover, for example, and with a little training and tying, it will quickly cover the patio roof, creating shade and a spectacular display of foliage and fruit.

The leaves are large and lovely, and create a shimmering green effect even before the grapes show themselves. Sunlight pouring through the bright green leaves and spattering on the floor below is a glorious sight. Then in the fall, as the grapes reach their peak of ripeness, the leaves begin to turn autumn colors. Even in winter, there is a kind of stark beauty to the weathered vines with their curly tendrils.

Size. Grapes need room to spread, and will quickly cover whatever support structure you provide. Unless you want to grow the vines a long distance horizontally, allow for at least 6 feet of trellis to support the vertical growth. Because you'll need to prune annually for good crops, it will be easy to keep your grape at this 6-foot height.

Recipe: Minted Melon and Grape Salad

Maggie says: This salad also makes a very nice light dessert and is especially pretty served in a brandy snifter or wineglass. For an attractive color contrast, use honeydew melon with red grapes or cantaloupe with green grapes.

1 cup plain yogurt

2 tablespoons honey

½ teaspoon grated fresh ginger, or

¼ teaspoon powdered ginger

2 tablespoons finely chopped fresh mint

2 cups seedless red or green grapes

1 medium honeydew or cantaloupe, peeled,

seeded, and cut into chunks

Lettuce leaves (optional)

Whole mint leaves, for garnish

1. To make the dressing, combine the yogurt, honey, ginger, and 1 tablespoon of the chopped mint in a blender, and blend until mixed. Refrigerate until needed.

2. Combine the grapes, melon chunks, and remaining tablespoon of chopped mint.

3. If serving as a salad, line a serving bowl with lettuce leaves, add the melon-grape mixture, and drizzle the dressing on top. If serving as a dessert, place in glass bowls or wineglasses, drizzle with the dressing, and garnish with the mint leaves.

Serves 5 to 6

Pollination. Virtually all grapes that you will want to grow are self-fertile. That means you will receive abundant crops of grapes without having to have another plant for pollination.

Hardiness. In areas of the world with very cold winters, grapes are usually taken down from their trellis and covered with soil to protect them from freezing. As a container gardener, you can accomplish the same thing simply by moving your container to a protected location for the winter. To make this possible, you'll need to do two things: make sure the container is easily moved (casters are a good idea), and have this portability in mind when you plan your pruning pattern (see below).

Don't forget that the roots of container plants are more vulnerable to cold temperatures than they would be if the plants were growing in the ground. The roots of grape plants will be killed at temperatures below 20°F. If your winter temperatures rarely fall below that, you will proba-

Grapes need a sturdy trellis to hold their heavy, luscious bounty.

bly not need to protect your plant. Where minimum winter temperatures fall between 20° and −15°F, you can keep your plant outside but you must protect the roots by wrapping the pot with an insulating material (see box on page 288). But if your winters are colder than −15°F, you'll have to move your grape plants, after they go dormant, to a protected location for the winter; see page 289 for suggestions. This is the point at which the form of your container, or your pruning style, becomes an issue.

Chilling Requirements. Grapes are grown in many regions of the world, from the humid tropics to Canada and Russia. Yet with all this experience, there is little detailed information on their chilling requirements. What we do know is that in warmer areas where there is no frost, grapes will grow continuously if the vines are repeatedly pruned. If you live in a warm region of the country, you'll probably get good crops by just leaving your grapevine outside all winter. If you live in a colder region, be sure to let your grapevine go through a period of light frost and go dormant outside before bringing it to a protected area; when the leaves fall, that's your cue that dormancy has begun.

Planting. You will find grapevines for sale as bare-root plants in the spring, or in nursery containers in spring, summer, or fall. Theoretically, you could plant them anytime they're available, but you'll probably find a large selection of varieties in spring.

The larger the pot you use for your grape, the longer it can remain there without replanting. For long-term growth, a 10-gallon pot will suffice, but a 15-gallon pot or a half whiskey barrel is ideal. Grapes have deep roots, so a deep pot is preferable to a shallow one. Use a coarse potting mix that drains well.

If you are planting a bare-root grape, it will probably be about a foot tall with a relatively small root system. Grapes are very sturdy plants and will grow quite a bit the first year. If you are not ready to plant immediately, you can keep the grape in a cool place for several days with the roots wrapped in wet paper. Before planting, inspect the vine. If there are any broken roots or roots that are too long to fit comfortably in the pot, prune them back. Fill the pot about halfway with potting mix and place your new grape plant in the center.

Continue filling the pot, holding the plant upright. Just above the top-most roots of the plant, you should see a place where the stem changes color. This is the crown, the point to which soil covered the plant in its previous location; it should be planted at this depth in the new pot. Fill the

pot with soil to about 1 inch from the top, adjusting the plant to the proper depth as you go.

If you're planting a nursery-potted grape, inspect the root system. If it has been in the pot for some time and the root mass is quite dense, be sure to loosen the roots somewhat. You can pull at larger exposed roots to separate them from the main body of roots; sometimes you'll have to beat on the roots with a stick to loosen them. Once you have freed up some of the main roots, you can prune them if necessary to fit the pot and plant the grape in the same way as you would a bare-root plant. After planting, water the grape well to eliminate air pockets and settle the planting mix.

If you haven't done so already, now is the time to consider how you want to train your grape plant. Because it is such a vigorous vine, it will need serious support. If you have it near a patio roof, arbor, wall, or fence, you can let it grow where it is, although you may need to add some latticework or similar construction so the vine will have something to grab onto. If you are intent on growing grapes but do not have a good climbing structure in place, you'll have to build a freestanding trellis and fasten it to your container. Make it *strong*.

You will have to do a fair amount of pruning to keep your plant confined to such a trellis, but it can look quite spectacular covered with bunches of grapes and fall foliage. A handsome system that we have admired uses a rectangular planter box, longer than it is tall, with sturdy cross beams attached to the back; the grapevine is trained to grow horizontally along the beams.

Take a moment now to familiarize yourself with the basic principles of grape pruning (below), and you'll see that you should have your support structure clearly in mind—better yet, in place—when the plant is put into the container.

Success with Grapes. The key to growing grapes is proper pruning, which we'll discuss shortly. Otherwise, your grape needs pretty much the same good, commonsense growing practices as other plants. By following a few basic rules, you can grow and enjoy colorful and delectable grapes almost anywhere in North America.

Watering. Water is a dangerous thing. Your grape needs enough of it to grow well, yet too much can damage or even kill the plant.

If you have planted a bare-root grape, its roots cannot use water for days or even weeks. After you have watered the vine well after planting, it will usually need no additional water until it starts to grow. During this time simply check the soil every few days to be sure it is not getting dry. Once the grape starts growing, it will begin using the water in the pot. Check the potting soil more frequently and water when it shows signs of drying. If the plant is in a large pot, a deep watering every five to seven days should be enough. You want to water just enough to keep it from wilting.

If you planted a grape that was in a nursery container, pay special attention to the area directly around the vine, where the original planting soil is. Because all the roots are concentrated here at first, this old soil can dry out very quickly while the surrounding new soil still feels moist. If you notice this, be sure to concentrate your watering close to the plant. Eventually the root system will grow into the new potting soil, and you can water normally.

In late August, start holding back on the water, providing just enough to keep the soil moist. This will slow down the growth rate, which is an important part of the plant's preparation for the colder temperatures of winter.

Fertilizing. Your grapevine should grow 3 to 5 feet a year and show healthy looking, medium to dark green leaves. Your goal is to fertilize just enough to keep the foliage green. More than that leads to trouble: scads of beautiful lush leaves but not much fruit.

Follow the same basic pattern of fertilizing as described for apples (see page 297), with one twist: grapes also need extra potassium when they are bearing fruit. You can meet this requirement by using a fertilizer high in potassium (the third number) or by adding greensand (see page 68), if you prefer the organic approach. Stop fertilizing altogether in late summer, as the vines are moving toward dormancy and need to slow down.

Pruning. Proper pruning is all-important for getting good crops from

Making a Grapevine Wreath

Those beautiful, elegantly simple grapevine wreaths that you see in gift shops and florists are surprisingly easy to make, and if you have a grapevine, you have the material right at hand in the long pieces that you prune off each spring. The trick is to make the wreath immediately after pruning, while the shoots are still flexible.

Start with the longest piece you have. Bring the two ends together, forming a circle. The finished wreath will be the size of that first circle. If your first piece isn't long enough to make a circle of the size you want, fasten two vines together with a bit of fine-gauge wire. If it's too long, use the excess to begin the wrapping process.

If possible, leave 3 or 4 inches of excess at the thin end of the vine and wrap the excess around the larger end, so the circle holds itself together. If you don't have any excess, use wire to tie the two ends together.

Now take the other pruned-off pieces, one at a time, and wind them around the base circle, tucking the ends under as you go. For a rustic look, leave the curlicues in place, and don't try too hard to keep the new additions smooth and tight.

That's all there is to it. The more vines you add, the thicker the wreath will become, but the circumference will not appreciably increase. As the vines dry out, they will tighten up a bit.

A grapevine wreath looks quite stylish just as is. Many people like to work in ribbons, fresh or dried flowers, bits of herbs to dry in place, cones and interesting seed heads, Christmas ornaments, and so on, creating a new look for each season.

a grapevine. If you don't do it, you will have a beautiful, lush vine that gives lovely shade but nary a grape to eat. Grape growers around the world have developed several basic techniques and patterns for pruning. The one we describe here, known as spur pruning, is not the only option; but we chose to feature it because it is a good all-purpose system and the best for containers that must be moved for winter shelter.

Spur pruning, like most other pruning styles, is based on a foundation of permanent branches trained into a T-formation. The location of the point where the main vertical stem branches out sideways to form the crossbar of the T is up to you, and making that decision depends on whether the container will need to be moved for the winter. So the first thing you must do is familiarize yourself with your winter weather patterns. If you'll be moving the container into a sheltered area for the winter, you will find that it is much easier to do if the branching point is relatively low, say 4 or 5 feet above the soil level.

Let's assume you planted your young grape in the spring; that's the most common time. Once the weather has warmed up, several shoots will begin growing from the base. When they are approximately 18 inches long, select one strong shoot, tie it gently to a bamboo stake, trellis, or other support, and prune off all the other shoots.

Allow this main stem to grow up the support until it reaches the point where you would like it to branch out sideways. Then let it grow about a foot longer, and cut back the shoot at your desired height. This extra foot of growth guarantees that the buds will have time to develop their full strength. (If winter shelter is not a concern, you may wish to let the main stem grow taller, to reach the top of a patio roof, perhaps. In that case, it may take two growing seasons to reach that height, but in every other way the following instructions apply.)

Below the cut you made, buds will begin growing. Select two that are pointing in opposite directions and remove all the others lower down. When the two chosen buds start to grow, tie them to your support in such a way that they are held horizontally. These will become what are called cordons, the permanent crosspiece of your T-structure. Keep training the cordons on a horizontal plane, and allow them to grow as far as they want the first year.

Now that you have established the basic T-framework for your grapevine, pruning for fruit production can begin. Early in the spring of the second year (or the first winter in milder climates), prune back the cordons to the point where they are about as thick as your index finger,

which will more than likely leave them around 2 feet long. It is best to make these cuts just past a downward-facing bud.

During the second summer, shoots will sprout from the cordons. Sometimes they will bear your first crop of grapes. The following spring (or second winter), prune back these shoots to the cordon, leaving just two buds on each one. If the shoots had fruit on them the previous fall, make the cut this way: find the point where the fruit clusters were, and go two buds beyond that point. New shoots will grow out from these buds during the third summer, and produce your first large crop of fruit. (The long stems that carry the fruit are sometimes called canes.)

After that, your annual pruning has two components: (1) completely remove the old canes that bore fruit the previous summer (you can use them to make grapevine wreaths, which is amazingly easy (see box at left); and (2) identify the new canes that grew the previous summer but did not produce fruit (the bark will look smoother), and cut them back so that just two buds remain. These new canes will produce fruit this summer.

If your container is staying put for the winter, prune early in spring. If you must move it for winter protection, you'll need to do the pruning in fall, after the leaves drop, in order to free the plant from its support. Similarly, you can allow the cordons to grow longer or keep them short, depending on the size and shape of your support and the need to simplify moving.

Insects and Diseases. Fortunately, grapes are not bothered by serious insect pests, and many varieties are disease-resistant.

Probably the most serious disease of grapes is powdery mildew. This fungus shows as a powdery grayish white coating on leaves, shoots, and fruit. It causes the leaves to curl and wither and the fruits to drop or split. Most American grape varieties (the ones that are recommended for most regions of the country) are not affected by powdery mildew, but European-type grapes, which are best for warm areas of California, Arizona, and the Deep South, do suffer from it. The best control is to dust your plant with sulfur, starting when shoots are 6 inches long and continuing about every two weeks until harvest. Be sure to follow label directions when using sulfur or any other spray or dust.

Harvesting. You should have your first crop of sweet, delicious vine-ripened grapes in the third summer after you planted your vine. Grapes ripen late, from September to late October depending on the variety and your climate. During summer and early fall, they will be hard, unappetizing little green berries. The first sign of ripening is a change in color and a softening of the fruit. From this point to full ripening is about four to six weeks. The final test is taste. You can't tell by appearance, for grapes will look ripe before they are fully sweet, so try a few before you pick full clusters.

After harvest, grapes can be stored for a couple of weeks in the refrigerator. For a beautiful dessert presentation, clip entire bunches from the vine, chill lightly, and serve on a white platter or shallow dish, perhaps with a rich, gooey cheese. The beautiful leaves from your grapevine can also earn a place on the dinner table, as liners for the cheese plate or hors d'oeuvres tray. The leaves have other uses too: if you enjoy making *dolmathes,* you'll appreciate having an endless supply of fresh grape leaves to stuff. And one or two leaves added to the bottom of jars of your home-canned pickles helps keep the pickles crip.

Varieties. Grapes are such an important horticultural crop worldwide that growers have produced over 8,000 named varieties; of these, about 2,000 are grown in California. Of course, you won't need to choose from such a vast number. In the cold-winter areas of the United States, the choice of varieties is probably limited to fewer than a dozen.

There are two main types of grapes, and many varieties in each type. The American grapes and their hybrids are best for northern growers. They are self-fertile, hardy, and able to ripen fruit in a short growing season. European-type grapes are well adapted to warm-season regions of California, the Southwest, and the Deep South. Listed below are a few of the best varieties of each type.

◼ American Grapes and Hybrids.

Canadice is a very sweet red seedless grape that was introduced in 1977 by the New York Agricultural

Experiment Station in Geneva, New York. A popular variety with gardeners, it produces abundant clusters of attractive and delicious fruit. Canadice is a very hardy plant, surviving temperatures to −15°F when planted in the ground, although in a container you will not subject it to such cold weather. This variety is great for fresh eating, and makes delicious juice, jelly, and wine.

A large blue-black seedless grape with a delicious spicy flavor, **Glenora** was introduced in 1976 by the Agricultural Experiment Station in Geneva, New York. Sweet and richly flavored, the grapes are produced in abundant, very large and showy clusters. Glenora is mildew-resistant and hardy, and puts on a beautiful show of red-and-orange leaf color in the fall.

Himrod is a very hardy white seedless grape that bears good crops of medium-size fruit, sweet, juicy, and delicious. Produced in large striking clusters, the grapes are absolutely wonderful for fresh eating, make delicate sweet juice, and can be dried into tasty raisins. The fruit ripens early, but it can be stored until Christmas in the refrigerator. Another introduction from the Agricultural Experiment Station in Geneva, New York, Himrod is somewhat disease-resistant.

Introduced by Oregon grape grower Bill Schulz, **Sweet Seduction** is an unusual variety with exceptional flavor. It produces beautiful golden yellow seedless grapes with a muscat-like taste that we usually associate with European grapes, making it unique among American types.

Vigorous and productive, Sweet Seduction bears large and attractive clusters of its seductively flavored fruit.

■ **European Varieties.** A very popular variety with both home gardeners and commercial growers, **Flame** bears large and heavy clusters of sweet, light red seedless grapes with uniquely crisp flesh and delicious flavor. You can purchase this variety in stores, but you'll find that home-grown fruit is sweeter and more flavorful. Flame is self-fertile, vigorous, and productive. It is well adapted to warm regions and requires long, hot summers to ripen its fruit.

The attractive **Black Monukka** produces striking long clusters of reddish black, seedless, oval fruit. The medium-size grapes are crisp and sweet, and are delicious for fresh eating. You can also dry the fruit for large, tasty raisins. When you see large raisins in specialty food markets, often they are from Black Monukka. Quite hardy for a European variety.

Muscat, also known as Muscat of Alexandria, is the variety associated with strong-flavored sweet grapes from the Middle East. It is one of the sweetest and most aromatic grapes you can grow at home. Muscat bears abundant crops of large, greenish amber, seeded grapes that hang in attractive, long loose clusters. You can enjoy these grapes fresh, and also make delicious wine and raisins from them. Muscat is self-fertile and requires a long and very warm summer to ripen its fruit.

Fruits

Peaches and Nectarines

GROW AS: **perennials (trees)**

PLANT SIZE: **4 to 6 feet**

START WITH: **grafted plants**

HARVEST SEASON: **mid to late summer**

SUN REQUIREMENTS: **full sun to partial shade**

MINIMUM SOIL DEPTH: **12 inches**

Sweet, delectable, and oh, so juicy, peaches and nectarines are a real summertime treat. They're right up there with vine-ripened tomatoes as the ultimate vehicle for a gardener's bragging rights. Like tomatoes, peaches grown for the supermarket have to be harvested early, while they are tough enough to withstand shipping, and like tomatoes, they never develop the rich, full, died-and-gone-to-heaven flavor of those that reach full ripeness while still on the plant. Imagine having your own tree-ripened fruit right outside your door!

Did you think that peach trees are too big for container growing? It's true that traditional trees, grown in the ground, reach 15 feet tall or more, but breeders have developed natural dwarf varieties (see Peach and Nectarine Basics, below) that don't exceed 6 feet; that makes container growing eminently doable.

With peaches and nectarines, container gardeners have an advantage over in-ground gardeners. Both these fruits are difficult to grow in wet climates, where diseases can damage tree and foliage. By growing them in containers, you can move the small trees to a protected location where leaf and bark diseases won't bother them.

With natural dwarf varieties and movable containers, just about anyone can grow peaches and nectarines. The rewards are priceless: in the spring you get to drink in the beauty and fragrance of the blossoms, and in summer you have the incomparable treat of biting into peaches and nectarines so lusciously ripe that the juices dribble down your chin and so wonderfully sweet that you won't care a bit.

Peach and Nectarine Basics.

Nectarines are basically peaches without fuzz. Both fruits are grown as grafted young trees, in the same way as apples (see page 292), with one important difference. Whereas apple rootstocks control the mature size of the tree, there is no rootstock for peaches and nectarines that can make a dwarf tree. Fortunately, fruit-tree specialists have found a way to create trees that naturally maintain a dwarf size. These natural dwarfs (also called genetic dwarfs) are much less vigorous than standard trees (most top out at 6 feet), but they produce full-size fruit with all the juicy sweetness and flavor of their larger cousins.

Pollination. Most peaches and nectarines are self-fertile, meaning they can bear fruit without the need of pollen from another tree. Some varieties, however, do need pollination from another variety, and those are noted in the Varieties section below. Where pollinators are needed, any other variety will work, as long as the two are within 20 feet of each other.

Hardiness and Chilling Requirements. Peaches and nectarines, when grown in a container, need their tender roots protected from cold weather. Anytime the temperatures fall below 20°F for more than a day or so, you should take protective measures (see page 289 for details). With peaches and nectarines, there is one additional element that must be protected against cold weather: the flowers.

The beautiful pink blossoms of peaches and nectarines appear earlier in the spring than do the flowers of many other fruit trees. In more northerly parts of the country, this early bloom can be hurt by frost,

sometimes so severely that no fruit is produced that year. Commercial orchardists use heaters to raise temperatures out of the danger zone. Since you probably have just one or two trees, and smaller ones at that, your trees are very easy to protect. Simply toss a blanket or sheet of plastic over the tree so that it reaches the ground all around the pot. Plastic alone will keep the temperature 5 degrees warmer than the air; a blanket will do even more. Be sure to remove the covering the next morning as soon as the air temperature is above freezing.

As with most other fruit trees, peaches and nectarines need to go through a period of winter chilling when the temperature is between 32° and 45°F (read the full story of winter chill on page 286). For most peaches and nectarines, the magic number is 500 hours. Almost anywhere in the United States your trees will get those hours automatically without any extra effort on your part; your only concern may be providing protection against severe cold (see page 289). For southern gardeners, there are dwarf peach and nectarine varieties that do not need as much winter chilling.

Planting. The basic process of planting fruit trees, whether bare-root or containerized, is described in detail in the section on apples (see page 290). Some of the naturally dwarfed peaches and nectarines are so small and slow growing that you may be able to use a smaller, shallower pot than you would use for apples. Many of these dwarfed trees are quite short and stand well without staking. However, if your tree is 3 or 4 feet tall and does not have a root system that can hold it upright, you should add a stake or some kind of lattice structure to support it.

Success with Peaches and Nectarines. For general care, peaches and nectarines need the same commonsense attention as other fruit trees: adequate fertilizing, adequate watering, and watchful attention in very cold weather, with protective measures if needed. For all these topics, the basic information given in the section on apples will also apply to peaches and nectarines, with just a few additions.

Peaches and nectarines are subject to a couple of diseases, described below, that thrive in damp conditions. So when you water these plants, make sure you put the water directly onto the soil and avoid sprinkling the tree itself. And as with other plants that go dormant in winter, start tapering off the watering and fertilizing in late summer.

Two aspects of growing peaches and nectarines need explicit discussion: pruning and diseases.

Pruning. Most peach and nectarine trees are pruned to form what is referred to in the nursery trade as a vase shape: the trunk is short, and at its top grow three or four evenly spaced branches, trained to grow up and out at a shallow angle (no more than 45 degrees). The center of the tree is open, with no main vertical branch or trunk. The basic shape is

rather like an upside-down cone or a flower vase that is broad at the top and narrow at the bottom. This flared shape allows good air movement through the tree, lets plenty of light in for optimum leaf and fruit growth, and helps keep the tree healthy and vigorous.

Most dwarf peaches and nectarines can be formed into vases. There are some dwarf varieties, however, that grow as a charming small shrub and don't need this intensive pruning. In fact, you couldn't train them to a vase shape if you tried. See pages 339 to 340 for more on these.

The process of forming a young tree into a vase shape is not difficult, even though some people get weak in the knees when you put pruners into their hands. Let's start from when you first plant your tree. What you get from the nursery or garden center will be either a very lightly branched young tree or what is called a whip—a single, thin trunk without branches. After planting your young tree, measure up 18 to 24 inches from the rim of the container and look for a place to cut. With a whip, this will be just above a bud. With a branched tree, it will be just above a branch. The idea is to keep the trunk permanently at this height, and to encourage side branches that will eventually become the main structure of the "vase."

Once you cut off the stem above your chosen point, all the buds below the cut will open and start to grow into branches. A month or two after the buds begin to grow, when the new branches are about 12 inches long, select three or four that are well spaced around the trunk and 2 to 4 inches apart vertically. They will be the permanent framework of the tree. Remove all the other young branches.

If you planted a whip, keep an eye on the branch that grows from the highest bud. Sometimes it tries to grow straight up and become a replacement trunk. You don't want that. Prune it off, back to the trunk. Also prune off the portion of the trunk below it, to the point just above where your next highest branch begins. Make this cut at a slight angle *away* from the direction of the branch to allow water to drain off and speed healing.

As the chosen branches grow, you may need to train them to keep them at the proper angle, no steeper than a 45-degree angle from the trunk. Young branches can be spread out by gently inserting a short piece of wood between the young branch and the trunk; some people use a clothespin.

After the vase shape is formed, you will need to do some maintenance pruning on the tree once a year. Do it when the tree is dormant: in winter if your winter weather is mild, or in early spring before buds begin to open. Start by removing any branches that cross and rub together, and any that have broken. When removing a branch, cut almost all the way back to the trunk or larger branch, but leave a short collar of raised stem just at its base. This collar contains actively growing cells that will help to quickly heal the cut. When cutting back a broken branch, you need only remove the part that is broken; find a spot below the break and about half an inch above a bud. This also promotes speedy healing.

After you have removed crossing branches and cut back broken ones, the next task is to reduce the new growth—the part of the branch that grew last summer—to about half its length. You can identify this new growth by its smooth, shiny bark. If you start at the tip of a branch and follow it back toward the trunk, you will see a point where the shiny new bark ends; farther back past that point, the bark is darker and rougher. That is the portion of the branch that grew two years ago. The dividing point is quite obvious. Measure the part of the branch that is new, and cut off half of it. This will stimulate more growth and a better fruit crop.

No matter what anyone says, there will always be some gardeners who would rather go to the dentist than tackle a major pruning job. If you're one (and there's no shame in it), we have some very good news. How about a peach tree that you don't have to prune at all, beyond a tender touch-up now and then?

Some varieties of dwarf peaches and nectarines grow more like a little bush than a tree. They have scads of small branches that are difficult, if not impossible, to form into a vase shape. These trees are very small, usually not more than 3 or 4 feet tall, and quite attractive, especially when loaded with full-size fruit. To prune these varieties, you need be concerned only with removing any dead or broken branches, thinning out crowded branches to at least 2 inches apart, and cutting back new growth annually (as with the other type, make the new growth shorter by half) for better fruit production.

Insects and Diseases. Peaches and nectarines have few insect problems but unfortunately can be affected by two potentially serious diseases: bacterial canker and peach-leaf curl. Both can severely damage peaches and nectarines, especially in a wet climate.

Bacterial canker shows up as an amber-colored blob on twigs, branches, or trunk. It is a sign that diseased tissue on the interior of the plant has broken into a surface wound, and the blob is actually sap that is trying to heal the wound. If you scrape the nearby bark, you will likely find dead tissue material, brown instead of a healthy green.

Bacterial canker is most prevalent in regions with lots of winter and spring rain. There are two principal ways you can prevent this disease from damaging your tree. One is to physically shelter the tree from rain, which we'll address shortly. The other is to spray the tree with a copper fungicide in combination with a second product known as a "sticker," which helps the fungicide adhere to the tree. This treatment won't kill the infection but will help prevent it from spreading, giving your tree time to heal itself. For best results, apply at least three sprays, the first in the fall before the rainy season begins, the second in December or January during a break in the weather, and the third in March.

Copper fungicide, also known as Bordeaux mixture, is marketed under several trade names. The sticker is a potassium resinate, and its only function is to keep the fungicide from immediately washing away in the rain. Stickers are sold under various trade names; one is called Sta-Stuk (you get the idea). The fungicide and the sticker are in separate containers, sometimes packaged as a duo; be sure to follow label directions for both.

The last two fungicide applications can also help prevent the second main disease of peaches and nectarines: peach-leaf curl. You can easily identify peach-leaf curl by the characteristic red splotches on the leaves, which cause the leaves to curl and become deformed. Different varieties of peaches and nectarines vary in the degree to which they are affected by peach-leaf curl. The most susceptible ones can be so impaired that they will not set fruit, or they may even be killed. This disease is also much more of a problem in regions with long, wet springs. A spray of copper fungicide in January, with another in February and again in March, will help prevent the opening buds from being infected.

As container gardeners, you have a way to deal with the threat of these two diseases that is not available to traditional gardeners: you can simply move the plant out of the rain. Put your peach or nectarine under a patio roof or under the eaves of your house or garage in the winter and spring. This will greatly reduce or even eliminate the damage from both these diseases.

Harvesting. Dwarf peaches and nectarines will often bloom and set fruit the year after you plant them, and they bear full-size fruit of surprisingly good quality.

To tell if your fruit is ripe, use the same test you would in the supermarket: press gently with your thumb. If the flesh gives slightly, it's ripe. Other signs of ripeness to watch for: the skin color changes (peaches go from green to golden orange; nectarines from green to red); if you tug gently, the fruit comes away from the branch easily; and the peaches give off a heavenly aroma.

Varieties. All of the following varieties were developed in a breeding program in California.

Nectarines. An attractive dwarf nectarine, **Necta-Zee** produces flavorful freestone fruit, bright red when ripe. It can grow to 6 feet tall and is self-fertile. Needs about 500 chilling hours.

Nectar Babe is another excellent dwarf nectarine that reaches 5 to 6 feet in height. Fruit is yellow-and-red freestone, large, sweet, and juicy. Nectar Babe requires about 500 hours of chilling and needs pollination by another peach or nectarine variety.

Peaches. A very attractive bush form of dwarf peach with sweet yellow freestone fruit, **Honey Babe** will grow to only about 4 feet in height. The branches naturally grow downward (a growth pattern known as weeping), and are covered with foliage so dense it conceals the fruit. This is one of the types that do not need forceful pruning. Honey Babe is self-fertile but will produce a heavier crop if pollinated by another peach or nectarine variety. Requires about 500 hours of chilling.

Early ripening and self-fertile, **Pix Zee** produces large, delicious freestone fruits with orange-yellow skin and a delightful fragrance. This dwarf variety will grow to about 6½ feet tall, and is an excellent choice for gardeners in warm climates, for it needs only about 150 chilling hours.

Another good variety for growers in the Deep South, **Bonanza** is a dwarf peach that requires only 250 chilling hours or less to properly bloom and set fruit. Bonanza is self-fertile and bears large yellow freestone fruit, sweet and flavorful. It grows to about 4 or 5 feet tall.

Fruits

Strawberries

GROW AS: **short-lived perennials or annuals**

PLANT SIZE: **12 inches**

START WITH: **plants**

HARVEST SEASON: **late May to mid July (June-bearing); June to first frost (everbearing)**

SUN REQUIREMENTS: **full sun**

MINIMUM SOIL DEPTH: **8 inches**

The first fruit of summer, strawberries hold a special spot in a gardener's heart. As soon as we see those snow-white blossoms we start the count-down, tenderly checking the plants every day, eagerly watching as the berries slowly turn from green to pink to red, and finally, unable to bear it any longer, picking the ripest one and biting into it right there on the spot. Your tongue knows, and your heart knows, that summer has arrived.

Strawberry Basics. Strawberries grow on leafy plants that stay relatively small: low mounds about 12 inches in diameter. The leaves are divided into three lobes, like clover, but they are much larger, slightly ribbed, and toothed along the edges. The flowers grow up out of the center of the plant on a stiff little stem that bears several small white flowers with centers of bright yellow stamens. As the berries begin to form and get heavier with size, they will droop down and be partially hidden among the leaves, where they will enlarge and ripen out of direct sun.

The main plants, the ones you'll be planting, are called mother plants; each mother plant sends out long, thin runners (they look like green string) that form smaller plants at the end, called daughter plants. It's this growth habit that makes strawberries especially suited to container growing; they are perfect in hanging baskets or tall tubs where the runners can hang down.

Strawberry plants are actually perennials, but their productive life is only about three years. Commercial growers continually replace mother plants with their daughters, which in turn produce their own daughters. In your container garden, you might want to consider just growing them as annuals, replacing old plants with vigorous new ones each year.

Strawberries are classified into

Recipe: Strawberries with Scented Geraniums and Crème Fraîche

C arole Saville, author of *Exotic Herbs*, maintains an extensive collection of herb plants in her California garden. She is well known for her herb cookery and has perfected the art of cooking with scented geraniums.

> **1 tablespoon finely minced rose-scented geranium leaves**
> **3 tablespoons sugar**
> **1 cup crème fraîche (see Note)**
> **2 pints fresh strawberries**
> **Scented geranium flowers, for garnish**

1. Combine the geranium leaves, 2 tablespoons of the sugar, and the crème fraîche in a small bowl. Cover the bowl with plastic wrap and refrigerate for at least 48 hours.

2. Remove the crème fraîche mixture from the refrigerator, scrape it into a fine-mesh sieve, and, using the back of a large spoon, push it through into a clean bowl. Discard the contents of the sieve. Cover the crème fraîche mixture with plastic wrap and refrigerate until ready to serve.

3. Rinse the strawberries and pat dry with paper towels. Hull the berries, slicing the larger ones into quarters. Sprinkle with the remaining sugar and toss to coat.

4. To serve, divide the berries among four small glass bowls or large wineglasses. Spoon some of the crème fraîche mixture over each serving, and garnish with scented geranium flowers.

(continued on next page)

(continued from previous page)

Note: If commercial crème fraîche is not available, a good version can be made at home.

Place 1 cup heavy cream (*not* ultrapasteurized) and 1 tablespoon buttermilk in a small bowl and stir well. Cover the bowl with plastic wrap and set it aside at room temperature until it thickens slightly, 12 to 24 hours, depending on the temperature. Once it has thickened, refrigerate until you are ready to use it. Crème fraîche will keep in the refrigerator for about a week.

Serves 4

three groups, based on how and when they make berries. June-bearing types produce one crop of large, high-quality berries starting in late May through late June. Another type is traditionally called everbearing, which is a bit of a misnomer; they usually produce two crops, one early in the summer and one in late summer, when the days are relatively short and relatively cool. The third type is day-neutral (a term that means their ability to flower and set fruit is not affected by the length of the daylight hours). Day-neutral varieties begin to bear in mid to late June and produce a continuous, light crop of berries all summer long, until cold temperatures and frost stop them. In some catalogs, the day-neutrals are consolidated with the everbearing types, with little distinction between them. Berries from these types are not usually as large as the June bearers, and are best eaten fresh rather than preserved as they tend to be a little softer in texture. The flavor, however, is excellent.

A fourth, very different type is the Alpine strawberry, a much smaller plant that does not produce runners. The dainty white flowers and sweet, intensely flavored, ½-inch fruits are produced throughout the growing season. It is possible to grow them from seed, but you will undoubtedly find that starting with plants is easier. In a container or window box they look quite stylish. You won't be picking quarts at any one time, but there will usually be a handful available—a true delicacy.

Planting. Strawberries are sold in 4-inch or 6-inch plastic pots at the nursery in early spring, and are easy to transfer from these pots into your containers. Containers need to be at least 8 inches deep, but more is better. Hanging baskets should be at least 12 inches across.

Fill the container with potting mix, and set the plants in place with the crown (the center core, where the leaves originate) just at the soil surface. When you're done, water the container thoroughly to settle everything in place. Add more soil if necessary to make sure the roots are well covered, but do not cover the crown or it can rot.

Success with Strawberries.

Strawberries are about the easiest fruit there is to grow. With just regular watering and fertilizing, they'll produce a crop the first year. The best way to tell if a plant needs water is to stick your finger down into the soil; if the top inch is dry, it needs a drink. Let the plant get too dry, and it will alert you by wilting.

Once your baby berries start actively growing, give them fertilizer every couple of weeks; use a formula meant for flowers or vegetables, with a ratio of approximately 1:2:1 (see Chapter 6).

As long as you start with clean, healthy plants and use a commercial potting mix, you aren't likely to have a problem with diseases, viruses, or insect pests. But slugs are everywhere, and you do need to watch out for them if your container is on a ground-level patio where these little devils might be lurking. If you see their silvery slime trail, take action (see Chapter 6) or they will decimate your beautiful strawberries. Birds

may also try to steal them, but a drape of netting over the plant will keep them out.

Harvesting.

This is easy: when the berries are bright red, pick them! Strawberries form in clusters, so be sure not to break off or damage any nearby green ones as you're picking the red beauties. That's all there is to it, except the part where you put one into your mouth, tilt your head back, close your eyes, and smile.

Varieties.

All varieties seem to do equally well in containers, so you just need to decide if you want June-bearing or everbearing, and then select a variety suited to your area.

For the Northwest, **Hood** is the number one June-bearer for its excellent flavor and high yield of large berries. **Quinault** tops the list for an everbearing type. **Allstar** is a good June-bearing variety for the Northeast and Mid-Atlantic regions. **Tristar** is an everbearing type with excellent flavor for all regions. It's pretty much a given that your local nursery will stock varieties that are appropriate to your area. Trust it.

P rofessional garden designers work with a charming concept called "borrowed landscape." It means that they incorporate into their planning the visual impact of nearby sights, be they a lovely tree in a neighbor's yard or a dramatic view in the distance. It's a way of making any garden seem larger and more cohesive, which makes this idea especially valuable to those whose garden space is limited.

Maggie started thinking about applying this notion to container gardens one day when she was visiting her mother, who lives on the six-

Theme Garden

Hanging Gardens of Babylon

teenth floor of a high-rise apartment building and has a small balcony that faces east. Anyone who lives in Portland, Oregon, instantly understands what that means: any balcony that is a few stories high and faces east provides a view of "our mountain"—the beautiful Mt. Hood, 11,235 feet high, with its distinctive upper profile perpetually covered in snow. This gorgeous sight is so cherished by Portlanders that they have been known to stop dead in the middle of the sidewalk to gaze at it when a (rare) blue sky gives them a clear view, grabbing fellow pedestrians—total strangers—and saying, "Look—the mountain's out." On such a day, Maggie's mother has only to step out onto her balcony to enjoy this picture-postcard scene.

Once, when Maggie was sharing this visual treat with her mother, it occurred to her that the sight could be enhanced with an archway framing the view, a living arch made of plants. In that way, her mother could make the mountain part of her balcony garden.

To make such a garden, you need (1) a balcony with a lovely view or an attractive focal point in the distance, and (2) permission from the building's management to install hooks in the ceiling of your balcony, along the outer edge. Suspend hanging baskets at staggered heights, with the lowest at the outer edges and the highest in the center, creating the sense of an arch framing the view.

We think you'll like the results better if the containers and their contents are visually similar; use containers of the same size and type, and choose plants within just one color family (one in addition to green, of course). This is a situation where a monochromatic color scheme could be quite striking. To accentuate the arch effect, use deeply trailing plants at the edges and more rounded forms in the center.

Some suggestions for plants

Chamomile, page 182

Cherry tomatoes, page 168

Creeping rosemary, page 242

Malabar spinach, page 151

Nasturtiums, page 376

Oregano, page 235

Pansies, page 382

Scented geraniums, page 262

Strawberries, page 342

Thyme, page 278

Trailing begonias, page 352

CHAPTER 10

EDIBLE
FLOWERS

Cooking with flowers adds an element of magic to meals. Daintily nibbling a rose petal, you could easily imagine you've been transported to the land of Titania and Oberon. And you can share that bit of enchantment with your family and guests by incorporating edible flowers from your container garden into salads, entrées, desserts, or beverages, and by using the blossoms as colorful garnishes on almost any dish.

In this section we offer broad suggestions about using edible flowers, plus a few recipe ideas. It is our hope that you will be inspired to come up with your own creative ways to cook with flowers, for that is a big part of the fun. Take a taste of a flower petal, close your eyes, and turn your imagination loose. If the petal tastes like lemon, what dishes would be enhanced by a lemony addition? How could you use the sweet, floral taste of rose petals or daylilies, or the peppery bite of nasturtiums?

Note that we have not described *all* the possible edible flowers, for some of them are not appropriate for container gardening. To expand your horizons, you may want to explore Cathy Wilkinson Barash's wonderful book *Edible Flowers from Garden to Palate.* She was a true pioneer in this area, and her book is considered the bible of edible flowers. In it you'll find many more types of flowers than we have described, and also terrific ideas for innovative ways to cook with them. We do believe, however, that from the assortment of possibilities presented here, you'll have plenty of blossoms to work with.

Also keep in mind that *the flowers of all herb plants are edible.* As a group they tend to be small and not particularly showy, but they can provide charming garnishes and, when added to foods, a colorful herb taste.

Be Safe

If you're serving food that contains edible flowers, it is your responsibility to know what you are doing. Safety requires scrupulous attention to several things.

1. This law is unbreakable: do not eat or serve anything that you do not know *for a fact* to be nontoxic. Make no assumptions; sometimes flowers that we think are closely related have very different chemical compositions, and just because one flower is safe to eat doesn't mean that its cousins are. Even if you are using the flowers only as a garnish and do not intend for people to actually eat them, they might; use only nontoxic flowers.

   Be aware that some of the flowers we consider edible (begonias, for example) contain elements that should not be eaten in great amounts. Usually the harmful elements are present in minute quantities, and you would have to consume an abnormally large amount of the flower to harm yourself, far more than any reasonable person would ever do. We'll let you know which flowers require caution.

2. Do not eat or serve flowers that have *ever* been sprayed with toxic chemicals—insecticides, fertilizers, herbicides, or any other such items that can leave harmful residues. By the same token, do not use flowers that have been treated with systemic versions of those same items (systemics are applied to the soil and taken up by the roots; they affect the plant's entire system, hence the name).

3. For that reason do not use flowers from the florist, even if they are otherwise edible. You just cannot know how they were treated at the greenhouse.

4. If you have small children in your life, teach them to be safe, too. Make sure they clearly understand that just because they see you harvest and eat some flowers does not mean they can pick and eat other flowers.

5. Many local poison-control agencies have produced a list of toxic and nontoxic plants that are likely to be

found in your region. Locate the phone number (post it by the phone if you haven't already), and ask about their resources.

Good Preparation Habits

After harvesting the flowers, you'll have a few simple tasks to prepare them for eating.

1. Use common sense: wash off any dirt or dust before using the flowers. And watch for bugs. A larger blossom may shelter a honeybee down inside. The best approach is to swish blossoms in lukewarm water, then lay them in a colander or spread them on paper towels for a few minutes; the little critters will just walk away.

2. Many flowers have a small, bitter-tasting area at the base of the petals, where the petal is attached to the stem. You can remove these "heels" one at a time, but here is a much faster way.

   With your left hand (or right hand if you're left-handed), grasp the entire flower at the top by gathering all the petals together into a bundle. With your other hand, use scissors to cut through the flower just above that heel. Now you have a handful of individual petals. This is much easier to do while the flower is still on the plant.

   After you've harvested the petals, snip off the leftover part of the flower head, for it will not produce another flower and will just look ratty if you leave it on the stem.

3. If you plan to use the entire flower rather than individual petals, and if you plan for people to actually eat the flower (rather than simply admire it as a garnish), first remove the pistil and stamens, the thin spikes that come up from the center of the flower. Snip them off with embroidery or manicure scissors. They won't hurt you, but their texture makes them not particularly palatable.

Edible Flowers

Begonias

GROW AS: **annuals (or perennials from saved tubers)**

PLANT SIZE: **8 to 18 inches**

START WITH: **transplants or tubers**

HARVEST SEASON: **early summer through fall**

SUN REQUIREMENTS: **partial shade**

MINIMUM SOIL DEPTH: **6 inches**

For luscious color, begonias are unparalleled. The range of hues is satisfyingly broad: all the reds, pinks, lilacs, corals, yellows, oranges, and creamy whites you could want. But it's the quality of the color that is so mesmerizing: the blossoms seem to have an inner light that makes them luminous. It's the warm glow of late-afternoon sunlight through colored glass, or the rich luster of antique silks.

This luminescence is all the more valued because so many begonias are beautiful pastels, ultrapale tints that in most other flowers tend to be overpowered by stronger colors. Even the palest begonias can hold their own in any planting. Their blossoms are so enchanting that our senses get all mixed up: we see color and think texture, or taste, or all three at once.

Begonia blossoms are large enough to have a strong visual impact (2 to 3 inches in diameter), and each one stays on the plant for weeks. Plants begin blooming in late May or early June, and with regular fertilizing will continue through the summer and fall, up till the first hard frost. Many varieties have a cascading growth pattern, for spectacular hanging containers.

The petals (the edible part) have a crisp texture and a pleasantly tart taste that adds a nice zing to salads.

Many container gardeners face shady conditions, and finding a flowering plant that will bloom enthusiastically in shade is a real challenge.

That's another reason begonias are such a prize: these beautiful plants thrive in partial or filtered shade and fizzle in strong, direct sun.

All in all, tuberous begonias are an exquisite addition to a container garden.

Begonia Basics. The genus *Begonia* contains several large groups, but the only one we are interested in is the type known as tuberous begonias, meaning that they are grown from tubers. (A tuber is one form of underground storage, somewhat like a bulb, and in fact is often lumped in with bulbs as one large group.)

How do you know which kind of begonia you're getting? In catalogs, look for "tuberous begonias" in the listings; what you get when you order is the tuber itself, along with planting instructions. Garden centers sell tubers in early spring; they come in packages with large labels showing a color photograph of the mature plant, so you know what color you're getting.

Later in the spring, you'll be able to buy small transplants at nurseries. This is a clear advantage if they are showing a flower, because then you know the exact color. But make certain you are purchasing a tuberous begonia, *not* the bedding plants commonly known as wax begonias. If the label isn't clear, and the staff can't tell you for sure, go somewhere else.

When your begonia starts blooming, you'll notice that the plant bears two kinds of flowers. The flat ones, with a single layer of petals, are the females; the frilly, showy ones are the males. The flowers appear at the end of a stem in groups of threes, occasionally twos. A common threesome is two female flowers with one male in the center. A flamboyant, gorgeous male, surrounded by two much more modest-looking females—make of that what you will.

Planting. The begonia tuber looks a bit like a tulip bulb that got squashed: about the same diameter, about the same color, but flat as can be, with a hollow spot in the center of one side. Plant it directly into the outdoor container, about 1 inch deep, hollow side up, after your spring frost date. Keep the soil damp but not soggy.

Make sure you mark the spot somehow, because it takes a while before you'll see sprouts and you don't want to accidentally dig into the tubers in the meantime. A way to avoid the problem is to plant them into a temporary container that you can keep separate until new growth is showing. Using that same idea, you can even get a serious head start on the blooming season by planting the tubers indoors in February or March, and moving them outside when the weather has warmed up.

Starting with a transplant is simplicity itself: just repot it into its permanent container when all danger of frost is past.

At the end of the season, you can remove the tubers from the pot and save them for next year. Wait until the leaves start to fall off the stems, then lift out the tubers, brush away the soil, and set them in the sun for a few days until they are very dry. Pack the tubers in a small bucket or tub filled with peat moss, and store them in a cool, dry spot. You can also use paper bags filled with a bed of peat moss. This is a very good idea if you have more than one kind because you can write the color right on the bag. Come next February, plant tubers 1 inch deep in an indoor container, set it in a warm, bright area, keep the soil damp, and wait for the pink sprouts to start poking up.

Success with Begonias.

Begonias like lots of water but not soggy soil. They're also heavy feeders. To keep the flowers coming, enrich your potting mixture with some compost, if possible, and fertilize often with liquid fertilizer; best of all, do both.

Water frequently but carefully. Try to water at the base of the plant, without soaking the leaves. The stems of the plants are soft and juicy, and the leaves are frequently quite large. When waterlogged, those big leaves can become so heavy they cause the main stem to break. Also, begonias can be bothered by powdery mildew, a plant disease that thrives in warm, damp environments. Keeping water off the leaves helps to control it.

Anything that produces as many blossoms as begonias do needs a lot of replacement fertilizer. Once a week, give the plants a drink of a complete fertilizer that is proportionately higher in phosphorus (the middle number on the package label).

And keep them out of bright sun.

Varieties.

Within the tuberous group, you'll be able to choose from several types. There are begonias with large flowers that closely resemble camellias, and they are referred to as the Camellia type; another is called the Carnation type because their tightly frilled petals look like florists' carnations. Some begonias stand softly upright, and some are bred to grow in a cascade. Each type comes in a wide range of drop-dead colors, from deeply saturated reds, oranges, and yellows to the softest pastels. Most blossoms are solid colors, but some varieties have petals in one color with an edging of a different color. A particularly rewarding variety is **Nonstop,** for its nonstop flowers in many gorgeous colors.

As you're making your choices, you will probably be most concerned with color, and second with growth habit (upright or cascading). Your best course is to study a catalog with color photos, and read the descriptions carefully. Or just go cruising in your favorite garden center, and let yourself be seduced by the sumptuous blossoms. Whatever you pick, you can hardly go wrong.

Maggie says: One year I allowed myself to get sweet-talked into buying a hanging planter from a community group that was selling them as a fundraiser. At the time I said yes, all I knew was that it was planted with begonias; no blossoms were showing, so I had no idea what color they were.

The garden gods must protect suckers like me, because what I ended up with is about the most gorgeous basket I've ever seen. The flowers are a soft creamy white with just a blush of pink, iridescent as mother of pearl and so shining pure it could break your heart.

Although the begonias were planted in a container meant to be hung, they are not the trailing, cascading type; the flowers sit up above the foliage, and so are best viewed from above. So I set the basket down on the stoop by my front door (northern exposure), where the flowers are (1) protected from hot sun, and (2) perfectly oriented for admiring visitors.

From this experience I learned several lessons. First, if a plant turns out to be different from what you imagined, that doesn't make it less wonderful. Modify your original vision, and you can still enjoy it. Second, when an eight-year-old cutie-pie asks you to buy something for a school fund-raiser, say yes, and something good will happen.

Cooking with Begonias. The part of the plant that you eat is the flower petals, which have a crisp texture, something like lettuce, and a distinctively sour tang. It's not puckery sour like vinegar, but more like the tartness of lemon. The sour taste, incidentally, comes from oxalic acid, which in very large quantities can be harmful. Oxalic acid has the effect of binding calcium in the body, with concurrent damage to the kidneys. A healthy person would have to eat something like a bushel basket every day all season to cause any major damage, but moderation is still a good idea, especially where there is a history of kidney disease.

Because of their tartness, begonia petals blend well in a salad of mixed greens with a vinaigrette dressing. They also work nicely in any vegetable dish that would be enhanced by a squeeze of fresh lemon: sautéed green beans, braised greens, roasted peppers, and so forth. Stack several petals together, slice horizontally into ribbons, and toss them in near the end of cooking. Use chopped petals in place of grated lemon peel in tabbouleh or lemon rice pilaf (use blossoms of sev-

eral colors, and you can call it Confetti Pilaf). Like all edible flowers, begonias have something of a floral undertone, which combined with the lemony tang is particularly nice in a fruit salad. And all these dishes are greatly enlivened by the beautiful colors of the flower petals.

Sweet and Tangy

Here's a very refreshing dessert for summer lunches or a teatime treat. In the center of a lovely large platter, put several small bowls of fruit-flavored yogurt. Surround them with masses of begonia petals in as many colors as possible. Invite your guests to use individual petals to scoop a bit of yogurt. The combination of sweet yogurt and tangy flower petal is delightful. If you serve several kinds of yogurt and more than one color of flower, your friends will have fun trying out mix-and-match combinations. And for a special summertime treat, make begonia sorbet (see page 358).

Cool and crisp on the tongue, sweet, tangy, light, and rich all at the same time, sorbet may well be the perfect light summertime dessert. Made with only sugar, water, and flavorings (usually some form of fruit), sorbet captures the unique taste of whatever fruit it embodies and holds it in cool crystalline form that is not quite like the fruit nor quite like ice but somehow embraces both. And because it contains no cream and usually not even milk, it is also fat free.

Theme Garden

Summer-time Sorbet

Sorbets capture not only the tastes of their fruit ingredients but their colors as well, in virtually unadulterated form. Strawberry sorbet is a far more intense deep pink than strawberry ice cream—more like strawberries. Mango sorbet is the rich color of mango flesh, and lemon sorbet is the light, almost translucent pale yellow of freshly squeezed lemon juice, not the artificially bright color of commercial lemon products.

So distinctive are these colors that the word *sorbet* itself has been borrowed by people describing things other than food to convey purity of color and a sense of coolness and sweetness. There is, for example, a variety of viola named Sorbet Mix, described in one catalog as having the colors of "blueberry, lemon chiffon, lavender ice, and French vanilla." You know what they look like just from the name.

That's the idea behind this garden—it represents sorbet both figuratively, in its freshness of color, and literally, for a delightful sorbet can be made from its plants.

The star of this garden is a great glorious tumble of **tuberous begonias.** Of all the wonderful edible flowers we have to choose from, for sheer oomph of color nothing can surpass the tuberous begonia. The range is impressive: everything from the most delicate ivory and many soft pastels through deeply saturated hues of red, orange, and yellow. But even more impressive is the luminous quality of the color; even the palest pastels seem to glow with inner light. A container filled with tuberous begonias, either all one color or a felicitous mixture, will absolutely knock your socks off.

This does not have to be a large garden to have impact. Use a

For details on
growing the plants in
this garden, see

Begonias, page 352
Mint, page 223
Violas, page 382

Recipe: Begonia Sorbet

For an extra-special presentation, top each serving with two small mint leaves and one crystallized Sorbet Mix viola, which you made in the spring when the violas were in bloom (see page 180 for instructions) and carefully saved for just this occasion.

> **1 can (12 ounces) frozen lemonade concentrate,**
>   **thawed**
> **3 or 4 bright-colored begonia blossoms,**
>   **coarsely chopped**
> **Whole begonia petals and mint leaves,**
>   **for garnish**

Mix the lemonade concentrate with 2 cans of water and pour into shallow pans or ice-cube trays. Place in the freezer for about an hour, or until frozen. Put the frozen mix in a food processor fitted with the steel blade and blend for a few seconds. Return to the pans and refreeze. Repeat the blending and refreezing several times for smoother texture. Add the chopped begonia petals during the last blending. Garnish each serving with additional whole begonia petals and mint leaves.

Mint version. Before mixing it with the lemonade concentrate, heat 2 cans of water to boiling and steep a handful (about ¼ cup) of fresh mint leaves in it for 5 minutes, then strain. Remeasure, and add more water if needed to make 2 cans of liquid.

Courtesy of Weidners' Gardens, Encinitas, California

medium-size container, the prettiest one you can find; this flower-filled garden seems to want a very decorative container, perhaps one with a floral design or a pastel color that complements the blossoms. Plant it chock full of the begonia tubers in spring after all danger of frost is past. You want the full, rich look of blossoms bursting out of the pot, so plant lots.

The sorbet garden has only one other ingredient: **mint.** Because of its very invasive root system, mint performs much better in its own pot. (Actually, mint performs quite nicely wherever it is; it's just that you, the gardener, will be happier if it has its own space.) So put your favorite kind in a small, pretty container, and set it beside the begonia. Both plants will do well in a semi-shady spot; in fact, the begonias prefer it.

You may want to plant, somewhere else, some of the Sorbet Mix **violas,** although the violas bloom very early in spring, long before the begonias are in blossom. If you want to serve violas with your sorbet, the best way to preserve them, and also the prettiest presentation for your dessert, is to crystallize them (see instructions on page 180).

Now for the sorbet. Back in the summer of 1998, I (Maggie) visited a nursery in the San Diego area that specializes in begonias. Their offering is unique; at least I've never seen anything like it. Each year they plant —*in the ground*—thousands of begonias in a half-acre area that is like a giant lath house, covered with a ceiling made of greenhouse cloth but no real walls or floors. Customers choose their plants, dig them up, and plop them into nursery pots they brought with them. I'm told that gardeners from miles around pass along the news: "The begonias are ready at Weidners'."

It was there I first became acquainted with begonia sorbet, although I have come across it in other places since then. This wonderfully simple recipe was originally developed by the owners of Weidners'; I have modified it to incorporate the taste of mint, which I think adds an extra dimension, but which you should surely consider optional.

Edible Flowers

Calendulas

GROW AS: **annuals**

PLANT SIZE: **12 to 24 inches**

START WITH: **seeds or transplants**

HARVEST SEASON: **summer and fall**

SUN REQUIREMENTS: **full sun**

MINIMUM SOIL DEPTH: **6 inches**

Calendula is a versatile flowering plant with many virtues: the petals give a rich golden color to foods, the flowers have medicinal properties to soothe rough skin and heal small wounds, and the bright, sassy yellows and oranges add a touch of sunshine to any garden. And if that isn't enough, this endearing plant will even do tricks for you: the blossoms close at night and reopen with the morning sun.

In fact, calendula, with its colors of the sun, has been used as a religious symbol for many centuries and across many cultures. Hindu temples were festooned with the flowers, and Buddhists considered it one of the sacred plants, perhaps because it was one source of the yellow dye used for the golden color of monks' robes. The ancient Egyptians, Greeks, and Romans all used calendula in religious rites as well as more temporal activities: in cooking, in medicine, and as a dye. With its long tradition in herbal medicine and folklore, calendula could as easily be placed in the Herbs chapter of this book, except for the fact that today we grow it mostly for the cheerful flowers.

Calendula Basics. The calendula flower is round and flat, rather like a daisy, about 2 inches in diameter. It has no fragrance. The stems and leaves are fuzzy but not especially noteworthy. The stars are the flowers—a bright, intense golden yellow that perks up both the garden and the gardener. Keep cutting and deadheading the flowers, and more will bloom; as cut flowers, they last very well indoors.

Calendulas are considered cool-weather plants, which in many parts of the country gives them a long bloom season, from late spring all the way through fall. In very mild climates, calendula blooms all winter and peters out in the summer. Gardeners who live at the beach face unusual weather challenges, and this is one plant that works very well there.

Planting. Start seeds indoors in March, and transfer to outdoor containers when the plants are about 2 inches tall. Or buy transplants at the garden center in mid spring.

Even though calendula is technically an annual, it reseeds itself quite easily and in an open garden can come back year after year. In a container garden you may get the same benefit if you deliberately let some of the flowers mature so their seeds fall onto the soil; just remember, come next spring, that the seedlings are not weeds.

Success with Calendula. This is such a sturdy little plant, it's hard to have bad luck with it. To get a long, steady show of flowers, stick to the basics: deadhead your plants often, fertilize regularly, and keep them watered.

Harvesting. Although at one time the leaves of the plant were used to stop the bleeding of large wounds, today we're interested only in the flowers. Harvesting is therefore a simple matter of snipping off the flower heads, along with part of the stem (for a handle).

To use the flowers in fresh dishes such as salads, simply swish the entire blossom in water to rinse off any dust, then pull off individual petals.

The flowers also dry very easily. Remove the stem, right up to the base of the flower, and place the flowers in one layer on paper towels or in a shallow basket, away from direct sunlight. When the petals are dry (check every day), pull them from the center core and store in a tightly covered container. They will keep their color and beneficial properties for months, until you're ready to use them in any of the ways suggested here.

Varieties. For container gardening there is only one species, *Calendula officinalis.*

Cooking with Calendula. It may have been one of the gastronomes of ancient Rome who first used calendula petals to give a golden color to foods. We know it has been used for many centuries as a way to color butter and cheese, and in modern kitchens it's often used in rice dishes and breads as a substitute for the astronomically expensive saffron. This "poor man's saffron" produces a very acceptable color but not the saffron taste; calendula has a somewhat bitter flavor.

For sprinkling over a salad or garnishing cooked vegetables, use fresh petals. In cooked dishes, either fresh or dried petals will give you good color. Fresh petals should be chopped finely, and the dried ones crushed or pulverized before adding to your recipe.

Other Uses. Calendula holds an important spot in the herbalist's medicine chest. The plant contains natural chemicals that help stop bleeding and heal wounds, so it has been used for hundreds of years as an emergency medicine. In the United States during the Civil War and also in Europe as late as World War I, medics used it to treat wounded soldiers, and patriotic American and European gardeners grew masses of calendulas to be shipped to the battlefields.

Calendula Legends

■ A young girl who walks barefoot among calendulas will acquire the gift of understanding the language of birds.

■ A girl who dreams about calendula will soon be married or inherit great wealth.

■ To find something of value that is lost or stolen, place a branch of calendula underneath your pillow. You will have a dream in which the location of the item will be revealed, along with the identity of the person responsible.

Today, in less ferocious circumstances, we can still take advantage of the beneficial properties of this salutary garden plant. Calendula is an excellent skin balm. It can be used to ease rough or chapped skin; to soothe sunburn, rashes, or insect bites; and to heal minor cuts and abrasions. The trick is, how to get the good stuff out of the petals? Here are several ideas.

In all these natural preparations, use fresh flowers if possible, for they contain the greatest concentration of medicinal properties. While things are "brewing," keep the container covered so the volatile chemicals do not evaporate.

■ Use either fresh or dried petals to brew up a very strong batch of medicinal tea (which is technically called an infusion). Strain out the petals and, if you won't be using the infusion immediately, store it in the refrigerator; it will keep for a few days. Dip a cotton ball into the liquid and pat it on the skin where needed, or immerse a washcloth in the herbal infusion, wring it out, and use it as a compress.

■ Add the infusion to your bathwater, and slip in for a long, soothing soak.

■ Use the same infusion, perhaps diluted with warm water, as a healing mouthwash and gargle after a trip to the dentist.

■ Make herbal vinegar, which can be used like the infusion but has the advantage of a long shelf life. Vinegar by itself is a good skin conditioner; with the added healing properties of calendula, it is an excellent treatment. The vinegary smell dissipates quickly, and the soothing qualities continue.

To make the vinegar, tear off fresh petals and pack them loosely into a jar. Add plain distilled vinegar to cover the petals, and set the jar on a counter for several days. When the vinegar is a rich color and the petals seem to be bleached, it's ready. Strain out and discard the petals, and store the vinegar in a clean jar.

■ Make a lotion from lanolin (which you can find in some pharmacies) or light vegetable oil such as almond or safflower oil. Gently heat the lanolin or oil, stir in calendula petals, cover, and turn off the heat. Let this sit for several hours, then strain off the spent petals.

Do not use this technique to make herb-flavored oils that you intend to eat; the danger of botulism is too high in home preparations of these low-acid oils.

■ Make a cream, using either petroleum jelly or calendula oil (see above) plus beeswax. This may come as a surprise, but all creams (even very expensive commercial brands) are essentially the same: an oil, melted wax, and the fragrance, which is carried in some kind of liquid, usually water. If you start with calendula-infused oil, and add to it a bit of melted beeswax, you'll get a cream; keep adding beeswax until you get the consistency you like.

Another technique for making cream is to gently melt petroleum jelly (a few seconds in the microwave works well for this) and pour it over calendula petals in a jar with a lid. Let this sit, tightly covered, for several days, then melt to liquid form and strain out the petals.

■ Make a soothing powder with cornstarch. Put dried petals and a small amount of cornstarch into a blender and blend until the petals are pulverized and blended with the cornstarch, then add more cornstarch and blend it all together. This is especially good for diaper rash.

Circumstances often dictate which technique you use. In December you won't have access to fresh flowers, and if you develop a winter rash you'll be glad you dried some blossoms last summer. If your children come home from a camping trip with tiny cuts all over their arms and legs, you want to help them right now, not several days from now, so you'd make an infusion for compresses rather than waiting for herbal vinegar to "brew."

Many people who enjoy natural health and beauty products are in the habit of making up a batch of lotion or cream while their calendula plants are in full bloom, and keeping it in their medicine chest.

Edible Flowers

Chrysanthemums

GROW AS: **annuals or perennials**

PLANT SIZE: **10 to 24 inches**

START WITH: **transplants**

HARVEST SEASON: **fall**

SUN REQUIREMENTS: **full sun**

MINIMUM SOIL DEPTH: **6 inches**

The chrysanthemum family is a large one, and includes such first cousins as Shasta daisy, painted daisy, marguerite daisy, and even one of the several plants known as dusty miller. Feverfew, another cousin, is listed in the Herbs chapter. Here, though, we are concentrating on just one species, the very familiar plant known to gardeners and horticulturists by the nondescript name florists' chrysanthemum.

This is the "mum" that shows up as a potted plant in every supermarket and flower shop in the country in September and October, with puffy flowers in autumnal shades of gold, yellow, bronze, or orange. You may have taken a pot to Aunt Shirley's for Thanksgiving dinner, or received one yourself as a hostess gift. Because we so often see them this way—in a pot wrapped in colored foil, with a matching bow—it may be something of a revelation to realize that chrysanthemums will grow quite happily in your outdoor container garden.

As is sometimes true of edible flowers, what chrysanthemums contribute to food is more a matter of color and novelty than flavor. But their contribution to your container garden more than makes up for any culinary shortfall.

Chrysanthemum Basics. It's no accident that we associate mums with autumn, for that is their natural bloom time. They are one member of the group of plants referred to as "short-day," meaning that their internal trigger for blossoms gets turned on when the days begin to get shorter. When you see them in the market out of their natural season, it is because a commercial greenhouse has simulated a short-day period, tricking the plants into thinking it's time to bloom.

The plants set buds in mid to late summer; the blossoms are in full force anywhere from six to twelve weeks later, depending on the variety. Well into the fall, when most other flowering plants have finished, mums are still putting on their show. Flowers are generally long lasting, blooming for as long as eight weeks, another reason for their popularity.

The array of choices is enormous. Chrysanthemum breeders have produced plants with flowers in many sizes and shapes (from tiny buttons to huge pom-poms) and in just about every color you would ever wish: white, yellow, orange, bronze, pink, red, purple, lavender, and many shades thereof.

Chrysanthemums have passionate fans, many of whom intensely and lovingly fuss over the plants to achieve the perfect flowers that win awards at flower shows. Much of the information in catalogs of mail-order nurseries that specialize in mums is directed at these customers, so you can learn a great deal from them.

Planting. Starting with small transplants purchased from the garden center is easy as pie; just plant them into your containers in the usual way. They usually appear in the nurseries in early summer. When you order from a mail-order catalog, you get small nursery-potted plants, ready for transplanting.

Should you be the recipient of a gift of potted mums, you can sometimes turn them into outdoor garden plants as well. You may wish to enjoy them indoors until the flowers are past their peak, and then transfer them into an outdoor container. Tip the contents out, and in all likelihood you'll see that the pot contains several individual plants, clumped close together. Separate the clump and you will have several new plants, each of which will grow

into a full bush by summer. Set each one into a small container with good-quality potting soil, keep it moist, and wait for new shoots to sprout from the base of the plant.

The time of year is a factor. Often gift chrysanthemum plants will arrive in your life in October or November. It may be too cold, depending on the climate, to set out the separated plants. In that case, the easiest course is to keep the gift pot intact and indoors until spring. Snip off dead flowers and keep the soil very lightly damp through the winter; what you'll have is a mildly interesting houseplant, with leaves but no flowers. When the weather warms up, divide the clump and put the individual plants into containers.

Success with Chrysanthemums. Your mums may be attractive to aphids (see Chapter 6 for treatments), but otherwise these are easy plants. They grow naturally into a bush shape, with lots of branches and masses of flowers. Chrysanthemum hobbyists maintain a careful regimen of pinching out new growth to encourage more branching, and then removing some of the flower buds to promote larger (but fewer) blossoms. Whether you choose to try some of those techniques is up to you. If you don't do any of it, you'll still have a great plant with handsome flowers in the fall.

In areas where winters are mild or moderate, your chrysanthemum will be a perennial, growing larger each year as new branches develop from the base. After several years the center of the plant may begin to die back, growing all the new healthy branches on the edges. This is your cue to divide the plant, saving smaller plants from the edges and discarding the bare center portion. The best time to do this is early spring, just as the plant is getting ready for a spurt of growth.

In very cold climates, you'll need to give your mums some winter protection if you want to maintain them as perennials. Move the container to your most sheltered spot, and wrap it with some kind of insulating material (see page 288 for suggestions). A bit more work, but safer, is to remove the plant from its big container, put it into a smaller pot, and keep it indoors through the winter. For extra insurance, you can do some of both: divide the plant at the roots, then move just one portion into an indoor container while sheltering the larger outdoor container from the elements. Easiest of all, you can decide to treat the plant as an annual and start over next spring with new transplants from the nursery.

Harvesting. Nothing to it: just pull off petals as needed. Or snip an entire blossom for a large garnish. The more you cut the flowers, the more the plant makes new blossoms.

Varieties. As you might expect with any flower that is so significant in the florist trade, plant breeders have put in thousands of hours developing new chrysanthemum cultivars, and more are introduced each year. It would not be helpful for us to name specific varieties, as they probably will have been supplanted by the time you

do your shopping. The best bet is to explore the mail-order catalog of a specialty nursery, or visit a well-stocked retail nursery and select whatever catches your fancy.

You may find it useful to know that mums are grouped into several large categories, distinguished by flower shape and growth habit. These categories are used primarily by nurseries that specialize in chrysanthemums; your garden center probably displays all mums together, regardless of category.

The type called **cushion mums** are especially nice for containers. They grow in small mounds, about 1 foot in diameter, often totally covered with blossoms. With this compact, tidy habit, they'd work nicely as the bottom layer of a mixed container garden. Flower color may be pink, red, salmon, white, yellow, copper, or bronze. All the others are sometimes grouped under the all-purpose heading **upright garden mums,** meaning that they are taller and more erect, 18 to 24 inches high. Other category names you may encounter in various catalogs are **button,** a reference to the very small flowers; **football,** the huge flowers made into autumn corsages; **spider** and **spoon,** which describe the shape of the flowers and the individual petals.

Cooking with Chrysanthemums. The flavor of chrysanthemum petals is a little on the bitter side, and so they are more appropriate with salads and main dishes than desserts. You may find, as some cooks do, that you care more about the color than the taste.

Edible Flowers

Daylilies

GROW AS: **perennials**

PLANT SIZE: **1 to 4 feet, depending on variety**

START WITH: **transplants**

HARVEST SEASON: **summer into fall**

SUN REQUIREMENTS: **full sun to partial shade**

MINIMUM SOIL DEPTH: **6 inches**

Of all the interesting tidbits concerning botanical naming, the daylily story is one of the sweetest. The genus to which all daylilies belong is *Hemerocallis,* a word derived from the Greek *hemera,* meaning "day," and *kallos,* meaning "beauty"; that is, "beautiful for a day" or "one day's beauty." This refers to the fact that each blossom lasts only one day. A flower that dies so quickly could as easily have been given a somber, funereal name, yet daylilies are named for their beauty, not their transience—a gentle reminder that gardens hold many metaphors for living a good life.

And lest you worry that it's all over in a snap, daylilies put on a gratifyingly long show of blooms. Each individual flower is open for just one day, but the plants produce dozens, even hundreds, of flower buds in a season. Some varieties, including the lovely Stella d'Oro, are constantly in bloom throughout the summer.

On a more prosaic note, the label *Hemerocallis* is important because it's your confirmation that you are acquiring a true daylily, and not a lily. "Daylily" is not a synonym for "lily"; they are two different plants entirely. The dramatic, fragrant flowers of lilies are undeniably stunning, but not edible.

Daylily Basics. Daylilies are perennials, with long, strappy leaves and flower stalks (known as scapes) that stand up above the foliage. Sometimes the foliage forms a shape like an opened Chinese fan: the leaves arch over into a sort of semicircle that is essentially flat from front to back, and the scapes emerge from the center. A mature plant has masses of these fans in a tight clump, forming an all-around mound that is quite attractive even before the flowers begin their show. Many daylilies are herbaceous, meaning that the plant dies to the ground in the winter and reemerges in the spring, but some keep their handsome foliage all year round. The herbaceous types tolerate cold winters better than the evergreen varieties.

367

The flower buds form at the upper end of the flower stalks; they open for one 24-hour period, then close and eventually wither away. Most types of daylily have one main period of flowering, which can last for a month or more, and some then put on a second burst of blossoms (in catalogs, look for varieties marked "remontant").

Planting. Start with a small plant, either from a mail-order nursery, a retail garden center, or a division (described below) from a friend's garden. Plant it in your outdoor container the same way as you would any transplant. Sometimes a 1-gallon container plant from the garden center actually contains, or can be gently separated into, several smaller plants; in that case, plant them out with about 6 inches of space in between.

Success with Daylilies. For growing daylilies, success is largely a matter of getting up in the morning. You'd be hard pressed to find an easier, more trouble-free flower. Daylilies prefer to be in sun but will tolerate partial shade. They like rich, fluffy soil with good drainage (and what plant does not?), but they will take whatever you give them with little complaint. They appreciate a dose of fertilizer during the season, and water when needed, but otherwise are pretty undemanding. Daylilies seem to be little troubled by insects, and diseases are practically unknown.

Your only major chore will be dividing, and even that you won't have to worry about for maybe five years. Daylilies multiply at their roots, which spread outward underground, so that each year the mound gets wider and wider. Eventually, the crowded conditions rob the plant of vigor, and its flower production diminishes. The solution is to divide the plant. Here's how.

In the fall when the bloom season has ended, dig up the entire plant. Lay it on a flat surface so you can get a good look at the roots. If you tease away some of the soil, you can clearly see that instead of one main stem with lots of branches, what you have is a mass of stems coming up from the thick, fleshy roots. Each one of those stems could in theory become a new plant, if only you could get them apart. The best way seems brutal but is actually kindest. Take a large, sharp kitchen knife and slice down through the plant, right through the root mass. Now you have two plants, each of which has one flat side; if you replant them, new growth will quickly fill in to soften that cut edge.

Or you can continue to divide. Slice the two halves in half again, for four new plants. Eventually you will find that you can pull the roots and stems apart with your fingers, if you wish. In this way you can take one very large daylily plant and convert it into many small plants. The smaller they are, the longer you can go before having to divide them again, but also the longer it will be before they bloom heavily. Like many other things in the garden, it's a trade-off.

Harvesting. The flowers are large and snap easily off the stalk. As with all edible flowers, you'll probably want to remove the pistil and stamens—very carefully, if you intend to keep the blossom intact. If not, just pull the petals apart and discard the rest.

Varieties. Alongside almost any rural road anywhere in the United States, you can see daylilies growing wild, their tall scapes topped with heavy orange flowers, nodding their heads in greeting as you pass, the way country folk do. From this original species, literally thousands of cultivars have been developed by breeders both amateur and professional.

So today we have daylilies in shades of burgundy, lavender, pink, coral, salmon, pale green, and creamy white, as well as the more common yellows and oranges. Most flowers are the familiar lily shape (like a funnel or a bell), although some varieties display frilled and ruffled petals, long spidery shapes, or double layers of petals with a fluffy look.

Choosing from a catalog can be daunting. Our advice is, start by focusing on size. Dwarf varieties, 12 to 18 inches tall, work best for most containers unless you want to put together a really large, bold combination planter. Next consider color, time of bloom, and whether foliage is evergreen or herbaceous. You can't go wrong with varieties honored by the American Hemerocallis Society: Honorable Mention (often abbreviated HM in catalogs), the Award of Merit (abbreviated AM), given to only 10 plants each year, or the Stout Medal (abbreviated SM), awarded to only the most outstanding types.

At a garden center, you will have fewer varieties to choose from (which you may consider a plus), but you often get to see them in bloom, so you know for sure what color flowers you're getting.

Maggie says: For containers I love Stella d'Oro, which has the golden yellow flowers you would expect from its name. It's small (total height, including scapes, 18 to 24 inches), foolproof (a Stout Medal winner), and seems to bloom forever. It is extremely popular, and therefore widely available—a real delight.

Cooking with Daylilies. The taste of most daylily flowers is floral and lightly sweet (an 11-year-old friend of ours thought Stella d'Oro petals tasted like honeysuckle), with a crisp texture. A few years ago *Sunset* magazine, the *ne plus ultra* for gardeners in the West, did a taste test involving the blossoms of nine familiar garden plants, and the tasters raved over the daylilies. They used the common roadside variety, *Hemerocallis fulva,* which reminded them of cucumber with a sweet aftertaste. Try the petals in green or fruit salads; add large, unopened buds to a vegetable stir-fry; toss shredded orange-colored petals into steamed green beans at the last minute.

Cathy Wilkinson Barash suggests a beautiful dessert idea: start with large blossoms and carefully remove stamens and pistil, keeping the flower intact. Lay the whole flower in a dessert dish and fill it with ice cream or sorbet, then sprinkle a few ribbons of petals over the top.

Edible Flowers

Dianthus

GROW AS: **annuals or perennials**

PLANT SIZE: **4 to 12 inches**

START WITH: **transplants or seeds**

HARVEST SEASON: **spring, early summer**

SUN REQUIREMENTS: **full sun**

MINIMUM SOIL DEPTH: **5 inches**

The language of gardeners is a fascinating thing. Technically, if you just say "dianthus" you could be referring to any of the several hundred species in the *Dianthus* genus. Among the members of this large group are the familiar florists' carnations (both full-size and minis) that you've seen a million times, and also the old-fashioned cottage-garden favorite with the winsome name sweet William. But in one of those quirky habits of nomenclature that have developed over time, gardeners generally use "dianthus" to mean just one portion of the genus: all the dainty little flowers known collectively by the common name "pinks."

In this case, pink is a noun, not an adjective. You can choose white pinks, red pinks, purple pinks, and pinks in every shade of pink. The name may derive from the fact that the edges of the flower petals have small notches, as if cut with pinking shears.

Many pinks have one other endearing quality: fragrance—the warm, spicy, and altogether surprising aroma of cloves. So pronounced is this fragrance that one group of these plants is known as "clove pinks," and several cultivars have "clove" or "spice" in their name. This delightful fragrance is as appealing to honeybees as it is to humans, and so by planting dianthus you are encouraging bees to visit your garden. In a vegetable garden, anything that brings bees is a very good thing indeed.

All in all, these are enchanting little plants. They come back for several years (most of them, anyway); they add a strong note of color; and if you choose the right ones, they smell heavenly.

Maggie says: I recently put together a mixed container of herbs with a pink theme—the color pink, that is. It contains chives (pink puffball flowers), tricolor sage (pink streaks on the leaves), a thyme with pink flowers, and two pinks: one with magenta flowers on upright stems, and one of the spreading, clumping kind with soft pink flowers. I have no idea what variety either of the pinks is, but I really don't care. I love their frilly little flowers and their sweet smell.

Pink Basics. If you're just starting to feel that you have this business of scientific names under control, you might assume that the pinks are one species, sweet William is another, and florists' carnations another. Life is seldom that simple. The flowers known as pinks comprise several separate species (with the common names maiden pinks, cottage pinks, Chinese pinks, and so on), and one subsection of *one* of those species is the florists' carnations (which are mostly grown in greenhouses). From the several species of pinks, many subspecies and cultivars have been developed by crossbreeding, and new ones show up each year. The main differences are in flower color, flower shape, or the way the plant grows.

Some pinks grow in the shape of small, spreading mounds that eventually cover an area like a very lumpy carpet, their flowers tight against the foliage. Others are more upright in habit, with flowers atop erect stems, but still modest in overall size. A few are annuals or biennials (usually sold as annuals), but most are perennials. The flowers themselves take one of two basic forms: one flat layer of petals (the general term for this configuration is "single"), or multiple layers, more reminiscent of the familiar florists' carnation (these are called "double"). In your garden center you're more likely to find single flowers—about the size of a nickel, with pretty frilled edges to the petals.

Planting. A number of *Dianthus* species can be started quite easily from seeds. Start seeds indoors three to four weeks ahead of the spring frost date, following the directions on the packet for spacing and depth. When the seedlings have several sets of true leaves, they are ready to move into the outdoor container; see Chapter 5 for seed-starting and planting instructions.

If you prefer to buy young plants from the garden center, you'll simply transplant them into your desired outdoor container in the usual way, also described in Chapter 5.

Success with Dianthus. Pinks do best in soil that drains quickly, which is probably what you already have in your containers. They bloom best in full sun, but in very hot climates will appreciate some protection from the afternoon sun. Most varieties bloom from spring through early summer, especially if you keep clipping off the dead flowers, and some put on a secondary bloom later in the summer.

Most dianthuses are perennials, but they typically don't last more than a few years. Even the sturdiest perennials may need some protection against freezing in very cold climates (see Chapter 1 for suggestions). The clumping, spreading types have a tendency to push clumps up out of the soil, especially when they are grown close to other plants. You can turn this to an advantage by separating some of the pushy clumps and potting them into separate smaller containers. If you then bring these smaller pots inside for the winter, you're guaranteed at

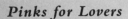
Pinks for Lovers

Since ancient times, pinks have been used in celebrations of love. When young lovers became engaged, their families announced the betrothal with a large party, featuring a ceremonial punch with pinks floating on top. The wedding itself was decorated with garlands woven of flowers and herbs, with pinks being a featured flower.

Today, we can continue this lovely tradition by making flower-laden ice cubes for punch at a bridal shower or engagement party. Here's how:

Harvest pinks by snipping them off close to the stem, but keep the whole flower head intact. Swish them through clear water to rinse away any dust. Fill ice trays halfway with water and float one perfect flower in each. Freeze. (This interim step ensures that the flower stays in position in the middle of the ice cube.) Then fill the trays the rest of the way, and freeze until solid.

You can adapt the idea by freezing a large ring (using a ring mold) or by making large rectangles of ice with recycled milk cartons. With the larger ice blocks, you can mix in other flowers and small snippets of herbs, creating small floral compositions to decorate the ice block.

least some winter survival. Come spring, each clump will be the start of a new planting.

Harvesting. Harvesting the flowers is a simple matter of snipping them off with scissors or hand pruners, and has the added bonus of stimulating the plant to produce more flowers. With practice, you can pinch the flower heads off at the base, but the stems are surprisingly sturdy and resist snapping by human hands.

Varieties. Among the half-dozen or so principal *Dianthus* species are literally hundreds of varieties and cultivars, with new ones being introduced each year. The original species, *Dianthus caryophyllus,* known in Elizabethan days as gillyflower, is today almost impossible to find in its true, original form. *D. plumarius* is the species known by the common name cottage pink; this is an old favorite, going back several hundred years, with many new cultivars.

Cross-breeding between *D. plumarius* and *D. caryophyllus* produced *D. allwoodii,* a modern group with dozens of varieties, most of them wonderfully fragrant.

D. deltoides, known as maiden pink, usually forms low, loose mats. The many cultivars of *D. chinensis,* Chinese pink, have brilliant colors but no fragrance.

There are more species; this is just a sampling to give you an idea what a rich, broad genus *Dianthus* is. Studying the selections in specialty catalogs, you can begin to develop a sense of the differences in growth habits, time of bloom, shape, color, and fragrance of flowers, and make your selections accordingly.

Or you may find it easier to just meander through your favorite garden center in spring and choose from what it has available. In addition to simplicity, this approach offers two very tangible advantages. What you primarily care about, in all likelihood, is color, and the only way to be sure what color the flowers will be is to purchase the plants while they are blooming. You'll also be able then to check that other delightful quality of pinks: the fragrance of their flowers.

Cooking with Dianthus. Before you do anything of a culinary nature, you'll want to remove the bitter-tasting white portion at the base of the petals. The easiest way to do this is to fold the flower petals into a clump in one hand and use scissors in the other hand to snip off the entire base; your first hand is now holding individual petals, minus their white stubs.

The petals are then ready for whatever your imagination can create. Think "floral" and "spicy" together; what does that combination suggest? For starters:

- Sprinkle flower petals over fruit salad.

- Add dianthus petals, finely chopped, to apple pie or berry cobbler.

- Combine flowers into the sauce for Harvard beets or German-style sweet-and-sour red cabbage.

Edible Flowers

Marigolds

GROW AS: **annuals**

PLANT SIZE: **8 to 12 inches**

START WITH: **transplants or seeds**

HARVEST SEASON: **summer and fall**

SUN REQUIREMENTS: **full sun**

MINIMUM SOIL DEPTH: **5 inches**

Many people love marigolds: bright, cheery, pom-pom flowers in sunshine shades of yellow and orange. Anyone who has ever grown them also knows about the stinky aroma of the leaves, and in fact many people plant them alongside vegetables, particularly tomatoes, because they're reputed to repel harmful pests like tomato hornworms.

We're not talking about *those* marigolds. They're not really edible—well, they won't kill you, but they have a very bitter taste. Grow the large, buxom flowers if you love their looks, and plant them next to your tomatoes if you wish. And you can certainly use the blossoms as handsome garnishes. But for edible marigolds, concentrate on the particular species commonly called either signet (from its former scientific name *Tagetes signata*) or gem marigold—same thing.

Marigold Basics. Signet marigolds are so different from the familiar garden marigolds that you might think they were an entirely different plant. Rather than puffy pompom flowers, the blossoms of signet marigolds are single (just one layer of petals) and quite small, usually about a half inch. These plants are incredible bloomers, absolutely covered with flowers from summer on into fall. The flowers have a warm spicy taste that has often been compared to tarragon's. And rather than the sharp, acrid smell of most marigold foliage, signets have a very pleasant lemony fragrance that is most apparent when you brush your hand over the soft, lacy leaves.

The plants maintain a small, tidy, well-rounded shape, and with their masses of flowers make a wonderful filler for your containers. Because of their restrained size, they're particularly good candidates for window boxes.

Planting. If you can find transplants of signet marigolds in your garden center, plant them into your containers, following the general directions in Chapter 5, as soon as freezing weather has passed. You may, however, have more luck finding (or ordering) seeds.

Start seeds indoors (see Chapter 5)

three to four weeks before your spring frost date. You can also simply wait until the outdoor weather is warm and sow seeds directly into your containers. The seeds germinate readily, but you'll have to keep the area moist and clear of other plants in the meantime.

Success with Marigolds. This is such an easy plant, it's hard to imagine anything going wrong unless you totally forget to water. For maximum success, place signet marigolds in a sunny spot and keep the dead flowers picked off. Otherwise, just enjoy.

Harvesting. Nothing to it: just snip off the flower heads whenever you need them. The more you snip, the more new flowers you'll have.

Varieties. Most of the signet marigolds found in seed catalogs are part of the Gem strain: **Lemon Gem, Golden Gem, Tangerine Gem.** The differences, as you might imagine, are in the color of the flowers, and the colors are just what you'd expect from the names: butter yellow, golden yellow, and yellow-orange. One mail-order company offers a cultivar named **Starfire,** with bicolor flowers. You may find other varieties; just be sure you're ordering seeds of *Tagetes tenuifolia* or *T. signata* (same thing).

Cooking with Marigolds. Because of their flavor (spicy rather than sweet) and their color (in the yellow/orange range), signet marigolds work best with entrees, vegetables, and salads rather than desserts.

Butterfly Heaven

Sitting quietly on your patio on a warm summer's afternoon, you may be visited by one of nature's loveliest, most graceful creatures, the butterfly.

Butterflies, like honeybees and some birds, subsist on the nectar they collect from flowers. They are enchanting guests: they don't make noise, they aren't going to sting you, and they aren't spooked by your presence. They alight gently on flowers, unselfconsciously displaying their beautiful coloration, then gently move on.

Many of the plants that are especially attractive to butterflies are not edible, and thus are not included in this book. But butterflies do have an affinity for signet marigolds, one more reason for adding these comely little flowers to your container garden.

■ Use as a garnish for mixed green salads, potato salad, or pasta salad.

■ Toss in with steamed or sautéed vegetables such as yellow and green zucchini or green beans.

■ The rich red of cooked beets is even more brilliant when a few golden yellow flowers are added at the last minute.

■ Accent chicken dishes with signet marigold flowers (tarragon is a classic herb with chicken, and as we've said, many people think signet marigolds have a tarragon-like taste).

Note: the white area at the base of the petal is very bitter tasting; cut it off before adding flower petals to your cooking.

Edible Flowers

Nasturtiums

GROW AS: **annuals**

PLANT SIZE: **6 to 12 inches high (dwarf types); 6 feet or more (trailing types)**

START WITH: **seeds**

HARVEST SEASON: **summer into early fall**

SUN REQUIREMENTS: **full to part sun**

MINIMUM SOIL DEPTH: **6 inches**

Robust taste, knockout color, and fast, easy growth—if ever there was a perfect candidate for the three-star general of the edible-flower realm, it's nasturtiums.

This is one of the few edible flowers whose taste contributes as much to foods as does its color. In fact, all parts of this gorgeous plant are edible: the leaves, the flowers, and the seeds. The leaves and flowers have a strong, peppery taste that will remind you of watercress.

Nasturtium Basics. Garden nasturtiums come in two basic types:

those that climb upward (or trail downward), and those that stay in relatively compact mounds (sometimes listed as "dwarf"). Just to complicate matters, there's a middle ground described in some catalogs as "cascading mounds." There are other variables you will want to consider—color and shape of flower, leaf color—but the question of growth habit comes first. If you're planning a large combination container with a trellis full of bright orange nasturtiums as a tall backdrop, and you inadvertently plant one of the compact dwarf types, you will never have what you want. Similarly, if you mistakenly plant a trailing vine in a small, low container, it will eventually puddle its growth all over the floor rather than forming the neat mound you intended.

Planting. Nasturtiums are one of those plants that do not transplant terribly well, so your best bet is to plant seeds directly into their ultimate container. The seeds are large and easy to handle, so it's simple to place them exactly where you want. Do it as early in the spring as possible, as soon as the danger of heavy frost is past. Seeds germinate quickly and grow fast. If you live in warm climates, with very mild winters, fall plantings will give you bright flowers in early spring.

Maggie says: One year I started the garden season with several packets of nasturtium seeds in different colors, and no good long-term plan about where each would ultimately go. I know that nasturtiums do best when direct-seeded, but I wasn't ready for that. So in April I started seeds in expandable peat pellets (see Chapter 5). This meant that I (1) did not miss the ideal planting time and (2) bought myself some time to figure out what to do later.

Nasturtiums have the happy habit of dropping their seeds onto the ground at the end of the season and then coming up next year without any effort from you. This is of course most noticeable in full-size, traditional gardens; in container gardens, the seeds could fall onto the sidewalk or patio floor rather than onto fertile soil. But if you are growing nasturtiums in a large container, you might notice some babies poking up next spring.

Success with Nasturtiums.

These bright, cheerful flowers are extremely easy to grow. They are at their best in coolish temperatures, so don't be surprised if they seem to shut down when the weather is very hot. For that reason they will appreciate some light shade in the hottest regions, although as a general rule these are full-sun plants.

For maximum success, keep these cautions in mind:

■ **Make sure the soil drains well.** In traditional gardens, nasturtiums do best in sandy soil. In your containers make sure you put them into soil that has lots of some supplement, such as perlite or vermiculite (see Chapter 5), that promotes drainage. Ideally, all your containers will have this kind of soil mixture, but if they do not, choose carefully which ones you use for nasturtiums.

■ **Go easy with the fertilizer.** Too much fertilizer promotes lots of leaf growth instead of flowers. Also, nasturtiums tolerate dry soil better than many garden flowers. Don't deliberately withhold water, but just keep this in mind as you're planning your garden: if life's chores get in the way, this is one plant that can go without water for a few days.

■ **Check regularly for aphids.** If there is a downside to nasturtiums, it is that they are attractive to aphids. Many traditional gardeners, in fact, grow nasturtiums as a trap crop, to draw aphids away from other plants. Check the undersides of leaves every day in hot weather, and take corrective action (see Chapter 6 for techniques) at first appearance. You may find it easier to simply snip off and discard the affected leaves; it won't hurt the plant.

Harvesting. Plucking a few leaves or flowers for tonight's salad is a simple matter of pinching them off the plant and washing them well. Be on the lookout for small insects deep inside the blossoms.

What's in a Name?

We are fascinated by the intriguing origins of plant names, and the nasturtium story is particularly interesting.

The word *nasturtium* is derived from two Latin words: *nasus,* meaning "nose," and *tortus,* meaning "twisted or tortured." The two words together designate something that twists or tortures the nose, as would a plant with a strong smell.

But here's the intriguing part. It's not nasturtiums (the bright orange flowers) that bear the Latin name *Nasturtium,* but the salad herb we know as watercress. Its full scientific name is *Nasturtium officinale.* Ever had a watercress sandwich? That unmistakable strong, peppery bite is very similar to the taste of nasturtium leaves. So watercress, which twists the nose, is formally named *Nasturtium.*

Why aren't nasturtiums (the flowers), which also twist the nose, included in the *Nasturtium* genus? It appears that at one time they were, but Carl Linnaeus, the Swedish scientist who devised modern plant and animal classification, concluded that there was enough of a difference between the two to put the floral nasturtiums into a separate genus. And he gave it an equally intriguing name.

Tropaeolum, the genus to which nasturtiums belong, is derived from a Greek word that means "trophy." But not just any kind of trophy: it seems that ancient Greek warriors kept the helmets and shields of defeated enemies as spoils of war and displayed them by hanging them on a tree trunk, thus announcing their victory to all who passed by. That tree trunk, laden with peaked helmets and rounded, convex shields, was called a *tropaion,* or "battle trophy."

Some 1,800 years later, when Linnaeus happened upon a tree with a flowering plant growing up the trunk, he noted that the leaves were somewhat rounded and slightly convex, and that the bright orange flowers had a round shape tapering to a pronounced peak. Seeing those two shapes covering the tree trunk, he was reminded of the Greek soldiers' tradition, and named the flower in honor of the trophy tree.

Varieties. The classic nasturtium flower is bright orange, with a single layer of petals and a pronounced "tail," technically called a spur. But as you might imagine, with years of plant breeding and developing, that's only the beginning of the story. Today's nasturtiums have both single and double flowers, in an amazing array of colors. You can choose from tangerine, pale buttery yellow, salmon, scarlet, apricot, rosy red, and dark mahogany red, as well as the familiar pure orange or golden yellow. Some types are packaged in mixed colors; look for the word "mix" or some synonym. The graceful rounded leaves may be lime green, deep blue-green, or bright green splashed with white. Just be sure you read the seed packet or catalog description carefully, and determine whether you're getting a compact or trailing type.

The compact variety **Whirlybird** features large flowers that sit up on top of the leaves, for a very dramatic color display. Whirlybird comes in lots of colors, and is often packaged as a mix.

Empress of India is noteworthy for its striking coloring: dark blue-green leaves and deep red flowers. This variety is available as a compact, mounding type as well as a trailer.

Alaska features very unusual and very attractive variegated leaves: bright green splashed strongly with a rich, creamy white. Flowers may be yellow, orange, cherry red, salmon, or crimson; also packaged as a mix.

Peach Melba was named for the famous dessert because of the flower coloration: petals are the soft yellow of peach flesh, with a raspberry red splash at the flower's throat.

Cooking with Nasturtiums.

Because the taste is so assertive, so distinctive, nasturtiums should be reserved for dishes where their peppery tang will not startle the tastebuds—tossed salads, for instance. As we have become more adventurous in our choice of salad greens, the leaves and flowers of nasturtiums fit right in. Here are some other ideas.

■ Use nasturtium flowers to garnish deviled eggs and potato salads.

■ Toss individual petals and finely chopped leaves into cold pasta salads.

■ Chop flower petals and add to cold soups such as vichyssoise or avocado bisque; garnish each serving with one whole flower.

■ Just for the sheer beauty of it, line the edge of a round or oval serving platter with nasturtium leaves. Their round, softly scalloped shape makes a lovely background for a mounded rice dish, lightly steamed yellow squash, or tomato aspic.

■ For a summertime luncheon, assemble individual salads designed in concentric circles. First lay down a base of nasturtium leaves, then an outer ring of sliced red or orange tomatoes, then a ring of cucumber slices, and an inner ring of sliced yellow tomatoes. For the centers, steam, chill, and hollow out whole pattypan squashes and stuff with tuna salad, egg salad, or tabbouleh, garnished with one perfect nasturtium blossom. Drizzle a vinaigrette dressing made with nasturtium vinegar (see pages 257 to 259) over all.

■ The notion of combining herbs and spices with fruits is well established in Mediterranean countries. One delicious dessert is fresh peach halves baked on a bed of crushed peppercorns, with a bit of sugar and a splash of lemon juice. It sounds startling until you taste it. To continue the theme, add petals of Peach Melba nasturtiums to the baking dish at the last minute, and top each serving with whole flowers.

■ Create your own special main-dish garnishes using individual nasturtium leaves topped with a small dab of some condiment appropriate to the entrée: horseradish sauce, mustard-cranberry relish, shredded carrots dressed with nasturtium vinaigrette, balls of herb butter. Choose the smaller leaves, and look for ones that are lightly cupped.

Theme Garden

A Royal Feast

Here is a wonderful, simple combination for a container with a trellis: Purple Peacock **pole beans** growing up the trellis, with Empress of India **nasturtiums** trailing down over the edges of the container. All summer long, this garden delights with a changing show of beautiful colors: blue-green, scarlet red, soft mauve, deep burgundy, bright green.

All bean plants are rather skimpy and sparse looking at the base. In this planter, trailing nasturtiums, all parts of which are edible, fill in the blah space and then tumble over the edge with their beautiful leaves and blazing flowers. (By the way, trailing nasturtiums are also climbers, and they will climb up the trellis along with the beans if you turn your back.)

The glory of this combination is the rich, regal colors, and that is why we have called it a royal feast. The nasturtium flowers are a deep, glowing scarlet red, set off nicely against blue-green foliage. The beans give a double dose of color: first the flowers (which are edible) in shades of soft purple and lilac, then the beans themselves, with rich, dark purple pods. When you harvest them for dinner, be ready for a surprise: once they hit boiling water, the purple pods turn green. Children love this little chemistry lesson.

Nasturtiums do better if you plant the seeds directly in the container; do that in early spring after all danger of frost has passed. If for some reason you weren't able to plant seeds, using small nasturtium transplants later in the season is a possibility, assuming you can find them in the garden center at that point, but they won't have the same vigor.

You'll need a strong trellis arrangement to support the beans; see page 40 for several ideas. Plant four or five bean seeds in front of each vertical member of the trellis as soon as the weather is warm (nighttime temperatures around 60°F).

Once the beans have passed their peak, cut down slightly on your watering and fertilizing, and the nasturtiums, which will last on into fall, will produce more flowers.

For details on
growing the plants in
this garden, see

Beans, page 81
Nasturtiums, page 376

Edible Flowers

Pansies, Violas, and Violets

GROW AS: **annuals or perennials**

PLANT SIZE: **4 to 12 inches, depending on type**

START WITH: **transplants or seeds**

HARVEST SEASON: **spring and fall**

SUN REQUIREMENTS: **full sun to shade, depending on type**

MINIMUM SOIL DEPTH: **3 inches**

Sweet, delicate blossoms that add color and quiet grace to your containers—that's the essence of these three closely related flowers. They bloom early in the spring, when a gardener's soul is more than ready for flowers. Then, as the first tinge of winter approaches, a new planting gives more flowers just when other things in the garden are shutting down. Many have a hauntingly sweet fragrance, and the palette of colors they offer is broad and varied enough to enhance almost any container combination the gardener's eye can imagine, or any dish the cook can create. To delight students of history and folklore, these plants are the subject of many charming tales and legends. And besides all that, the flowers themselves have an appealing look that can only be described as cute.

Viola Basics. In this chapter we have grouped together three plants with a very close botanical relationship. Even though we know them by three different common names, they all belong to the same genus— *Viola*—and share the same growing needs. So close is their connection, they are sometimes confused with one another. Knowing scientific names comes in handy.

Pansies (*Viola wittrockiana*) constitute the largest group of these three cousins. You know what pansies look like, but you may not realize just how many cultivars there are, in every color of the rainbow, and in both solid hues and multicolored patterns of all types. Some display a pattern of darker splotches near the center of the blossom that with a bit of imagination looks like a face; many children think they look like kitten faces.

Violas (*Viola cornuta*) look like pansies, except they are smaller; while some pansy flowers are as big as teacups, violas are about the size of a nickel. They are also hardier than pansies and more readily withstand cold weather. At your garden center, you'll probably find that the range of color choices is more limited.

Johnny-jump-ups are in fact a separate species (*Viola tricolor*), but we include them with violas because they are so similar in size and growth habit. As you might imagine from the Latin name, each flower has three colors: purple, yellow, and white.

Violas give us another lesson in the fickleness of common names. As with dianthus, the genus name has come to be the common name of *one* species in that genus. You can drive yourself nuts with this—all violas are *Violas* but not all *Violas* are violas—or you can simply accept it and get on with life.

Violets are easy to recognize. In all likelihood the flowers you call violets are the species *Viola odorata,* known as sweet violets. There are other violet species, but they are less commonly offered in retail nurseries. Violets may be purple, blue-violet, pink, or white. Keep in mind that, unlike pansies and violas, which are typically considered annuals, violets come back every year. (African violets, by the way, are *not* related to violets; don't eat them.)

Planting. Pansies and violas are usually grown as annuals, and are easy to start from seed. In winter and early spring, start seeds indoors, following the general instructions in Chapter 5. When seedlings are about 2 inches tall, transplant them into outdoor containers. This will give you a rich crop of pansies for your spring garden. If you also want a second crop for fall and winter, you can start seeds indoors or out. If outdoors, we recommend using a separate container as a propagator, since your mixed containers are going full blast with tomatoes or cucumbers and may not have room for tiny seedlings.

Or you can take the simpler route and buy small plants at the garden center; they are widely available in both spring and fall. The trade-offs are the usual ones: ordering seeds gives you access to many more varieties; buying started plants saves work. If you decide to buy plants, wait until they are showing their flowers so you can see what color you'll be getting.

With violets, which are perennial, you will most likely start with transplants, either from a retail or mail-order nursery, or from a friend's garden. Violets multiply by sending out underground runners, and eventually will spread to cover an entire area with their sweet little flowers and lovely leaves. Anyone who has planted violets in a traditional garden will have, after a few years, a veritable violet factory, and will probably be pleased to give you a few babies. Every gardener knows instinctively that sharing plants is good karma.

Johnny-jump-ups also grow readily from seed, whether you plant seeds or not. They get the jaunty name from their habit of vigorous self-sowing (coming up next year from seeds

What's in a Name?

Johnny-jump-up, the little viola with the energetic name, has been known by many other fanciful epithets. In some cases the reason for the name is obvious; in others, it's anybody's guess.

Herb trinity (from its three colors)

Heartsease (used medicinally in the Middle Ages)

Monkey faces (some think the markings resemble the faces of kittens, some think people, why not monkeys?)

Love-in-sun-flower (Shakespeare used this)

Peeping Tom

Love-in-idleness

Meet-her-in-the-entry-kiss-her-in-the-buttery

dropped this year), often quite some distance away. This is more noticeable in traditional gardens, where there is ample soil to receive the migrating seeds, but if you have several large containers, don't be surprised if next year some of these Johnnys jump up in a neighboring pot.

When planting, keep in mind that pansies, violas, and Johnny-jump-ups will grow nicely in either sun or partial shade; violets need some shade, and grow best either in a northern exposure or underneath larger plants.

Success with Pansies, Violas, and Violets.
With these three cousins, success is largely a matter of timing. All flourish in coolish

weather, and then start to pout when it gets hot.

If you planted pansies or violas in the spring, don't be surprised if they look bedraggled by mid summer, with long, lanky stems and increasingly puny flowers. At that point you have two choices: (1) you can prune them very heavily, cutting back almost to the soil line (which means you are sacrificing any remaining flowers), and hope they will regenerate when the fall weather comes; or (2) you can rip them out completely and buy new ones at the end of summer. If winters are mild in your area, these fall-planted pansies will often carry through to next spring, and will surprise you with delicious color in March or April.

Because pansies and violas are so widely available and are on the market in both spring and fall, it's easy to pick up one or two and tuck them into a container or window box wherever you have a bare spot. They'll never get to be an ungainly size, and when they start to get scraggly they're easy to replace. In other words, they are the perfect plants for quick-in-and-out treatment, adding bright color and perhaps fragrance just when you need it.

Violets are another story. They bloom very early (February or March) and then cease producing flowers; but unlike pansies, the plants retain a tidy, compact shape between bloom times. The leaves are small, heart-shaped, and sometimes richly colored with red undersides; so that even when they're not blooming, violets are sweet little plants. Rather than treating them as in-and-out plants, you're better off

Napoleon's Violets

With their shy, secretive appearance, their heartbreakingly delicate aroma, and their habit of blooming so early in the year, violets have captured the imagination through the ages, playing a central role in many myths, legends, and historical anecdotes. Consider, for instance, the emperor Napoleon.

In May 1814, having suffered a series of military and political defeats, Napoleon was forced into exile on the small Mediterranean island of Elba. He urged his supporters, scattered around France, to continue the struggle, pledging to them that he would "return with the violets"; in other words, in February. Napoleon loyalists adopted the violet as their emblem, the symbol by which they recognized one another; in their secret meetings, they referred to their leader as Caporal Violet—Corporal Violet.

Napoleon kept his word. On February 26, 1815, he secretly left the island and returned to Paris, where he raised new armies and began the military campaign historians call the Hundred Days, a campaign that ended with his final defeat at Waterloo.

letting them stay in place year after year, the better to woo you with their springtime fragrance.

All three plants yearn for rich, moist soil (imagine the floor of a dense forest: cool, damp, shady, with a thick layer of decaying leaves). In your containers, this means a regular program of watering and fertilizing. Deadhead regularly. And that's really all you need to be concerned with until the summer doldrums arrive, for in most respects these are carefree plants.

Harvesting. It's the flowers that you will use in cooking, so harvesting is a simple matter of picking them as needed, which has the extra benefit of encouraging the plant to keep producing more blossoms.

This triumvirate of flowers lends itself well to several methods of preservation. Pansies and violas, because they are essentially flat, are good candidates for flower pressing; violets can be candied (see page 180) or made into syrup (see page 387).

Varieties. Let's start with violets, because there are fewer choices. For blossoms in a rich, classic purple, a good choice is **Royal Robe.** For pink flowers, look for **Rosina. White Czar** has, as you can guess, pure white flowers, and there is also a plain **Czar,** with bright blue flowers. If you're lucky enough to have a friend with a garden bed full of violets, and your friend offers to share, you may end up with a variety whose name you don't know; but you will know the color of the flowers, and furthermore you'll have a treasure from the heart—and that is always better.

Violas, remember, are like miniature pansies but come in fewer colors. Like pansies, viola blossoms may be all one color or multicolored, although

Myths and Folklore

In the language of flowers, pansies stand for thoughts, as in "You are in my thoughts." In fact, the flower is named after the French word *pensée,* which means "thoughts," or "ideas." Many who see the shape of a face in the common pansy markings interpret it as the face of someone deep in thought.

Violets, with their small flowers so often hidden under the foliage, represent modesty.

In Roman mythology, we find the story of how the violet got its name. It seems that Jupiter, the god of all the universe, had fallen in love with the lovely Io (her name was the diminutive of the Greek name Ione, which is Viola in Latin). When Jupiter's wife Juno found out, she threatened to have her rival put to death. To save Io, Jupiter changed her into a white heifer, and caused small purple flowers to spring up wherever she stepped to give her sustenance. These flowers he named violets, the diminutive of Viola, the Roman version of his beloved's name.

---

solid colors are more common. Here are two examples from a recent catalog. The flowers of the aptly named **Cuty** are a cheerful mix of purple, blue, and white petals with yellow eyes. A charming new introduction is **Sorbet,** which comes in half a dozen solid colors in pastel tones, with names like **Lemon Chiffon** and **Lavender Ice.**

Pansies have almost as many colors, shades, and tints as a paint store. Browsing through just one catalog, we found them in solid white, orange, yellow, gold, red, tangerine, mahogany, blue, purple, lavender, pink, and a purple so dark it was practically black. And we found color combinations almost beyond counting: magenta and white, light pink and dark pink, rose red and dark red, yellow and brick red, purple and gold and white, orange and yellow, blue and yellow, and on and on.

In addition to specific colors and color combinations, seed companies offer mixed packets of viola and pansy seeds; look for a word like "mix," "mixture," or "blend" in the name. With these seeds, you never know for sure what color flower any one plant will produce until it blooms. That's either a charming surprise or a color-scheme disappointment, depending on your outlook.

Since color is really the whole point of adding pansies and violas to your containers, you may find it makes more sense to simply cruise the aisles of your favorite garden center and choose whatever colors fit into your plans, without regard for their specific names. Buy plants that are already showing a blossom or two, and you'll know the color for sure. You will also be able to tell whether the flower is fragrant. Not all pansies are, but it's a delightful bonus.

Cooking with Pansies, Violas, and Violets. All three of these

flowers add a great boost of color and visual charm to your dishes. Taste is secondary to looks, but because the palette of possibilities is so broad, you can add pansies (and, to a lesser extent, violas) as a garnish to just about any dish, and create something lovely and memorable.

Here are a few ideas to get you started:

▩ Make flower-filled ice cubes from yellow and purple violas (see page 372 for instructions) and use them in lemonade.

▩ The next time you make oven-fried chicken, add lots of paprika to your crumb mixture so that the cooked chicken has a rich orangey color. Serve on a white platter, encircled with large dark blue pansies.

▩ A colorful, healthy appetizer: yogurt–cream cheese dip with lots of chopped herbs, garnished with small-flowered red or pink pansies, surrounded with toasted slices of French bread, which are in turn garnished with large pansies in the same colors.

▩ For a September ice-cream party: purchase several flavors of ice cream, frozen yogurt, and sorbet; go for color variation. Scoop out ice cream balls, lay them out on a cookie sheet or large plastic tray, and freeze. Set out bowls of pansies and violas in as many different colors as you can manage. (At other times of the year, you can substitute or add other flowers.) At party time, pile the ice-cream balls into a large, prechilled glass bowl and invite guests to dig in.

The fun is combining flower petals and different flavors of ice cream.

If some of the ice cream remains in the bowl, it will eventually melt into a multicolored, multiflavored slush. Don't let it go to waste. Shred any remaining flowers into bits and throw them in, and add ginger ale or seltzer for a farewell punch.

▩ Violets, either candied or plain, are a classic way to beautify petits fours for the tea tray. Directions for candying violets are on page 180, but you can also purchase them ready-made in specialty bakeries and confectionery shops.

▩ There is no cake decoration more beautiful than a ring of brilliantly colored pansies against white or pale pastel icing.

Sweet Violet Nectar

The flowers of violets are too soon gone, but their seductive fragrance can be preserved in violet syrup, which is easy to make.

Fill a glass jar or bowl with a handful or two of flowers. Cover with boiling water. Let steep for several hours or overnight, then strain.

The liquid will be pale green. Add lemon juice, drop by drop, and it will gradually turn pink.

Measure the water, and add twice that amount of granulated sugar. Simmer over low heat until the sugar is thoroughly melted. Remove from heat, cool, and transfer to glass bottles for storage. Use violet syrup to sweeten and color beverages, but don't overdo it as it functions as a mild natural laxative.

I n a time long ago, when gods and goddesses walked the earth disguised as mortals, a beautiful maiden named Persephone caught the
eye of Hades, the god of the Underworld. As she strolled through a
meadow picking wildflowers, Persephone felt the earth open up
beneath her feet when she reached for a particularly lovely flower.
Out of the opening thundered the fierce Hades, who grabbed Persephone,
threw her into his chariot, and disappeared back into the abyss.

Persephone was the daughter of Zeus, the greatest of all Greek gods,
and Demeter, the goddess of agriculture. In
despair over the loss of her daughter, the
grieving Demeter neglected her duty to provide for the spring crops, and before long the
entire populace was threatened with famine.
Zeus, concerned for the welfare of his sub-
jects, intervened with Hades and negotiated
for Persephone's return, but Hades would not
let her leave permanently.

Theme Garden
A Green Spring-time

It was arranged that Persephone would
be allowed to return to the earth and be
reunited with her mother for half the year,
and that she would spend the other half in the Underworld. This is why
each spring, when the goddess of agriculture is filled with joy at her
daughter's return, seeds sprout and break through the earth's crust and
green plants begin to grow, only to die and return underground in winter.

This garden celebrates the legend of Persephone with a glorious
burst of early springtime vegetables and flowers.

In a medium to large container with a trellis, sow seeds of climbing
peas, either snap peas or English peas, or a mix of both. Sow the seeds
close to the bottom of the trellis, and plant them as early in spring as you
possibly can—as soon as the soil is neither frozen solid nor totally waterlogged. Here in the Pacific Northwest, we use Presidents' Day as our
pea-planting rule of thumb. In parts of the Northeast, St. Patrick's Day
serves the same purpose.

All around the surface of the potting soil, set out small plants of several
kinds of **lettuce,** as well as any other spring greens that catch your fancy.
You may have started them from seed in February or March, or purchased
transplants from the garden center. Incorporate contrasting colors and textures into this garden understory by planting several different varieties,

including some of the cut-and-come-again types and mesclun blends.

Intermingle spring **pansies** among the lettuce plants. For a soft springtime color scheme, choose small-flowered pansies in pastel blue or pink.

Add one or more clumps of **chives.** Their spiky green leaves appear early in spring, a perky sign of the delicious taste to come; later in the spring, their lavender pom-pom flowers will accentuate the colors of the pansies.

Except for the chives, all these plants are cool-season annuals and will die—or seriously pout—once summer weather arrives. At that point we recommend that you remove all the spring plants and replace them with

summer-loving ones (one possibility: the Romeo and Juliet garden on pages 188 to 190). Work carefully around the chives because you want to maintain them for future years. Next spring, when the first tiny shoots shoulder up through the soil, remember to thank Persephone.

For details on
growing the plants in
this garden, see

Chives, page 191
Lettuce, page 109
Pansies, page 382
Peas, page 125

Edible Flowers

Roses

GROW AS: **perennials**

PLANT SIZE: **1 to 3 feet**

START WITH: **plants**

HARVEST SEASON: **summer**

SUN REQUIREMENTS: **full sun**

MINIMUM SOIL DEPTH: **12 inches**

Roses have been the world's most beloved flower since practically the beginning of time, and they are worthy of the passionate affection they inspire.

But can roses really be grown in containers? Yes, as long as you choose the right ones. If the word *rose* calls forth a mental picture of a single long-stemmed beauty, one perfect flower at the end of a long stem, nestled in with 11 others in a shiny white florist's box, then you'll need to expand your horizons and become acquainted with the various categories of roses.

Rose Basics. Roses have existed on earth in their wild form for millions of years, and they have been grown by mankind for pleasure and for healing for at least 5,000 of those years. When early humans began to cultivate the wild roses that grew around them, they set in motion a process of floriculture that eventually led to the development of many new strains of roses, and that continues to this day.

A seminal date in rose history is 1867, when the first hybrid tea rose was unveiled in France. Today, rose fanciers use that year as the beginning of what are referred to as "modern" roses; all types of roses in existence before that date are "old" roses, many of which are enjoying a well-deserved surge in popularity. The 1867 date is significant for us because the roses recommended for container growing are all modern types.

The number of rose varieties increased exponentially after 1867, as breeders around the world found enthusiastic customers for everything they could come up with. Today there are more than 20,000 different roses; to make discussion simpler, they are grouped into categories. Depending on which professional you ask, there are between 20 and 35 categories, and there is still honest debate about where the dividing lines are. (The final word on the matter belongs to the American Rose Society; see page 399.)

To choose an appropriate rose for your container, concentrate on the following four categories.

The first category we recommend for containers is the **polyantha,** which means "many flowers."

The first polyantha roses hit the market in the late nineteenth century, and since then hundreds of cultivars have been introduced. Polyanthas are distinguished by their bloom pattern: large clusters of many small flowers at the ends of their stems. They tend to be smaller plants overall, which makes them ideal for our purposes. Another wonderful feature: they bloom continuously all summer long.

Another significant development welcomed enthusiastically by container gardeners is the **miniature** rose. This type is just what you would imagine from the name: a miniaturized version of a classic rosebush. Some plants are so tiny they could fit in a teacup, but the standard size is around 1 foot. Miniatures show the complete range of flower shapes seen in full-size plants, they come in every rose color known, and many new ones are introduced every year. And for something that seems so fairylike and dainty, they are surprisingly hardy.

A third category of special interest to container gardeners is the **patio** rose. This is something of an in-betweener: larger than miniatures, smaller than polyanthas. Patio roses are generally between 1 and 2 feet tall, form a nicely shaped mound, and bloom heavily. As a category, patio roses are better known in England than in the United States, but some of the larger mail-order nurseries now carry a good selection. In 1999, the American Rose Society adopted a new category it calls mini-flora, which comprises plants that in size are midway between floribundas (the next step up from polyanthas) and miniatures. As a practi-cal matter, we think of patio roses and mini-floras as being quite similar.

Finally, there are **ground cover** roses. They spread out horizontally and stay relatively low to the ground—the classic definition of a ground cover—and that makes them perfect for containers, especially if you like the idea of roses tumbling over the sides. You may find ground cover roses in well-stocked retail garden centers, but more likely in mail-order catalogs of rose growers.

Planting. The roses you purchase at the garden center, as well as from mail-order suppliers, will probably be packaged as bare-root plants (see page 290). The best time to plant them, in general, is spring. That is when you're most likely to find them for sale in retail nurseries, and most mail-order nurseries schedule their shipping dates so that plants arrive at your best planting time. The exception is miniatures: they are almost always sold as potted plants, which means they can be planted at any time; also, some mail-order nurseries ship all their roses in pots.

To plant bare-root roses, follow the general directions on page 290. We've seen good results from fortifying the potting soil with compost mixed in at the bottom (roses are heavy feeders). The process is this: fill the container about one-fourth full with potting soil, add a layer of compost to about the one-third level, and mix them together very well. If you can't find a good source for compost, use slow-release fertilizer granules (see Chapter 5) and stir them into your potting mix before planting. You might also add some hydrogel crystals (roses are also heavy

Roses Not for Containers

Once you begin noticing the many types of roses in display gardens and mail-order catalogs, it is easy to become infected with the dread gardeners' disease "gimme-itis." They all look so gorgeous (that is, after all, the point of the beautiful photos) that we want every single one.

Resist. It may be true that a rose is a rose is a rose, but not when it comes to container gardening. The types described here are best enjoyed in your municipal rose garden or a friend's yard.

Old Roses. All the varieties known and grown before 1867, including those that have been reintroduced in recent years. Although old roses are getting a great deal of attention these days, and although it is true that their fragrance and taste are superior to those of many modern roses, most of them are simply too large for containers. Enjoy reading about them, and enjoy them in someone else's garden.

Species Roses. This is an all-purpose term meaning types that grow wild, or varieties propagated from wild roses that retain all the original characteristics. One popular species rose that comes highly recommended for culinary purposes is the rugosa rose (*Rosa rugosa*), but unfortunately its growth habit is too lusty for containers.

The following are modern roses that for one reason or another are not appropriate for containers.

Hybrid Teas. The long-stemmed beauties that you send your sweetie on Valentine's Day are hybrid teas. They win blue ribbons at rose competitions and they make lovers swoon, but they don't flourish in containers, and they particularly don't like anything else nestled nearby, so they don't work well in container combinations.

Shrub Roses. This is an all-purpose term for roses that grow into large shrubs, with beautiful arching sprays of flowers. They are vigorous, hardy, and sturdy, and they make wonderful hedges and dramatic accents in the landscape. But they won't work in containers; most are at least 6 feet tall and wide, and many are larger still.

Grandifloras. A modern rose category known for its vigorous growth and large size; that's why "grand" is in the name, and that's your cue that these roses are too large for successful container growing.

Here are two modern rose types that might possibly work, with some extra attention from you.

Floribundas. For our purposes, floribundas belong in the marginal range. They are smaller than grandifloras, but larger than polyanthas. This means you'll have to study the catalog descriptions carefully, looking for specific floribunda cultivars that are relatively small for their class.

Climbing Roses. Roses do not climb naturally in the same way that pole beans do, winding their stems around a support; gardeners have to help them by tying the stems onto a strong trellis or some other kind of support. It is possible to grow climbing roses in containers, but you must realize what you're getting into. While there are a few climbing varieties that are relatively small, most climbers are large, vigorous plants that will overwhelm the trellis and swamp your container. So unless you have room for a very sturdy trellis or a way to let the rose gambol over the side of your house or up a tree, a climbing rose would not be a good choice. Unless, that is, you are willing to keep the size under control by constantly pruning the new growth, which pretty much defeats the original purpose.

drinkers). Then continue as described for all bare-root plants.

Planting roses that come in nursery containers is just like planting anything else from containers, but remember to incorporate extra fertilizer and hydrogel into the potting soil first.

Keep in mind that your rose will be in the container for many years. This will affect your choice of pots in terms of size (except for miniatures, large is better than small) and material (stay away from short-lived pots). It also means that you'll need to give some thought to what else goes in the same container. Either combine roses with other perennials so you never have to dig into the soil, or, if you wish to plant annuals, choose those with very shallow roots so you won't disturb the root system of the rose when planting the annuals.

Success with Roses. Mention your interest in growing roses, and you'll hear horror stories about how temperamental they are, how hard they are to grow, how much work they entail, and so forth. We readily admit that roses are not as easy as, say, daylilies, but neither are they worthy of the bad rap they too often get.

Watering. Even in the ground in a traditional garden, roses need lots of water. In containers, which dry out much faster, they are especially vulnerable. Roses must never be allowed to dry out completely. Adding hydrogel crystals will help, but you still need to check the soil faithfully; in summer, you may have to water roses every single day. Don't skimp, and don't get careless.

How you water is also important. Water the soil directly, and don't water from above; the idea is not to get the leaves wet. Damp leaves lead to mildew, black spot, and rust—fungal diseases that thrive in cool, damp environments. It's preferable to water in the morning, so the sun has a chance to dry away any dampness during the day. If life's circumstances force you to do your watering in the evening, be especially careful not to wet the leaves.

Fertilizing. Roses by their nature need lots of nutrients; however, because of all the watering you are doing, you're continuously washing away the nutrients in the potting mixture. The solution, happily, is simple: fertilize frequently to replace lost nutrients.

A high-blooming plant such as a rose needs a complete fertilizer that is a bit higher in phosphorus (the middle number). Any general flower fertilizer with a ratio close to 1:2:1 (see Chapter 5) will work, although many gardeners prefer to use one of the commercial fertilizers specially formulated for roses. While the rose is actively blooming, apply fertilizer once a week. Begin to taper off in mid August, and stop altogether as soon as the leaves drop.

Pruning. We prune any plant for two purposes: to promote its health by removing diseased or problematic limbs, and to control its shape by directing its growth. Both are important for roses, but even more important is a related phenomenon: in plants that flower in the way many roses do, pruning for shape has the extra effect of promoting the production of flowers.

Here's how it works. Speaking in very general terms, roses produce their blossoms out at the end of the stem (in roses it's called a cane), rather than all along the stem as some flowering plants do. Also, speaking very generally, roses start growing each spring at the point where they stopped growing the previous year. Left to their own devices, then, the canes just keep getting longer and longer each year, so that eventually you have a very silly-looking plant with long, spindly stems and a few lonesome flowers at the ends.

Pruning is what keeps that from happening.

In your mind's eye, picture a yardstick and then imagine it is a rose cane. All along the cane, every few inches, there are buds that represent potential new stems; in the spring, as the plant comes to life after winter dormancy, those buds start to thicken. Pick a spot on the virtual yardstick where you want new stems to begin, and imagine cutting just above the bud that is closest to that spot. If your cut is at the 12-inch mark, then the one or two buds just below that point will form new canes, and flowers will form at the end of those canes. The first 12 inches from the soil line will be bare, except perhaps for some leaves. If you choose to cut lower down, at the 6-inch mark, say, then your rosebush will have bare stems for 6 inches, then new canes and flowers.

Now convert that imaginary yardstick into a real stem; even though it may not be as perfectly straight as a yardstick, the concept remains: prune back last year's growth to the point where you want this year's growth to begin. You won't have a rose where you make your cut; you'll have the start of a new cane.

Keep these principles in mind:

1. Pruning stimulates growth. The buds immediately below the cut open, and new growth follows.

2. In most cases, pruning is best done in the spring. Because pruning stimulates growth (see Principle 1), you don't want to do it just as the weather is starting to turn cool, or the tender new growth will freeze.

The Language of Roses

In Victorian England, chaste young ladies and their suitors used floral bouquets to send each other messages of love. For this purpose many flowers and herbs were assigned special meanings, but it was the rose, that most storied of all flowers, that often carried the most complex, most subtle messages.

Red rose	I love you.
Red rosebud	You are pure and lovely.
White rose	I am worthy of you. We must keep our love a secret. I cannot accept your attentions.
Withered white rose	I know you have been unfaithful.
White rosebud	I am too young to be speaking of love.
Red and white roses together	Unity; we are together as one.
Yellow rose	I love someone else. My love for you has faded. I think of you as a friend. I am jealous of the one who has your affection. You have my heart; try to care for me.
Pink rose	You are a graceful, tender beauty.
Faded rose	Beauty is fleeting (a very versatile phrase, with multiple uses and interpretations).

Certain rose varieties carried very specific meanings. The centifolia, one of the old roses, meant "My heart is in flames." La France (the original hybrid tea rose, introduced in France in 1867) was very precise: "Meet me by moonlight."

Communications of the heart are, of course, ripe for misinterpretation, and we can only wonder how these young lovers managed to declare their true feelings when some of the flowers had more than one meaning. Then, as now, love was hard.

3. Choose a bud that is facing outward, rather than in toward the middle of the plant, and make your cut just above it.

The other reason for pruning, to remove diseased or problematic limbs, is psychologically easier. Whenever you see a stem that is obviously dead, cut it off at the soil line. Cut back any broken stems below the break. And anytime two stems cross and rub against each other, one of them has to go; remove the one that is pointing in toward the center of the plant, cutting at the soil line. Do this clean-up pruning first, and the strategy needed to prune for shape will be easier to see.

Weatherizing. Roses are tough plants, but they do need to be protected from extreme heat and extreme cold.

In very hot weather, the danger is to the roots, and the solution is to keep the soil as cool as possible. If convenient, move the container into the shade in the hottest part of the afternoon, but don't forget to move it back: roses need at least six hours of sun a day to bloom. A more convenient, and more permanent, solution is double-potting (see page 4). Place the container with the rose inside a larger container, fill the space between them with something like wood chips or moss, and keep that perpetually moist. The layer of insulation will protect the tender roots from overheating.

Double-potting requires planning. Since your original container is likely to be large and thus rather heavy, lifting it into another, still larger container will not be easy. If your summers are scorchers, it is wiser to create this double-pot arrangement *before* planting, and just leave it intact all year. The insulating layer will also help protect the soil against severe cold come wintertime.

Roses are vulnerable to freezing in areas with hard winters. In traditional gardens, the surrounding earth acts as insulation; in containers, there is no such protection. Where winters are bitterly cold, move the entire container into a more protected area, such as a garage or cool indoor room. If that's not possible, wrap the container in a thick blanket of insulating material (see page 288 for some suggestions) and move it to the most sheltered outdoor spot you have.

Pests and Diseases. The biggest insect problem you will have, if any, is probably aphids. They love the juicy buds of roses, so keep your eyes open as soon as the weather turns warm and the flower buds get fat. See Chapter 6 for controls.

Roses are more susceptible to diseases than most of the other flowers you might consider growing in containers, and that is probably the source of their bad reputation as picky plants. But none of these diseases is an automatic life sentence, and they're actually quite easy to get under control, especially if you take action at the first sign of trouble. In this regard you have an edge over traditional gardeners, since in containers roses are close at hand and right at eye level, and thus easy to monitor.

Three fungal diseases are the biggest problem for roses: black spot, rust, and mildew. Thanks to their very descriptive names, they're easy to recognize. Black spot causes small black spots on the leaves, ranging in size from a pinpoint to a pencil eraser. Rust shows up as a spatter of rusty red specks on the leaves. And mildew appears as a splotchy coating of gray powder all over the leaves and buds. In truth none of the three will kill your plant, and often you can get by with ignoring the whole thing—except they're ugly as sin, especially the mildew.

The best cure is prevention. First, realize that these diseases thrive in environments that are wet, cool, and thick with vegetation. Good air circulation is their enemy, so keep the roses

Rose Trivia

The rose has been a prominent part of civilized life for many centuries. It is probably inevitable, then, that so many fables, legends, and folktales should have attached themselves to this most favored flower. From the many fascinating tidbits, we share a few of our favorites.

In the time of early Christianity, rose petals were pulverized and mixed with water to make a paste, which was formed into beads and strung together as prayer beads. And that is why we call it a rosary.

Venus, the goddess of love, was hit by an arrow from Cupid's quiver and the drops of her red blood fell on a nearby flower. From that day to now, roses, especially red roses, have been the emblem of love.

The first time Marc Antony visited Cleopatra, she covered her floors with rose petals several inches deep so that he would stir up the fragrance, and be stirred in turn, as he came near her. In the Middle Ages, however, prostitutes were required to wear a rose in public so that all might recognize them; it was a mark of disgrace.

Venus appears in another legend about roses, concerning the symbolism of silence. It is said that Harpocrates, the god of silence, stumbled upon Venus making love with a handsome young mortal. To buy his silence, Cupid, her son, presented Harpocrates with the first rose ever seen.

In ancient Rome it was common knowledge that any discussion held under a rose was to be kept secret, and never repeated outside that room. Originally, a rose was suspended over the table where the participants were seated; later, roses were carved into the ceiling of the meeting room. The Latin phrase *sub rosa*, "under the rose," is still used to describe a secret communication.

---

and all surrounding plants pruned enough to promote airflow.

Many serious rose growers use a preventive spray every spring: a dormant spray that combines a horticultural oil with lime sulfur to smother insect eggs and fungus spores. A homemade, nontoxic alternative you can use for edible flowers is the baking-soda spray described on page 76.

If one of the Nasty Threesome shows up anyway, first of all remove the infected leaves and put them in the garbage. Then spray the plant thoroughly with the baking-soda solution, covering the tops and bottoms of all leaves; repeat every couple of days as needed.

Harvesting. Snip off the whole rose and its stem, so as not to leave an unsightly bare stem on the plant. Wash the flower carefully; roses, with their many folds of petals, are apt to collect dirt.

To use the petals individually, grasp the rose in one hand and cut the entire flower away from the base with scissors; make your cut high enough so that the bitter-tasting white heel at the base of the petals is left behind. (Then, of course, snip off the stem, for aesthetic reasons.)

Roses also dry beautifully, either an entire blossom or bud, or individual petals. The colors tend to darken, and the fragrance usually fades away, but it does mean you can have rose petals in wintertime. Dry them the same way you do herbs: spread individual petals out flat; hang whole flowers on stems upside down, just like herb bundles (see box on pages 170 to 171).

Any blossom left on the plant will eventually form a fruit, called a hip, about the size and shape of a cranberry. The fruits are attractive in their own right, and a favorite snack for birds. Rose hips are very high in vitamin C and, as you may already know, can be used to make a delicious caffeine-free herbal tea.

Varieties. One difficulty with suggesting specific cultivars of roses is that there are so many of them, with dozens more introduced every year. This year's favorite may be impossible to find next year, as growers develop new beauties and retailers succumb to their charms. It is with some trepidation, then, that we make our recommendations.

■ Polyantha
Angel Face (mauve, fragrant)
Cecile Brünner, a.k.a. **Sweetheart Rose** (light pink)
China Doll (deep pink)
Lovely Fairy (darker pink)
Margo Koster (orange-pink blend)
Perle d'Or, a.k.a. **Yellow Cecile Brünner** (yellow-orange)

The Fairy (light pink, cascading)
White Pet (white, fragrant)

■ Patio
Gourmet Popcorn (white with yellow centers)
Regensburg (deep red with white overlay)

■ Miniature
Winsome (lavender)
Jean Mermoz (pink)
Ralph Moore (red; 2000 ARS award winner)
Applause (orange-pink; 2000 ARS award winner)
Lemon Gems (yellow; 2000 ARS award winner)
Sweet Chariot (purple, fragrant)
Cinderella (white, fragrant)

■ Ground Cover
Arctic Sunrise (white)
Gourmet Pheasant (deep pink)
Minilights (yellow)
Robin Red Breast (dark red)

Some ground-cover roses attain a height of 2 to 3 feet, but others, including those suggested here, are much smaller plants.

Floribundas have a growth habit similar to that of polyanthas, but they are larger overall and so most are unsuitable for any but extremely large containers. Two that do work well in containers as they are smaller than most others in their category are **Margaret Merril** (white) and **Sunsprite** (yellow, very fragrant).

Perhaps the best advice we can give you is to acquire the catalogs of rose nurseries (see Appendix) and

Searching for the Perfect Rose

One way to go about choosing roses is to follow the guidance of the experts at the American Rose Society in Shreveport, Louisiana. Help from this highly respected nonprofit organization comes in two forms:

1. Every year, the ARS evaluates all roses commercially available in the United States, and assigns to each a numerical rating that reflects its overall quality. The ratings (grouped by rose categories) are presented in annual handbooks, along with lists of the top-rated roses in each category, Award of Excellence winners, and AARS winners (described below).

2. In addition to the numerical ratings, the ARS designates a few outstanding miniature roses to receive the Award of Excellence; any miniature from this list is an excellent candidate

for your container garden. A related nonprofit organization, All-America Rose Selection, chooses outstanding cultivars for its prestigious AARS winner award. Many are too large for containers, but any miniature or polyantha AARS winner would also be an excellent candidate.

The handbooks contain no photographs, so a really thorough search for the ideal rose is a two-step process: pick a few top-rated candidates from the ARS list, then use mail-order catalogs to see what they look like. The handbook can be purchased from the American Rose Society (see Appendix).

If you have Internet access, the ARS website (www.ars.org) is an astonishingly rich resource of rose information, including an explanation of the rating system and other publications of interest.

become acquainted with their offerings. Look at the photographs and read the descriptive details, paying close attention to what the growers say about the size of mature plants. AARS winners and ARS Awards of Excellence for Miniature Roses (see box above) are usually highlighted in the catalogs.

One small word of warning: you're likely to find inconsistencies in how individual roses are categorized; one grower may include a certain plant in the list of polyanthas, while another may put that same rose in with the patios, or even the miniatures. Don't let this worry you. In the long run, it doesn't really matter which category a rose is assigned to as

long as you're getting a plant that is an appropriate size for containers.

Shopping for roses via mail order offers several advantages: you get to see the newest cultivars; you get complete, dependable information about the size of the plant, which is critical for container gardeners; and it's a lot of fun.

Cooking with Roses. The citizens of ancient Rome, who knew how to throw a party, were especially fond of foods prepared with roses. They had rose wine, rose cakes and pastries, rose sauces for meats and game, and between courses they nibbled on rose petals sprinkled all over the banquet tables. For those of us who think we're ultrahip by incorporating fresh flowers into our cuisine, it's rather humbling to realize that this was an established food fad more than 2,000 years ago.

But that makes it no less delicious. The intoxicating sweetness that we associate with the most fragrant roses can be captured in cooking, adding a note of elegance and grace to many kinds of dishes.

Speaking very generally, the more fragrant a rose is, the stronger its flavor. Individual flavors vary from spicy to fruity, but always with the foundation of "rose." There's no other way to describe it: a rose petal tastes like a rose smells.

Because the flavor is something our taste buds identify as sweet, roses are especially appropriate for desserts and beverages.

Try adding chopped rose petals to:

▦ apple pies, tarts, or baked apples;

▦ custards and puddings (especially vanilla);

▦ cakes and cupcakes;

▦ sweet quick breads, such as applesauce or apricot bread;

▦ cream cheese, with nuts and chopped fruit, for a tea-sandwich spread.

Or steep shredded rose petals in hot water for half an hour to extract flavor and color. Strain out the petals and add the rose liquid to lemonade, fruit punch, or white wine spritzers.

Whole petals, flowers, and rosebuds can be used in these ways:

▦ Sprinkle petals of yellow, orange, or coral roses into spinach salads;

make vinaigrette dressing with rose vinegar (make just like herb vinegar; see box on pages 257 to 259).

▦ Cut petals of dark red roses into ribbons, add to carrot-pineapple salad; garnish with whole flowers.

▦ Add petals to fruit salad; garnish with whole flowers.

▦ Freeze tiny rosebuds into ice cubes (see page 372) and add to punch or iced rose-hip tea at a bride's luncheon.

▦ From an early-twentieth-century herbal comes this idea for tea sandwiches, adapted for modern cooks. First, prepare rose-scented butter: thoroughly cover one or two sticks of unsalted butter with rose petals by rolling them in lightly crushed petals. Wrap each stick tightly in plastic wrap, and chill overnight. For the sandwiches, scrape away the petals and spread the rose-scented butter in an even layer on thin-sliced bread. Trim the crusts from the buttered bread, and cut the bread into fingers or triangles. Lay fresh petals between two slices of bread, letting some of the petals peek out over the edge.

▦ Make a composed salad using whole roses with flat, open flowers (the kind with just one layer of petals). Carefully snip off the stamens and pistil so that each blossom becomes a shallow cup. Arrange several of these rose cups on a bed of mixed greens, and fill each one with an assortment of goodies: melon balls, strawberries standing on end, or small balls of flavored cream cheese. Drizzle a lemon-honey dressing over everything.

Edible Flowers

Sunflowers

GROW AS: **annuals**

PLANT SIZE: **2 feet (dwarf types)**

START WITH: **seeds or transplants**

HARVEST SEASON: **late summer, fall**

SUN REQUIREMENTS: **full sun**

MINIMUM SOIL DEPTH: **12 inches**

T he gentle giant of the American prairie . . . the flower that captivated Vincent van Gogh . . . the solemn religious symbol of the Aztecs . . . the favorite floral hiding place for children. This cheerful flower named for the sun is so well loved for its happy countenance, it's no wonder that it has found such a prominent place in the gardens of so many cultures, past and present.

One of the fascinating aspects of the study of plants is the way they help us track the great movements of history. We may not be able to remember kings and dates, but anyone who loves gardens and flowers can visualize the people of long-ago cultures working in their gardens, and thus get a very real sense of what was happening in their world at that time.

Many familiar garden flowers and food plants are indigenous to the temperate areas of Asia and the Middle East. When European explorers began their journeys to the East in the fifteenth century, their primary goal was commerce, but an important secondary outcome was the expansion of scientific knowledge.

Most of the expeditions included naturalists, who were as thrilled to find unknown specimens of plants and animals as the ships' captains were to discover unknown lands. And so plants native to the East were introduced to the West, where many of them thrived and became part of the natural landscape.

A couple of centuries later, when settlers from Europe colonized the New World, they brought with them the seeds of the plants they had come to depend on, and so the botanical thread was extended from Asia to Europe and thence to the Americas—almost full circle.

But sometimes the circle turned the opposite way. The first Europeans to visit the New World found some plants that were unknown to them, including significant food crops that had sustained native Americans for millennia: corn, squash, beans, and peppers both hot and sweet. They also reported a stunning flower; tall as a tree, strong and supple, with an enormous flower head that moved throughout the day to turn its face to the sun it so closely resembled in shape and color.

Returning home, these Europeans brought with them seeds of this exotic plant, and soon sunflowers were to be found in the gardens of Europe:

- In France, where years later Vincent van Gogh was enchanted by vast fields of them.

- In the Netherlands, where their ability to soak up large amounts of water was put to good use in the reclamation of low-lying marshlands.

- In southern Russia, where the open spaces of the Russian prairie were the perfect ground for cultivation. Today, close to 90 percent of the world's commercial crop of sunflowers comes from Russia.

Back in the New World, the hefty flower with the nutritious seeds flourished throughout North America, especially on the Great Plains. Today visitors to Kansas, the Sunflower State, send home postcards of the mammoth plants. And wherever it is grown, the cheerful sunflower never fails to warm the heart of those who encounter it.

Sunflower Basics. Sunflowers are annual plants: they go from a seed to a tall plant bearing bright-faced flowers and a big seed head all in one season. That cycle—seed to flower and back to seed—is something we all understand intellectually, but in sunflowers we get to observe it in a very memorable way. That's one reason sunflowers are so good for children to grow: few lessons in science are this much fun.

The familiar tall plant that comes to mind when you think of sunflow-ers usually has just one large blossom at the top. But newer varieties have been developed that form numerous branches, creating a shape more like a shrub than a tree, and these are more suitable for containers.

The cheery blooms are beautiful in cut-flower arrangements. The brightly colored petals are edible, and are very pretty sprinkled onto green salads. But if you want to have sun-flower seeds to munch on, you must leave the flowers on the plant to fully mature, at which point the petals will have completely died off. You can, in other words, have edible flowers or edible seeds, but not both—at least not from the same flower head.

Planting. Sunflower seeds are large, easy to handle, and germinate quickly. Start seeds indoors two or three weeks before the spring frost date, then set the seedlings out into your containers when all danger of frost has passed. Or if your growing season is long enough, you can plant seeds directly into the container. Most of the dwarf types reach bloom time in 60 to 75 days.

You may also find sunflower transplants for sale at the garden center in the spring; these can be tempting, but be careful. Large garden centers typically offer only the familiar tall plants, since that's what most people expect. But full-size sunflowers are simply too large for containers, and are practically guaranteed to blow over come the first good wind. Nursery labels, alas, are not always exact. The only way we know to be absolutely sure of getting a dwarf variety that will work in containers is to order seed from a mail-order catalog.

Success with Sunflowers.

These gigantic flowers are quite easy to grow. They tolerate hot, dry weather better than most flowers. Although no one recommends actually letting the plants go dry, it probably isn't a mortal error if you miss watering now and then. To encourage sunflowers to reach full maturity, fertilize and water regularly. Late in the summer you may see rust or powdery mildew on the leaves (about the time these diseases show up on your cucumbers), but seldom are they fatal; see Chapter 6 for controls.

Harvesting. To use the petals, simply pull them from the flowers. If you're careful, you can remove *a few* individual petals and leave the flower on the plant for the seeds to mature.

If you love roasted sunflower seeds, you'll find it very satisfying to grow them yourself—that is, if you can harvest them before the birds do. Something like 40 species of North American birds enjoy sunflower seeds as food, and you're sure to have a few of them where you live. To keep the birds away, cover the ripening seed head with protective fabric or tie on a large paper bag. When the seeds are fat and move easily when you wiggle them, they're ready. In the long run, though, you may find it even more pleasing to leave the seeds to the birds. Then you can simply sit back and watch the show, as dozens of these beautiful creatures drop by your patio for lunch.

Cooking with Sunflowers. As a container gardener, you have the choice of using sunflowers at any one of three stages:

1. The immature buds can be steamed or sautéed and served like artichokes. (This is a treat that only those who grow sunflowers can enjoy. When the buds are fat enough to have some substance, but *before* they begin to open up into a flower, cut them off with your pruners.)

2. The bright-colored petals can be used much in the same ways as marigold flowers (see page 375); there is a distinct bitter tang to their flavor.

3. The mature seeds are a nutritious snack.

Varieties. You may be interested to know that the tallest sunflower on record is more than 25 feet high, and the largest recorded flower head is more than 32 inches across. But not all sunflowers are the height of a two-story building with a flower the size of a garbage-can lid. Happily for container gardeners, flower breeders have developed dwarf varieties with short, branching trunks and smaller flowers. And they have given us a variety of flower colors and shapes, too. While the familiar flat flower head, with just one layer of golden yellow petals surrounding a dark center, is the most common, you can also find flowers in other hues (burgundy red, burnt orange, bronze, white, and two-toned) and double flowers in the shape of fluffy pompoms. Here are several appropriate for growing in containers.

A Renaissance Recipe

In the late 1500s, the Englishman John Gerard made quite a name for himself as a leading apothecary, a businessman who grew herbs commercially and prepared them for healing potions. In modern terms, an apothecary was a combination drug manufacturer and pharmacist. Gerard is known to us today primarily as the author of *Herbal,* published in 1597. This very comprehensive book, describing all the medicinal plants then known, served as a textbook for practitioners of herbal medicine for centuries.

He did not, however, strictly limit himself to medicine, but occasionally indulged in culinary fancy. Regarding sunflowers, he wrote: "We have found by triall, that the buds before they be flowered, boiled and eaten with butter, vinegar and pepper, after the manner of artichokes, an exceeding pleasant meat, surpassing the artichoke far in procuring bodily lust. The same buds neere unto the top broiled upon a gridiron and afterwards eaten with oile, vinegar, and pepper have the like property."

The artichoke is, if you stop and think about it, an unopened flower bud, so it's not at all surprising that our ancestors viewed unopened sunflowers in the same way. Whether either is successful at procuring bodily lust is a personal and highly private matter into which we shall not intrude.

Cathy Wilkinson Barash, who includes a recipe for a modern version of sautéed sunflower buds in her book *Edible Flowers,* recommends briefly blanching them in boiling water first, to leach out any bitterness.

Sunspot is a rather small plant (2 feet high) that produces astonishingly large flowers: 10 inches across, with a very large seed head in the center.

The well-branched **Sundance Kid** reaches a height of approximately 1½ feet, with flowers 4 to 6 inches in diameter. The flowers themselves may be different colors, from pure yellow through and through to a darker bronze-and-gold blend.

An award-winning **Music Box** is a bit over 2 feet tall and bears lots of 4-inch flowers on its many branches. From one packet, you'll get sunflowers in a range of colors.

Big Smile is a full-size (5-inch) classic flower—bright golden yellow petals around a dark center—on a plant that rarely tops 1 foot tall.

Pacino produces soft yellow flowers 4 to 5 inches across. Plants stay about 1½ feet in containers, and produce lots of side branches.

Teddy Bear is sure to delight children. Most sunflowers are flat as a dinner plate; this one is rounded and very frilly and fluffy, rather like a marigold on steroids. The 6-inch flower is bright golden yellow, with no visible seed center, and fuzzy to the touch. Plants may reach 2½ to 3 feet in height.

Edible Flowers

Tulips

GROW AS: **annuals or short-lived perennials**

PLANT SIZE: **12 to 18 inches**

START WITH: **bulbs**

HARVEST SEASON: **spring**

SUN REQUIREMENTS: **full sun**

MINIMUM SOIL DEPTH: **6 inches**

All gardening is, to one degree or another, an act of faith. You put something into soil and you expect or hope or pray that it will flourish. This is true with small transplants and shrubs, on which you can already see the promise of future glory, but know intuitively that it comes with no guarantees. It is true with seeds, which hold their destiny encased in a small, plain-looking package that bears no visible relation to the plants' ultimate form. And it is especially true with tulips, with their counterintuitive timing.

We put tulips (and other spring-flowering bulbs) into the earth in the fall, just as all the other plants are in the process of shutting down for the winter. If all goes well during the cold season, we will be rewarded with a burst of glorious color the following spring. In the meantime, we and all around us are turning inward, coming inside, consciously and deliberately moving away from the natural world outdoors. While they are developing underground, the tulip bulbs are completely hidden from sight, depriving us of even the kind of stark winter beauty that many trees and shrubs display. It is easy to forget that tulips exist.

There is something poignant and surreal about planting just before winter. It feels illogical, even backward. But tulips cannot be grown in any other way, which is why planting them represents the purest form of a gardener's faith.

The outcome of that faith is a brilliant flash of some of the most intense color you will ever see in nature, at the time you most need it: just when you think you can't bear another cold, dreary winter day. That such beauty is also good to eat is an unexpected bonus.

Tulip Basics. Tulip bulbs contain the embryonic raw material for long, strappy leaves and (usually) just one flower stalk. Most flowers are large and vibrantly colored, lasting on the plant for about two weeks. Depending on variety, the blossoms will appear in March, April, or May. By choosing carefully from the many types and classes available, it's possible to enjoy tulips over a long span of time. They make wonderful cut flowers, and add a strong note of color to your cuisine.

Just about every tulip bulb you plant is guaranteed to produce a gorgeous flower the following spring. Whether it comes back the second spring is another matter. When they reach a certain level of maturity, tulips reproduce themselves by growing small bulblets, called offsets, attached to the mother bulb. The mother bulb, knowing it has done its duty, starts a mortal slide downward. In commercial fields, the offsets are harvested and planted for future inventory. We could do that, too, except that they take several years to reach the flowering stage; in the meantime, there are no flowers. So it is a foregone conclusion that at a certain point, a tulip bulb will decline and flower production will go on hiatus. The difficulty is that you cannot tell by looking whether a bulb you purchased is at that point.

Caution

Although most people can tolerate tulips without difficulty, you should be aware that an allergic reaction is possible. Some people experience a rash on their hands after handling tulips. Another reaction comes from eating the flowers: nausea, vomiting, and heart palpitations. This is rare, but not unknown.

If you already know that you are prone to severe reactions to allergens, proceed carefully, and limit yourself to one or two petals. For the same reason, exercise caution with guests; unless you're certain about their allergic tendencies, use other flowers.

Sometimes a bulb will flower for two or three years, sometimes not.

As a practical matter, therefore, many people treat tulips as annuals and plant new bulbs every fall. To avoid disappointment, we recommend that you do likewise.

Planting. A tulip bulb has the general shape of a very large teardrop, with one more-or-less flat end and one pointed end. Plant the bulbs with the pointed end up. Here's the basic process.

First dig out a space for the bulbs. How deep? One rule of thumb is two to three times as deep as the bulb is fat; 6 inches is a good round number. Sprinkle some phosphorus-rich fertilizer in the bottom of the hole, either bone meal or commercial bulb food. Set the bulbs in place, quite close together, and cover with your potting mix. Mark the area in some way so you won't accidentally dig into the bulbs next spring if you plant other things in that same container. If your winters are severe, put the pot in a sheltered location, or cover the soil with mulch, or both.

It is also possible to add tulip bulbs to an established container in which you already have a small tree or other perennials; you just have to be a bit more careful with your digging. Also, if the container where you wish to have tulips next spring still houses flourishing tomatoes or cucumbers in September or October, you'll have to work around them. Usually it's only a matter of lifting the vines aside temporarily while you insert the tulip bulbs underneath.

How the Tulip Got Its Name

Anna Pavord has given us all a treasure with her wonderful, lyrical book *The Tulip: The Story of a Flower That Has Made Men Mad* (1999). In a most engaging way, she relates the history of this luscious flower, and includes this delightful and altogether reasonable guess about the origin of its name.

In the 1550s a Flemish diplomat by the name of Busbecq was sent by Emperor Ferdinand I, ruler of the Holy Roman Empire (Germany and Italy), to Constantinople (today's Istanbul) as ambassador to the court of Suleiman the Magnificent, leader of the Ottoman Empire (what we now call Turkey and the Middle East). Busbecq is credited with bringing home to Europe not only the bulbs of the tulip, which were very popular with the Turks, but the name of the flower as well.

The Turks called tulips *lale,* but Busbecq, in a letter back home, reported that the Turkish name for the flowers was *tulipam.* The two names sound not at all alike; how could he have made such a mistake?

At that time it was the fashion in Constantinople to wear a single tulip flower tucked into one's turban. Anna Pavord speculates that Busbecq, out strolling with his interpreter, pointed to a flower worn in a turban and asked the name of it; the interpreter misunderstood and gave the name of the turban—*tulband*—rather than the flower. And Busbecq, rendering the Turkish word phonetically, altered its spelling when writing about it.

Those of you who live in the South or the Sun Belt have one extra step. Tulips need to go through a period of cold weather to form roots and to activate the embryo inside the bulb. If Mother Nature does not provide that cold period, you'll have to step in. Acquire your bulbs no later than November 1, and store them in the refrigerator for six to eight weeks. Around Christmastime, plant them in the containers. It's a nice thing to do in the week between Christmas and New Year's.

Tulips need to be planted in potting soil that drains readily, so they don't rot during the winter. If you had a traditional garden, you might also have to take special precautions against underground animals or insects that munch on bulbs, but as a container gardener, you completely avoid that problem.

Success with Tulips. Once you make peace with the fact that you may not be able to keep tulips from year to year, the rest is easy, for tulips are remarkably free of diseases and other problems. Starting with fresh bulbs, all you really have to do is enjoy the gorgeous results. But if you do want to try to rejuvenate the bulbs for next year, here's what to do.

Once the flowering is done (the flower head simply disintegrates as the individual petals fall off), cut off and discard the stem and leave the foliage in place. It will gradually turn yellow, and that's your cue to remove it. You can tell when the proper time has arrived because the leaves pull away easily with a gentle tug. As they mature, the leaves transmit energy down to the bulb for winter storage; that's why you must leave the plants in place until the process is complete, even though they look ugly in the interim. You can disguise the yellowing foliage by tucking in some annuals around them.

Continue to fertilize the container (which you will do anyway if other things are planted in it) through the summer and again early next spring, when the pointy tips of the foliage first emerge, and keep your fingers crossed. If you get leaves but no flowers the second spring, remove the spent bulbs and start over with new ones in the fall; a second year of fertilizing isn't going to help.

Harvesting. Snip off the entire flower (and remove the remainder of the stem from the plant for aesthetic reasons). To use the whole flower,

carefully take out the stamens and pistil; for individual petals, simply pull them from the base. Just remember that, unlike most of the flowers we suggest in this book, tulips don't rebloom after cutting. Except for some very specialized types that produce multiple stems, one tulip bulb is going to make one flower, and once it's gone, it's gone.

Varieties. Rather than name individual varieties of tulip, of which there are a gazillion, it may be more useful to you if we acquaint you with some general classifications.

One way of categorizing modern tulips is by time of bloom. Thus you will see that many mail-order companies group their offerings into "early," "midseason," and "late" (March, April, and May, respectively), and in fact official classifications of tulip groupings include single early, single late, double early, and double late. Other group names you may encounter refer to the shape of the blossom itself: lily-flowered and peony-flowered are what you would imagine from the names; parrot tulips have petals with very feathery edges; fringed tulips have a very frilly look.

Darwin tulips and Darwin hybrids, with their familiar squarish flowers in dynamite colors, are among the most popular and most common types; they are midseason bloomers. Triumph types were crossbred from Darwins and so have very similar blossoms but extra-sturdy stems. So-called cottage tulips are egg-shaped late bloomers.

Tulip Companions

Kale, with its handsome, very decorative leaves, pairs very attractively with tulips. The slender, smooth tulip foliage makes a nice textural contrast with the frilled kale, and the large, luminous flowers are nicely set off against the dark leaves of the kale.

Two nice color schemes: pink or lavender tulips with Red Russian kale; yellow tulips with Black Tuscan kale.

And every one of these comes in such a range of fabulous colors and color combinations that you'll have no trouble finding ones that make your color scheme sizzle and pop.

As if that weren't enough, you can also choose from a wide range of species tulips, sometimes called botanical tulips. Like other species plants, these are the original, wild forms of the flower, cultivated by modern growers but retaining all the original traits of the wild plant. Species tulips are small, low-growing, and early blooming; a very pretty arrangement is to use them as a lower tier underneath full-size tulips.

All these types can be ordered from mail-order catalogs, where you'll find so many temptations your head will spin. Or you may prefer to buy from your local garden center. Happily, retail nurseries and garden centers inevitably remind us when it's time to plant tulips by setting out an enticing array of bulbs. Some are packaged in groups of five to ten, with a large photograph showing the flower in bloom. You can also buy from bulk bins, filled with individual bulbs; choose the fattest, firmest bulbs you can find.

Cooking with Tulips. The undertaste of tulip petals is usually described as being reminiscent of fresh garden peas, which makes tulip blossoms especially appropriate for entrées and salads. Their dazzling colors also contribute panache to desserts, and we won't overlook that aspect, but when you're looking for flowers that lend themselves to main dishes, think tulips.

▧ Cathy Wilkinson Barash, who has given us so many wonderful ideas in her books on edible flowers, suggests stuffing whole blossoms with tuna salad (remove the stamens and pistil first). You can expand that idea in any direction: pasta or rice salads, tabbouleh, potato and roast beef salad, coleslaw, marinated cucumber salad, and so forth.

▧ Cut petals into thin ribbons and sprinkle over steamed vegetables. Look for good color combinations: orange or yellow with spinach, white or pale apricot with peas, dark red or purple with potatoes.

▧ For a luncheon salad, first line the plates with dark green lettuce leaves and tuck in a few brilliantly colored tulip petals—perhaps pure lavender or a two-toned pink.

▧ Here are a few possibilities for your hors d'oeuvres tray:

▪ Marinated mushrooms accented with whole petals of deep orange tulips.

▪ Sliced pâté on a bed of bright red tulip petals.

▪ A spread of cream cheese and diced smoked oysters, showing bright specks of shredded yellow tulip petals.

▪ Rounds of English cucumber, spread with softened cream cheese, then topped with one magenta tulip petal and a few curls of lemon zest.

V ictoria ruled the British Empire for 63 years, longer than any other monarch before or since. She assumed the throne in 1837 when she was 18 years old, and was still active as ruler when she died at the age of 81. During her reign Great Britain became the leading world power. Largely free from war during the period, England developed into the world's first urban industrialized society, and with that came the mix of economic prosperity and social problems that remain the hallmark of the modern age.

Theme Garden

Victorian Splendor

Today our main impression of Victorian society is that it was uptight, repressed, and prudish. But human nature is seldom one-dimensional, and Victorian England was far more contradictory than it was clear-cut. While Victoria was queen, Wordsworth and Shelley wrote some of the most sensual poetry in the English language; Charlotte Brontë captured the dilemma of an entire generation of women with her story of the young Jane Eyre, struggling between sexual desire and a sense of duty; Charles Dickens goaded the country into passing child labor laws with his strong novels of urban poverty; and Charles Darwin challenged traditional religious views with the publication of *On the Origin of Species*.

That same sense of contradiction can be seen in the decorative styles of the day. We think of Victorian interiors as terribly formal, stiff, over-stuffed, and overdecorated, and often they were. But in protest against that overblown style, the architect and painter William Morris founded the Arts and Crafts school that remains so popular today.

In gardening we can see that same shift. Early in the Victorian period, gardens indoors and out were formal and artificial; in England, the most untropical climate imaginable, large tropical plants were the height of fashion. Near the end of the nineteenth century, under the influence of garden designers like Gertrude Jekyll, things began to loosen up. The lush, flower-packed, but definitely unrigid Jekyll style is best recognized in what we today call the cottage garden, filled with old-fashioned, well-loved flowers (although in Jekyll's day no one would have considered them old-fashioned).

If we can say anything definitive about the Victorians, it is that they had a passion for flowers, flowers, and more flowers. And that is why our

Victorian container garden is stuffed with them, along with highly decorative herbs. But in keeping with the theme of this book, all the flowers are edible.

To accentuate the Victorian look, you might consider planting this garden in an antique or white wicker container. If you find something wonderful, the container itself becomes part of the overall look, and you'll want to make sure it gets a place of honor. At the same time, of course, make sure it's large enough to hold all the plants you intend to include.

For details on growing the plants in this garden, see

Lavender, page 205
Roses, page 390
Sage, page 252
Scented geraniums, page 262
Thyme, page 278
Tulips, page 405
Violets, violas, and pansies, page 382

One style that we have admired is made of white wicker; it is essentially a long rectangle set on legs, and has a sweet, old-fashioned appeal. We'll describe this garden as if it were in such a planter—that is, long and skinny—but you can readily adjust it to a garden-in-the-round if need be. Also, in the spirit of the Victorians, we will create a symmetrical, slightly formal arrangement.

In the center, one scrumptious **rose.** Depending on the size of your container, select either a polyantha or a patio type (polyanthas are the larger of the two). Choose a color that you love, for it will establish the color scheme for your garden. Anything white, pale peach or apricot, soft pink, or pale lavender will look lovely. On either side, a large **lavender.** The species known as Spanish lavender has flowers much showier than most lavenders. Next to the lavenders, one or more **miniature roses** in colors that harmonize with the lavender and the large rose.

Between the lavenders and the large rose, and slightly in front of them, place two **rose-scented geraniums.** They will not be the most floriferous plants in your garden, but will give off an incomparable rose fragrance when touched. On either side of the geraniums, more miniature roses.

Fill in the balance of the front row with **violets, violas,** and **pansies** in shades of soft purple and pink, and with decorative herbs, including tricolor **sage** and cascading **thyme,** perhaps Silver Lemon, delicately edged in white. Aim for a full, lush look; put in *lots* of plants.

This garden will give you flowers from early spring (the violets and pansies) through fall (roses). All these plants will last for a number of years, except for the pansies, which you will want to replace each spring, and the geraniums, which will be killed by severe cold. If you fall in love with your geraniums, take cuttings in late summer and root them indoors in the winter, ready to go back into the planter come spring.

You may wish to embellish the planter with several pretty pots of pastel **tulips** arranged near the base. Among the prettiest and most Victorian-looking are the ones with fringed petals. Because tulips are most successful when planted anew each year, we suggest you use separate containers that can be easily moved aside when the tulips are finished blooming.

To create a similar look in a large round container, put the tallest rose in the center, the lavenders, miniature roses, and geraniums around it, and the herbs and smaller flowers in the outermost ring. Plant tulip bulbs in a separate pot, and sink it into the soil of the larger container; when the tulips are past, lift out that pot and set it aside for replanting in the fall.

APPENDIX

U.S.D.A. HARDINESS ZONE MAP

T he U.S. Department of Agriculture has developed a nation-wide system of hardiness zones, indicating the *average* coldest winter temperatures. This map designates 11 major zones, with the lowest numbers denoting the lowest average temperatures. The numbering system has been widely adopted by the horticultural industry, and zone information for individual perennial plants is included in most garden catalog descriptions (as in "this variety hardy in zones 6–8" or "to zone 8").

We container gardeners have much more control over the vagaries of winter than do our in-the-ground-garden counterparts because containers can be more easily protected against or moved away from severe weather conditions.

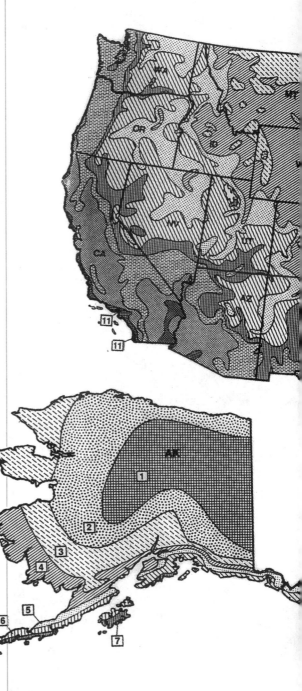

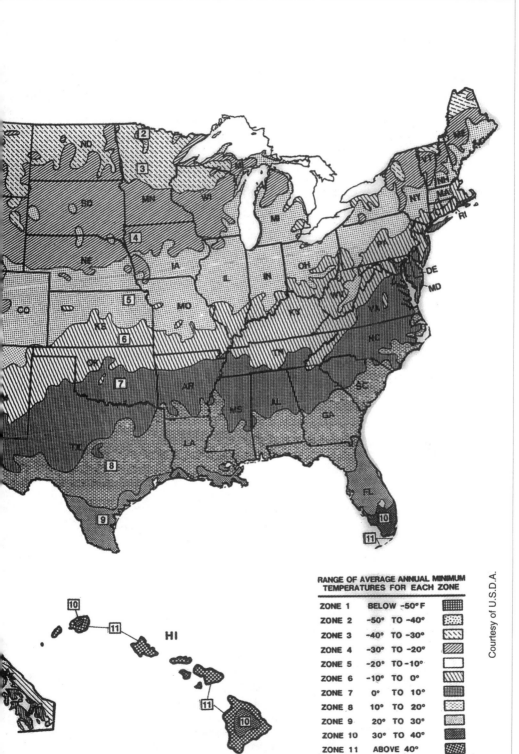

RANGE OF AVERAGE ANNUAL MINIMUM
TEMPERATURES FOR EACH ZONE

ZONE 1	BELOW -50° F	
ZONE 2	-50° TO -40°	
ZONE 3	-40° TO -30°	
ZONE 4	-30° TO -20°	
ZONE 5	-20° TO -10°	
ZONE 6	-10° TO 0°	
ZONE 7	0° TO 10°	
ZONE 8	10° TO 20°	
ZONE 9	20° TO 30°	
ZONE 10	30° TO 40°	
ZONE 11	ABOVE 40°	

Courtesy of U.S.D.A.

MAIL-ORDER SOURCES

The companies and organizations listed here represent by no means all the mail-order options; they are simply ones we know and admire. To find others, explore ads in recent issues of gardening magazines or browse the Internet.

Companies by Specialty

Vegetables

Abundant Life Seed Foundation
The Cook's Garden
The Gourmet Gardener
Harris Seeds
Johnny's Selected Seeds
Nichols Garden Nursery
Park Seed Company
Renee's Garden
Richters Herb Specialists
Seeds of Change
Shepherd's Garden Seeds
Territorial Seed Company
Tomato Growers Supply Company
Veseys Seed Ltd.
W. Atlee Burpee Company

Herbs

Abundant Life Seed Foundation
The Cook's Garden
Dabney Herbs
The Gourmet Gardener
Harris Seeds
Jackson & Perkins
Johnny's Selected Seeds
Killdeer Farms
Nichols Garden Nursery
One Green World
Park Seed Company
Raintree Nursery
Rasland Farm
Renee's Garden
Richters Herb Specialists
The Sandy Mush Herb Nursery
Seeds of Change
Shepherd's Garden Seeds
Territorial Seed Company

The Thyme Garden Herb Company
Veseys Seed Ltd.
W. Atlee Burpee Company
Wayside Gardens

Fruits

Bay Laurel Nursery
Jené's Tropicals
Nichols Garden Nursery
One Green World
Park Seed Company
Raintree Nursery
Renee's Garden
Seeds of Change
Shepherd's Garden Seeds
Territorial Seed Company
W. Atlee Burpee Company
Wayside Gardens

Edible Flowers

Abundant Life Seed Foundation
Bluestone Perennials
Caprice Farm Nursery
The Cook's Garden
Dutch Gardens
Edmunds' Roses
The Gourmet Gardener
Harris Seeds
Heirloom Old Garden Roses
Jackson & Perkins
Johnny's Selected Seeds
Justice Miniature Roses
Nichols Garden Nursery
Oakes Daylilies
Olallie Daylily Gardens
Park Seed Company
Raintree Nursery
Renee's Garden

Seeds of Change
Shepherd's Garden Seeds
Territorial Seed Company
Van Bourgondien Dutch Bulbs and
  Perennials
Van Dyck's Flower Farms
Veseys Seed Ltd.
W. Atlee Burpee Company
Wayside Gardens
Weidners' Gardens

Other

American Rose Society
Granny's Garden Socks
Gardener's Supply Company
Gardens Alive!
Kinsman Company
Peaceful Valley Farm Supply

Company Contact
Information

ABUNDANT LIFE SEED FOUNDATION
P.O. Box 772
Port Townsend, WA 98368-0772
Phone: (360) 385-5660
Fax: (360) 385-7455
E-mail: abundant@olypen.com
Web: www.abundantlifeseed.org
Catalog: $2
Vegetables, herbs, and *edible flowers.* This is a
nonprofit educational foundation that raises
and collects the seeds of open-pollinated
cultivars grown without chemicals.

AMERICAN ROSE SOCIETY
P.O. Box 30,000
Shreveport, LA 71130-0030
Phone: (318) 938-5402
Fax: (318) 938-5405
E-mail: ars@ars-hq.org
Web: www.ars.org
Nonprofit organization that promotes
rose-growing in all settings. Extremely
useful website. Publishes *Handbook for
Selecting Roses,* $4 includes shipping.

BAY LAUREL NURSERY
2500 El Camino Real
Atascadero, CA 93422
Phone: (805) 466-3406

Fax: (805) 466-6455
E-mail: info@baylaurelnursery.com
Web: www.baylaurelnursery.com
Catalog: free and online
Fruit: Peaches, figs, and more.

BLUESTONE PERENNIALS
7721 Middle Ridge Road
Madison, OH 44057-3096
Phone: (800) 852-5243
Fax: (440) 428-7198
E-mail: bluestone@bluestone
  perennials.com
Web: www.bluestoneperennials.com
Catalog: free
Edible flowers: Chrysanthemums—lots of
them.

CAPRICE FARM NURSERY
10944 Mill Creek Road SE
Aumsville, OR 97325
Phone: (503) 749-1397
Fax: (503) 749-4097
E-mail cyndicap@gte.net
Web: www.capricefarm.com
Catalog: free
Edible flowers: Ninety kinds of daylilies.

THE COOK'S GARDEN
P.O. Box 535
Londonderry, VT 05148
Phone: (800) 457-9703
Fax: (800) 457-9705
E-mail: info@cooksgarden.com
Web: www.cooksgarden.com
Catalog: free
Vegetables: Good selection of some of the
more unusual varieties of vegetables;
tomatoes, beans, chard, carrots, eggplant,
cucumber, lettuce and salad greens, squash.
Specialize in seed collections. *Herbs:* Good
selection of standard and gourmet herbs;
seeds and plants. *Edible flowers:* Sunflowers,
nasturtiums, marigolds. *Other:* Books,
tools, kitchen and garden supplies.

DABNEY HERBS
P.O. Box 22061
Louisville, KY 40252
Phone: (502) 893-5198
Fax: (502) 893-5198
E-mail: dabneyherb@win.net

Web: www.dabneyherbs.com
Catalog: $2
Herbs: Full listing of popular and unusual herbs (plants and seeds), including lavender, lemongrass, lemon verbena, pineapple sage, oregano, marjoram, chamomile, fennel, feverfew, parsley, scented geraniums, more. *Other:* Books.

DUTCH GARDENS
P.O. Box 2037
Lakewood, NJ 08701
Phone: (800) 818-3861
Fax: (732) 942-3802
E-mail: info@dutchgardens.com
Web: www.dutchgardens.com
Catalog: free
Edible flowers: Tulips, tuberous begonias, daylilies. Stunning photographs.

EDMUNDS' ROSES
6235 SW Kahle Road
Wilsonville, OR 97070
Phone: (888) 481-7673
Fax: (503) 682-1275
E-mail: edmunds@edmundsroses.com
Web: www.edmundsroses.com
Catalog: free
Edible flowers: Roses. *Other:* Felco secateurs, goatskin gloves, watering kits. Beautiful catalog with good plant descriptions.

GARDENER'S SUPPLY COMPANY
128 Intervale Road
Burlington, VT 05401
Phone: (888) 833-1412
Fax: (800) 551-6712
E-mail: info@gardeners.com
Web: www.gardeners.com
Catalog: free
Other: No seeds or plants, but everything else you might need: plant trellises, tools, outdoor furniture and accessories, containers, plant stakes, much more.

GARDENS ALIVE!
5100 Schenley Place
Lawrenceburg, IN 47025
Phone: (812) 537-8650
Fax: (812) 537-5108
E-mail: gardenhelp@gardensalive.com
Web: gardensalive.com

Catalog: free
Other: Organic fertilizers and organic controls for pests and diseases; garden tools and supplies.

THE GOURMET GARDENER
12287 117th Drive
Live Oak, FL 32060
Phone: (888) 404-4769
Fax: (407) 650-2691
E-mail: information@gourmet gardener.com
Web: www.gourmetgardener.com
Catalog: free
Vegetables: unusual gourmet varieties.
Herbs: Basil, bergamot, burnet, chamomile, many others. *Edible flowers:* Calendula, dianthus, marigold, nasturtium, violet, plus an edible flower collection. *Other:* Books, gifts.

GRANNY'S GARDEN SOCKS
30 Blue Jay Lane
Noxon, MT 59853
Phone: (800) 639-9692
Fax: (406) 847-2299
E-mail: gardensock@blackfoot.net
Web: www.gardensock.com
Other: Hanging planters of heavy-duty plastic, for use on railings, decks, posts.

HARRIS SEEDS
P.O. Box 24966
Rochester, NY 14624-0966
Phone: (800) 514-4441
Fax: (877) 892-9197
Web: www.harrisseeds.com
Catalog: free
Vegetables: Very pretty catalog, extensive selection of good varieties. *Herbs:* Small selection of the standards. *Edible flowers:* Marigolds, dianthus, pansies and violas, calendula, sunflowers. *Other:* Growing and greenhouse supplies.

HEIRLOOM OLD GARDEN ROSES
24062 NE Riverside Drive
St. Paul, OR 97137
Phone: (503) 538-1576
Fax: (503) 538-5902
E-mail: info@heirloomroses.com
Web: www.heirloomroses.com
Catalog: $5 (color)

Edible flowers: Roses, roses, and more roses. *Other:* Books on growing roses. Catalog has lovely photos, extensive descriptions, and history; well worth the cost.

JACKSON & PERKINS
1 Rose Lane
Medford, OR 97501
Phone: (800) 292-4769
Fax: (800) 242-0329
E-mail: service@jacksonandperkins.com
Web: www.jacksonandperkins.com
Catalog: free
Herbs: Lavender. *Edible flowers:* Best known for roses; also offers tuberous begonias, other flowers. *Other:* Gifts, gloves, tools.

JENÉ'S TROPICALS
6831 Central Avenue
St. Petersburg, FL 33710
Phone: (727) 344-1668
Fax: (727) 381-4415
E-mail: jtropical@attglobal.net
Web: www.tropicalfruit.com
Fruit: Apples, blueberries, citrus, currants, figs, grapes, nectarines, peaches, strawberries.

JOHNNY'S SELECTED SEEDS
184 Foss Hill Road
Albion, ME 04910
Phone: (207) 437-4357
Fax: (800) 437-4290
E-mail: johnnys@johnnyseeds.com
Web: www.johnnyseeds.com
Catalog: free
Vegetables: Wide selection of container-recommended varieties, good growing information. *Herbs:* Seeds only. *Edible flowers:* Calendula, nasturtiums, sunflowers, violas. *Other:* Tools, supplies, accessories, books.

JUSTICE MINIATURE ROSES
5947 SW Kahle Road
Wilsonville, OR 97070
Phone: (503) 682-2370
E-mail: justrose@gte.net
Web: nurseryguide.com/members/11309
Catalog: free
Edible flowers: Hundreds of miniature roses.

KILLDEER FARMS
21606 NW 51st Avenue
Ridgefield, WA 98642
Phone: (360) 887-1790
Fax: (360) 887-3009
E-mail: geraniums@killdeerfarms.com
Web: www.killdeerfarms.com
Catalogs: text only, free;
    color photos, $3
Herbs: More than a hundred varieties of scented geraniums.

KINSMAN COMPANY
P.O. Box 428
Pipersville, PA 18947
Fax: (215) 766-5624
Phone: (800) 733-4146
E-mail: webmaster@kinsman
    garden.com
Web: www.kinsmangarden.com
Catalog: free
Other: Not a nursery per se, but stocks a very nice selection of handsome trellises in wood or metal, decorative planters both freestanding and hanging, unusual pots, and tools.

NICHOLS GARDEN NURSERY
1190 Old Salem Road NE
Albany, OR 97321-4580
Phone: (800) 422-3985
Fax: (800) 231-5306
E-mail: customersupport@
    nicholsgardennursery.com
Web: www.nicholsgardennursery.com
Catalog: free
Vegetables: Good selection of new and unusual vegetables, along with old favorites. *Herbs:* Extensive selection of both common and rare herbs; stevia, lavender, lemongrass, lemon verbena, rosemary, saffron crocus, sweet bay, salad burnet, much more. Seeds and plants. *Fruit:* Alpine strawberries. *Edible flowers:* Pansies, tagetes marigolds, nasturtiums, sunflowers. *Other:* Books, kitchen tools.

OAKES DAYLILIES
P.O. Box 268
Corryton, TN 37721
Phone: (800) 532-9545
Fax: (865) 688-8186
E-mail: webmaster@oakesdaylilies.com
Web: www.oakesdaylilies.com
Catalog: free
Edible flowers: Just daylilies, over 700 listings.

419

OLALLIE DAYLILY GARDENS
129 Augur Hole Road
South Newfane, VT 05351
Phone: (802) 348-6614
Fax: (802) 348-9881
E-mail: info@daylilygarden.com
Web: www.daylilygarden.com
Catalog: free, or collectors color catalog for $1
Edible flowers: Only daylilies.

ONE GREEN WORLD
28696 South Cramer Road
Molalla, OR 97038-8576
Phone: (877) 353-4028
Fax: (800) 418-9983
E-mail: ogw@cybcon.com
Web: www.onegreenworld.com
Catalog: free
Herbs: Stevia. *Fruits:* apples, blueberries, crab apples, currants, figs, gooseberries, grapes, nectarines, peaches, strawberries. *Other:* Books on growing fruits. Excellent catalog, reliable information.

PARK SEED COMPANY
1 Parkton Avenue
Greenwood, SC 29649
Phone: (800) 845-3369
Fax: (864) 941-4206
E-mail: info@parkseed.com
Web: www.parkseed.com
Catalog: free
Vegetables: Extensive selection of almost all vegetables, including heirlooms. Good information and growing instructions. Seeds and plants. *Herbs:* Basil, parsley, mint, tarragon, sweet woodruff, thyme, marjoram, lavender, monarda, borage; seeds and plants. *Fruit:* Strawberry, blueberry, grapes, columnar apple. *Edible flowers:* Sunflowers, dianthus, tuberous begonias, daylilies, marigolds, nasturtiums, pansies and violas. For tulips and daylilies, request bulb catalog. *Other:* Trellises and plant supports, good selection of gardening supplies. Excellent all-around catalog. Well-established company.

PEACEFUL VALLEY FARM SUPPLY
P.O. Box 2209
Grass Valley, CA 95945
Phone: (888) 784-1722

Fax: (530) 272-4794
E-mail: contact@groworganic.com
Web: www.groworganic.com
Other: Broad and fascinating selection of gardening supplies, tools, and accessories.

RAINTREE NURSERY
391 Butts Road
Morton, WA 98356
Phone: (360) 496-6400
Fax: (888) 770-8358
E-mail: info@raintreenursery.com
Web: www.raintreenursery.com
Catalog: free
Herbs: Lemongrass, stevia. *Fruits:* Very wide selection of many fruits, including blueberries, strawberries, currants, gooseberries, apples (including columnars), peaches (including genetic dwarfs), grapes, citrus, figs. *Edible flowers:* Daylilies. *Other:* Books, kitchen supplies, trellises. Catalog has excellent growing information.

RASLAND FARM
6778 Herb Farm Road
Godwin, NC 28344-9712
Phone: (910) 567-2705
Fax: (888) 567-2705
E-mail: rasland@intrstar.net
Web: www.alcasoft.com/rasland
Catalog: free
Herbs: Good selection of plants; also books and dried herb blends. Minimum order $25.

RENEE'S GARDEN
7389 West Zayante Road
Felton, CA 95018
Phone: (888) 880-7228
Fax: (831) 335-7227
E-mail: webmaster@reneesgarden.com
Web: www.reneesgarden.com
Vegetables: Heirloom and gourmet vegetables. *Herbs:* Basil, chives, cilantro, lavender, oregano, parsley, thyme. *Fruit:* Alpine strawberries. *Edible flowers:* Sunflowers, nasturtiums, pansies, calendula. Does not sell by mail-order in the usual sense; seeds are sold online, in retail garden centers (call 888-880-7228 for nearest location), or through John Scheepers, Inc. (860-567-6086).

RICHTERS HERB SPECIALISTS
357 Highway 47
Goodwood, Ontario, L0C-1A0, Canada
Phone: (905) 640-6677
Fax: (905) 640-6641
E-mail: inquiry@richters.com
Web: www.richters.com
Catalog: free
Vegetables: Small selection includes several
Asian greens; seeds. *Herbs:* Very extensive
selection; seeds and plants. *Other:* A few
tools and pest-control supplies; wide selec-
tion of books on herbs. Richters is a
favorite of herb gardeners in the U.S. as
well as Canada, and is well-equipped to
ship to American customers.

THE SANDY MUSH HERB NURSERY
316 Surrett Cove Road
Leicester, NC 28748-5517
Phone: (828) 683-2014
Fax: (828) 683-2014
E-mail: sandymushherbs@mindspring.com
Web: www.brwn.org/sandymushherbs
Catalog: $6
Herbs: Specialist in herbs and herb collec-
tions; many varieties of lavender.

SEEDS OF CHANGE
P.O. Box 15700
Santa Fe, NM 87506
Phone: (888) 762-7333
Fax: (888) 329-4762
E-mail: gardener@seedsofchange.com
Web: www.seedsofchange.com
Catalog: free
Vegetables: Heirloom and traditional vari-
eties. *Herbs:* Many unusual kinds, along
with standards (basil, bergamot, mint,
oregano, chives, garlic chives). *Fruits:*
Apples. *Edible flowers:* Calendula,
marigolds, sunflowers. *Other:* Books, tools,
posters. Pretty, helpful catalog.

SHEPHERD'S GARDEN SEEDS
30 Irene Street
Torrington, CT 06790-6658
Phone: (860) 482-3638
Fax: (860) 482-0532
E-mail: custsrv@shepherdseeds.com
Web: www.shepherdseeds.com
Catalog: free

Vegetables: Good selection of unusual
varieties and old favorites; great selection
of lettuce and salad greens and Oriental
vegetables; lots of peppers and tomatoes.
Herbs: Good selection, good descriptions
and uses. Many different kinds of basil,
borage, cilantro, chervil, sage, pineapple
sage, rosemary, lemongrass, bay, thyme,
lavender, saffron crocus, scented
geraniums. Catalog loaded with good
information on culture and use. *Fruits:*
Blueberries, currants, gooseberries, grapes.
Edible flowers: Calendula, sunflowers,
dianthus, marigolds, nasturtiums, violas.
Other: Trellises, tools.

THE THYME GARDEN HERB COMPANY
20546 Alsea Highway
Alsea, OR 97324
Phone: (541) 487-8671
Fax (call first): (541) 487-8671
E-mail: herbs@thymegarden.com
Web: www.thymegarden.com
Catalog: $2
Herbs: Extremely broad selection of herbs,
including more than forty types of thyme;
seeds and plants, dried herbs and herb blends.

TOMATO GROWERS SUPPLY COMPANY
P.O. Box 2237
Fort Myers, FL 33902
Phone: (888) 478-7333
Fax: (888) 768-3476
Web: www.tomatogrowers.com
Catalog: free
Vegetables: Tomatoes and peppers—that's
what they sell. You owe it to yourself to
get the catalog and see the photos! *Other:*
Books, posters, supplies.

TERRITORIAL SEED COMPANY
P.O. Box 158
Cottage Grove, OR 97424-0061
Phone: (541) 942-9547
Fax: (888) 657-3131
E-mail: tetrl@territorial-seed.com
Web: www.territorial-seed.com
Catalog: free
Vegetables: Very broad selection.
Herbs: A wide selection of seeds and some
plants (stevia, tarragon, others). *Fruits:*
Strawberries (including alpine), blueberries.

Edible flowers: Marigolds, nasturtiums, pansies and violas, many sunflowers, unusual scented geraniums. *Other:* Books, tools, gardening and cooking supplies. Very helpful, detailed catalog, with great information.

VAN BOURGONDIEN DUTCH BULBS AND PERENNIALS
P.O. Box 1000
Babylon, NY 11702
Phone: (800) 622-9997
Fax: (888) 327-4268
E-mail: blooms@dutchbulbs.com
Web: www.dutchbulbs.com
Edible flowers: Tulips, daylilies, tuberous begonias.

VAN DYCK'S FLOWER FARMS
P.O. Box 430
Brightwaters, NY 11718-0430
Phone: (800) 248-2852
Fax: (800) 639-2452
E-mail: jan@vandycks.com
Web: www.vandycks.com
Catalog: free
Edible flowers: Tulips, daylilies, and more.

VESEYS SEED LTD.
P.O. Box 9000
Calais, ME 04619
Phone: (800) 363-7333
Fax: (800) 686-0329
E-mail: Weseys@veseys.com
Web: www.veseys.com
Vegetables: Very wide selection, including many good container varieties. *Herbs:* Seeds for a good selection of the basics. *Edible flowers:* Calendula, dianthus, marigold, nasturtiums, pansies and violas, and lots of sunflowers. *Other:* Tools and supplies, books. Veseys is a Canadian company, and specializes in varieties that do well in northern climates; their motto is "seeds for shorter seasons."

W. ATLEE BURPEE COMPANY
300 Park Avenue
Warminster, PA 18974
Phone: (800) 333-5808
Fax: (800) 487-5530
E-mail: burpeecs@surfnetwork.net

Web: www.burpee.com
Catalog: free
Vegetables: Large selection of vegetables with many varieties of each listed; good descriptions and information. Mostly seeds, some plants available. *Herbs:* Good selection of most of the more common herbs; plants and seeds. *Fruits:* strawberries, blueberries, grapes. *Edible flowers:* Tuberous begonias, daylilies, dianthus, sunflowers, pansies, nasturtiums, marigolds. *Other:* Seed-starting supplies, tools. One of the oldest and best seed companies, very extensive catalog.

WAYSIDE GARDENS
1 Garden Lane
Hodges, SC 29695
Phone: (800) 845-1124
Fax: (800) 817-1124
E-mail: info@waysidegardens.com
Web: www.waysidegardens.com
Catalog: free
Herbs: Standard and unusual plants including catmint, saffron crocus, coconut thyme, pineapple sage, lemongrass, bay, and more. *Fruit:* Fig, alpine strawberry. *Edible flowers:* Roses, tulips, daylilies, dianthus, violas. *Other:* Trellises, labels.

WEIDNERS' GARDENS
695 Normandy Road
Encinitas, CA 92024
Phone: (760) 436-2194
Fax: (760) 436-3681
E-mail: staff@weidners.com
Web: www.weidners.com
Edible flowers: Begonias, pansies. Unfortunately, you can't order them by mail, but if you find yourself in the San Diego area, be sure to drop by. Bring your shovel and a few empty pots. In summer you can dig up your choice of begonias from a half-acre field; in the fall, it is filled with 20,000 dig-your-own pansies.

INDEX